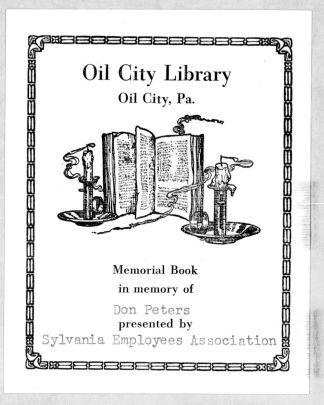

A Saga of Wealth

Books by James Presley:

A Saga of Wealth   1978
Food Power: Nutrition and Your Child's Behavior   1978
(In collaboration with Hugh Powers, M.D.)
Human Life Styling: Keeping Whole in the 20th Century   1975
(In collaboration with John C. McCamy, M.D.)
Public Defender   1974
(In collaboration with Gerald W. Getty)
Vitamin B$_6$:The Doctor's Report   1973
(In collaboration with John M. Ellis, M.D.)
Please, Doctor, Do Something!   1972
(In collaboration with Joe D. Nichols, M.D.)
Center of the Storm: Memoirs of John T. Scopes   1967
(In collaboration with John T. Scopes)

A Saga of Wealth;

The Rise of the Texas Oilmen

by James Presley

G. P. Putnam's Sons • New York

SBN: 399-11852-7

Library of Congress Cataloging in Publication Data

Presley, James.
    A saga of wealth.

    Bibliography
    Includes index
    1, Petroleum industry and trade—Texas—History.
2. Wealth—Texas—History.   3.   Texas—Industries—
History.   I.   Title.
HD9567.T3P73 1978   338.2'7'28209764   78-136

PRINTED IN THE UNITED STATES OF AMERICA

Acknowledgments

Without the cooperation of hundreds of persons, I could not have written this book as it exists and in the time it took. Most of all I owe a deep debt of gratitude to the oilmen—and oilwomen—and observers of the industry who talked with me at length, despite their busy schedules. Their names are listed in the interviews portion of the oral history section of the bibliography.

Grateful acknowledgment is made to the following for permission to reprint previously published material:

Esquire: For material from "Just Plain H. L. Hunt," by Tom Buckley in *Esquire,* January, 1967.

The New Yorker: For material from "Where Are They Now? Mr. Davis and His Millions," by Stanley Walker in *The New Yorker,* November 26, 1949.

Prentice-Hall, Inc.: For material from the book *Hugh Roy Cullen: A Story of American Opportunity* by Ed Kilman and Theon Wright. © 1954 by Prentice-Hall, Inc. Published by Prentice-Hall, Inc., Englewood Cliffs, New Jersey.

The University of Texas Press and Robert C. Cotner: For selected quotes and paraphrased material from *Addresses and State Papers of James Stephen Hogg,* edited by Robert C. Cotner, Copyright 1951 by

The University of Texas Press; and *James Stephen Hogg: A Biography* by Robert C. Cotner, Copyright 1959 by The University of Texas Press. Used with permission of Robert C. Cotner and The University of Texas Press.

Mrs. H. L. Hunt and the publishers H. L. H. Products and Parade Press: For material from *Alpaca Revisited* by H. L. Hunt, Copyright 1967 by H. L. Hunt; *H. L. Hunt Early Days* by H. L. Hunt, Copyright 1973 by Parade Press; and *Hunt Heritage: The Republic and Our Families* by H. L. Hunt, Copyright 1973 by Parade Press.

Claud B. Hamill permitted me to quote freely from *We Drilled Spindletop!* by Curtis G. Hamill, his father. Glenn H. McCarthy was kind enough to remove restrictions on the use of an earlier interview in the Pioneers in Texas Oil Oral History Project at the University of Texas at Austin; Mrs. Henry W. Barton did the same on a transcript of an interview with her late father, Walter Cline. Edgar W. Owen and James A. Clark were repeatedly helpful on pinning down details.

In the academic community I am indebted especially to Professor Joe B. Frantz of the Department of History at the University of Texas at Austin for his always helpful advice and interest in preserving my tape-recorded interviews for the Oral Business History Project at UT-Austin. Mrs. Carol Sadler and her associates at the Oral Business History Project provided helpful transcripts. I am also grateful for the useful suggestions from UT-Austin Professors Barnes F. Lathrop and Robert C. Cotner, Governor Jim Hogg's biographer.

Librarians and archivists at UT-Austin were especially kept busy guiding me through holdings, and I wish to single out Dr. Chester V. Kielman, librarian-archivist at the Barker Texas History Center, and his assistant, Robert A. Tissing, who supplied me with material from the Pioneers in Texas Oil Oral History Project, as well as Sara Rumbo and Mary Beth Fleischer at the Texas Collection and J. C. Martin at the Texas Newspaper Collection. Other librarians made life easier for me at UT-Austin's Main Library and its Business and Economics Library, the Fondren Library and Science-Engineering Library at Southern Methodist University, Austin Public Library, Texas State Library, Palmer Memorial Library at Texarkana, Texarkana Public Library, and the libraries of Texas A&M University and East Texas State University. Helen Click and Frances Howze at the Palmer Memorial Library obtained vitally needed materials through interlibrary loan.

Corbett Anderson's skillful artwork is responsible for the map of Texas' oil and gas fields. I am also grateful for the many persons who helped provide the photographs which are reproduced herein. Particularly helpful were Richard E. Drew, photographic and film services coordinator at the American Petroleum Institute, and Jack Rolf, director of operations for the Oil Information Committee of the Texas Mid-Continent Oil & Gas Association.

Others who contributed information and otherwise assisted include Texas Land Commissioner Bob Armstrong, Judge James E. Barlow, Stanley Brown, Trebbie Brown, James W. Byrd, Bill and Bonnie Cadwell, Ed Campbell, William Clayton, Thomas W. Crouch, Kemper Diehl, Irene Elliott, Evelyn Golz, Charles R. Graham, Annye Hall, Harry Heinecke, Frederic W. and Georgie Heinke, Kay Holmquist, Jean Jackson, Bobby H. Johnson, Emily Jones, Kent Keeth, Margaret Linkous, Elizabeth Mavropoulis, Edward Miller, the late Mrs. Lloyd Murray, Nancy Parker, Roy D. Payne, H. H. Pickens, Bill Poynter, Mary Beth Rogers, Earl A. Ross, Monroe Scoggins, Charles W. Seedle, Floyd Sexton, John Sidney Smith, the late Vesta Stephens, Calvin Sutton, Tomas Torrans, Victor Treat, Bill Williams, Welch Wright, Mrs. Edwin Yerger, and Marshall Young.

There is no way I can adequately express my appreciation for Gilbert and Cora McAllister over the past twenty years. Gilbert carefully read the first five chapters in an earlier version and gave me the benefit of his honest reactions, which made me write better.

Harvey Ginsberg, who was first my editor at Putnam's, got me started and kept me going with his enthusiasm for the project; Hugh G. Howard, my editor upon completion of the manuscript, was as perceptive, professional, and fair as a writer has a right to expect. Blanche C. Gregory, my literary agent for the past dozen years, was an inspiration, a comfort, and a source of encouragement from the beginning. Elizabeth Wright, once again, helped type the final manuscript, often under adverse circumstances as we approached delivery time.

My mother-in-law, Frances Burton, and Birdie Porter were helpful in more than a few ways. My father, J. A. Presley, to whom this book is dedicated, not only encouraged but offered valuable insights into the ways of traders.

The cooperation of my immediate family was crucial. Our

children, John and Ann, cheerfully did all they could to make writing conditions optimal. My wife, Fran, offered me suggestions on the book and saved me countless hours by making those endless trips to the library, bookstore, post office, office suppliers, and repair shops, all the time keeping the family operating efficiently.

Only I, of course, am responsible for any errors or other shortcomings of the book.

JAMES PRESLEY

This book is dedicated
with loving appreciation and gratitude
to my father, James Alex Presley,
and
to the memory of my mother, Opal Wright Presley (1906–1962)

Being a Conversation
Between
FAIN GILLOCK, an Old-Time Oilman,
and
MODY BOATRIGHT, a University Professor

GILLOCK: The oil business, as you may understand, is so filled with miracles that we never get through talking about it or telling stories. And when you get through, even the professional liar couldn't misrepresent things too badly because these miracles still happen.

BOATRIGHT: If what he said wasn't true, it might happen next week.

GILLOCK: That's true. You take the history of your oil development in Texas—reads like fiction.

BOATRIGHT: It certainly does.

GILLOCK: And you can't enlarge upon it—it's just happened, and they are facts, and we have to accept them as being true stories. I know so many of them that if I repeat the stories, it would be difficult for a stranger to believe.

BOATRIGHT: Well, I want you to repeat them. We don't care whether strangers believe them or not.

—Pioneers in Texas Oil, Oral History Project
of the University of Texas at Austin

CONTENTS

INTRODUCTION

The oilman came late in Texas history.

First, there were the Indians, nearly 12,000 years before the first commercial production of petroleum. By the time the Spanish arrived in the sixteenth century four distinct Indian cultures flourished: Caddo in the east, Coahuitecan and Karankawa on the coast and in the south, pueblo tribes in the far west, and nomads on the plains.

The Spanish unfurled the first of six flags that were to fly over Texas. Álonso Álvarez de Pineda claimed the land for his country from aboard ship as he sailed along the Gulf Coast in 1519. Explorations by Alvar Núñez Cabeza de Vaca, Francisco Vásquez de Coronado, and Hernando de Soto followed during the century.

The French fleur-de-lis fluttered briefly and feebly. In the late seventeenth century René-Robert Cavelier, sieur de La Salle, established Fort St. Louis on Matagorda Bay. But the French incursion had little lasting effect except to spur Spain to reaffirm its rights to the land. Spanish settlements appeared in San Antonio, Goliad, and Nacogdoches in the eighteenth century, keeping Texas a part of New Spain which was governed from Mexico City.

When Mexico won its independence from Spain in 1821, Texas, as a part of Mexico, came under the third national flag in a brief but dramatic period. The same year—1821—colonists began arriving in Texas from the United States. Fifteen years later there were about 20,000 settlers and 4,000 black slaves. In 1836 Texans—predominantly Anglo-Americans—declared their independence from Mexico. General Antonio López de Santa Anna marched north from Mexico City to put down the rebels. He wiped out the defenders of the Alamo in San Antonio, then almost drove Sam Houston's army out of the state. But on the afternoon of April 21, 1836, while the Mexican army was relishing siesta time, the Texans swooped down upon Santa Anna's unsuspecting soldiers, routed them, and captured their leader.

For nearly ten uneasy years the fourth flag, that of the Republic of Texas, symbolized a sprawling buffer zone between the expanding United States and Mexico. Then, in 1845, Texas came under a fifth flag when it became the only state to join the Union by treaty. The Mexicans, of course, still considered Texas theirs. The annexation precipitated the Mexican War, which ended with a triumphant United States marching to the Pacific. Texas saw its cotton culture and slaveholding economy grow until the Civil War.

The sixth flag to fly over the Lone Star State was that of the Confederacy, as Texas seceded from the Union in 1861 over the protests of old Sam Houston, governor and a Unionist. The state was spared the bloody fighting experienced in many parts of the South, but the last battle of the war was fought in Texas near Brownsville on the Rio Grande, almost a month after Lee had surrendered at Appomattox. Ironically, the Confederates won.

During the postwar years the state adjusted to the reality of being a conquered land. Union troops occupied it, and for a time radical Republicans governed; in 1870 Texas was readmitted to the Union, and in 1874 conservative Democrats regained control of the state government.

Reconstruction was accompanied by the growth of the cattle business and a concentrated war on the Indians. As early as 1866 cattle drives headed north to Kansas and Nebraska. In the early 1870's federal troops undertook a major campaign against the Indians, who had stepped up their raids during the Civil War. The Indians were subdued in 1875, and the survivors relegated to reservations in the Indian Territory. But many portions of the state remained wild and woolly, enabling the Texas Rangers to earn their fame maintaining law and order during this era.

Steadily Texas grew, its population, its agriculture, its ranches, and its business. The state government, anxious to increase population by luring settlers, generously rewarded railroads with millions of acres of free land for laying tracks, until the double iron rails were as common as cow trails. But the railroads were a mixed blessing; they allowed a two-way flow of passengers and freight, helping "build" Texas, while spreading the influence of out-of-state capital, of which the railroads themselves were the prime example. Passenger and freight rates were controlled from the East. Other out-of-state corporations found Texas to be a fertile field for profit, often to the disgruntlement of the residents. Some called Texas a "truck patch." Anger followed frustration, and alert politicians called for, and passed, state laws to regulate the "outsiders"—laws that were still on the books at the time of the first development of the region's petroleum deposits.

The discovery of oil opened up a new era in the state's—and the nation's—history, bringing a new meaning to the American frontier experience. The early roaring oil camps marked the beginning of a new and rowdy way of life that survived deep into the twentieth century, after the rest of the American—and world—frontier had vanished. Frontier behavior moved to wherever there were new oil fields.

Oil played a dominant role in making Texas what it is today, jerking it into industrialism and booming its spindly cities into throbbing metropolises. Without the fantastic wealth of this natural resource, Texas today might be just another large southwestern state noted for its livestock, agriculture, wide open spaces, and, perhaps, tourism; after all, it does offer a convenient route to Mexico. Instead, the petroleum giant has found its niche as the richest state in natural resources, which, in turn, has attracted other kinds of money, ensuring it abundant millionaires and political clout.

How did it all come about? What were these oil frontiersmen like? What happened to the great wealth? How did the money affect those who ended up with it? This book is an attempt to answer those questions.

A Saga of Wealth

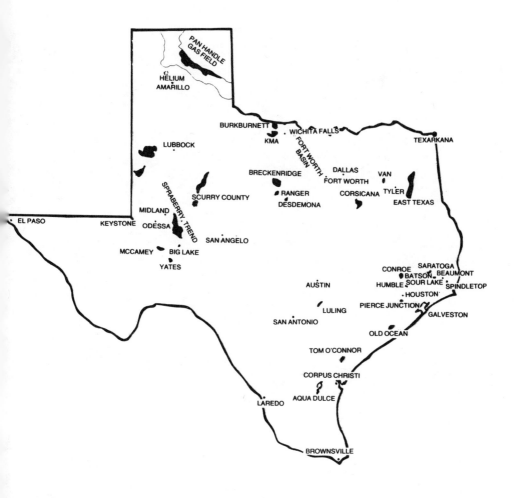

A few of the thousands of oil and gas fields in Texas, including most of those mentioned in the book. (Fields west of Lubbock are Levelland, Slaughter, and Wasson.) If all fields were depicted, they would stretch from Laredo to Brownsville all along the Gulf Coast to the Louisiana boundary; from the south of San Antonio in a northeasterly direction to the east of the East Texas field; in West Texas from west of Lubbock, Odessa-Midland, and the Yates field across to the Wichita Falls–Fort Worth Basin area; and east of the Panhandle gas field.

I

Outsiders, Keep Out!

1

Elaborate historical irony that it is, the debut of the Texas oil industry came hard on the heels of the state's most dramatic reform movement, which featured pitched battles with railroads and other out-of-state trusts in the late nineteenth century.

Eventually the reform laws growing out of this struggle against monopoly had their impact on the oil business. In this way, reformers helped shape the social and legal environment in which the industry would first grow. Their timing made it seem as if the early lawmakers had tailored the statutes to fit the rambunctious oil industry of the future, with special attention to out-of-state capital that would be attracted by the bounteous bonanzas.

Had the prescient laws been enforced to the letter, they would have severely restricted the role of "foreign" capital, for on paper they gave a slight advantage to Texans over outsiders. But making laws is one thing; making them work and seeing that one's successors enforce them are another. However, the changed legal and social climate did make economic opportunity possible for many Texans who otherwise might have lost out altogether.

Of the reformers, the one whose influence stretched farthest and lasted longest was James Stephen Hogg, an unforgettable politician who ultimately became an oilman.

Fiery, eloquent, huge-bodied, good-natured, blue-eyed Jim Hogg was a Texan's Texan. As the most dynamic vote getter to hit the state since old Sam Houston had vanquished the tyrant Santa Anna at the Battle of San Jacinto in 1836, Hogg symbolized the spirit of his times. He was a transitional man, from the old to the new: In the early years of his career, while a state official, he wore a beard as full as any Confederate veteran's; then in mid-career he shaved his face clean, as if to leave no doubt that he represented a new generation, with new styles and new views.

Today our impression of Hogg comes from the photographs of his smooth face. He was a trust-busting attorney general, then a fighting, controversial, and the state's first native-born governor. The six-foot-three Hogg won every state office he sought. If he had wished, he probably could have gone on to the United States Senate. In the 1890's his name was mentioned as a possible Democratic candidate for President, and if William Jennings Bryan had won the White House in 1896, he would have invited Hogg to be his attorney general.[1] Although Hogg has been dead for decades, an election year rarely passes in Texas that his name isn't invoked.

Physically—except for his usually pleasant face—Hogg looked like the stereotyped version of the fat-cat robber baron of his day. In his later years his weight ranged between 250 and 300 pounds. Tall though he was, there was no escaping the truth: He was a fat man and, not surprisingly, sensitive about remarks that juxtaposed his Scottish surname with his obesity. Years after he left the governor's office, while in London, he declined an invitation from King Edward VII because he feared his massive body would look ridiculous in knee trousers and silk stockings.[2]

The circumstances of Hogg's early life go far to explain the course he was to take. A feeling for the underdog and a respect for law and justice came straight out of his childhood and youth. He was born, prophetically perhaps, in the midst of a rainstorm, March 24, 1851, at the family plantation near Rusk, Texas, in a region of pine trees and rolling hills that eight decades later was to produce one of the world's great oil reserves. The Hogg family enjoyed wealth and status. They owned fifteen slaves and more than 2,000 acres of land. Jim's Alabama-born lawyer father, Joseph Hogg, had arrived in

Texas in the days of the Republic and had served in its Congress, in the Annexation Convention of 1845, and in the State Senate.

Young Jim seemed headed for a comfortable, predictable future when the Civil War intervened and the prosperous life abruptly ended with a string of shattering events. In 1862, when Jim was eleven, his father died of fever while in command of his Confederate brigade at Corinth, Mississippi. The next year his mother died. At twelve he was an orphan in the midst of a war the South could not win.

Thrust into the world on his own, young Hogg had to fend for himself. Like Abraham Lincoln before him, he read by a pine-knot fire to gain his education. Privation and misfortune became a part of his life. After the war was over, he was cheated of a year's cotton money—more than $500—that he had earned as a share cropper. Not long after that some local ruffians tried to murder him one night and very nearly succeeded, as they sought revenge on the big, strapping farm youth, who, some time before, had helped the sheriff arrest them. They shot him in the back. With a pistol ball lodged near his spine, young Hogg hovered between life and death. A doctor probed the wound with a pine stick but was unable to remove the bullet. Somehow the tenacious patient recovered. He was to suffer excruciating pain from the lead near his spine until ten years later, when he decided to endure it no longer. During the noon recess of court one day he summoned a physician and without anesthetics had the metal dug out and the wound stitched in time for the afternoon session of court.[3]

These discouraging events only spurred young Hogg onward in a determined struggle to make something of his life. "Hardship," he wrote, "is the native soil of manhood and self-reliance. He who cannot abide the storm without flinching lies down by the wayside to be over-looked or forgotten." [4]

While still a boy, he worked as a printer's apprentice and later as an editor for a series of small-town weekly newspapers in eastern Texas. At twenty he launched the triweekly Longview *News*, and the next year, 1872, he established the Quitman *News* in another town. Through journalism he mastered the English language.

Running a newspaper wasn't enough for the large, awkward young man. At night he studied law; by the time he was admitted to the bar he had married and had launched his political career by winning the post of justice of the peace on a platform of "Enforce the Law!" He later won the county attorney's office using the same slogan. He never backed off from a fight and during one speech stepped down from the stump to thrash a heckler whose remarks had become too personal. As county attorney he enforced the law as he had promised, even prosecuting his own friends for Sunday horse trading.

His backcountry charisma soon swept him into the newly created office of district attorney—criminal prosecutor for six counties—where, as in the past, he stood unequivocally for the majesty of the law and due process. He lashed out against mob action and built a reputation for antiracism that endeared him to the blacks who lived in East Texas. When he left politics briefly to practice law in Tyler, the "capital" of East Texas, he became a popular speaker before black audiences and was instrumental in "redeeming" the county from the Republicans in 1884 by swaying over enough black voters.[5]

The times were ripe for Hogg. Farmers, workingmen, and independent voters seethed with discontent over the shoddy service and cavalier treatment they received from the out-of-state corporations. When Hogg decided to seek the Democratic nomination for attorney general in 1886, his issues were waiting for him. He won the nomination by acclamation and coasted to victory in the fall.

In the state capital at Austin thirty-five-year-old Attorney General Hogg found Augean stables awaiting their political Hercules. Hogg's first goal became to enforce the state's insurance laws strictly. He filed suits to oust forty "wildcat" fire insurance companies. When they responded with countersuits, he roared with righteous indignation, "The whole thing is a monstrosity, and I am going to assault it if it stops immigration, makes the newspapers mad, 'busts Texas,' and buries myself forever." [6] He won his suits; those firms that returned to do business were mindful of the laws on capitalization.

Another cause was less easily handled. A new State Capitol was being built in Austin, under contract with a Chicago syndicate. The state had paid the syndicate 3 million acres of land in the Texas Panhandle, on which the syndicate had established the sprawling XIT Ranch.

Because of huge English and Scottish holdings in West Texas, the Texans were sensitive to foreign ownership, and the contract with the Chicago syndicate specified American ownership of the ranch. But the financiers ran short of funds and began selling stock—illegally—in England. When the syndicate attempted to change the wording of the contract, Hogg refused to allow it.

That was merely one aspect of the Capitol controversy. The dome was built in Belgium, but because of the discriminatory railway rates, it cost more to ship it from Galveston to Austin, about 200 miles, than across the Atlantic. Rubbing salt into the wound, the Chicago syndicate imported granite cutters from Scotland to shape the native Texas stone. When the new building was dedicated in May, 1888, the roof leaked.[7]

Hogg forced the syndicate to repair the roof and the whole experience, coupled with other shenanigans by foreign and out-of-state interests, inspired the legislature to pass, later while Hogg was governor, an alien land law. No foreigner—one not a citizen of the United States—was allowed to own land in Texas. Another law severely restricted the landowning privileges of corporations, with a fifteen-year deadline for disposal of land not needed for the conduct of business. These were body blows to absentee landlordism.

Hogg's most memorable struggles were with the railroads. Texas had granted railroad promoters 10,240 acres of public lands for every mile of track built; the companies could then sell the land to finance their rail laying. Eventually rail companies had been handed nearly 40 million acres, the size of six or seven Eastern states—and about 22 percent of Texas' area. Although only two other states had more rail miles, Texas was plagued with high rates, poor service, and overcapitalized lines.[8] As attorney general Hogg sued the nine trunk-line members of the noncompeting, rate-setting Texas Traffic Association, charging them with illegal monopoly. Winning a permanent injunction, he forced them to disband. In another suit he recovered millions of acres of public land—about the size of Rhode Island—that railroads had acquired unlawfully.

What Hogg did openly in the courts, however, could not undo what was agreed upon in secret between the companies. The railroads went underground with gentlemen's agreements that left no substantial evidence for the rampaging young attorney general.

Stiffer laws were needed, and consulting frequently with Hogg, legislators in 1889 passed the state's first antitrust bill, aimed at railroad combines and other out-of-state corporations. Texas became the second state—by four weeks, after Kansas—to enact such laws, logical reforms for a state in which out-of-state monopolies and foreign landowners appeared to be dominating economic life.[9] Preceding the federal Sherman Antitrust Act of 1890 and bearing the heavy imprint of Hogg's thinking, the Texas law has been described as "a dragnet of great sweep and close mesh." [10]

If, of course, one moved to Texas and set up business, that person or company was no longer an outsider. So long as a business was operated in conformity with the state's laws, that business was welcomed. Texas was building, and emigration from other parts of the country was encouraged. Hogg's thinking was not antibusiness, but a juridical attempt to ensure fair competition.

Armed with the newly passed weapon, Hogg waged an aggressive campaign for safer rail lines and for compliance with the law, exhibiting the same vigor with which he had stamped out Sunday horse trading back in the piney woods. As suit followed suit, Hogg engaged the rail companies in pitched battles. State law required a Texas headquarters for Texas operations, and when old rail magnate Jay Gould moved the International and Great Northern offices and shops from Texas in revenge for the lawsuits, Hogg forced the firm to return to Texas. Later he forced the Texas and New Orleans to return its offices and shops from New Orleans to Houston.

As 1890 rolled around, the logical leading candidate for governor was trust-busting, never-say-die Jim Hogg. But he had reservations. "The honest truth is," he wrote a friend, "I am too poor to hold such an office." [11] A few months later he reluctantly agreed to run. His announcement was the signal for the railroad interests to muster their forces as never before. Jay Gould took the candidacy so personally that he made a special trip to Texas to help defeat Hogg. Although the rail magnate claimed he was touring for his health, everywhere he went he spoke out against Hogg. "The attitude of the Attorney General is such as to cause some fright among capitalists," Gould warned in Dallas.[12] If Gould's words weren't specific enough, the state's big-city press spelled it out: With Hogg as governor, business would suffer.

Gould was not the first to attack Hogg. The year before, a railroad lobbyist had publicly denounced Hogg's lawsuits against the rail companies as encouraging to "anarchists and communists." [13] It was not to be the last instance in which charges of "communism" were flung at a Texas reformer, and the accusation, no doubt, played a part in Hogg's decision to carry the fight to its logical conclusion—the establishment of a regulatory commission especially for railroads.

Unfazed, Hogg called for a three-man railroad commission and compared Texas' rates with those of states where railroads were regulated. In Georgia, lumber was hauled 100 miles for $14 a carload; Gould's Texas and Pacific line charged $80. Texas ice factories paid $80 to ship a carload of ice 200 miles within the state, while St. Louis competitors sent a carload 1,000 miles for $60.[14] "Enforce the laws, show no quarter to any man who will practice frauds on the people by inflated, fictitious securities," thundered Hogg from the stump. "Let capital know that in Texas a written obligation means what it says, and that all public securities will be strictly scrutinized by a state jealous of her reputation for honesty in all things." [15] In the convention that summer in San Antonio the thirty-nine-year-old Hogg won the Democratic nomination by a landslide. He swamped his Republican foe in the general election.

The moment the railroad officials had so adroitly avoided for so long was now before them. Lobbyists labored day and night in the capital city, Austin. Legislators were treated like princes. Those who would accept had their choice of shad roe, sirloins, porterhouses, and English mutton chops, washed down with the rarest of wines and the strongest of liquors, along with weekend junkets to the Gulf Coast. Other politicians, filled with free food and drink, won handsomely at card games hosted by lobbyists. As if this were not insurance enough, prominent Texans were recruited to caution the inexperienced young legislators, most of them fresh from the farm or small towns. Their words built up to a one-theme chorus with varying lyrics: "Don't be too hard on the railroads. . . . We need them. . . . Hogg is a demagogue. . . . He wants too much power. . . . Hogg's just too radical." [16]

Hogg counterattacked by individually exposing the underhanded tactics of the lobby to each legislator and by letting each one know he intended to take the fight to the people, if necessary. The lights burned late in the governor's mansion as Hogg conferred with legislators in an all-out effort to keep the bill strong. Ultimately Hogg's regulatory bill passed by a comfortable margin.

To head the first Railroad Commission, Governor Hogg wanted someone honest, prominent, and beyond reproach. The man best suited, he felt, was United States Senator John H. Reagan, who had been postmaster general of the Confederacy. The governor invited seventy-year-old Reagan to the mansion and handed him a copy of the new law.

After reading it, Reagan looked up, surprised. "How was it that such a law as this got through? It is the best commission law I ever saw."

Hogg, pleased, said, "It is the best law that has been passed in Texas in many a day and in habilitating the commission I am going to reach up and get the curtains of heaven to clothe it in, even if I have to pull somebody out of the United States Senate!" [17]

In June, 1891, the Texas Railroad Commission held its first meeting. Decades later the Railroad Commission became the state's regulatory agency for the oil industry as well, and it still is. Over the years its importance to petroleum production came to overshadow its original significance. In more recent history, reactions to its effectiveness have been mixed. Some reformers have periodically criticized many of its commissioners for too often favoring the major companies, instead of regulating the industry as impartial referees. To some extent the commission also has been limited by its statutory mandate to ensure conservation of resources, at the expense of other regulatory possibilities. But, then, evolution may take many turns.

2

Hogg's reforms made him a national figure. In his native state the whirlwind of controversy raged around him until his death. His supporters perceived him as an almost perfect man, his mind constantly preoccupied with the welfare of the common people. The anti-Hogg faction viewed him as "a gigantic swashbuckler of more tongue than brains," and the Galveston and Dallas *News* denounced him as the "completest and most perfect specimen of the demagogue that the nineteenth and all other centuries have produced." [18]

The most revealing clue of all to his character, though, may have been the circumstances under which he left the governor's mansion in January, 1895. He was nearly forty-four years old. He was thousands of dollars in debt, and he had to borrow money with which to pay his personal bills until he established a private law practice. After four terms in two of the highest public offices that the Lone Star State had to offer, Jim Hogg's bank balance came to $135.[19]

3

During his second term as attorney general Hogg was alerted to the monopolistic practices of John D. Rockefeller's Standard Oil Company. In 1894, while Hogg was rounding out his last year in the governor's mansion, Standard dominated the market for oil and kerosene in the Southwest. In Texas, Rockefeller's corporation accomplished this through the Waters Pierce Oil Company.

Following a months-long investigation of the Waters Pierce operations, Texas Attorney General Charles A. Culberson felt the evidence was strong enough to take the company to court for violating the state's antitrust act. Suit was filed, and in 1894 indictments were handed down in Waco against John D. Rockefeller et al. of Standard and Henry Clay Pierce et al. of Waters Pierce. Governor Hogg sought extradition of Rockefeller from New York and Standard official Henry M. Flagler from Florida. When New York and Florida refused to extradite the two men, the trial proceeded against the division manager of Waters Pierce. He was convicted a year after Hogg left office. Fined $50 for being a party to "a conspiracy against trade," the manager declined to pay the fine, was jailed, and won his point when the Texas Court of Criminal Appeals ruled that the state had not proved the defendant was "knowingly" a party to conspiracy.

The legislature strengthened the state antitrust act, and the attorney general's office charged after Waters Pierce with renewed vigor. In 1896 Attorney General Martin M. Crane noted that Waters Pierce, for its own benefit, as well as for the Standard trust, controlled "ninety-nine per cent of the oil business of Texas, amounting to one-half million barrels annually." Waters Pierce eliminated competition by rebating customers who would decline to handle other oil and by underselling rivals and putting them out of business, then, in triumph, raising prices unreasonably. Through transfers of stock to Standard Oil, Waters Pierce remained a part of the trust it was sworn not to be.

Attorney General Crane went for the jugular vein. He sued to force the company to forfeit its Texas charter and won. In June, 1897, a jury in Austin rendered a verdict against Waters Pierce. The company's state charter was canceled, and Waters Pierce was prohibited from doing any business within Texas. This time the trial court's decision stuck. The State Court of Civil Appeals and the State Supreme Court upheld the judgment, and in 1900 the United States Supreme Court sustained the lower court's rulings.[20]

Just when their own native oil resources were developing, the trust-busting Texans had let the nation know what they thought about Standard Oil and its surrogates, but it was not the last they were to hear of Waters Pierce.

4

The accepted economic facts of life in those days were depicted in geography classes with catechistic thoroughness.

"What is Pennsylvania noted for?" the teacher would ask.

"Coal and oil," the children would respond.

"What is Texas noted for?"

"Cattle and cotton."

Decades later a veteran oilman, Claude Witherspoon, wryly recalled those scenes from his own childhood in Corsicana. "There wasn't supposed to be any oil or gas south of the Mason-Dixon line at that time," he said. "Well, I drilled a gas well in that schoolyard, right where we were studying, after I got in the business." [21]

For most of the nineteenth century nobody dreamed that Texas would ever become an oil-producing state. Since the day in 1859 when Edwin L. Drake had brought in his Titusville well, Pennsylvania had dominated the fledgling American oil industry. Although Texas' first well had been drilled not long after the Drake well, production had been negligible for decades. In 1866 Lyne Taliaferro Barret, using a very crude rotarylike device, had found oil at 106 feet in Nacogdoches County in the eastern part of Texas. It produced only ten barrels a day, and Barret went back to farming.[22]

As late as 1889 the Dallas *Morning News* published a long, detailed two-column "Survey of the Geology of Texas" that gave petroleum the least attention, after guano, coal, metallic ores, mineral waters and gases, and salt deposits. One sentence was all the future industry received: "Petroleum springs, including heavy lubricating oils, are known to eastern Texas and the work of studying this geological character will soon be begun." [23] During an eight-year period ending in 1895 Texas produced no more than sixty barrels a year, "about enough to oil the guns of the Texas Rangers," one waggish commentator observed. Even as late as 1900 the economy was almost totally supported by agriculture, timber, and their products.[24]

5

The oil that heralded Texas' earliest commercial field came with more irritation than jubilation. It almost spoiled a community's drinking water.

In the 1890's the little town of Corsicana, just south of Dallas, was looking for a reliable water supply. Eventually a special company was chartered to put down three artesian wells within the city limits. The drilling sites soon became the focus of social activity as townspeople clustered to observe and comment.

The drillers worked with an old cable tool rig and a wooden derrick. When they reached a depth of 1,035 feet, crude oil began rising to the surface.[25] After metal casing was sunk to seal off the oil, the petroleum continued to rise to the surface and was diverted into a ditch that drained 150 gallons a day. Despite this irksome interruption, the water well was finally completed at 2,470 feet, and that, with the other two wells, provided Corsicana with its water supply for many years.

Two profit-minded local businessmen sent a sample of the crude

\

oil to a laboratory operated by a Standard Oil affiliate in Oil City, Pennsylvania. The oil was of commercial quality which meant, in that preautomobile era when only five automobiles and no trucks were registered in the entire county, that it was good for burning in lamps.

A local company was organized. One partner was a Pennsylvanian, who may have been a roving scout for Pennsylvania wildcatters John H. Galey and James M. Guffey. The news spread fast. By September, 1895, Galey and Guffey were committing money to drill for Corsicana's oil. Soon afterward they dispatched rigs and crews to the scene. After slight initial success, however, they lost interest and sold out two years later.

A new company, composed of local businessmen, took up the search for oil but was also afflicted by the twin plagues that were repeatedly to frustrate early Texas oil development: the lack of capital and a scarcity of knowledgeable operators. As time went on, Texans were to become experienced—*the* experts, in fact—in drilling and producing oil. But they were never to solve completely the need to seek funds from outside the state. New York and Chicago were financial centers. A man could find money near at hand, maybe, for small-scale drilling. But if he had something big, especially a bonanza, he necessarily had to persuade "outsiders"—major oil companies or wealthy financiers and investors—to help him develop his field. On a smaller scale, the Corsicana experience was the beginning of this pattern of going out of state for capital.

Corsicana's mayor, James E. Whiteselle, wrote Joseph S. Cullinan, a Washington, Pennsylvania, oilman with close ties to the Standard Oil empire. In the fall of 1897, when Cullinan was en route to California on a business trip, the Corsicanians met him in Dallas and took him to their town.

At thirty-six, mustached, strong-jawed "Buckskin Joe" Cullinan, as he had been known during the days when he was a tough crew boss, was an aggressive, strictly business, closed-mouthed oilman. The first son of Irish immigrants, the Pennsylvania native had worked his way from a laborer's job to a Standard Oil executive position. Now mature and polished, his "buckskin" qualities dormant within a muscular frame nearly six feet tall, Cullinan was intimately familiar with all aspects of the business.[26]

"They didn't know anything about Cullinan, nor any of the rest of these folks," recalled local banker Arthur Elliot years afterward. "And they wired the Sam Houston Bank and got the wire back that Cullinan and those he represented—they would recognize his checks for one million dollars or more. Well, you know, a million dollars in those days was some money." [27]

The men who stood behind Cullinan in his first Texas venture were friends from his Standard days: Calvin N. Payne and Henry C. Folger, Jr., both officials in the Rockefeller organization. With their backing Cullinan formed a company that made Corsicana Texas' first oil boomtown, as Cullinan drilled what today would be considered very shallow wells, 1,000 to 2,000 feet deep. Derricks soon towered over housetops within the city itself as Cullinan completed well after well.[28]

From the beginning, Cullinan was thought to be connected with Standard Oil, a belief that he made no great effort to suppress. Early in his Texas venture, he was quoted as saying, "I am representing myself and capital back of me, but I am not making this deal for the Standard Oil Company. Still, this contract will not conflict or be inimical to the interests of the Standard people." Evidence indicates that Cullinan first went to Texas as an independent and attempted to raise capital from non-Standard sources; only when that failed did he go to his Standard friends.[29]

Corsicana was like a beachhead, the first one of the Texas oil frontier, with the next jumping-off point unknown. Cullinan's refinery was one of the first west of the Mississippi, and a surging local pride announced itself the day some of the town's citizens stood atop a tank car of "crude" with a banner that proclaimed:

CORSICANA PETROLEUM OIL.
GREATEST DISCOVERY EVER MADE IN TEXAS, QUALITY
AS GOOD AS
PENNSYLVANIA'S. QUANTITY UNLIMITED.[30]

If the actions of the Texas trustbusters had signaled, in effect, "Outsiders, Keep Out!," the sign at Corsicana negated it by erecting an unspoken, but powerful, message that beckoned, "Outsiders, Flock In!" While the curators of the state's legal machinery brooded over how to keep Standard Oil's tentacles from controlling trade, Standard-linked money was busily developing the local resources.

In 1898 the Corsicana field produced more than a half million barrels of oil.[31] These first signs of wealth and boom soon attracted immigrants of a type that could hardly have been foreseen a decade earlier. In a way they did not know themselves, the Texans were getting ready, emotionally, for Spindletop. In only a very small way, however—for there was no precedent for Spindletop.

II

SPINDLETOP—WHERE IT ALL BEGAN

1

The great Beaumont field that launched Texas as a major oil state, built three cities, opened up the rich Gulf Coast, broke the worldwide monopoly of Standard Oil, and ushered in the age of liquid fuel began as a dream in the head of one man.

Spindletop traces its genesis to slender, hump-shouldered Pattillo Higgins, a one-armed jack-of-all-trades, who began talking up his visions of a prosperous, oil-rich Beaumont a decade before the first gusher blew in. No man could have been a better promoter for the field than Higgins. Born in Beaumont in 1863, he demonstrated in his youth that toughness of spirit required to make a successful oil promoter. One day young "Bud" Higgins was threatened with a switching by his teacher for not bringing his grammar book. "Well, I tell you," husky young Bud said, "I don't believe you can whip me. I don't believe you can whip me!" The schoolmaster never forced the issue. He laid down his stick and told the boy to return to his seat.[1]

Several years later, Higgins lost his left arm in a shooting episode. One version is that he lost his arm as the result of being shot in the hand during an accident in his youth. But others who knew both Higgins and Beaumont said he lost the arm after a shooting fight with a man named Bill Patterson. Patterson lost his life, and Higgins went free in what apparently was ruled justifiable homicide. One contemporary described Patterson as an officer. Another account has it that Higgins was acting as a constable.[2] Whichever was the truth, Higgins was as unyielding as the steel forged in his father's blacksmith shop.

After he quit school, the boy worked at whatever he could find in the small town of 9,000 in the flat coastal region. "I could build anything I wanted to build," he once told an interviewer. He became a cabinetmaker, sold fish (once catching a 600-pound sturgeon in the Gulf, he claimed), worked on a railroad, and wheeled sawdust for a sawmill. In the sawmill he learned about machinery, which was to become a lifelong fascination.

Later Higgins set up a brick plant. During a business trip up north to buy equipment, he saw for the first time—in Dayton, Ohio—brick material being burned with oil as fuel. He witnessed a similar sight in Indianapolis. Oil produced an even, easily regulated heat, an obvious improvement over the logwood fire he had been using. He also visited oil fields during his trip and learned the surface signs used to find oil and gas. With the still-fresh memory of what he had seen, he was determined to find petroleum. In the Gulf Coast area of Texas, he believed, there was oil, a conclusion based upon gaseous smells he had noticed there.[3] He sold his brick plant and entered the real estate business.

By this time Higgins had long since lived down his wilder days. He had become a deacon in Beaumont's First Baptist Church, where he also taught a class of girls. One day he took his Sunday school class on an outing to the "sour springs" near Beaumont. Each of the five springs was eight feet deep. Containing blue, green, and yellow waters with smells redolent of lemon phosphate, kerosene, and rotten eggs, the water had been used for health aids, either for drinking or bathing. Its properties were various; either constipation or diarrhea might result.[4] After studying every clue he could find, Higgins decided the springs lay on an oil field.

The focus of his attentions was a circular mound rising above the surrounding swampy land in an elbow of the Neches River. The immediate area gave off a sulfuric smell from a sulfur spring and surface gas. Higgins and others had set fire to the gas and watched, fascinated. "You could burn it by taking a tin can and heading up the bubble there and strike a match and she'd flash and maybe burn," he recalled years later.[5]

Big Hill, as it was known, was about fifteen feet higher than the surrounding terrain. The name Spindletop was to come later, borrowed indirectly from that of a popular picnic spot called Spindletop Springs, about a mile away on the banks of the Neches River: When the schooners came down the Neches without their sails up, the long, slender, bare masts stuck up like exaggerated spearlike metal spindles used to hold the yarn in an old-fashioned spinning wheel. Hence, the name Spindletop Springs. When a promoter applied Spindletop Heights to his acreage during the boom, thereafter Spindletop was applied to the hill and the field.[6]

Higgins read everything he could find about geology. He developed a theory that the mound was caused by a rock structure pushing up from beneath. Under the rock, he believed, was oil. Despite a discouraging opinion from the United States Geological Survey that the Gulf Coast was not a likely oil region, Higgins maintained his conviction that the hill would produce. When he encountered a "For Sale" sign on the north edge, he knew the golden moment had come. The tract involved 1,077 acres.

Higgins pondered the situation through a sleepless night. The next day he sought to convince a number of Beaumont's leading citizens of the hill's potential. After a string of disappointing interviews he decided to go to George W. Carroll, president and general manager of the Beaumont Lumber Company. He took Carroll out to the scene.

"Now, Mr. Carroll," he said, "I believe it's an oil field, and gas, and a good chance for a big sulfur mine. Now if it turns out like I believe it will, it'll be worth millions of dollars." [7]

Carroll, the town's leading Baptist and a neatly groomed man whose gray-flecked beard flowed to the top button of his waistcoat, was persuaded to invest the $1,000 option price if Higgins could secure a joint loan to cover the rest of the price at $6 an acre. This Higgins did. There remained the matter of adding other acreage on the hill. Higgins was not able to buy the other tracts, but Captain George W. O'Brien, a leading lawyer in the town who owned 1,350 acres, and John F. Lanier, with 273 acres, were willing to put their land into a company that would exploit its minerals. This was the beginning of the Gladys City Oil, Gas, and Manufacturing Company, named, as a tribute to Higgins as a teacher, after Gladys Bingham, a little Episcopalian girl who attended Higgins's Baptist Sunday school classes. The company was chartered in 1892. Twenty-eight-year-old Higgins, himself a draftsman, drew part of the letterhead.[8]

To drill the first well, the company contracted with a Dallas man who subcontracted the job to redheaded Walter B. Sharp, then twenty-three years of age and destined to become a pioneer of the Gulf Coast's oil fields. But Sharp's drill bogged in quicksand, and he gave it up at 418 feet, less than one-third of the depth stipulated in the contract.[9] Another abortive attempt by another drilling contractor also failed, this time because of the cable tool equipment used, the wrong kind of a rig for the Gulf Coast's soft strata. A cable tool rig literally pounds the hole down, as the heavily weighted drill smashes up and down; then the cuttings are bailed out of the hole. It works best in hard rock. On the other hand, a rotary drill—as the word implies—rotates, all the while boring deeper into the earth. On the Gulf Coast, the rotary bit was indispensable.

By then Higgins and his partners were strained financially. Unhappy with the leasing terms the others had foisted on him, Higgins sold his stock in the company, as well as some of his own land, to appease his creditors. He was left with only thirty-three acres on one slope of Big Hill and some scattered lots, but he refused to let go of his dream, which he continued to preach to anyone who would listen, even after one of the state's geologists had condemned the area as bereft of oil.

Eventually the local men lost their patience at Higgins' endless sales pitch of the great fortune to be made. "Well, Pattillo," he was told one day. "I know very little about oil, and you too, and I wish you'd quit bothering me with it." [10]

2

Higgins' faith in the hill seemed to be the only argument for its potential. Beaumont, with a population of about 9,000 people in the center of a rice-growing area, was "just a place in the road," unlikely to attract oil seekers. The leading hotel, the Crosby, was little more than a wooden shack. There were a train depot and a few other buildings. "That's all it was," said one old-timer. "And the rest of Beaumont, there was nothing to it. Just like any other little town that's trying to exist." [11]

Higgins did everything he could think of to lure in new believers. At one point he wrote a letter to John D. Rockefeller, Jr., who turned it over to Standard's Forest Oil Company of Kansas City. A man was sent to Beaumont. Higgins took him over the terrain and painted word pictures of fantastic buried wealth. Standard's man was unimpressed.[12]

When all seemed lost, Higgins tried a new gambit. His former partners would lease the land to him or to others, but he had exhausted all known avenues in trying to raise funds. Why not advertise? Higgins bought space in a manufacturing journal, to find a man with enough money to carry on what others had deemed worthless. But Higgins did not phrase it like that. The bait he dangled was the hope of millions in return.

3

A solitary reply came, signed by Anthony F. Lucas in Louisiana. In April, 1899, Lucas arrived in Beaumont, and Higgins took him out to the long-neglected hill.

Mustached and heavy-jawed, Captain Lucas, as he was known, was a tall, handsome man. He was the adventurer Higgins needed, with the background and ambition it would take.

Born in 1855 on Austria's Dalmatian coast, Lucas had been graduated as a mining engineer from the Polytechnic Institute at Graz. He later trained as a naval officer and was commissioned a lieutenant in the Austrian navy. Instead of going to sea, he took a leave of absence in 1879 to visit an uncle in Saginaw, Michigan. He decided to remain in the United States and was naturalized a citizen at Norfolk, Virginia, in 1885. Soon afterward he married Caroline Fitzgerald, a genteel Georgia belle. In 1893 he became the resident engineer at the Petit Anse salt mines in Louisiana, which he supervised for Myles & Company of New Orleans for about three years. After this, Lucas drilled in southern Louisiana, where he found salt and minor petroleum deposits.[13]

Lucas admitted to Higgins that he was looking for sulfur, really, but it would be all right if they found oil, too. He explained that he had seen mounds formed by underground salt domes pushing upward, and oil was often found around them. In June, 1899, he signed a lease for 663 acres, with an option to buy, for which he agreed to pay the Gladys City company $31,150. He made a down payment of $11,150 cash, with the remainder to be paid by the end of a two-year period. Higgins was to have a 10 percent interest in Lucas' options and an equal percentage from Carroll if the scheme succeeded. The same month Lucas started drilling, using a light rotary rig.

Lucas' first well went to 575 feet, then failed when gas pressure in the hole caused his light piping to collapse. However, it did show gas and oil before he was forced to stop. Lucas' funds were exhausted, and he needed assistance before starting again with heavier equipment. His few meager oil samples were not enough to convince anyone in Beaumont, so he headed east, to interview, among others, Henry C. Folger of Standard Oil. Folger sent Calvin Payne from Pennsylvania to study the site. Arriving with Joe Cullinan, now in Corsicana, Payne condemned it. Later a U.S. geologist also rated it a poor location.

When Lucas was about to give up hope and discontinue drilling, Dr. William Battle Phillips, professor of geology at the University of Texas, offered encouragement. Phillips thought the idea was worthwhile. He gave Lucas a letter of introduction to Guffey and Galey, the Pittsburgh oil firm that had earlier invested in the Corsicana drilling. Lucas scurried off to Corsicana and met John H. Galey, who was there on company business. Then the two of them headed to Pittsburgh for a conference with James McClurg Guffey.

The Higgins-Lucas geological theory was accepted. Guffey agreed to back the drilling of three wells—provided the first one was promising—and urged Lucas to lease as much property as possible in the area. Lucas' share, however, was whittled thin, and Guffey insisted that Lucas tell nobody, not even Higgins, of the details of their arrangement. Lucas leased thousands of acres more, covering the area of the mound except for Higgins' thirty-three acres and other small holdings. This he did at a personal sacrifice; Mrs. Lucas had to sell their furniture.[14]

Once Guffey and Galey's requirements had been met, Galey

headed for Beaumont. He arrived on a day that Lucas was out of town. Mrs. Lucas took him to the big hill. At the sulfur springs he stopped and pondered, then planted a stake about fifty feet away. There, he announced, the well would be drilled. When Lucas returned later, the two men agreed that each of the three wells would be drilled to a depth of 1,200 feet. Then Galey said, "Captain, I know a man who can drill that well to twelve hundred feet if it can be done at all. I consider him the most capable drilling contractor in this country. Go to Corsicana and see if a trade can be made. His name is Jim Hamill." [15]

4

The Hamill brothers—Jim, Curt, and Al—were Pennsylvania-born. Heavyset Jim, the eldest, had gone to work early as a tool dresser on a cable tool drilling rig that dug many artesian water wells in Texas. Shorter, broad-faced Curt ran a farm and dairy. Al, the baby brother, had been sent to Pennsylvania to live with an aunt; when he grew old enough, he headed for Texas to work with his brother Jim. [16]

At the discovery of oil in Corsicana, Jim and Al Hamill went into the oil drilling business. In 1898 Curt left his farm and dairy at Waco, Texas, to work with his brothers as a tool dresser at $55 a month. It was good pay, even though a working day lasted twelve hours, and sometimes eighteen. Soon the Hamills bought a rotary drilling rig.

Lucas made a deal with Jim Hamill, who served as business manager for the brothers, for $2 a foot for the well. Guffey and Galey would provide the pipe. In early October, 1899, the Hamills shipped their rotary rig via train from Corsicana to Beaumont. Al Hamill arrived with the rig and immediately purchased lumber for the derrick and bark-covered slabs to fuel the boiler that would provide the steam to power the drill. Then, to the amazement of Lucas, the brawny young man unloaded the carload of pipe by himself, skidding it down the side of the rail car. As soon as the rest of the crew arrived, a slush pit was dug. The slush pit was to contain waste materials washed out of the hole. Then another pit was dug, into which water could be pumped to make steam. The boiler was soon moved by mule team to the drilling site.

They began building a wooden derrick, though none of them had ever built one before. They knew how large the base had to be and the size at the top. From that they made a pattern, as a seamstress would for a dress.

One day, as he waited alone on the derrick sills, Curt Hamill was greeted by a one-armed man driving a buggy, who introduced himself as Pattillo Higgins.

"If you get this well down, you're going to bring in an oil well," Higgins predicted.

"What makes you think there is oil here, Mr. Higgins?"

Then Higgins, who at that time knew nothing of Lucas' agreement with the easterners, confided in him a secret that he had told only one other person—his original partner, George Carroll.

"I had a vision and a dream. I dreamed I saw houses over this hill and it bothered me so much that the next morning I went down to the livery stable and got me a horse and a post auger and came out here and spent a whole day on the hill. I drilled six post-holes as deep as the auger would go and carried the formation in to Mr. Carroll and told him of my dream. Mr. Carroll said he would have the samples analyzed.

"The following night I had another dream. This time I saw derricks over this hill with fluid going high in the air. I awoke sitting up in bed. The following morning I went back to see Mr. Carroll, but he was out in the woods and I didn't get to see him until after night. I told him of the second dream, and that I would like to buy some land on the hill.

"Mr. Carroll said, 'Pattillo, I know some men that might join us and we will purchase some land out there.' " [17]

5

The Hamill crew built the derrick out of wet, green timber in less than two weeks. Then early one fall morning they began—spudding in, it is called—by boring into the soil with a twelve-inch bit.

They experienced a number of difficulties. After several hundred feet they struck a stratum of coarse water sand that caused them to lose the water they were pumping into the well. Curt Hamill thought muddy water would help. A preacher named Cheney, who owned the mules they had used on the pits, solved the problem. He drove his herd of cattle over and kept them moving through the pit for four hours, until there was a good supply of mud. This was pumped into the hole to hold back the troublesome sand while they drilled through it.

They moved along, drilling through some sticky gumbo mud and surviving a small gas blowout that blew water out of the hole and damaged their rotary drill. They reached 870 feet in early December. About three o'clock one morning Al Hamill noticed the pump was working more freely and the rotary was turning more easily. He smelled gas. Daylight came, and there was oil on top of their mud ditch. Captain Lucas telegraphed Galey.

The old wildcatter hurried to Beaumont as fast as trains could convey him. It took three days. He ordered a four-inch pipe set in the hole, perforated where the oil had come forth. A very fine, soft sand came up inside the new pipe—without oil. Next they put two-inch pipe inside the four-inch pipe to wash out the sand, but that didn't work. Everyone was thoroughly discouraged, and Galey saw no way to solve the problem. He decided to abandon the hole and try a new location where such fine sand wouldn't bother them.

At this point Mrs. Lucas, a determined woman, spoke up.

"Mr. Galey," she said, "the contract calls for drilling this well to twelve hundred feet. I'm not satisfied with this test. I feel that every effort should be made to carry this well down to twelve hundred feet. We need to know what there is down that far." They decided to continue drilling.[18]

Three men—Curt and Al Hamill and Peck Byrd—operated the rig day and night until Christmas Eve, rotating turns on night shifts. The two Hamill brothers caught the train to Corsicana for the holidays and right after Christmas Curt returned with his family, including his one-year-old son, Claud, who decades later was to become a prominent oilman in his own right. By New Year's Day, 1901, all the crew were back at work. They drilled through shale and gumbo, then struck a hard rock that shut them down. The old drilling bit was badly worn, and they had to replace it.

As they were running the drill pipe with the new bit back into the well, with about 700 feet of pipe in, the drilling mud began to boil up. Pressure was rising. Curt Hamill was on a ladder up in the derrick. Then the drill pipe began moving as if it were about to fly out through the top of the derrick.

Suddenly the pipe catapulted through the derrick, knocking the boiler smokestack down and cascading lengths of pipe all about. Rocks coughed out of the hole, followed by the smell and sound of gas. Then it came: a frothy black liquid bubbling from the six-inch hole in the earth, flowing higher and higher, until it shot up through the top of the derrick. *Oil!*

Curt, blinded by mud and oil, never was sure, to the day he died more than seventy years later, how he got down from the derrick. Oil was everywhere. The derrick floor was slippery with it. Curt heard Al and Peck Byrd yelling for him to get away. But the machinery was still running, so he struggled across the slick derrick floor and kicked the clutch off, to prevent the pressure from throwing the equipment into the crown block at the top and tearing the derrick down. Al and Byrd were still shouting at him. With oil in his eyes, somehow he stumbled toward them.

Finally safe and wiping oil out of his eyes with his shirttail, he realized how close he had been to death. He could see the pipe lengths scattered where they had been blown out of the hole. It seemed miraculous that none had struck him.

As they stood watching the six-inch jet of oil rising more than 100 feet over the derrick, Curt remembered the fire in the boiler.

"We've got to get that fire out!" he yelled. The trio ran with buckets of water to the boiler and doused the firebox until the flames were gone. It was another miracle that the oil hadn't caught fire from the boiler before they were finished.[19]

The oil that would open up the great Spindletop field was roaring out from 1,020 feet.[20] It was ten-thirty on the morning of Friday, January 10, 1901, a date that marked the beginning of a new era in the history of petroleum and of Texas.

6

Peck Byrd scurried to notify Captain Lucas. The captain wasn't home, so Byrd left word and returned to the well. Located by his wife at a dry goods store, the captain dashed to his buckboard and, with his old horse in a dead run, headed for the hill. The drilling crew saw him racing over the horizon. He was rolling so fast that when his buckboard came up to the gate, the horse stopped abruptly, throwing Lucas out of the vehicle in an almost comical fashion. A very heavy man, whom they'd never seen excited before over anything, now Lucas was extremely agitated.

"Al! Al! What is it?" Lucas shouted.

"Why, it's oil, Captain." [21]

The large captain grabbed young Hamill and hugged him until he seemed likely to squeeze him in two. "Thank God, thank God!" he bellowed. Then he hugged Curt Hamill and Peck Byrd.

Elated though they were, Lucas and his team were ill prepared for such good fortune. They knew no way to stop the wild flowing well, had no tanks in which to store oil. As soon as he regained his composure, Lucas rushed off to send a telegram to Galey in Pittsburgh. But Galey wasn't in the home office, and it took three days to locate him in West Virginia and get him on a train to Texas.[22]

7

By early afternoon the first sightseers were pouring in from Beaumont. Some had heard the roar of the gusher. Others had seen it. The rest of the town had learned by word of mouth. They walked, drove buggies, rode horseback. Hundreds of people crowded around the fenced-in cow pasture, excitedly viewing the earth's towering ejaculation.

The news spread fast. About five o'clock veteran photographer Frank J. Trost arrived on the afternoon train from Port Arthur. The days were short that time of the year, and it was late in the day to be taking a photograph. Dark clouds, threatening rain, hung low over the Gulf Coast horizon. Nonetheless, Trost set up his tripod about 250 feet from the Lucas well, as it was to be called. The wind was blowing in strong gusts, and a heavy oil spray drifted out across the prairie. Trost clicked his shutter, caught the next train home, worked all night, and was back in Beaumont the next morning with 130 copies of the photograph, all that he could produce in the time he had had. These he sold for 50 cents each. Thirty minutes later he had none left, but a neat profit. Thereafter he sold as many as he could turn out, printing 45,000 copies over the next six weeks. The photograph was published on the front pages of newspapers all over the United States and in foreign countries. It brought him fame and a small fortune.[23]

The dreamer who had started it all, Pattillo Higgins, was in the adjoining county looking at timberland on the day that the Lucas well blew in. At nearly five o'clock that afternoon, as he rode through Beaumont, an old friend hollered at him from the sidewalk. "Bud, did you know you were the wisest man in the world?"

He told Higgins about the well. It was too late now for the tired Higgins to go out to the well after his long trip. The next day he could see and smell the oil from four miles away, in town. He went out to see it firsthand. When he returned, he began organizing the Higgins Oil Company.

But the events leading up to the gusher, cutting him out of the major share that he had yearned for, left a sour taste in his mouth. Until the day he died, he was to allot scant credit to Captain Lucas and the Hamill team.

"They didn't bring the well in," he said. "It brought itself in. If it hadn't have brought itself in, we would have been all starved to death and everything else, and Beaumont would have been an old cow pen—that's all." [24]

8

The roaring gusher performed for ten days, precipitating the wildest rush since the discovery of gold in California. By Sunday 1,000 people had flocked in, and the influx never slackened until the boom was over. The Lucas well sprayed oil over the prairie for miles, saturating grass and soil. Cow tracks were filled with oil. As a milling crowd viewed the well that Sunday, one man lighted a cigar and thoughtlessly threw the match down. With the earth soaked with oil, a fire suddenly flared up. The crowd stampeded like cattle. Peck Byrd and the Hamills began beating out the fire, and a Pennsylvanian in the crowd, who knew the oil business, took off his coat and whipped at the flames. Others did the same. The fire was finally subdued, at the cost of blistered hands and faces and burned clothing.[25]

The flow of the gusher was estimated at somewhere between 70,000 and 100,000 barrels per day. The wasting oil was almost immediately a problem, and men worked with teams of mules to build levees to keep the oil out of the nearby streams. Sulfuric gas fumes from the spray fanned out all the way into Beaumont and discolored the buildings. Ten days after the eruption, every house in Beaumont needed painting.

But what were they to do with a wild well?

When old Galey arrived from the East several days later, Al Hamill met him and took him to his room at the Crosby Hotel. Soon Captain Lucas joined them. A little later Joe Cullinan, who had wasted no time in rushing down from Corsicana, joined the deliberations.

Peck Byrd, whose father had been a civil engineer, had drawn a plan on a brown paper bag. A man named Elmer Dobbins, who had got it from Byrd, sold it to Al Hamill for $500. Al made a deal with Galey to cap the well for $1,000. The next day the Hamill crew rounded up timber, clamps, railroad irons, and valves. Some parts had to come from St. Louis. They fashioned a carriage assembly with a large gate valve to control the flow of oil. Rocks were still coughing up from the depths, along with the oil, so they waited until their valves would be safe.

Just before noon on the tenth day of the black spouter's life, Jim Hamill decided the time was ripe. Al, because he was the unmarried brother, spent most of the afternoon sawing off the pipe protector, working under an unrelenting deluge of oil. The work was extremely hazardous, for a spark from the saw's bite could set off an explosion. Al then dressed the threads on the pipe, with a pair of goggles taped over his eyes and a slicker hat and coat to drain off the oil. By the end of the tense afternoon he had the filing done, and they could screw on the T or the collar. Then they moved the entire assembly over the well, and Curt rushed in and closed the valve. The only injury was to Curt, who was temporarily overcome by gas but soon recovered. He became the first gas casualty on the Gulf Coast.[26]

Oil soaked the countryside. One day, less than a month, later a huge fire broke out as a spark from a locomotive turned the waste oil into an inferno. Men working in the field set a counterfire at the other end. The two fires met in a roar and a flash like lightning, jarring the ground. Black smoke billowed to the next county. Many people, black and white, went to church in Beaumont and prayed. They thought the world was coming to an end.[27]

On the contrary, it was soon throbbing with new life.

9

In today's era of television, understanding how an oil strike like the Lucas well at Spindletop could instantaneously attract mobs of oil-crazed investors and fortune seekers is easy. In 1901, when newspapers and telegraphers conveyed the news that word of mouth didn't handle, the news spread almost as swiftly as it would today. At the Southern Pacific ticket office in Houston, men laid down their money for tickets and then tore out to catch the train, leaving their change behind. Some trains were so overloaded that latecomers could hardly hang on.[28]

Soon after the Lucas well had come in, quiet, sleepy little Beaumont became, in the words of a *Harper's Weekly* writer who surveyed the scene, "the dirtiest, noisiest, busiest, and most interesting town on the continent to-day." [29] The focus of the day-and-night pandemonium was the Crosby Hotel, a ramshackle one-story frame building with a second story in the rear and chinaberry trees in the front. The hotel was across the street from the Southern Pacific Railway station. In older, preoil days the twelve-foot pine porch that swept around two sides of the Crosby was the best place in town to prop one's feet on the banister, smoke, and talk. Suddenly clogged with bustling humanity, the Crosby was more like a modern subway station during a rush hour.

As more drilling got under way and new wells came in, the Crosby porch was partitioned off into narrow, six-foot squares, with each space renting for $100 a month as a real estate "office." Planks divided the stalls. The wall was decorated with blueprints of the great oil field. Although gold and silver were commonly used for smaller transactions, stacks of greenbacks soon appeared—more money than most people had ever seen before. Hundreds of thousands of dollars changed hands as well-dressed people mingled with roughnecks in high-topped boots and slickers in a smoke-filled atmosphere. There was only one bank in Beaumont at the time, the First National, and according to one contemporary, "they just shipped money in there by the sackfuls. Got where the bank wouldn't accept any deposits, because they had it piled in sacks around the lobby."

The lure was enough to drive anyone into a frenzy of expectation; three of the first six wells were capable of producing more than all of the fields in Russia, which had been ranked first in the world in oil production. Soon the upstart Spindletop field was producing more oil than the rest of the world combined.[30]

Rumors, trades, and theories filled the air. Everyone had an explanation of how oil flowed under the earth. Many thought that there was a broad underground river of oil that started in Pennsylvania and that the Lucas gusher was caused by pressure from the north. Everyone wanted a gusher and wanted to organize an oil company. More than 1,000 oil companies were ogranized in this period, as the boom extended into the surrounding county. One broker offered 10-acre blocks of one 5,000-acre survey from a platform in front of the Crosby, beginning each morning at ten o'clock. The survey was twenty-five miles from Spindletop. The man started the price at $10 an acre and advanced it to around $300 by $10 increments. It was a time of big thoughts and big money. One man, discovering a $10 bill in his bankroll, contemptuously tore it up and discarded it in the wastebasket.

"How did you happen to get in my pocket?" he addressed it scornfully.[31]

Claude L. Witherspoon, a Corsicana native in his late twenties, who had already learned a lot about the business by the time he arrived in Beaumont, was moving through the mob when a fellow named Bright seized him by the arm.

"Say, what have you got to sell? What have you got to sell?" Bright wanted to know.

"Well, what's the matter here?" said Witherspoon. "Have people gone crazy?"

"You got anything to sell?"

"Why, yes," said Witherspoon, his memory suddenly refreshed, "I've got a hundred and twenty acres up here about three miles above Beaumont."

"What'll you take for it?"

Witherspoon was ready to part with it forever for $50, but first he warily asked, "Bright, what'll you give me?"

"You can sell it. I believe I can get you five thousand dollars for it."

"Well, I believe I'll take it."

"Sign this contract, sign this contract." [32]

Four brothers in a vaudeville act left the theater in Beaumont, borrowed money, and formed a company that brought in a well. One eastern writer told of two men he had seen on the train from New Orleans. In Beaumont he saw them poring over a map. The next morning half-page newspaper ads announced the existence of the What-Not Oil Company, which offered its $500,000 capital stock at 50 cents on the dollar. One of the men he'd seen on the train was its president; the other was secretary and treasurer.[33]

10

The newly arrived residents of Beaumont ate and slept wherever they could. Many paid $1.50 to $2 a night to sleep on a porch. Some, like H. P. Nichols, paid $3 to sleep in the straw of Broussard's livery stable loft. "I'm certain I never heard a more wonderful exhibition of snoring," said Nichols. "The voices covered the entire range from basso profundo to coloratura soprano." Millionaires slept next to workingmen.

The Beaumont water was often "soupy" with an odor redolent of alligators, bullfrogs, and fish. Everyone soon learned that drinking it could bring on severe stomach cramps and bowel trouble, climaxed by diarrhea. The malady became known as the Beaumonts. Facilities were limited, and when a man was afflicted with a severe case of the Beaumonts, he might frantically bid as high as 50 cents to secure the immediate use of a toilet. Later the experienced visitors purchased uncontaminated drinking water, and the oil companies provided safe water for their own people.

At first tents went up as if an army had arrived, but with lumber cheap and plentiful, little shacks soon sprang up at the oil field, out in the woods, wherever space was available. Men and their families lived as close as they could to the derricks. Overnight the Spindletop field had transformed Beaumont into a crowded, bustling town on the make.

"And," as one old-timer put it, "the mud was everywhere, good God Almighty, everywhere." [34]

As it drew all kinds, classes, sizes, and shapes of people into its vortex, the boom set a heady pattern for those that were to come in Texas and other states. Quick, sensational profits were the magnet. Speculators and swindlers, honest workmen and salesmen of all descriptions, millionaires and paupers, gamblers and prostitutes—they all came, many of them to die penniless because they went to Spindletop.

While the scenes of swarming humanity served as adrenaline to many a man, others were at least temporarily dismayed by what they witnessed on the the way to Spindletop. One merchant, the father of author George Sessions Perry, told of his train's stopping briefly in a small town north of Beaumont. One of his fellow passengers opened the window and hailed a townsman.

"What town is this?" asked the passenger, assaying with some disdain what he could see of the town.

"Liberty!" the proud Texan shot back.

"Give me death!" blurted the traveler, slamming his window shut.[35]

Had it not been for the profit-maddened mass of humanity he found at his destination, the passenger probably would not have through much better of Beaumont. In the mornings, when the rain thrashed down in sheets, driving people off the streets, the town was lonely-looking, gray, dirty, dreary. The mud of a boomtown is the same as the mud of war, and mules and ox teams, groaning under loads of heavy oil field machinery, flopped and struggled in the mud as abrasive mule skinners cursed and shouted.

Men looking for honest work flocked in with the rest. Anything close to oil field experience counted. If one was from an oil town or even an oil-producing state, he was automatically credited with the knowledge needed. Pennsylvanians and West Virginians could get jobs with a minimum of questions. Anyone from Corsicana had a good chance of becoming a driller. If a Texan wasn't from Corsicana, well, naturally he didn't know anything about drilling.

Dangerous though the work often was, its rewards were more attractive than those of the farm. Many, like seventeen-year-old R. R. Hobson, signed a "death warrant"—a piece of paper attesting that the signer was a white man, twenty-one years of age, realized the work was dangerous, and assumed all risks. It protected the employer from responsibility in the event of an injury on the job.[36]

Although several hundred Chinese lived in Beaumont, operating laundries and restaurants, and there were Italian immigrant farmers in the area, the milking of Big Hill was dominated by white, native-born Americans. The black man, while he was there, was at the bottom. For a time blacks dug earthen tanks in which to store oil and lived in a section called South Africa. They did their work, singing and bantering among themselves, and bothered no one. But some of the whites, emphasizing their intent with gunshots, drove the black men from the field.[37] Producing black gold was deemed white man's work.

With the influx of saloons, dance halls, whorehouses, and gambling dens, Beaumont became the wildest town in North America. Some places operated twenty-four hours a day—"ladies and all"—and many featured dancing upstairs where local four-piece bands—fiddle, guitar, violin, and bass viol—played "Over the Waves," "Beautiful Ohio," and other popular tunes of the day.[38] Boisterous drillers, gunmen, pimps, gamblers, and businessmen mingled in the smoky gambling dives, taking their chances at craps, roulette, poker, and faro, all the time swearing, arguing, drinking.

Fighting became a way of life. Most northerners, who believed in fighting with their fists, were dismayed when the lusty frontiersmen whipped out knives and six-shooters. The frequent scuffles sometimes ended in death. As for the majesty of the law, one contemporary summed it up: "Well, they'd mostly count it among themselves who was the best man. Why, he was the law." "It was free America then," said another. "Free America, do as you please, yes, sir."[39]

As the little town somehow absorbed 50,000 uninvited guests, the consequences became both painful and gaudy. If a man flashed a roll of money, he could be certain someone would relieve him of it. If a prostitute or a gambler failed, a more violent individual would try. Dead men needed no money, and the muddy Neches River could handle the "floaters."

The atmosphere, like that of all booms, was one of here-today, gone-tomorrow. Drilling operator Jack Ennis swapped jeweler Harry Hilburn a Spindletop lease for a tray of unmounted diamonds. That night Ennis took the diamonds with him to the Reservation— "Why, it was a bunch of whorehouses, what it was"—on the wild end of Crockett Street. After he had got high from drinking beer, Ennis grasped the sparkling tray and flung it away from him with a grand gesture, littering the floor with diamonds. All the women in the house instantaneously deserted their temporary companions and raced pell-mell for the rolling stones. "Scramble for them, you girls!" Ennis yelled joyously.[40]

Fifty years later Columbia University professor-author William A. Owens, a native Texan, asked Carl F. Mirus, who had been at the great field, about some of the songs the men sang.

"Well," said Mirus, "I don't ever recall the oil folks' ever getting to where they sang. They might have used wine and women, but they never indulged in song."

"Well," persisted Owens, "that's the thing I'm trying to find out. Why didn't they indulge in song?"

"Because usually they were so busy with the other two that they didn't have time to sing." [41]

11

Oil fever is highly infectious. One of the earliest investors in the Spindletop field was former Governor Jim Hogg.

Hogg could scarcely believe what he heard of the Beaumont wonder until he ran into his friend O. B. Colquitt of Dallas. Colquitt, who had a half dozen small wells in Corsicana, urged Hogg to lease or buy in Beaumont. Hogg shook his head; he didn't have the money or the time—he was busy practicing law. Colquitt argued that the big ex-governor could become rich, and Hogg finally decided to take a look.

When Colquitt stepped off the train in Beaumont about a week later, the first sight he saw was that of Hogg on the porch of the Crosby Hotel. Hogg had already made some money on lease deals and was one of Spindletop's heartiest boosters.[42]

By the next month Hogg had joined forces with James Swayne of Fort Worth, a state representative and Hogg's floor leader during his gubernatorial days. Needing land and capital, Hogg and Swayne invited in three others, with each of the five partners scraping up $40,000. It was the beginning of the Hogg-Swayne Syndicate, unincorporated probably because of Hogg's antipathy toward the word "corporation."

Hogg's entry into the oil business constituted an abrupt shift in focus, but not one out of character with his past. The veteran trustbuster had always encouraged honest businessmen who competed fairly. By becoming an entrepreneur himself in one of the most competitive situations imaginable, all the while complying with the laws, he was exhibiting no inconsistency with his earlier role. Hogg's reforms had aimed at ensuring honesty and fairness in business. There is no evidence that he departed from that code as an oilman.

On the eastern side of the Spindletop mound there were fifteen acres that Swayne hoped to obtain for the company. He tried to persuade the owner to join in a $2 million company, with $500,000 allowed for the land, but Captain Lucas had already leased the property and the mineral rights were controlled by the Guffey Petroleum Company. After negotiating with Guffey, the syndicate secured the mineral rights in the fifteen acres from Guffey for $180,000, along with rights to a well being drilled. They paid the owner $105,000 for the surface rights. Once the titles were cleared and the pending lawsuits settled, the fifteen acres had cost $310,000. It was soon worth twice that.

Why did Guffey sell to the Hogg-Swayne Syndicate? Sometime later Guffey indicated he had done it to ensure the goodwill of Hogg, who was a political power in a region where "Yankees" were not welcomed with open arms. Guffey and his associates may have been interested in building as many strong Texas friendships as they could, not only as insurance against any possible future legal attack upon them as easterners and outsiders, but also to gain allies in event of a collision with the giant Standard.

A wild frenzy followed. The syndicate was in debt. Hogg suggested selling small blocks to extricate themselves. They did. In one astonishing transaction, two and a half acres went for $200,000. One company paid $50,000 for one-twentieth of an acre. Another group bought one-twenty-fourth of an acre for $15,000. As the mad rush continued, the syndicate was soon out of debt, while others scrambled to purchase quarters, sixteenths, and thirty-seconds of an acre. Acreage became so subdivided that on the original Hogg-Swayne tract derricks were jammed together so closely that men could walk from one derrick to the other without touching the ground. Lured by the assurance of quick profits, some buyers subdivided their property even further. Leases grew so small that they had no room for a boiler, which had to be placed on the road nearby—Boiler Avenue.

The syndicate retained half of the Hogg-Swayne tract. By the end of 1901 there were 214 producing wells in the Beaumont area, operated by 100 companies. Of those wells, 120 were on the original, Hogg-Swayne tract, while the entire Spindletop field covered 200 acres. By then there were two other overcrowded drilling sites, situated on a five-acre location.[43]

Inevitably the jammed-up wells lowered the gas pressure in the field, the technical importance of which was not then recognized. Conservation was an unknown word. Spindletop became an early, classic, and notorious example of the doleful consequences of the "law of capture," a rule borrowed from English common law that allowed a man to flow all the oil he could from his lease, without concern for the welfare of his neighbor-competitor. The lessons of greed and waste that Spindletop offered were not to be understood and uniformly heeded for more than three decades. Every person with an interest in a well concentrated on pumping all he could out of the earth, as fast as he could.

12

As he had in politics a decade earlier, former Governor Jim Hogg became a living legend in Beaumont. When in town, he usually went to Spindletop several times a week. He always stepped up to the derrick floor of a drilling well and shook hands with all the roughnecks. He was jolly, had plenty of stories to tell, and everybody liked him.

Because of his size, he was a spectacle. In order to check on his interests at Spindletop, he had to wade almost waist deep in weeds and assorted trash. When he returned to town, his boots were greasy with oil. He was a remarkable sight with his 240-pound body filling a chair at a Pearl Street café while bootblacks worked over his boots.[44]

For a time Hogg lived at the Oaks Hotel, a wooden frame building outside the downtown Beaumont business district. One hot morning, after a flash flood had created a small lake downtown, Hogg hired a flat-bottomed skiff, pulled by a brawny black man, to tow him to his destination. He sat in a huge rocking chair, his trouser legs rolled over his knees, and shielded himself from the broiling sun with a big red-and-white umbrella. As the black man pulled his fare down Calder Avenue, everybody walking in water on the sidewalks stopped to stare. It was the only traffic on the street that soggy day.

"That was in the days before the movies," said one man. "If we'd have had those days a movie like we do today, of current events, they'd shown that all over the United States." [45]

Even in that hectic atmosphere, the welfare of Texas seems never to have left Hogg's mind. One day in the Crosby House, Hogg and Judge R. E. Brooks, one of his partners, were discussing the price of oil when the big ex-governor had a sudden inspiration.

"Ed, you know, I believe I'll have the legislature pass a law that the people of Texas will never have to pay over twenty cents a barrel for oil produced in their state here."

"Well, hold on here, Governor," the startled judge blurted out. "We're in the oil business. We don't care how high the oil goes!" [46]

13

While Spindletop produced and new gushers roared in, many of the important decisions relating to the field took place far from Texas. In his deal with James M. Guffey, Lucas had been left with one-eighth of the partnership, with five-eighths going to Guffey, a quarter to old Galey. Guffey, a ruddy-faced Pittsburgher with long, curly white hair and a flair for wheeling and dealing in both politics and business, then went to Pittsburgh banker Andrew W. Mellon, borrowing $300,000 for the new partnership.

Guffey and his associates had found competitors swarming all over the hill. Lucas had failed to tie up all the oil-laden tracts and had leased a lot of worthless land. Guffey now asked Mellon again for funds, to build a refinery, a pipeline, and all the other facilities to turn the property into a high-profit investment. As new wells came in, Mellon was won over. The J. M. Guffey Petroleum Company was capitalized at $15 million. Guffey, president of the company, bought out Galey and Lucas, as planned. He paid them, together, less than $800,000, plus some stock. The Mellons and other wealthy Pittsburghers took large blocks of the stock. Before the year had ended, a separate company, the Gulf Refining Company of Texas, had been organized for refining operations. Andrew and Richard Mellon took large shares of the stock.

When the glut of oil from the prodigious field pushed the price down to three cents a barrel, the Mellons dispatched their young nephew William L. Mellon, a shrewd, resourceful, and energetic oil veteran in his thirties, to Beaumont. When Will Mellon returned to Pennsylvania, the choice was clear: Either invest over $12 million more or get out from under the burden.

Andrew Mellon went to New York to sell out to the Standard Oil Company. Rockefeller officials Henry H. Rogers and John D. Archbold weren't interested.

As Rogers put it, "After the way Mr. Rockefeller has been treated by the State of Texas, he'll never put another dime down there."

The Mellons had no choice but to stay in the oil business. Young Will Mellon became executive vice-president of both Guffey Petroleum and Gulf Refining.

In 1907, when Oklahoma's gigantic Glenn pool was discovered, the Mellons and their associates organized the Gulf Oil Corporation. By then old Guffey had been shorn of his power. He sold his stock and bowed out.[47] A new major company had been founded on Texas oil, but full control had early been thrust into the hands of eastern capitalists, and the Mellon family, already blessed with a huge fortune, found itself further enriched.

14

The day after the Lucas well came in, Joe Cullinan arrived from Corsicana. Impressed by what he saw, Cullinan tried again to interest Standard Oil. Two months later Standard officials personally investigated Spindletop and again declined to become involved.

Late in March, 1901, Cullinan made his move. He organized the Texas Fuel Company, for the purchasing of oil and the operation of a pipeline. Cullinan had a 37,000-barrel storage tank twenty miles south of the field. When Spindletop's flush production flooded the market with 3-cent-a-barrel and 5-cent oil, Cullinan bought the cheap oil, stored it, and waited for prices to climb.

Meanwhile, the Hogg-Swayne Syndicate was making money, but with most of their acreage sold and the price of crude oil ridiculously low, they needed a pipeline and a refinery to exploit their holdings properly. That fall the syndicate came to an agreement with Cullinan. Contributing pipeline right-of-way and a refinery site option in Port Arthur, from which the oil could be shipped, Hogg-Swayne subscribed to half of Texas Fuel's $50,000 capital stock. This maneuver linked Hogg-Swayne, composed mainly of lawyers and politicians who knew little about oil but held choice acreage, with Cullinan, an oilman experienced in all phases of the business.[48]

Urgently needing capital for expansion, Hogg-Swayne was forced to look outside Texas. Hogg, a proved persuader, was chosen to head east to hunt down well-heeled investors. In the fall, accompanied by his pretty nineteen-year-old daughter, Ima, the widower Hogg left for New York. He especially hoped to interest capitalist John W. Gates. The two men had known each other since Gates had been a drummer, or traveling salesman, for barbed wire in Texas two decades before.

Forty-five-year-old "Bet-a-Million" Gates, as he was known as a result of huge winnings at English tracks, was, above all, a gambler. Whether in business or at the gaming table, he followed one philosophy: "Never lose your nerve. Make up your mind what it is you want to do—and then go after it." With a dollar cigar always in his mouth, the bulky, unpredictable schemer never lost his nerve.

Before Spindletop, Illinois-born Gates and others had put together the $90 million American Steel and Wire Company. Gates' boardroom fights became legend. He was never accepted socially by New York's Four Hundred. He spit, he was profane, and easterners perceived him as "a gross, uncouth Westerner who ate peas with his knife and whose belch could be heard through the Waldorf's Peacock Alley."

Gates would bet on anything. In Chicago he'd wagered $1,000 on which drop of rain would slide down the bottom of a windowpane first. He often flipped coins for $10,000 a toss, and one never-denied story has it that he settled a $30,000 argument with Charles Schwab over American Steel and Wire holdings with a double-or-nothing flip—which he won.[49]

"I think no man should bet unless he's sure he's right," he said. "And when he's sure he's right he should be willing to bet every dollar he owns. That's the way I bet. For me there's no fun in betting just a few thousand. I want to lay down enough to hurt the other fellow if he loses, and enough to hurt me if I lose."[50]

His outlook was ready-made for the oil business, where risks were great but potential rewards higher.

Jim Hogg and his daughter, Ima, stayed at the Waldorf-Astoria while in New York. Hogg's talks with Gates progressed slowly, but Gates did express some interest in the big Texan's proposition. Hogg was optimistic and confided to his daughter, "Something very wonderful may come of this."

Young Ima, a woman who all her years was to see things as they were, was shocked at some of the inconsistencies in this millionaire's character. Gates, she observed, had a lovely wife, and they lived beautifully. He exhibited a very active mind with "an amazing lot of information," but his flawed education shone through it all.

"He would use bad grammar, which astonished me," reported Ima. "I couldn't understand why a man with as much presence as he had and really very impressive personality should not have learned how to speak good English."

Half a century later Ima Hogg still shuddered over "those peculiar grammatical errors."[51]

15

Gates came into the venture. For additional financing, the Texans approached white-haired, gimlet-eyed Arnold Schlaet, who represented the Lapham-United States Leather interests in New York. Of $450,000 pledged through the issuance of certificates, only $282,000 had to be paid in cash. Of this amount, German-born Schlaet contributed $125,000 and Gates, $25,000, with Hogg-Swayne and Cullinan each putting up $66,000. Gates wanted to add $100,000 to his share, but the wary Schlaet had persuaded Cullinan to keep Gates' contribution low. In April, 1902, a merger of Texas properties and know-how with New York money resulted in the organization of The Texas Company, with offices in Beaumont and New York. Joe Cullinan became its first president, Schlaet vice-president.

Hogg, Gates, and Cullinan agreed that the main office should never be moved from Texas—a stipulation that was not put into writing. Five of the nine original directors, including Pennsylvania-born Cullinan were citizens of Texas; the other four were New Yorkers and Chicagoans. Cullinan promised that all state laws would be complied with and a majority of the board would be from Texas.[52]

Although he held Texas Company stock until his death, Hogg himself had little to do with the company thereafter. As the years passed and the company needed even more money for expansion, eastern capital—the Gates and Schlaet interests—moved into the driver's seat. The Texans simply didn't have the money required. Within a few years Cullinan was the only one of the original Texans left on the board.

When Jim Hogg learned of the easterners' further acquisition, he was visibly disturbed. He stopped a friend one day in the lobby of the Crosby Hotel and told him, "The Texas Company is beginning to smell like Standard Oil, and I'm going to get out of it at the first favorable opportunity." [53]

Hogg's words had the ring of prophecy. At first Cullinan ran the Texas Company virtually as a one-man show, mostly from the field, but Schlaet and the Gates interests steadily chipped away at his position. In 1913 Cullinan lost control of his board's executive committee. Defeat in a proxy fight followed, and he resigned as president.[54] The pioneering era was over, and with control totally out of Texas hands, the company might have been renamed, more realistically, The New York Company.

16

Halfway around the world from Texas one morning in early 1901, a dynamic, soft-spoken, plain-looking, heavyset man sat down to breakfast after his horseback ride. His paper brought news of the Lucas gusher at Spindletop. Sir Marcus Samuel, an English Jew with social and political ambitions, adjusted his pince-nez glasses to scrutinize the article that other Englishmen scarcely noted. With old Queen Victoria terminally ill, her subjects' attention had been focused on her and her sixty-year-old son, who was to succeed her as Edward VII. Sir Marcus' heart must have thumped with youthful excitement as he read of the Texas well, for its prodigious promise represented a dream he had nurtured for years.

Sir Marcus had foreseen the age of liquid fuel, and he instantly viewed the Texas gusher as the missing link in his campaign to persuade the world's shipowners to change over from coal to oil. Although the Russians ran a few ships on oil, the British held 70 percent of the world's ocean trade, and Sir Marcus wanted to convert the Royal Navy into an oil-burning armada. He also saw the suggested conversion as an opportunity to add new tankers to his own fleet for shipping oil to Europe.

Sir Marcus' oil activities had been restricted previously to the Orient. Born into a lower-middle-class shopkeeping family in London's squalid East End, Sir Marcus had made his first fortune before he was thirty, trading with the Far East. The family sold shell boxes and general merchandise, and it was for this family trademark, "Shell," that Sir Marcus had named his private limited company, formed in 1897 to handle oil shipments. Although unknown in Texas because of its concentration in the Orient, Shell was the second largest oil company in the world.

Immediately after breakfast Sir Marcus moved into action, cabling his agent in New York to seek out Colonel James Guffey. The Englishman's early efforts were exercises in frustration. Guffey was courting the Mellons, and subsequent reports left Sir Marcus filled with anxiety: Standard Oil had shipped 5,000 barrels of the new Texas crude oil "for experimental purposes" and had sent the steamer back for more.

Sir Marcus seemed to face one hurdle after another. While seeking a contract with Guffey, he learned that an obscure broker held an option on Guffey oil for the entire European trade. The broker, it turned out, was acting secretly for Standard's English subsidiary and, consistent with the cutthroat ethics of the day, was working to keep Guffey and Shell from getting together. Sir Marcus "nearly went mad" when he heard of this but was reassured when Guffey informed him that as soon as the earlier option expired, he was ready to ship oil to Shell in virtually unlimited quantities.

Realizing the critical moment was at hand, Sir Marcus dispatched his brother-in-law to New York to push negotiations as soon as the other option expired. At meetings with Guffey and the Mellons, the Shell agents were impressed by the potential of the Texas field. There seemed to be no likelihood of an end to the oil at Spindletop. A contract was signed. The Guffey Company was to sell half its total production for twenty-one years, primarily in the form of liquid fuel, at a fixed price of 25 cents per barrel, plus 50 percent of the profit netted from sale of the oil. The minimum amount would involve about 14.7 million barrels.[55]

In committing himself to bucking Standard's worldwide monopoly, Sir Marcus had staked everything—his capital, his credit, his reputation, all risked on the basis of slight hard data. He had only his brother-in-law's assessment of the Americans; he did not understand Texas' laws, no American lawyer was hired to draft the contract; no scientific proof had been sought of the field's "unlimited" capacity. Bet-a-Million Gates or a latter-day Texas wheeler-dealer couldn't have taken a more grandiose step.

Sir Marcus' difficulties began to multiply. Sir Henri Deterding's Royal Dutch firm was breaking Shell's monopoly in the Dutch East Indies, and the British Royal Navy was dragging with its experiments with oil as fuel. The only optimistic news came from Germany, where oil had been tested extensively as fuel. Soon, after a complicated financial maneuver, Shell had a contract with the Hamburg-Amerika Line, which was to be the mainstay in marketing Texas oil in Europe. By mid-July, 1901, six months after the

Lucas well had spewed forth, a tanker left Port Arthur with the first Spindletop oil bound for Europe.

Reconsidering their original hesitation, Standard officials made overtures to Shell, suggesting a merger that, drawing in the Royal Dutch, would control the world market. Sir Marcus realized the plan would lead to Standard's swallowing and digesting Shell completely and withdrew from negotiations.

As Sir Marcus' political fortunes rose—he became lord mayor elect of London in 1902—his Texas venture fell apart. The "unlimited" supplies dwindled. Water began appearing in the oil, and the Lucas well and half the others stopped producing. Sir Marcus' dream seemed frustrated. The next spring he ordered four of his steamships modified to transport cattle from Texas to England, a humiliating comedown from his earlier visions. His contract with the Americans was in a shambles. The Mellons couldn't supply the oil, at the new higher prices, without destroying themselves—quite unlikely behavior. Andrew Mellon visited Sir Marcus at his English country place, where they concluded terms that gave the Mellons a new lease on life.[56]

Sir Marcus' grand hopes were smashed. He had succeeded in breaking the Standard stranglehold, but more to the benefit of the Mellons than to himself. A few years later the Royal Dutch company devoured Sir Marcus' Shell through a merger.

17

A recurrent question was: "What is Standard up to?" Standard Oil seemed to be everywhere, yet nowhere. Officially, the behemoth indicated complete disinterest in Texas, but most oilmen took for granted the Rockefeller corporation was involved in exploiting the field in some manner. Every time Cullinan, Guffey, or even Standard's old foe Hogg made a new business move, a rumor would link him to Standard. But the evidence never developed.

Standard, however, was very much present. It bought substantial quantities of crude oil from the Texas Company and other major Spindletop producers. In late 1901 George A. Burt, a bluff, swaggering former railroad executive with a flair for any level of society, appeared upon the scene, soon to ingratiate himself into the good graces of prominent Beaumonters. He was Standard's front man—a well-kept secret until after he had built a massive $5 million refinery. Then, to the bemusement of the local sons, a new company—Security Oil Company—was chartered under Texas law, took over the refinery, and Burt, his job done, faded away. A New York banker became president of Security, and the masquerade continued until 1906, when Security and another Standard-backed company were ousted for violating the state's antitrust laws. A few years later Standard money surfaced again, this time as the Magnolia Petroleum Company.[57]

Although Standard had secured by subterfuge several footholds in Texas, public opinion and the official attitude toward the octopus undoubtedly blunted its usual aggressiveness. Had it not been for the state's antitrust laws and official attitude, Standard would have been more open and active, sharply limiting companies like Gulf, Higgins Oil and Fuel Company, Houston Oil Company, Texas Company, Rio Bravo Oil Company, and Sun Oil.

Sun Oil had been operating in Toledo, Ohio, since 1886, but the boom offered the means of a lively expansion. When first word of the Lucas gusher reached Joseph N. Pew, head of the Sun Oil Company, he recognized it as the opportunity he had been waiting for. Immediately he dispatched a nephew to Beaumont to survey the scene personally. A glowing report came back.

Cautious but encouraged, Pew sent another nephew, J. Edgar Pew, to Texas, this time for an extended visit. Heartened by the reactions, Joseph Pew bought land back East at Marcus Hook, twenty miles from Philadelphia, and began building a refinery. Later he bought land in the Beaumont area and had both metal and earthen tanks built for oil storage. Next came a pipeline from the field to the storage facilities. When the price of oil hit rock bottom, he had the tanks filled.

J. Edgar Pew was the ideal man to run Sun's Texas holdings. He became a "naturalized" Texan, blending in with local people and rearing a family there. Most of all, he was competitive. He liked to play cards, golf, baseball, football—anything in which he had an opportunity to excel. He was made for the times.

More than a year later the Pews' big opportunity came when the properties of the Lone Star and Crescent Oil Company went up for public auction on May 30, 1902. It was a million-dollar company that had been caught in the squeeze of long-term contracts, plummeting prices, and declining production. Edgar Pew opened the bidding at a high $100,000. Caught off-balance, his potential competitors kept quiet, enabling him to acquire the property at one-tenth its value.

There was one more hitch. He had to deposit one-fourth of the purchase price by the end of the business day. The day—May 30—was Memorial Day, a bank holiday. If he did not raise the money, the next day the company would again go on the block and his competitors might come to their senses and try to outbid him. But Edgar Pew was the lucky kind; in golf, his ball often would hit a tree, then ricochet onto the green. That day, as he passed an old barbershop, he learned it was to become the Gulf National Bank in the morning. He went inside and introduced himself to the cashier and explained that he needed $25,000 on the spot. The man knew who Pew was and made the loan. It was the beginning of lively growth for the hitherto-small company. Sun Oil's operations in Texas remained extensive thereafter.

Ironically, the money that young Pew borrowed that day came from the bank that S. G. Bayne, the New Yorker, had set up to handle the affairs of Standard Oil's Burt refinery.[58]

The vacuum created by Standard's seeming absence in the early stage also left the way open later for other, native companies, such as Humble Oil and Refining Company, organized in 1917 through the merger of several Texas properties. All nine of Humble's founders and original directors came out of the early Gulf Coast fields.

William Stamps Farish and Robert Lee Blaffer, later to become presidents of Humble, met in a rooming house at Beaumont in 1902. Farish, a graduate of the University of Mississippi law school, had been sent to Spindletop by his promoter uncle. Within two years after his arrival he had organized a partnership with young Blaffer, of a German-American family in New Orleans, who had gone to Beaumont as an oil buyer for the Southern Pacific Railroad. After 1904 they drilled for others and traded in leases. In 1905 they moved to Houston; the new Humble field, near a town named after former Justice of the Peace Pleasant Humble, was only several miles away. The partners lived in a shack at the field, with hardly enough money for food, and Blaffer reportedly put up his gold watch for security to pay their drilling crew. But a few years later they were on their way up.

Their future partners came from a variety of backgrounds. Two were drillers and producers: Ohio-born Charles B. Goddard started as a roughneck at Spindletop, and Walter W. Fondren, a Tennessee farmer's son who had been orphaned at ten, had arrived in Texas at the age of seventeen with a pair of overalls and 30 cents; Fondren became a helper on a rig at Corsicana in 1897 and went to Spindletop as a skilled driller. Harry C. Wiess, only thirteen when Spindletop roared in, was a well-off Beaumonter who had earned a civil engineering degree at Princeton. Two early directors were attorneys—Lobel A. Carlton and Edgar E. Townes. Lumber and real estate magnate Jesse H. Jones was to become one of the biggest men in Houston's future.

Tall, robust, handsome Ross S. Sterling, a native Texan, saw one early business venture wiped out by the Galveston flood of 1900. Coming back, he operated a feed store at Sour Lake during the boom that followed Spindletop. Establishing businesses in Saratoga, Dayton, and Humble with his brothers, he became known as "the hardest-working white man you ever saw in your life." He bought a number of small banks and in 1909 invested in oil properties for the first time, buying two producing wells in the Humble field. It was a good start for a man who was to become governor of Texas in the early 1930's.

In 1911, while still in his thirties, Sterling became the leader in organizing the Humble Oil Company, named after the field. Although it concentrated in the Houston area at first, when Texas production fell off it operated also in Oklahoma. When the Humble Oil and Refining Company was organized, Ross Sterling and his brother Frank became directors and their oil company contributed its properties and name to the new enterprise.

Ironically, the Humble Oil and Refining Company came into being as the result of a bill that the larger Texas Company (Texaco) had been trying to lobby through the Texas legislature. Up till then state law did not permit an oil company to be "integrated," or operating in all phases of the business—production, transportation (pipelines), refining, and marketing. The men who were to form Humble had opposed the earlier unsuccessful attempts by Texaco to change the statute. But when the bill finally passed in 1917,

Humble—not the Texas Company—was the first to incorporate under the new law, as the various abilities and properties of all these men and others were consolidated into a legal entity that constituted an integrated company with a subsidiary pipeline company.

The all-Texas nature of the Humble company was to be short-lived. Overtures soon came from Standard Oil Company (New Jersey). Standard wanted 60 percent of Humble's stock. The Texans, though they needed capital for expansion, resisted at first; then, in 1919, Humble sold one-half its stock to Standard for $20 million, $17 million of it in cash. Sterling, as president of Humble, agreed to sell additional shares of his personal stock, to assure control for Standard, and this stock was held by Standard president Walter C. Teagle as an individual, in order not to violate Texas law.

An old Spindletopper, Ed Prather, who had been associated with many of Humble's founders, had a joshing, yet prophetic explanation for the high price Standard had paid for the company: "They aren't paying that much for any property; they're paying it for those boys! They don't have men like that up there. Before you and I die, those boys will be running the Standard Oil Company!"

He was accurate enough. William Farish was the first Humble president who went on to become president of Standard.[59]

With adequate financing, the new companies—including the strictly Texas ones—were able to compete with Standard on nearly equal footing, one result of which was that a bit less of the state's wealth went north.

How much did Standard profit from Spindletop? A fair enough assessment came on the fiftieth anniversary of the discovery when David Rockefeller, grandson of old John D., Sr., belatedly and tersely, but officially, acknowledged his grandfather's gain.

"It was important to my own family," he said, "for the Standard Oil Company benefited from it to a considerable extent." [60]

18

Spindletop was an extravagance of waste. Overpromoted, over-drilled, overproduced, the field was a prodigy that could never live up to what was expected of it. Promoters gave the business and the field a bad name, bilking thousands on the basis of minuscule tracts and, frequently, nonexistent production. Many remembered the field as "Swindletop." Worst of all, the law of capture prevailed in the ugliest way. Because of the jammed-up wells and wasteful practices, fire—the greatest waster of all—was a constant threat, the worst example of which was the Ten Acre Fire that engulfed the Hogg-Swayne tract in 1902.

Everyone seemed to suffer from an incurable boom fever, believing the field's future was unlimited. Some oilmen would open up their wells, say, on a Sunday afternoon, simply to impress their guests. While they strolled around, just looking, the oil ran off in a ditch in a display of conspicuous production and waste as notorious as anything Thorstein Veblen might have described.

"It'll last forever, that well," said H. A. Rathke, explaining the attitude of the time. "That meant a thousand years from now all we have to do is just open this valve and we'd have all the oil we want. That's what they thought. That's the reason they wasn't cautious." [61]

The day of retribution came, and the great field petered out. By 1904, when Captain Anthony Lucas, returned from two years of prospecting in Mexico, it was all a sorry shambles. Walking over the derrick-littered maze, the captain shook his head. Too many wells, for one thing, when half a dozen might have done the job better.

"The cow was milked too hard," he said, "and moreover, she was not milked intelligently." [62]

Spindletop taught an expensive lesson that was to go unheeded for a long time. If the never-ending gold mine fizzled, well, there were plenty of others, weren't there? The oil frontier spurted on, to Sour Lake, Saratoga, Batson's Prairie, and other boomtowns along the Gulf Coast. But many of the patterns of things to come had been established at Spindletop. One-eighth became the standard landowner's royalty thereafter. At Spindletop Texans learned that to achieve gigantic growth in the oil business, they had to go out of the state—to the East, where the big money was—for help in developing the native resources. Some learned that the price of such grand success was to flirt with, or succumb to, control by eastern capital.

Spindletop and the fields that succeeded it changed the direction of industrial and, eventually, social history. Sir Marcus Samuel's dream was to come abundantly true. In early 1904 the general manager of the Southern Pacific Railroad announced that its 1,400 locomotives were to be converted into oil burners. Other major railroads followed. What Sir Marcus and others did not foresee was the era of individual transportation units that grew up with the age of liquid fuel. In the early days of the automobile's development, electric and even steam-powered cars competed freely with the internal-combustion engine. Gasoline, the first fraction out of distilled crude petroleum, wasn't important until about 1910; soon after, gasoline exceeded kerosene in sales. From then on the oil industry and the automobile grew together, with an impact on the future that can never be precisely gauged. In time, gasoline—so inflammable it was once a source of extreme annoyance to any refinery—became a "necessity." The circumstances suggest that the old saw "Necessity is the mother of invention" may also be true in its reverse: If enough of a new material can be found, new uses will be found for it, just as oil brought about plastics and other industries, which in turn changed society and its technology.

The Texans in on the early days of the boom did not uniformly profit from it. Jim Hogg, who helped shape the legal environment in which Spindletop occurred, did not live to see the outcome of his efforts in the oil business. He did not become rich. He had little cash. On top of this he lost money in a bank investment in Beaumont. "All this stuff about James Stephen making millions is the veriest rot and makes me tired," his son Will wrote to Ima, by then studying music in New York. "He will do well if he gets out with comfort." [63] Hogg held Texas Company stock that his three sons and daughter were to dispose of after his death in 1906. His most substantial material legacy to them was land he had purchased away from the Spindletop area. Years later it produced oil for his children and made them millions.

The man who set all this in motion, Pattillo Higgins, typified another general pattern that was to appear in other booms. He was left out of the larger rewards from the field he had promoted. Excluded from the Guffey company at the outset, Higgins sued his former partners for the one-tenth he felt was due him. Eventually settlements were made. Higgins organized the Higgins Oil and Fuel Company and drilled some early producing wells before prospecting on other leases. Then, in 1902, Patrick Calhoun, a New York lawyer, bought 60 percent of the stock in Higgins' company, after which Higgins sold his own stock, and Calhoun and John Henry Kirby, a Houston lumberman, promoted the huge Houston Oil Company, using Higgins' stock to absorb other companies. Higgins left Beaumont a few years later, moving first to Houston and, in 1919, to San Antonio, where he died in 1955 at ninety-two.[64] During the intervening years, he had been active and successful in several fields, including those at Goose Creek and Barber's Hill, and had remained in the oil business till the day he died.[65]

He had a lot to look back on. The results of his nineteenth-century dream had been far-reaching. The growth of three Texas cities—Beaumont, Port Arthur, and Houston—could be traced to Spindletop. Standard Oil's monopoly had been broken. The age of liquid fuel had become a national joyride. Texas was the major oil state. If Higgins felt he was the father of some of this, he could hardly be blamed. If he had moments of tortured disappointment at not sharing in the profits more, who can criticize him?

III

THE SCANDAL OF THE SENATOR AND STANDARD OIL

1

As the author of a 1907 article in *The Independent* wrote, Senator Joseph Weldon Bailey possessed "inimitable self-assurance." The reporter followed him on the floor of the United States Senate, where, with head thrown back and long hair drifting over his forehead, Bailey was an orator in the Roman tradition. He was a large-statured, pugnacious man, whose eyes flashed and chest expanded as he shook his fist at foes present and absent.

"Bailey is great," wrote the reporter. "He knows it and means that the world should know it. If it were any other senator besides Bailey there would be little, if any, notice given of his trouble in Texas outside of its border." [1]

Joe Bailey was the junior United States senator from Texas, and the trouble to which the reporter referred was one of the scandals of the day, encompassing political favors, the allegation of a bribe— and oil. Furthermore, it was Standard Oil, a name anathema to most Texans and, by 1907, a national target. The Bailey controversy, as it came to be known, was to survive as an enduring symbol of the sometime coziness between politicians and oilmen which has persisted from frontier times to the present day.

The neatly dressed Bailey with his noble features cut a fine figure even by Washington standards. Despite his youth and his lack of seniority, he was acknowledged as an able lawyer and as one of the foremost Democratic leaders in the country. "In the Senate," one wrote of him, "the Republicans respect him very much, fear him a little, and like him a great deal." [2]

Bailey was born in the midst of the Civil War in 1863 at Crystal Springs, Mississippi, near the Union Army lines. Vicksburg had fallen, and the Confederacy was living on borrowed time. The elder Bailey was a small merchant with no slaves or land, but fervently pro-South.

Like young Jim Hogg, a foe in later years, Joe Bailey grew up during Reconstruction. Although he lived in the Deep South, where the ravages of war were felt the deepest, Bailey had advantages the Texan never had. The war had divided one wing of his family, which had members in Pennsylvania; in peacetime the split was healed, and an uncle from the North underwrote young Joe's college costs.

Bailey attended a series of schools—Mississippi College, the University of Mississippi, the University of Virginia law school, and, finally, Lebanon Law School in Tennessee. In 1883, at the age of nineteen, he was admitted to the bar, returned to Hazlehurst, Mississippi, and almost immediately plunged into politics. In his first race he defeated his father for delegate to the state Democratic convention. The issue was railroad regulation. Young Joe favored regulation.

He soon delved into other more touchy matters. Half the voters in Copiah County were black. Bailey became one of the leaders at a white mass meeting at the county seat, organized to minimize the black men's power at the polls. In the election that followed, black voters were intimidated and subjected to illegal acts. A Senate investigating committee that held hearings in New Orleans made it clear that Bailey had played a leading role in the event. For this and other reasons, he left Mississippi a year later.

In 1885 Bailey settled in Gainesville, in the prairie country of North Texas. He married a Mississippi belle the following year and lost no time in involving himself in local and state politics. In 1890, at the age of twenty-seven, he was elected to the Congress over the incumbent, becoming the youngest member of the new Congress. [3]

Bailey served in the House of Representatives for ten years. During this period he publicly supported Jim Hogg, but Hogg did not trust the youthful politician.[4] Neither did Ima Hogg, the governor's daughter. Bailey, she observed, would always whisper, rather than speak openly, to her father.[5] Events were to confirm Hogg's suspicions. Disgruntled by the Populist demands adopted by the Democrats in 1896, Bailey opposed the nomination of William Jennings Bryan. That fall, as Bryan was losing to McKinley in the presidential race, Bailey was reelected to the House and became the Democratic nominee for speaker, a remarkable leap for a man completing only his third term.[6] Bailey's star was ascendant.

Tensions between Hogg and Bailey increased when Bailey, commanding a growing body of supporters, announced his candidacy for the Senate in 1900. The incumbent was Horace Chilton, a longtime friend of Jim Hogg. Chilton, ailing at the time and unable to undertake a vigorous campaign, withdrew from the race. That made Bailey a shoo-in, and in January, 1901, the state legislature— following the mandate of the July Democratic primary—elected him. He was thirty-seven years old.

The clean-shaven new Senator with the musical voice and magnetic personality attracted large crowds wherever he spoke. In Texas he served as an anchor for the conservative anti-Hogg forces. Nationally, leading Democrats suggested him as presidential nominee for 1904.[7] Bailey's position in the early part of this century was intriguingly similar to that of a latter-day Texan, Lyndon B. Johnson. It is risky to carry the comparison too far, but after his election in 1948 Johnson rose rapidly to Senate majority leader and toward the end of the 1950's had become a southern conservative favorite for President. Although Johnson continued to marshal liberal support in Texas, some of his harshest critics were liberals who accused him of increasing friendliness toward the business Establishment. As stump speakers both men ranked at the top. (LBJ's television performances, on the other hand, were stiff and formal.) Johnson, of course, held more power in the Senate, held higher office, and ended up more liberal than Bailey.

2

In March, 1900, Texas' attorney general, Martin M. Crane, won his case against Waters Pierce Oil Company before the United States Supreme Court. The High Court affirmed the action of the

Texas courts in a judgment of ouster and injunction because of the restraint of trade. An important legal point, however, was that the evidence was ruled insufficient to prove that Standard Oil controlled Waters Pierce.[8]

Waters Pierce had a fortune at stake in Texas—300 distribution stations and an investment of a half million dollars. The firm was being thrust out just as a growing market for illuminating oil was developing. The president of the company, Henry Clay Pierce, stood to lose hundreds of thousands of dollars.

Waters Pierce was a Missouri-chartered company, so St. Louis-based Pierce turned to a fellow Missourian, former Governor David R. Francis. Francis had served as Grover Cleveland's secretary of the interior and knew the leading politicians in Washington. He knew a strong Texas lawyer for the crisis: Congressman Joe Bailey.

In late April, 1900, Francis wired Bailey, asking him to stop in St. Louis on his way to Washington. Pierce, then forty-eight, was a native of Watertown, New York, who had gone to St. Louis at the close of the Civil War. At just seventeen he had become the cashier of a bank. After saving a few thousand dollars, he secured a partnership in a St. Louis oil company, and in 1869 he acquired his partner's interest. The firm became the leading oil company west of Ohio. About 1870 Pierce surveyed Texas for its sales potential, soon afterward forming Waters Pierce and Company.[9]

Precisely what happened at that St. Louis conference between the solon and the oilman is still the subject of contention. The only existing account of their conversation is Bailey's version—offered in his defense years after the event. According to Bailey's account, Pierce explained that Texas was trying to drive out his oil company, and Bailey replied that the people of Texas would not tolerate the methods of Standard Oil.

To this Pierce responded, "Mr. Bailey, the Standard Oil Company has no control of the Waters Pierce Oil Company. The Waters Pierce Oil Company is an independent concern and not controlled by any trust."

"Why," Bailey said, surprised, "Mr. Pierce, I thought that was what they convicted you of down in Texas."

"That's precisely the same mistake that so many of our people make," said Pierce. "Instead of convicting us of being a trust, they expressly acquitted of us being a trust."

"What did they convict you of, then?"

"Because one of our agents made an illegal contract."

"If that is the only offense," said Bailey, "it seems to me it will be easy enough to pay a fine commensurate with that offense and then go in and behave yourself and you will have no futher trouble."

Bailey said that he would speak to the state's attorney general in Pierce's behalf.

"I will be very glad to pay you for your services," the oilman said.

"Mr. Pierce," Bailey said, bristling, "you can't pay me for that kind of service."

"Are you not a lawyer?" countered Pierce.

"Yes, but I practice law, not influence." [10]

What Bailey failed to disclose, when he first publicly discussed this conversation sometime later, was that he had borrowed $5,000 from Pierce on that occasion. He was purchasing a large ranch in Texas and urgently needed the money. Pierce made the loan himself, anxious that Bailey waste no time in pleading Waters Pierce's cause. Bailey signed a note for $3,300 and soon afterward drew by draft the remainder of the sum.[11]

The personal loan became a well-kept secret for years. If it had remained a strictly personal matter between the two men, no one would ever have known. But without telling Bailey, Pierce subsequently placed the sum on his company books under "account of Texas legal expenses." [12] The discovery of this evidence years later was to have a significant impact.

Following their conference in St. Louis, Pierce accompanied Bailey back to Texas, where—the evidence seems clear—the senator exerted his influence in behalf of Waters Pierce. In Waco, where proceedings against the company had begun, Bailey and Pierce met with the district attorney, the trial judge, and the lawyers who had represented the state. Bailey sought a compromise of the civil suit and dismissal of criminal charges, but the district attorney would not yield.[13] They then went on to Austin, the state capital, where Bailey discussed the case with Governor Joseph D. Sayers. The governor assured him the state did not want to drive out legitimate business. As long as the firm operated according to law it would be encouraged to remain. Next, Bailey visited the attorney general, his old friend Tom Smith, with whom he had gone to school at the University of Mississippi. He suggested, since Pierce had promised the company was not in a trust, that Smith let Pierce pay a fine and continue business. Smith explained that this was not possible under the judgment of the court. For the first time, Bailey later reported, he read the judgment himself and understood the attorney general's point. The court's ruling had "perpetually" enjoined the company from doing business in Texas.

His business completed at the State Capitol, Bailey met Pierce in an Austin tavern and advised him, "The only thing which you can do is to dissolve this offending corporation, organize you a new one and come into this state with clean hands and obey the law, and you will have no trouble." [14]

Apparently acting on Bailey's advice, Pierce and the company's directors voted to dissolve the company on May 28, 1900. The next day they submitted a formal application for a new charter from the state of Missouri and were chartered anew. They then applied for a new Texas permit. Attorney General Smith, having been informed by Missouri officials that the old company was dissolved and a new one formed, advised the Texas secretary of state that the application must be granted. On May 31 Waters Pierce was back in operation.[15]

3

Waters Pierce, a symbol to many of Standard Oil's monopoly, was being watched closely. Ex-Governor Jim Hogg was particularly dubious of the overnight transformation, and as a lawyer and private citizen he expressed his doubts two months later to the state bar association. The occasion was a paper presented by another lawyer in which it was argued that, having adhered to the legal formalities, Waters Pierce's new charter might have been delayed but could not have been denied.

"It cannot change its status in a day by merely changing its suit of clothes," Hogg boomed back. "This corporation was found criminally guilty, and it has never been whipped of its crime. There was a law there prescribing a penalty of fifty dollars a day for every person belonging to that trust, but it hasn't been enforced. Yet their president comes into Texas, a confessed criminal, stalks into the state capitol, treating with the state officials, unwhipped of justice. That is what holds our laws in contempt.

"I know I tread upon ticklish ground, but, by gatlins, I have been used to it all my life! . . . You may snigger and smile and smirk and be derisive to me and the stand I take, but I say it is a crime to hint or connive at endorsement in any form of the declaration that the anti-trust laws of our state can be enforced against trusts by driving them into a new charter. If we do that, we declare it is impossible to enforce the laws in Texas against the strong, while the penitentiary is full of the weak." [16]

Hogg's salvo made the matter a public issue at a time when it could only embarrass Congressman Bailey, then about to win nomination to Chilton's U.S. Senate seat. Undoubtedly, because of his deeply rooted antipathy to trusts, Hogg would have raised the question if he had never heard of Joe Bailey. But now he had the opportunity to lambaste indirectly, and possibly to sidetrack, the man who was nudging his friend Chilton out of the Senate.

Bailey feared the political repercussions if the issue was allowed to smolder. At the Democratic state convention that summer he felt compelled to present his version of what had happened. The loan, not yet public knowledge, was never mentioned. His speech was the first in a series of fusillades traded by Bailey and Hogg forces at the convention.

A test of strength began, with Bailey forces controlling the machinery at the convention. After three key reform issues were voted down by the pro-Bailey majority on the platform committee, Hogg forces took the planks of the minority report—no free passes except to railroad workers, no corporation money in elections, and termination of insolvent corporations—to the floor of the convention.

When Hogg began to speak in support of the reform planks, he was immediately served notice that the convention hall was Bailey territory. Someone yelled, "Give him three seconds!" Howls, cheers, hisses, and jeers swept over the hall, drowning him out.

"Are you afraid to hear a question discussed?" Hogg demanded. "Is it possible—" He paused. "When free speech becomes suppressed—" He could not continue. He glanced at the front rows, where hecklers were jeering him. "Gentlemen, I know you are drunk."

Gaveling for order proved futile, but Hogg refused to yield the floor. The howling continued, Hogg's anger rising all the while. Then he began shouting back.

"I see a lot of lop-eared scoundrels here who don't want to hear free speech," he bellowed. "A man who is cowardly enough, who is bad enough not to hear a speech, is not a Democrat and is a fool besides!" Some began cheering the massive old warrior. He shouted another volley of barbed words at the hecklers, as cheers rang from the audience. "I speak for those who are at home while you are here trying to tear down the institutions by your villainy tonight." More cheers. "I have faced a mob when the mob had the nerve to face me and I never shrank from death and no lot of white-livered curs can suppress my voice in a Democratic convention." Amid cheering, he pointed to seats at one side of the hall. "There sits over there a cowardly whelp who would take a position in a convention to try and cry down a gentleman."

Hogg was building an overwhelming momentum, but before he could proceed further, fistfights erupted. The local sheriff and convention sergeants at arms burst into the chaotic gathering, breaking up the brawlers, settling down the unruly crowd. Determinedly Hogg stood glaring at the troublemakers, his face flushed, his hands clenched into fists.

"Cowards," he roared. "No bully, no group of bullies, can drive me away from here."

Soon the hall grew quiet, and Hogg spoke for an hour without interruption in support of the three amendments to the platform. Others rose to speak against the amendments, often with stinging personal remarks at the big ex-governor, but order reigned thereafter. At one-thirty in the morning, the balloting ended. Hogg had won his fight, 561¼ to 401¾.[17] The vote was certain to keep the Bailey-Pierce issue alive into the fall.

Despite growing suspicions, there seemed to be no solid evidence against Bailey, and he remained the heir apparent to Chilton's Senate seat. His position became even stronger when one of his friends was named speaker of the Texas House of Representatives after the new state legislature convened in January, 1901. Then came the jarring note: A resolution calling for an investigation of Bailey was introduced.

With Bailey's friends in command of the legislature, the investigation could have been headed off. But when John Nance Garner, a young representative, sought out Bailey's views, Bailey asked that the resolution not be voted down.

The hearing, not surprisingly, revealed no damning evidence.

Hurriedly, forty minutes before the balloting for the Senate seat was to start, the House exonerated Bailey completely of any legal or moral wrongdoing, and he was elected to the Senate by a 137 to 6 vote of both chambers, with 15 members not voting. Bailey delivered a speech of appreciation and caught the next train for Washington.[18]

4

The years passed. Spindletop had come and passed its prime. On March 3, 1906, Jim Hogg died of a heart attack at the age of fifty-four. The same month the attorney general of Missouri, Herbert S. Hadley, released a concatenation of revelatory thunderclaps that were to reach all the way to Texas—and to Washington.

Hadley had filed suit against Waters Pierce Oil Company and Standard Oil for violating Missouri's antitrust laws. Witnesses testified that a son-in-law of Standard Oil vice-president John D. Archbold held a majority of Waters Pierce stock—68 percent—for Standard and that Standard had owned and controlled Waters Pierce from its early years. The suspicions of many Texans were confirmed.[19]

Bailey was up for reelection. While the Missouri proceedings dredged up a few memories of his dealings with oilman Pierce, a journalistic event outside Texas initiated a new confrontation for Bailey. In the July issue of William Randolph Hearst's *Cosmopolitan Magazine,* Bailey was depicted as a tool of the trusts. The article, entitled "The Treason of the Senate," fanned the controversy into a national matter more than any other single event. The article cited rumors of Bailey's love of fast horses and cardplaying which had necessitated more and more money. The attack so stung Bailey that he replied personally to the "muckrakers" on the floor of the Senate, first ridiculing Hearst as a political failure and then defending himself for his business and other moneymaking activities out of the Senate.

"Mr. President," he addressed the presiding officer, "I despise those public men who think they must remain poor in order to be considered honest. I am not one of them. If my constituents want a man who is willing to go to the poorhouse in his old age in order to stay in the Senate during his middle age, they will have to find another Senator. I intend to make every dollar that I can honestly make, without neglecting or interfering with my public duty; and there is no other man in this country who would not do the same, if he has sense enough to keep a churchyard.

"Mr. President, it is a great temptation for me to say what I think about these people, but that would offend the dignity and propriety of the Senate, and I forbear."

The vice-president had to remind the people in the galleries that the Senate rules did not permit applause.[20]

By early September Bailey had more than Hearst to fret over. From the witness stand in St. Louis, Henry Clay Pierce told how Standard Oil had obtained its controlling interest in Waters Pierce back in 1882.[21] Pierce also testified that in 1905 Bailey had been hired by Pierce to work out the tangled status of four Tennessee corporations involving $13 million interests in coal, a railroad, and a construction firm. Bailey's relationship with Pierce suddenly loomed larger than most people had suspected.[22]

With this new ammunition from Missouri, the Texas attorney general, R. V. Davidson, and his assistant, Jewell Lightfoot, began preparing a fresh antitrust suit against Waters Pierce. Almost immediately they filed suit for ouster, injunction, and $5 million in penalties. The company was charged with obtaining its permit by fraud, being controlled by Standard Oil, and being party to a Standard Oil trust agreement.

A few days later a "good government," or political reform, club in Houston announced its public stand against Bailey for his role in the company's reentry into Texas. Anti-Bailey political clubs began to form.[23]

The senator took to the stump in his own defense. He went into great detail describing his dealings with Pierce—without mentioning the loan—and discounted the accusations assailing him as the work of William Randolph Hearst, who, said Bailey, was out to destroy him.

Winding up one speech, Bailey alluded to his receiving a senator's salary of $5,000 a year. "But, my countrymen," he declaimed, "when I work over half of my time for you at $5,000 a year, don't you think I ought to be permitted to work the other half of my time for Mrs. Bailey and the boys?" Applause and shouts of "Yes!" interrupted him. "Do you think a man's fit to be your senator who, in order to occupy that high place in his middle age, will take his wife's feeble hand and with tottering steps lead her to the poorhouse when they are old?" [24]

Martin Crane, the reform attorney general of earlier days, campaigned against Bailey. Crane urged the legislature to ignore the primary vote—which had come before the full impact of the Missouri disclosures and had no legal force anyway—and refuse to reelect Bailey.

In his fiery orations, Crane approached Bailey's version of the transaction with scorn. "He said he was not paid for it. I accept his statement. But, good Lord, what an indignity he put on us for nothing!" The crowd roared with laughter, applause, and cheers. "Proud old Texas humiliated, her laws spat upon, her courts defied, all because H. Clay Pierce promised to be good."

Bailey responded by asserting that he had never acted as an attorney for Waters Pierce Company itself. He blamed the newspaper magnate Hearst for dividing the Democratic party and for trying to destroy him and deprive the country of his services.[25]

The heated debate changed few minds.

A final shock that hit Bailey's cause was more damning than anything previously unearthed. John P. Gruet, Sr., a former secretary for Waters Pierce Company, produced papers which established the existence of the $5,000 loan. Since this was the first public disclosure of the personal transaction between Pierce and Bailey, the anti-Bailey politicians seized upon it as the evidence they had long awaited. Gruet, of course, had his own reasons for revealing the papers. He was suing Pierce for back salary. Four years before, he had taken vouchers from the company's files without telling Pierce— or Bailey, who did not know they existed until Gruet announced it.

The Gruet papers spelled out the hard facts of the long-secret financial dealings. Bailey had received $3,300 the first time he met Pierce, followed by a $1,500 draft and a $200 check. The initial $5,000 appeared to be but the first in a series of loans. Bailey had signed a note for $8,000, and on one occasion Pierce had sent Bailey $1,750. The evidence was so convincing that the Dallas *News* and the Galveston *News,* the most powerful papers in the state, announced against Bailey's cause—thereby ending the neutrality which they had maintained during the controversy.[26] A showdown could not be postponed any longer.

5

In the wake of the Gruet disclosures, Bailey wrote to the Texas attorney general and offered to resign if evidence could be produced that he was guilty of improper conduct.[27] Since his term had only a few months to go, this would seem to be little more than an implicit recognition by him that a public investigation was inevitable. At the short-lived hearings of 1901, little more than a sop to public opinion, there had been no hint of Pierce's advancing money to Bailey, and many Texans now began to wonder why the senator had concealed this aspect of his dealings with the Standard oilman.

Ironically, when the state's legislators convened in Austin in January, 1907, they first reelected Bailey to the Senate by substantial margins in both chambers, *then* attempted to determine whether he was fit for the office. It was generally understood, however, that if he were not vindicated by the investigation, he would resign. Many legislators felt morally bound by their constituents' votes in the 1906 Democratic primary to seat Bailey.[28]

Prosecutor William A. Cocke, a legislator from San Antonio with a dark, curly cowlick, then drafted forty-two charges against Bailey.

John F. Gruet, Sr., provided the prosecution's most telling evidence as Martin Crane led him through his testimony. Gruet testified that Waters Pierce, like other distributing companies controlled by the monopoly, received its supplies from Standard Oil plants, including one at Corsicana and the Security Oil refinery at Beaumont.

"Now," asked Crane, "did that Standard Oil Company from 26 Broadway [in New York] assume or exert any supervision over the business of the Waters Pierce Oil Company?"

"Why, certainly, always," said Gruet.[29]

The examination soon moved into the matter of the loans Pierce had made to Bailey. Gruet explained how in one complicated transaction Bailey had received $1,750 on Pierce's personal draft, after which Pierce had gone into the company's till for the amount and ordered it charged "against legal expenses on account of Texas legislation." He also told of a similar event in which Pierce had lent Bailey $8,000, then had taken Bailey's note into the firm's bills receivable and reimbursed his personal expense from the company's funds.

"How were those loans finally disposed of by the Waters Pierce Oil Company on the books?"

"All charged to profit and loss," replied Gruet.

"All?"

"All of them. Legal expense would be charged over to profit and loss. Bills receivable, if they were not paid, were charged to profit and loss."

"Well, were either the $3,300 note or the $8,000 note, or the $1,750, ever paid?"

"Not during my time. They never were received by the Waters Pierce Oil Company." [30]

In defense of Bailey, former Governor Francis of Missouri, who had brought Bailey and Pierce together, told how he had personally repaid Pierce $4,000 of the original loan to Bailey. Explaining that he had had financial dealings with Bailey that were not related to Pierce, Francis testified that Bailey had asked him to repay the money to Pierce.[31]

In his own behalf, Bailey testified that he had never received any money from Waters Pierce Company but only from Pierce himself, for expenses or as loans.[32]

Bailey's examiner then delved into an $8,000 loan from Pierce, which the senator had negotiated in New York.

"Very well, Senator, has this $8,000 note ever been paid by you?"

"It has," replied Bailey.

"In full?"

"In full."

Bailey explained that he had repaid it out of a larger loan he had secured from a St. Louis bank.

Inevitably, the questioning turned to Bailey's familiarity with 26 Broadway in New York, Standard Oil's headquarters. He had been there only twice, he insisted. On one occasion he had stormed in to demand whether Waters Pierce was in a trust with Standard Oil— and had been assured that it was not. And he had visited 26 Broadway on one other occasion.

"When the oil discovery at Beaumont was made," he said, "the Standard Oil Company asked me for my opinion whether they could transact business lawfully in Texas. I gave them a written opinion that they could not, and I told them if they attempted it the officers would be prosecuted and put in prison and their property would be absorbed in fines and penalties. After I sent them that written opinion they asked me if I was willing to explain it. I went there and reiterated it. I guess they laughed in their sleeve about it, because it seems now that they were operating the Corsicana refinery at that time."

Apparently Standard paid Bailey a fee of $2,500 for his 1901 opinion.[33]

The senator admitted that Pierce's statement—that his company was free of Standard Oil domination—was incorrect and had misled him. Bailey had believed that the corporation had been dissolved and that Pierce had reentered Texas with clean hands.

"I am able to say directly and positively that I was deceived about it." [34]

Suddenly, as if a curtain had crashed heavily upon the stage, the investigation ended. The abrupt majority vote of the seven-man committee left numerous legislators disgruntled. For one thing, Senator Bailey had refused to allow Prosecutor Cocke to cross-examine him, and the four-man majority of the House investigating committee had cut short further inquiry by clearing Bailey of all taint. Three members of the committee dissented in minority reports—two calling for extended hearings to clarify several crucial issues, one noting that "at most the evidence shows a course of dealing on his part deemed by many to be inconsistent with sound public policy, and indiscreet." [35]

The results left both sides dissatisfied. Pro-Bailey forces wanted a clear-cut vindication; anti-Bailey men desired further investigation. The State Senate did not report at all, and the House adopted the majority report by a 70 to 41 margin. It was after 9 P.M. when the vote came. Bailey was carried on the shoulders of his supporters to the speaker's platform, where for the next hour he unburdened himself of a blistering, vindictive attack.

"These infidels who have waged war on me have made their own graves," he declaimed with unrelieved bitterness. "We are going to lay them gently in those newly made graves. We are going to bury them face down so that the harder they scratch to get out, the deeper they will go to their eternal resting place."

Then he entrained for Washington, to begin his second term in the Senate.[36]

The controversy was left unresolved and draped in ambiguity. One could point at the public record and claim Bailey was horrendously guilty—or "as clean as a hound's tooth," to borrow a phrase from a more recent political crisis. He had used his influence with officials on Pierce's behalf, and he obviously had profited by employment with the oilman on other matters and had borrowed money from him. But had this been improper? Had he actually accepted a reward for his services in Texas? Although the legislature, dominated by pro-Bailey forces, had replied with a resounding no, the questions lingered, like acrid smoke over a battlefield, for years.

6

Six months later in 1906, Waters Pierce Oil Company was found guilty of violating the antitrust law each day since it had been reestablished in 1900. Ordered out of Texas and fined $1,623,900, the company appealed, but in 1909 the United States Supreme Court affirmed the lower court's decision. By then interest had pushed the penalty to $1,808,483.30, the largest fine ever collected by the state of Texas. Officers carried suitcases of money to the State Capitol when it was paid.

H. Clay Pierce, indicted on criminal charges involving the antitrust affidavit he had made in 1900, was tried by a jury and acquitted in December, 1909, in time to witness the sale of his company's properties by the state receiver under court orders. A friend of his, Colonel Sam W. Fordyce, from St. Louis was the only bidder, and they formed a new company, the Pierce Fordyce Oil Association, which was soon operating.[37]

The same year Texas filed suit against eleven Standard Oil defendants, seeking combined penalties of more than $75 million. After lengthy court battles, judgments brought either ouster, injunction, or fines against the Security Oil Company, Navarro Refining Company, Union Tank Line Company, and Standard Oil of

Indiana. Although Standard Oil itself was not specifically forbidden to operate in Texas, its officers evidently were sufficiently gun-shy as to conduct their business in a more cautious manner thereafter. The era was to climax in Standard's dissolution in 1911 through federal efforts.[38]

Bailey's power waned. As his second term grew short, he returned to Texas less and less. In 1912 he announced his retirement from the Senate and opened a law office in Washington. He was forty-nine years old.

His old nemesis, the Hearst press, took advantage of the occasion to castigate him anew, reactivating the old charges, reprinting copies of Bailey's notes and other transactions with Pierce, labeling him "the black swan of Gainesville," and relegating him to the company of Benedict Arnold.[39]

IV

MUD 'N' BLOOD IN ROARING RANGER

1

For thirty years after Spindletop, the oil frontier pulsed spasmodically over the face of Texas, until every section of the state seemed laced with derricks and pipelines.

To have experienced one boom was to have seen them all. The master plot was this: In a drought-stricken, depressed area where almost no one believed a smudge of oil was to be found, someone would persist and strike oil. Everyone within ten to twenty miles or more immediately rushed to the scene of the flowing well. The stampede, in all its wildness, invariably followed—leasing, drilling, trading, carousing, gambling, letting blood.

Ranger, about 100 miles west of Fort Worth, is a classic illustration of the basic pattern.

The Ranger discovery, in the fall of 1917, along with a series of West Texas strikes that followed, will rank among the most explosive oil booms ever seen. In a world dominated by the war in Europe, with the United States and its allies needing all the oil they could find, it came at the right moment to stir the nation's imagination.

To the old-timer searching for surface geological signs of oil deposits, West Texas had little to recommend itself. It didn't look like oil land, not at all like Pennsylvania and West Virginia. "I'll drink all the oil in West Texas!" was exclaimed for so many years that it became a cliché, and for several years prior to Ranger all Texas was threatened with desertion by oilmen. In the aftermath of the Spindletop and early Gulf Coast discoveries, California had asserted its supremacy in oil production and by the end of 1910 had produced 375 million barrels, primarily from the rich San Joaquin Valley fields. But north of Texas a new oil giant was stirring. The challenge to California came from Oklahoma, beginning with the Cushing discovery in 1912; by 1915 the Sooner State had taken the lead. Even the booms of Kansas—Augusta and El Dorado—overshadowed Texas, where only small fields opened, such as Electra in 1911. Oklahoma and California were to continue to be the giants for several years. Even with the new booms that began with Ranger, Texas was not to take the number one spot till the end of the 1920's.

One disgusted geologist during this pre-Ranger period quit the Producers Oil Company and turned over his files to young Wallace E. Pratt with this advice: "Why do you waste your time in Texas? Why don't you come up to Oklahoma where the oil is?" Pratt .emained in Texas and eventually became the chief geologist of the Humble company and one of the industry's most distinguished figures.[1] Ranger, and other booms in the region, set Texas off again after the lull which had followed the opening of the prolific Gulf Coast.

Ranger's 600 or so inhabitants lived in a dry belt, producing cotton, peanuts, and cattle when drought did not intervene. There wasn't much to the town—a run-down railroad station, a blacksmith shop, a few stores. The only dramatic events previously witnessed in the county were a cyclone that killed thirty-five persons and a bank robbery at Cisco in 1887 that had netted the bandits $5,000 in silver. The story is told that the gunmen threatened to return and clean out the town, whereupon the lieutenant governor of Texas, who lived in Cisco at the time, frantically telegraphed the governor in Austin: "Bank held up. Robbers threaten to return and rob the town. What can be done?" The governor promptly wired back his solution: "Suggest you burn the town and evacuate." [2]

In 1917, W. K. Gordon, an engineer supervising the Texas Pacific

Coal Company's mine in nearby Thurber, saw the possibilities of oil and convinced his company to take about 25,000 acres near Ranger for 25 cents an acre. The first well produced gas, for which there was no market. Gordon ordered a second well be drilled, on John McCleskey's farm. When a reasonable depth turned up nothing, the company ordered the hole abandoned. Gordon would not quit; he persuaded the president to let him continue. At 3,485 feet he struck oil.[3]

Thirteen-year-old John Rust was shaking the dirt out of peanut vines in his father's field, adjoining John McCleskey's farm, on the afternoon of October 21, 1917. Suddenly he saw a terrifying sight with a sound to match. Something very deep green blew far over the derrick. It was accompanied by a roar, and the boy, afraid "the world was going to turn inside out or something," sprinted out of the peanut patch and down the hill toward town, two and a half miles away. When he reached the dusty old main street, he yelled to everybody he saw that something had gone wrong at the oil well.

Almost everybody in town rushed out to the McCleskey well. Young Rust, still shaken by his experience, joined his parents and watched the excitement from a safe distance. The next day outsiders began to swarm in from everywhere, in everything that could be ridden. Young Rust never returned to his peanut patch.[4]

2

Mud and blood. Those two words linked Ranger to almost all of its brother boomtowns. In the fall of 1917, when the rains broke the drought, thousands of teams of mules and horses streamed over the unpaved roads and streets, pulling heavily loaded wagons, until ruts were dug to impassable depths. Every automobile had a chain and shovel as standard equipment, but usually a team of mules was required to pull a car out of a mudhole. One woman set up a "detour" sign near one quagmire on what passed for a highway in those days. Her detour route led over a little bridge, where she stationed herself to collect a 25-cent toll. She started early one morning and was doing exceedingly well when someone realized, about three-thirty that afternoon, that she didn't own the bridge.[5]

Other newcomers avoided mudholes simply by cutting barbed-wire fences and driving across the land. The farmers were outnumbered, and soon few effective fences remained.

In town the mud presented the same problems it had in Beaumont. Crossing the street mud-free on a scow or a slide cost a dime, sometimes a quarter. At the bank one wore rubber boots; the lobby was ankle deep in mud. Two big express horses, tangled in their harness after a rain had flooded the area, drowned in a low place in the street.[6]

Violence followed the oil frontier like a starved coyote stalking a prairie dog. "Ever' kind of money-gitter came here to make legitimate sales or to just plain rob," one old-timer said.[7] Plain robbing, and plain killing, came to be accepted. Reportedly, one constable was shot at—and missed—a total of twenty-seven times in *one* night. Dead bodies in the street created no excitement.[8] Killers were rarely found, more rarely punished. One man was found guilty of murder, fined $100, and ordered to leave town.[9] Robbery was accepted as a logical hazard of possessing money.

Even hardened men were shaken by the wildness. Blackie, a floater-bootlegger whose surname is lost to posterity, was a veteran of the gold and silver mining booms in the West and in Alaska. He thought he had seen it all, but one day, while he was selling bootleg whiskey in Ranger, another floater approached him.

"Blackie, anybody bothering you?" the tough asked.

"Well, no, I guess not," said Blackie.

"Any law, any preachers, anybody you want to get rid of, I guarantee for a hundred dollars."

Blackie was shocked. He had never before seen a man solicit a murder for $100.[10]

Probably the man who contributed the most to restoring law and order to Ranger was Byron Parrish, a former Texas Ranger. In his early forties, six-foot, 200-pound Parrish was reputed to be the fastest draw in the whole western country. Drafted as chief of police, he wore a .45 six-shooter on each hip, a big white hat, silver spurs, gold pieces for cuff links and shirt studs, a diamond on one hand and an amethyst on the other. The first demonstration of his marksmanship must have precipitated a panicky exodus of many fainthearted crooks. Parrish had someone toss an empty dime milk can into the air; he kept it there until his pistols were empty. Hollywood couldn't have created a more colorful lawman.

One day, after criminals had tried to ambush him and had failed, Parrish went after Bob Quantrell, the "king" of Ranger's underworld. Tall, broad-shouldered Quantrell had served time in the Texas state prison at Huntsville and now ran a gambling hall. Parrish located him in the bank, stuck a .45 in his face, disarmed him, whacked him over the head with his own pistol, and marched him to the railroad station. Enraged though he was, Quantrell was never seen again in Ranger.[11]

The scenario had been written for the booms even before Ranger. Back in Batson, one of the wildest of the Gulf Coast booms that followed Spindletop, a saloonkeeper named Brown asked his newly arrived friend, a gambler, "Well, what do you think of our place?"

The gambler who had seen more than a few dingy scenes in his day, replied, "I do not say that everybody here in Batson is a son of a bitch, but I do say that every son of a bitch is here that could get here." [12]

3

The Texas Pacific and Oil Company—as it was now called, adding "oil" to its name—farmed out leases to other companies for development, and unleased acreage went to the swiftest, best-heeled landmen. Within two years almost $200 million of petroleum were produced within a forty-mile area as the boom fanned out from Ranger.[13] At its peak, $1 million of oil flowed every three days. By the time the boom had ended two-thirds of a billion dollars had been spent on leases, drilling, and construction.[14]

Some people came with money, hoping to multiply it; others came empty-pocketed, seeking their fortunes. Some left as millionaires; others, on foot. Young John Rust, who became a modest entrepreneur by merchandising water at five cents per cup, told of one hungry, penniless stranger. The man went to a nearby town, where he bought a lease with a $6,000 personal check—worthless, of course—and rushed back to Ranger, where he peddled the lease for a $14,000 certified check. He deposited the second check first thing in the morning, before his own check had cleared. Six months later the man was a millionaire.[15]

Cliff M. Caldwell lay on a cot in a crowded Ranger rooming house and overheard men in the adjoining room deciding where to spend $100,000 on leases. Rising very early in the morning, he hurried to the area they had named and bought all the leases he could at $5 an acre. By noon he was back in Ranger, reselling the leases to the men he had overheard. The large profit gave him his start.[16]

New hotels were built and soon were filled with the famous and the obscure. Rex Beach, "the Victor Hugo of the North," collected material for *Flowing Gold,* one of his thirty-odd novels. Evangelist Billy Sunday, following a revival in Fort Worth, visited Ranger—where he bathed his hands in oil and at night preached to a throng of 5,000 in the streets. Former President William Howard Taft lectured one night in the city; the next morning he walked unrecognized through the bustling hubbub. John Ringling, the circus king, built a railroad through the oil fields, and he and his wife lived in a palatial private car at nearby Eastland. George Lewis "Tex" Rickard, the Texas native who had punched cattle as a youth, hunted gold in the Yukon, and operated a gambling house in Nevada before becoming one of boxing's biggest promoters, came back to invest in oil. He, in turn, brought in Jess Willard, the world's heavyweight champion.

The boom was, above all, a time to get rich. At nearby Cisco, the site of the notorious 1887 bank robbery, Conrad Hilton purchased the Mobley Hotel, launching a long and profitable career in the hotel business. Trains came through Cisco at 2 and 4 A.M. The vacancies left by departing early risers were filled by the incoming guests, a "hot bed" system that kept his occupancy rate high. Hilton built hotels in Dallas, Waco, San Angelo, and other Texas cities before branching out to New York, Chicago, and Los Angeles.[17]

Landon Cullum and Bill Wrather found that agile wits may at times substitute for money. They drove all night in a Model T Ford when they heard of the McCleskey well and arrived to see the well blowing oil, the town packed, and prices already beyond their pocketbooks. They went looking for wildcat acreage, eventually to Hog Creek, or Desdemona as some called it.

The problem was, how could they avoid alerting their competitors? They invited a dozen landowners to a schoolhouse meeting one night. Explaining that they did not want to discriminate by paying one more than the other, they offered $1 for each *farm's* lease; in return they would drill a well, which would help all of them. The property owners went for it. For the sum of $12, Cullum and Wrather leased about 3,000 acres, then kept going until they had a total of 6,000 under lease.

They soon faced a dilemma that had plagued many another Texas oilman—the lack of capital to develop the leases properly. There was not enough money in Wichita Falls, where they had backers, so Wrather took a train to Pittsburgh to talk with Michael L. Benedum and Joseph C. Trees, famous and successful wildcatters. The easterners joined eagerly, and Cullum and Wrather were assured of wealth. When the two partners sold out, they were millionaires.[18]

The discovery well at Desdemona, Duke No. 1, was drilled by Tom Dees and Oscar True, Texans from Midlothian, near Dallas. They sold their group's half interest to the Magnolia Petroleum Company, receiving in return for each $100 share $10,280. Fourteen-year-old Les True, Oscar's son, was present the night Duke No. 1 blew in and was forever fascinated with the oil business; years later he was to become president of the Magnolia Pipeline Company.[19]

From Oklahoma came Jake L. Hamon, Sr., father of the latter-day Dallas oilman of the same name. Hamon had become rich in the Oklahoma oil fields and was a power in Republican politics, eventually playing a crucial role in Warren G. Harding's presidential nomination.

While drilling wells in the new Texas field, Hamon organized the Wichita Falls, Ranger, and Fort Worth Railroad, also known as the Hamon-Kell or the Oil Belt Railway, an expensive but potentially enriching operation. Hamon had to go to court to secure permission to cross the Texas and Pacific line at Ranger over T & P's stormy objections. On the night of the same day they began, a crew of 200 laborers and twenty-mule teams completed the crossing by torchlight. Texas and Pacific's traffic was tied up for hours, as armed men guarded Hamon's workers. Hamon's fight for his railroad's construction proved to be worth millions. In 1919 the Ranger freight depot did more business than Dallas, Fort Worth, and New Orleans combined.[20]

Native sons also did well for themselves. C. U. Connellee, who had laid out the county seat, Eastland, as a surveyor, became its wealthiest citizen. He built a racetrack, grandstand and all, and in partnership with former Senator Joseph W. Bailey raised racehorses. Later, near where his log cabin home had once stood, he built the Connellee Theater, the largest showhouse between Fort Worth and El Paso, bringing in stars of the day like Lasses White and Raymond Hitchcock. Hitchcock created a mild sensation by taking a stroll in spats and a derby, with a cane tucked under his arm—the picture of refinement.[21]

The colorful flocked in from every direction. Jack Kelley, a soldier of fortune who had fought with Francisco Madero in the Mexican Revolution, once netted $15,000 on a trade and immediately celebrated with champagne. First he drank it; he liked it so much that he, very drunk by then, had his hotel tub filled with it and took a bath.[22] Suave, courteous Count Van Maurik de Beaufort, a veteran officer of the Belgian army who had bought a lease and a well at Desdemona, appeared in glistening boots and neatly pressed khaki trousers, with a silk handkerchief in his coat pocket even on the hottest of summer days. Once, when a drunken tool dresser flung a harsh oath at him, de Beaufort ignored it, but a few days later, when he came upon the man alone, he administered a thorough beating. He explained, "A gentleman does not have a brawl in public." [23]

In Ranger, that was a new idea.

4

Many landowners became rich overnight. Others missed out entirely. Some made it, only to lose it all. John McCleskey, on whose farm it had all started, built the McCleskey Hotel downtown but died of typhoid fever—not from eating too many canned peaches, as the popular version had it—before he could fully enjoy his wealth.[24] A farmer named Higginbotham had struggled all his life on his 160 acres near Breckenridge; his wife had died and he had reared a large family of girls. "Lord, I just never had ten dollars I could call my own," he said. "If I took in a dollar, I already owed it." But with sixteen wells on the farm and oil selling for $3.50 a barrel, he had soon collected $3 million for his share.[25]

Others did not flourish so well. One farmer, offered a $100,000 bonus for his leases, held out for $1 million, never received a cent, and oil was never found on his land. Another family, enriched by their land's oil, left the Ranger district in style in a Pullman car to enjoy their new life as members of the landed aristocracy. It was a short-lived experience. Unwise investments ate up their money, and they returned home in a covered wagon with a team of mules. The wagon contained all their worldly possessions.

The patriarch of the family accepted his fate philosophically.

"I wasn't intended to be a rich man." [26]

5

Ranger and the other boomtowns were recognized by Lord Curzon, a month after the Armistice in 1918, when he noted that "American oil, and hardly any other, made up that 'wave of petroleum' on which the war was won." [27] But even then the end was in sight. The law of capture prevailed, and competitive drilling proved to be as catastrophic to the Ranger field as it had been at Spindletop. The reckless flaring off of gas had depleted the reservoir's energy. Wells stopped producing before the oil was gone from them. By 1920 the picture was dreary.[28]

The bust caught many a man short. Tom Harrell, who had been the county tax collector when the McCleskey well blew in, had turned from his snug $200-a-month county office to trading leases. He knew every farmer in the county. Within a short time he was worth $7 million, owned half a dozen cars, and operated from the entire floor of one office building. But with the war over and the need for crude oil decreased, the price fell to $1 a barrel, and the field fizzled from overdrilling. Gushers went on the pump; new drilling found dry holes. Within a ninety-day period Harrell lost all he had.

"Well," he managed to muster, "it was a lot of fun while it lasted." [29]

6

The Ranger era brought tumultuous chaotic settings that equaled, if not eclipsed, the California gold rush, the Alaskan stampede, and diamond strikes in South Africa and Australia. "All were epic in their way," wrote novelist Rex Beach, "but none bred a wilder insanity than did the discovery of oil in the Red River district." [30]

Burkburnett was a little town north of Wichita Falls near the Red River that is the boundary with Oklahoma. The discovery well in July, 1918, was a kind of neighborly enterprise to "poor-boy" a well—as cheaply as possible, "on a shoestring"—on S. L. Fowler's farm. Fowler's wife had insisted on drilling a well before they gave up on the drought-browned land and moved. Neighbor Walter Cline, a thirty-five-year-old veteran of the Gulf Coast booms, had an idle drilling rig, so Fowler, Cline, and their cronies put up several thousand dollars, drew up a one-paragraph partnership agreement, and drilled. Soon oil was running down the dried-up cotton rows. Cline immediately approached J. G. "Uncle Gash" Hardin, the richest man in town, with an offer to lease his 200-acre cow pasture near the Fowler farm. Cline quickly realized a large profit off the Hardin lease, and the Fowler Farm Oil Company, which had been capitalized for $12,000, sold for $1.8 million.

The Fowler well was a "poor man's pool," where the oil was close to the surface and the drilling easy, and the little men arrived before the large companies saw how valuable it was. Derricks sprang up in yards and town lots, wherever anyone thought oil might be. Walter Cline replaced his topless old flivver with a $4,500 automobile. Everything that Ranger had—except, perhaps, soliciting for $100 killings—this brother boom had.[31]

The exceptions to the patterns established by Ranger were few. One was Electra in North Texas, a town built and controlled by rancher W. T. "Tom" Waggoner, who owned about 300,000 acres. He named the town after his daughter.

Despite an anecdote that suggests discovery of oil angered him because he had been drilling for water for his cattle, old Tom Waggoner was happy over the discovery of oil on his land. The

Electra field, leased by the Texas Company, opened in 1911, six years before Ranger. The field was developed at a less fevered pace. Although there was some bootlegging, there were no open saloons or any of the other roughness of the typical oil town, because Waggoner owned and controlled the land. One longtime resident said he never saw a fistfight in Electra.[32]

Long after Ranger had flopped, the more orderly Electra was still flourishing. By 1923 the town's bank deposits had increased 1,000 percent, to $2 million, and people were ordering Studebakers, Fords, and other automobiles faster than distributors could supply them.[33]

7

For long years "conservation" was an ugly word to many oilmen. The lessons of Ranger and other booms were required to enlighten the industry.

Laws preceded practice. In July, 1917, the Texas Railroad Commission created by Jim Hogg, was awarded jurisdiction over pipelines by the legislature. Two years later the lawmakers ordered the conservation of oil and gas, forbade waste, and assigned responsibility for enforcement to the Railroad Commission. It was a trend that was to lead to present-day regulations governing production.[34]

The law of capture prevailed through the 1920's. To suggest a measured, orderly schedule of exploitation was wild-eyed, revolutionary, even un-American thinking. And perhaps, considering the past pattern of practically unlimited exploitation of natural resources, it was un-American. Although conservation had its advocates, the general feeling that supply was practically endless remained strong. The waste of natural gas was almost incomprehensible. It was one of the salient memories of oil writer Jay Hall, who grew up in the Ranger area. "When I was a kid in Hogtown or Desdemona, I have seen as many as three and four gas wells blowing at one time," he said. "They would keep you awake at night. You just couldn't *sleep.* Some of them would be on fire. That went on for days. There was never an attempt to put it out. That was for two reasons. One was that it was a difficult job, and nobody was pushing them; the other was that if the well blew long enough, it would blow in some oil. I've seen oilmen almost cry when they'd get a gas well. They didn't know what to *do* with it. It was a liability. No market for it." [35]

A few pioneers saw the need to prorate and conserve—there was "a community of interest in the bottom hole pressure." Conserving maintained a stable gas pressure that would help keep flowing oil in different parts of a field. These men realized that the law of capture did not help the nation or the oil industry. In West Texas, W. B. Hamilton organized an oil and gas bureau within the region's Chamber of Commerce to study the petroleum reserves. In 1928 he proposed that the Railroad Commission prorate the oil production in a number of West Texas pools to prevent waste of gas and prevent water encroachment—the underground salt water that kept much of the oil from being recovered. One of his few allies among the major companies was William S. Farish, president of Humble. Officials of Gulf in Houston, Magnolia in Dallas, and Standard of New Jersey opposed him. Gulf finally decided to go along, while Magnolia stubbornly resisted. Independents, for the most part, opposed the innovation just as fiercely.

In the Yates field of West Texas, proration demonstrated its effectiveness. With drilling limited and the field systematically developed, from two to five times as much oil per acre was recovered as in fields where oilmen refused the new methods. In time prices were stabilized for the consumers. Proration brought order to the oil patch and controlled waste and expense. The Yates field was a learning experience and provided a precedent when the unruly East Texas field in the following decade made the old ways obsolete.[36]

8

The 1920's were wondrous days. In the central portion of the state, the Luling, Mexia, and Powell fields opened up. At Spindletop on the Gulf Coast, M. Frank Yount drilled on the flanks of the historic old field with new methods and brought in a new boom as exciting as the first one, though much calmer. The Santa Rita discovery in 1923 opened the Big Lake pool in West Texas and, like a concatenation of Chinese firecrackers exploding on a long string, led to one field after another—McCamey, Crane-Upton, Winkler, and Yates pools. One could see how an outsider could gain the mistaken impression that finding oil in Texas was as simple as punching a hole in the ground.

The 1920's were the heyday of the Panhandle. In late 1918 natural gas was discovered in what became the great Panhandle field, to be recognized as the world's largest gas field. Drilling had followed an assessment by Dr. Charles N. Gould, a University of Oklahoma geologist who had once said, "I hate oil geology." Ultimately the gas area extended north across the Oklahoma Panhandle into Kansas, with several thousand gas wells producing more than 100 million cubic feet of gas daily to supply cities as far off as Denver, Chicago, Dallas, and Minneapolis. In 1926 a boom within a boom came to the Panhandle when oil was discovered near where the town of Borger was to arise as soon as an Oklahoma townsite promoter could rush in and found it. Borger earned the dubious distinction of being probably the toughest town on the Texas oil frontier. Men carried "courtesy rolls" of money to appease holdup men who might otherwise lose their tempers at netting no money and beat up or shoot the victims.[37]

As remarkable as these discoveries were, there was more. Near Amarillo, helium reserves were found that "greatly exceeded that known in the rest of the world at the time." Humble Oil and Refining Company owned much of the land, but Humble geologist Wallace Pratt persuaded his company to sell the land to the federal government at cost because of its value to national security. In 1929 the government began extracting the helium at its Cliffside plant. For years, four wells there produced most of the world's helium.[38]

The new discoveries came at an opportune time, when liquid fuel was becoming vital to American society. In 1920 there were 9,239,161 registered vehicles, about fifteen times the total of 1911. The horse-and-buggy economy was fading into history. Ironically, the West Texas that had been considered the oilman's graveyard had become instrumental in moving the nation. With the booms came the first concentrated migration of people and industry into the semiarid region. Of the eighty-five counties generally recognized as West Texas, oil or gas lay under 80 percent of them.[39]

In 1928 Texas took the leadership in oil production, ending the struggle for top place between Oklahoma and California. One West

Texas well on a test flowed 5,316.6 barrels an hour, or 127,598 barrels a day—a fantastic figure. Had proration not slowed the daily output of these prolific fields they would have spewed forth more than the entire country was then producing.[40]

Texas was to maintain its number one position for the next five decades. As far as petroleum was concerned, it was still frontier country.

V

OIL FOR THE LAMPS OF LEARNING

1

Although much of its wealth has gone out of state, Texas has clung tightly to a portion earmarked for a special use—education. Since the 1920's petroleum income has flowed into the coffers of the University of Texas. Today its endowment—based on oil and gas—is one of the richest in the nation, battling Yale for second place behind Harvard.[1] On a lesser scale, both the state's public schools and private educational institutions have received monies from native resources.

Nobody expected the University of Texas and its sister school, Texas A&M University, to become rich when the state of Texas gave the university system land in 1876. Then the only thing to do with land was to rent it for grazing or sell it outright to settlers. The school eventually was left with 2 million undesirable acres that just happened to have a great deal of oil under them, which no one knew about.

When Texas was a republic, its legislators allotted an endowment of 50 leagues (211,400 acres) for two yet-to-be-established state universities. Then, in 1856, the lawmakers arranged to sell all of the 50 leagues. The nonexistent universities were back to nothing.

The Agricultural and Mechanical College of Texas opened in

1876 as a land-grant college, and in 1883 the main campus of the University of Texas opened. By then the legislature had donated 2 million acres—mostly unwanted land in West Texas—in lieu of money. One surveyor called it "so sorry looking that I hesitated about undertaking the work." [2] By 1916 the university had 2,067,-105 acres under grazing leases, bringing in an annual income of $176,369.03—less than 10 cents per acre.[3] The following year a new law unwittingly shaped the school's future; it stated that income from minerals on the university's lands would go into its permanent fund.[4]

The first discovery on the University of Texas lands began in the head of one man, who was unable to cash in on it. Rupert P. Ricker's part was brief. Ricker, a graduate of the University of Texas Law School, returned from World War I in time for the Ranger boom. He blocked up—leasing contiguous holdings—431,360 acres of university land in four West Texas counties for 10 cents an acre and had thirty days in which to pay the $43,136 lease fee. He was unable to raise the money, but Frank T. Pickrell, a sergeant in Ricker's company during the war, and an associate of Pickrell's assumed the leases. They paid Ricker $500 for his troubles, and he was out of it.

Pickrell chose half the acreage, let the rest of the lease lapse, and went east to look for money. To finance the drilling, Pickrell's company conducted a school for salesmen in the World Tower Building on East Fortieth Street in New York to sell "certificates of interest." In New York several Catholic investors, hesitant over the deal, consulted their priest, who suggested, "Ask Santa Rita, the saint of the impossible, for guidance." They did, and when Pickrell started drilling, he, following their instructions, climbed to the top of the derrick, crumbled a dried rose into the dry western air, and said, "I christen thee Santa Rita."

The usual hardships followed as a crew drilled in the lonely, flat, barren land. Sometimes cowboys were even recruited to help. The payoff came on May 28, 1923, when the well came hissing in. Though not an enormous well, it opened up the Big Lake pool and led to the development of the Permian Basin, one of the nation's most prolific regions.

For several months no one was interested in one little well in the middle of nowhere. Then the veteran Pittsburgh wildcatter Michael

L. Benedum agreed to drill test wells. Two of the eight wells were dry holes, and none was promising—until the last one came in as a 1,500-barrel-a-day producer. The boom was on.

As the Big Lake field opened up, the desolate countryside was lighted after sundown by a large, pinkish glow for about twenty miles. The burning residue gas created a ball of fire that looked like "the devil's own giant candle," as the unwelcomed gas was flared off. One flare burned night and day for years.

The "saint of the impossible" had tapped a source that, combined with holdings in other fields, would convey hundreds of millions of dollars into the coffers of the University of Texas.[5]

Today the old Santa Rita rig stands on the Austin campus, pumping on certain days each year, a symbol of the wealth that petroleum has brought to the school.

2

As of the fiscal year ending in 1975 the University of Texas System's permanent fund possessed assets of $781,771,634.49. Practically the entire sum came from oil and gas royalties, lease rentals, and bonuses. Since the university did not finance its own drilling, the revenue came from its leasing agreements. The assets have been invested in bonds and stocks, the income from which is spent each year. Two-thirds goes to the University of Texas at Austin, one-third to Texas A&M University. Primarily the money has gone toward new buildings, fulfilling a need not provided for in the state's constitution.[6]

The mineral wealth has been the major factor in twenty-five or so modern buildings on the Austin campus. The overall impact on the school has, of course, been considerable. "Compare the University of Texas and the University of Missouri, which has no oil wells but does have lead and other metal resources," said Ed Owen, a geologist-oilman who has taught at the University of Texas. "I got my master's at Missouri in 1916, and I'm sure it was more advanced than the University of Texas was at that time—and now there's no comparison in size or in programs offered. Texas has gone way out from them and, I think, mostly because of the oil resources and the oil industry." [7]

Some, however, argue that oil's influences have not all been benevolent. Ronnie Dugger, publisher of the liberal *Texas Observer,* believes the university's "institutional implication in the oil industry jeopardizes its independence." Friendships with oil industry leaders, he asserts, influence politicians, and the school's regents, tending to identify with those who pay the oil royalties, are likely to frown on faculty members and students critical of the industry. Grants from oil companies shape the direction that research may take. Numerically, though, as he points out, oilmen have played a relatively small role in the governing of the university. Of the 150 regents who served during the ninety-year stretch from 1881 to 1971, only 12 were listed as oilmen.[8]

Criticism of oil and gas laws, from within the University of Texas itself, has most often come from the student body. Probably the most publicized instance occurred in 1956, when Willie Morris, then editor of the student-run *Daily Texan,* commented unfavorably on the Fulbright-Harris natural gas bill. The board of regents moved to censor the newspaper, requiring approval of its editorials. One regent was quoted as saying, "The *Texan* has gone out of bounds in discussing issues pertaining to oil and gas because 66 percent of Texas tax money comes from oil and gas." Morris, who was to go on to become editor of *Harper's* magazine and an award-winning author, won his battle against censorship, but in later years the board was to tighten control over the student newspaper. Morris concluded that "a student editor in Texas could blaspheme the Holy Spirit and the Apostle Paul, but irreverence stopped at the wellhead." [9]

3

Just as the University of Texas profited by legislative neglect and accident, so did the state's public school fund. The fund's greatest enrichment began with the Yates pool in West Texas in 1926.

The discovery—named after Ira G. Yates, a weathered old westerner with a prominent nose and a no-nonsense face one would expect of a Texas rancher in a Zane Grey novel—was in the rugged, expansive Pecos country of sagebrush and greasewood. While rancher Yates was becoming a millionaire, the public school fund acquired a windfall from "vacancies."

A vacancy is a piece of land that no individual or company owns or claims. This makes it legally "vacant" and automatically the possession of the state of Texas. By law, since the nineteenth century, the yield from such lands—originally sales or rentals—goes into a special fund for the public schools. Such tracts were always overlooked or "useless" land that no one wanted—until oil came. Ten years after the Yates pool discovery, the Texas public school fund had gained $6.5 million from it, with millions more to come. Part of the field was on already recognized public school lands. Valuable vacancy strips just added icing to the cake.[10] The most famous of the strips was 4 miles long and about 660 feet wide. Situated north of the Pecos River, it was bounded on both north and south by producing oil fields. When the strip was drilled, the state's public schools automatically collected. Forty years later the little "oversight" had given up more than 13 million barrels of oil.[11]

By 1975, less than half a century after the Yates discovery, total deposits of the permanent school fund amounted to more than $1.2 billion. About a fifth had come from the tidelands the state had leased in the Gulf of Mexico. More than 4 million acres are in these submerged lands, and their income goes into the public school fund.

The money in the permanent school fund, like that of the University of Texas' permanent fund, is never spent, with interest from its investments allocated to public education. Spread over the state's many schools, the income has not made any individual schools rich. Yet, as Land Commisioner Bob Armstrong explained, the fund provides "that 'extra' dollar that the taxpayers do not have to take out of their pockets." In 1975 Armstrong predicted that the state lands' income from oil and gas would be $100 million annually for at least a decade.[12]

4

It is probable that public schools in Texas' oil-producing counties have benefitted indirectly even more from this natural resource. Refineries, oil and gas properties, and other such assets go on the property rolls in the taxing counties, eventually enabling the fortunate districts to sport splendid physical plants that otherwise they could not afford. The public schools of Midland and Odessa in West Texas' Permian Basin provide a case in point.

Gifts and bequests from individual oilmen have gone to many institutions of higher education. Statistics are more difficult to compile than those for the state university, but the total impact has been considerable. Contributions have come in many forms: scholarships, endowed chairs, buildings, library collections, art collections, huge outright gifts. Enormous sums have gone to the many colleges and universities in Texas—and in other states as well.

Houston oilman Hugh Roy Cullen gave a huge portion of his fortune to the University of Houston. To the present day the Cullen fortune has accounted for gifts of more than $50 million. The money has been spent for buildings, land for expansion, and general academic programs. Cullen's gifts were the largest factor in the school's evolution from a small junior college to the leading urban university in Texas.[13]

The proceeds of the permanent school fund can be cited, but measuring with any precision the impact petroleum has had on Texas education is probably impossible. However, an examination of one facet of public school revenues is possibly useful, that of federal aid. This can provide an idea of the extent to which a state depends on outside assistance for its school system, which in turn gives an estimate of how well-off the state may be.

In Texas, petroleum's role can be shown only by implication, because it is a major source of wealth. During 1972–73 total revenues for Texas elementary and secondary schools amounted to nearly $3 billion. Only 12 percent of this came from the federal government. In order to keep the variables as few as possible, we can compare this to the federal contribution to the four states that touch Texas. Each of them received a higher portion of federal money, in ratio to total revenues, than did Texas: Arkansas, 17.1 percent; Louisiana, 13.9 percent; Oklahoma, 13.2 percent; and New Mexico, 19 percent. Only the two oil states—Louisiana and Oklahoma—came close to Texas.

In higher education during the same period the University of Texas at Austin is the salient symbol of petroleum's impact. Partially because of its permanent fund, derived largely from petroleum income, the school has become one of the nation's leading universities in spite of frequently niggardly appropriations from the state legislature. Yet even here the quantitative clues only indicate and do not prove: During fiscal year 1974 the University of

Texas at Austin ranked fourth in the nation in total enrollment— 44,934 students—but only thirty-seventh in the amount of federal money received. As a hint of Texas' greater wealth, all three universities with larger enrollments ranked much higher in the amount of federal aid received—the University of Minnesota, seventh; Ohio State University, twenty-first; and Michigan State University, twenty-sixth. Harvard, incidentally, was the fourth-ranked recipient; Yale, fourteenth.

In at least one set of statistics that come closer to reflecting quality of education, the number of volumes in the school's library, the University of Texas at Austin holds a prominent position, even though the permanent fund's income has gone for buildings instead of books. In 1973–74 the University of Texas ranked tenth in the nation among university libraries, with 3,518,690 volumes, close on the heels of Indiana University. Harvard, the leader, had more than 9 million; runner-up Yale, 6.35 million.[14] But, then, they had enjoyed a few hundred years' head start. Texas had not seriously started competing until well into the twentieth century.

VI

EAST TEXAS—THE GRANDDADDY OF THEM
ALL

1

At an age when most men seek the solace of a rocking chair,
Columbus Marion Joiner was, albeit unwittingly, carving his niche
in history. He was seventy years old when he drilled the discovery
well of the gigantic oil field in East Texas that, at the time of its
discovery, was by far the largest ever found.

Born in 1860 on an Alabama farm, Joiner was of Jim Hogg's
generation. Young Joiner grew up in a log house and was orphaned
at an early age. By the time he was twelve he was working in the
cotton and corn fields, and once he picked 400 pounds of cotton in
one day—a prodigious accomplishment—to win a 25-cent bonus. In
later life, he told people that he attended school for a total of only
seven weeks, but the older sister who reared him had taught him to
read from the family Bible and to write by copying the Book of
Genesis. He became an inveterate reader and was later to add to his
reputation by frequently quoting Shakespeare and the Bible.

In his late teens he traveled throughout the South, going as far
west as Texas. Later he ran a store in Tennessee, studied law, and
served a two-year term in the state House of Representatives. In
1897, when he was thirty-seven, he moved his family to Ardmore,
Oklahoma, where he leased Choctaw Indian lands to white farmers.

By 1906 he owned 12,000 acres of farmland, valued at almost $200,000. The next year an economic panic made him a poor man once again. More than two decades would pass before he recouped his fortunes.

Eventually Joiner turned to the Oklahoma oil fields. He met a gray-haired, heavy-bodied man with a prodigious appetite who was to play a crucial role in his life. This man, who would be remembered as Dr. A. D. Lloyd, claimed to be a geologist.

"Doc" Lloyd, six years older than Joiner, was six feet tall and weighed 320 pounds A gregarious man, he was viewed by the overwhelming majority of oilmen as a promoter rather than as a self-taught geologist. His name was originally Joseph Idelbert Durham. While working as a drugstore clerk in Cincinnati, he had studied medicine but then had swapped the workaday world to pursue a gold rush in Idaho, where he had worked as a government chemist examining ore. Through study and the force of his personality, he became a mining engineer, which took him gold hunting to the Yukon and Mexico. At one time he even sold patent medicine with what he called Dr. Alonzo Durham's Great Medicine Show.

"Dr." Durham of the booming voice and roving eye changed his name to A. D. Lloyd, perhaps because of his reputation as a charmer of the ladies. With a new name, presumably, he escaped harassment when he left them. His story was that he had been married six times and had fathered many children.

Dad Joiner and Doc Lloyd teamed up first in Oklahoma, where they almost discovered both the Seminole and Cement fields—at Seminole they failed to strike oil, stopping their drill 200 feet short. Lloyd had said oil was in both places. Later oil was found by other companies.

In 1925 Dad Joiner sought a new career in Texas. Five years earlier he had bought leases on 320 acres in Rusk County, Texas, from an Oklahoma syndicate. After inspecting the terrain and becoming convinced oil was there, he traveled frequently between Ardmore and Rusk County. With his wife remaining in Ardmore to run a boardinghouse—and to guarantee a steady income—he set up headquarters. Operating out of a one-chair office in downtown Dallas, Dad Joiner began searching for the pot of gold at the end of the rainbow.[1]

2

In East Texas, Dad Joiner found eager ears for his promises of economic growth among the natives of the poverty-stricken region of gently rolling hills, sawmills, cotton, sweet potatoes, and corn. He liked what he saw and leased more land. By the end of 1926 Joiner had leased more than 4,000 acres at nominal expense to himself.

But Joiner soon realized he needed another man to move his operation in the right direction. Where was Dr. A. D. Lloyd? On his trail one day, Joiner learned from a room clerk that his old partner was supposed to be in Mexico but would soon return to Fort Worth. A few days later, while Joiner was napping in the lobby of the Texas Hotel in Fort Worth, Lloyd lumbered in. Shortly afterward the two men drove to Rusk County in Doc Lloyd's new car.[2]

While Doc Lloyd explored Rusk County, applying what he knew of surface geology, Dad Joiner syndicated about 500 acres of his leases to raise money. The large-bellied Lloyd became his "geologist."

Lloyd's geological reports soon entered circulation. One was presented to W. Dow Hamm, district geologist for the old Roxana Oil Company at Ardmore, Oklahoma, Joiner's hometown. Hamm's young secretary lived at Mrs. Joiner's boardinghouse. Through her, Joiner submitted Lloyd's report on the East Texas acreage to Hamm.

The very brief report, signed by "Dr. A. D. Lloyd," consisted of two pages. One page had a map of the United States with the locations of its major oil fields, such as Signal Hill, Spindletop, and Bradford, Pennsylvania, as well as those in Oklahoma, Arkansas, and Kansas. Lines were drawn from all of these fields so that they intersected in East Texas. The last paragraph of the text was one that Hamm was never to forget.

"Gentlemen," it read, "all these major oil trends, intersecting as they do here in East Texas, bring about a state known in the oil business as the apex of the apex, a situation not found anywhere else in the world."

What "apex of the apex" meant, Hamm did not know; from a

professional point of view, it was gibberish. The lack of technical background in the report appeared obvious to him. "I didn't have the heart to tell Joiner how worthless this map was," said Hamm, who was later to become Atlantic-Richfield's chief geologist. "I told my secretary I was sorry. I didn't know anything good about it, but I didn't know anything bad either." [3]

3

The honey-worded Joiner somehow managed to make a start with rusty drill pipe and high hopes in August, 1927. His crew spudded in on the widow Daisy Bradford's 975½-acre farm. From that point on, it was the same old wildcatter's story: They were plagued by breakdowns and short of money; one misfortune followed another. Twice holes had to be abandoned when drill pipes became stuck or twisted off. Nearly two years after they had started, Joiner ordered a third attempt, the Daisy Bradford No. 3. By then he had a new driller, a man named Ed C. Laster. With a rickety, worn-out rig and local laborers who had to quit from time to time to tend their crops, Laster did the best he could. He had to improvise for boiler fuel as for everything else, sometimes burning green, uncured wood, sometimes old tires. Once things were so desperate that Joiner ordered the well to operate only on Sundays, so that potential investors, visiting from Dallas, would see them drilling when they came.[4]

The only shot in the arm that the poor-boy drilling operation had was in the fall of 1929 when the Van oil field came in. The Pure Oil Company had the majority of acreage, and the production was prorated and controlled by the major companies in it; nonetheless, it was proof of oil in the area, even if it was forty miles away.[5] Oil talk grew.

Despite the disappointments, Laster kept drilling. In the summer of 1930 he examined his core barrel and discovered he had nine inches of very good oil sand. He called Joiner, who was in Dallas. Instead of rushing over, Joiner promised to send Doc Lloyd to take over. The prospects of Lloyd's taking charge of the well stung Laster to the quick and led to strife from then on. Only by securing the backing of the landowners was Laster able to remain in control of the drilling.[6]

The well was tested on September 5, 1930. Along with Joiner's friends and supporters, a number of others were there, including two men from El Dorado, Arkansas—H. L. Hunt and P. G. "Pete" Lake. Hunt, already a wealthy man from his Arkansas wells, had drilled close to the Van field but had been unable to lease any worthwhile acreage. Lake, who ran a clothing store in El Dorado, often backed Hunt on oil deals.

The next step was to run casing and complete the well—in other words, to bring it in as a producing oil well. But because of Joiner's muddled financial condition, this took another month.[7]

A few days later the weekly Henderson *Times,* the nearest town's newspaper, splashed its front page with an inch high, eight-column headline: JOINER FINDS OIL ON MILLER FARM. (Locally the property was still known as the "Miller place," after Mrs. Bradford's father.)

The story quoted Ed "Lasseter," head driller, as saying, "I believe we have the biggest thing yet found in Texas."

A crowd of 2,000 converged upon the drilling site. One man, it was reported, had disposed of a forty-acre lease near the well that weekend to a major company for $16,000.[8] Others were devoting their time to clearing up titles on land in the Joiner well area.[9] Thousands began to pour into Henderson, even though the hole was still a long way from being an oil well.

About the middle of September Doc Lloyd was interviewed in the Henderson *Times* office.

"Boys," the beefy, exuberant old man bellowed, "this is the fourth time Joiner has found pay sand upon my recommendation and we're not going to let it get away from us this time!" [10]

4

Early in October, Laster was ready to bring the well in. Cement had been set several days before. The news had gone by telephone, word of mouth, and mail carriers who discussed it with their rural patrons. Five thousand or more people flocked to the Bradford farm, taking their lunches. Daisy Bradford's nephew set up a stand selling soda pop and hot dogs.

Dad Joiner drove up to the well in a dusty old Ford. He waved at the crowd and made his way to the derrick floor amid the pine trees. Scouts from several oil companies stood in somber discussion, while the swabbing of the hole continued.

The vigil lasted for three days. Some slept in their automobiles, others in wagons. Some left for meals, then returned. Finally, late on the afternoon of October 5, 1930, the swab came up with oil on it, followed by a gurgling down in the hole.

"Put out those fires! Put out your cigarettes! Quick!" yelled Laster. Men raced to turn off the boilers. Any spark could start a disastrous fire.

A roar rumbled from the well, and a stream of oil shot over the derrick. "Oil! Oil!" thousands cried at once. Men jumped up and down, throwing straw hats into the air as if celebrating the end of a war. A deputy sheriff fired his pistol at the oil and had to be restrained.

Joiner, exhausted by the wait, turned pale as he leaned against the derrick.

"I always dreamed it," he told Laster, "but I never believed it."

Once the geyser was free of water and mud, Laster closed it off, diverting the oil into a tank.

Joiner asked D. Harold Byrd, a young oilman who had lent him rig equipment at a crucial stage, to gauge the oil's flow and not tell anyone else. Byrd gauged it, then whispered, "She's flowing at the rate of sixty-eight hundred barrels a day!"

It was more than Joiner could keep to himself.

"Sixty-eight hundred barrels! Unbelievable!" he shouted incredulously.

Everyone within earshot—thousands—now knew the facts in detail, and the race was on.[11]

5

A few weeks after the well was completed, an oilman said, "They've found a kitten, and somewhere near will be found the old mammy cat." There was no hard evidence yet—there was only one well as yet, and it did not even flow all the time, so that its twenty-four-hour potential was much less than was first indicated—but the idea spread. Maybe it was from years of stored-up hopes; perhaps it was the payoff on the years that Joiner and Lloyd had preached the golden gospel.

Almost immediately Joiner was besieged by creditors, and a receivership suit was filed.

On a Saturday morning in late October the Rusk County District Court convened for a preliminary hearing. As the crowd leaned forward breathlessly, Judge Robert T. Brown announced, "Gentlemen, Mr. Joiner is too ill to be here today. Other interests may set a date in the future for a definite hearing. Personally, I feel that a man who has been three years getting a baby is entitled to nurse it awhile!"

The audience, many of whom knew how hard it was to save their mortgaged farms, broke loose with cheers until the sheriff had to rap for order.[12]

6

H. L. Hunt watched Joiner's legal difficulties with mounting interest. By the end of October Hunt had bought all the leases he could afford on the eastern side of the Joiner well and was now spudding in his own well, offsetting Joiner's well to the south. An offset well is one that is situated opposite a well on adjoining property, as close to it as possible.

Hunt had about 100 wells in Arkansas and Louisiana and a substantial bankroll, but an extensive oil investment with vast acreage can deplete even the largest bankroll in a very short time. By the time he had bought what he considered key leases and paid for the drilling of his own well, Hunt had, by his own account, only $109 to his name. And as he observed the "peculiar behavior" of the Joiner well, he was not sure he had spent his money wisely.

He had never seen anything like the Joiner well. It would make a "head" of several hundred barrels of oil, then cease to flow. "Flowing by heads" refers to a well that flows intermittently, then subsides until it accumulates another head of gas pressure that causes the oil to flow again. Each day the process would be repeated. Hunt concluded that the oil was feeding slowly into a thin section of the Woodbine sand, as the producing stratum was called by geologists, and that this came from a thicker source west of the well.

Hunt concluded that the field was west, instead of east, of the

Joiner well. If his conclusion were correct, much of Joiner's lease block—that to the east—would be dry; that to the west would be extremely valuable.[13]

Joiner's troubles seemed to compound day by day. After Judge Brown had postponed the receivership proceedings against Joiner in Henderson, certificate holders, afraid they would lose their investments, filed another suit in Dallas. At a hearing in late October, Joiner's attorney presented a petition for voluntary receivership on behalf of his client. Joiner was unable to satisfy all his investors, either by developing or selling his holdings. He was to have no respite. His first success in the oil business was rapidly ensnarled in litigation. Finally, a receivership was appointed.

It was in this setting that H. L. Hunt, a veteran entrepreneur used to taking huge risks without blinking an eye, offered to buy all of Joiner's leases, covering about 4,000 acres.

If he had tried to, Haroldson Lafayette Hunt, Jr., couldn't have dreamed up a more appropriate background as training for this crucial moment in his variegated career. He was born on February 17, 1889, on a 500-acre farm near Ramsey, Illinois. Hunt's grandfather, a captain in the Confederate Army, had been shot to death by a band of Quantrill's guerrillas.

His father, Haroldson Lafayette Hunt, Sr., had taken the remnants of the family north in 1865, walking from Arkansas to Illinois. He intended to go where the money was and insisted there wouldn't be any money in the South for fifty years. Although a Confederate veteran in Union territory, "Hash" Hunt, as he was called, became the first Republican elected sheriff of Fayette County, Illinois.

Hash Hunt married the daughter of a Union Army chaplain. H. L., Jr., the youngest of eight children, was his mother's favorite. His nickname, June, was an abbreviation of "Junior." From anecdotes supplied by his siblings, "June" Hunt was later able to establish that he had learned to read before he was three. "I barely remember when I began reading but I remember listening to my mother, who was highly educated, incessantly reading to me from the Bible in Greek, Latin, French, and German, then translating the passage into English for my benefit," he wrote. Most of his early education came from the St. Louis *Globe-Democrat,* which he read from cover to cover. Inevitably he gained a reputation in the region as a child prodigy. Long before he was old enough to start school, his older siblings brought him their readers, and he devoured them all. He never attended grade school, except for the noontime ball games of "three-cornered cat," after which he remounted his horse and rode back home.[14]

At sixteen, young Hunt left home and headed west. He washed dishes in western Kansas, topped sugar beets in Colorado, banded sheep in Utah, hauled gravel in California. On the Irvine Ranch in California he first worked as a mule skinner and then planted eucalyptus trees. He missed the San Francisco earthquake of 1906 by a few days when he left to try out for a semipro baseball team in Nevada. Failing to make the team, he hired out as a lumberjack in Arizona. He and his brother Leonard, who was along for some of the travels, made a cattle feed crop in the Texas Panhandle. When Leonard returned to Illinois to teach school, "June" went on to Saskatchewan. There, in 1910, he learned that Leonard had died.[15]

As a child H. L. Hunt, Jr., had beaten his older brothers at Authors. In his later journeys, the six-foot youth played cards everywhere he went. Not long after leaving home, he had won more than $200 at cards from a friend and had used the money to enter Valparaiso University in Indiana. He talked himself into enrollment, despite his never having been to school, and signed up for Latin, algebra, rhetoric, zoology, and history. He played a lot of poker, too, but was second in his class when a severe case of tonsillitis forced him to drop out.

In 1911, when Hunt was twenty-two, his father died. With a family legacy and, presumably, any gambling winnings he may have had by this time, he headed south to make his fortune. His father had told him of "the unbelievably rich alluvial soil" in the delta country along the Mississippi. At Lake Village, Arkansas, he made a down payment on a 960-acre plantation and began an up-and-down existence that lasted almost a decade. He planted cotton on the plantation, but for two straight years floods ruined his crops. Thereafter his luck improved. By the end of World War I, with successful crops behind him, he was prosperous.

Hunt, though still a "blue-bellied Yankee" to some of the old-timers in that part of the old Confederacy, got along well enough. He married Lyda Bunker, a local belle from a prominent family. As a postwar land boom began, he sold his plantation and purchased another. For several years he bought and sold land. At one point he was worth, in his own words, "a couple of hundred thousand dollars."

Although he had earned a reputation as a poker player, usually winning from older, experienced gamblers, gambling in another sense broke him. When the postwar depression hit in 1921, his gamble on cotton futures ended dismally as fluctuating prices caught him off guard, and he finally exhausted his cash resources. His plantation properties were mortgaged for $200,000 but were not worth that on the market. When the price of cotton skidded to $50 a bale, the bottom fell out of the land boom, and his fortune was gone. At thirty-two he was penniless.[16]

At this point the El Dorado oil field, ninety miles away, came in. Never one to drag his feet and curse vain luck, though he didn't even have enough cash for expenses, he borrowed $50—requiring three cosigners—and headed for the oil boom.

Stories have circulated that Hunt won his first oil lease in a poker game. His own version—which sounds reasonable enough—is that he got his start by buying leases without cash and then selling them, for cash, at a higher price before he paid off the first man. After several months he secured a small lease of his own, bought an old rig, drilled a well, and broke even on it. From then on he was in the oil business, learning his lessons sometimes expensively. One story was that he remained solvent by winning weekend poker games and using his winnings to pay off his crew. But he did bring in some gushers, and a few years later he drilled forty wells in the Smackover field extension, netting himself $600,000 when he sold a half interest.[17]

A man who always knew when to bluff and when to raise, Hunt enhanced his reputation as a poker player during his El Dorado days. "When I learned I was the best poker player in the world was during the El Dorado oil boom," he told Tom Buckley for an *Esquire* article in 1967. "The talent, the high-powered talent from all over the country, was there." He asserted that the old pros, who knew everything there was about cheating, believed he must have been cheating because he was so successful. But, Hunt explained, he had a photographic memory, remembered every card that was played and the order in which they had been discarded before the last shuffle.[18]

After El Dorado he never left the oil business. He studied the

Florida land boom in 1925, but seeing the values were artificial, he left without exercising options he had bought. Instead, he returned to Louisiana, where he found some profitable shallow production. In the late 1920's he went to Ballinger, in West Texas, and in early 1930 he drilled a well at Ben Wheeler, near the Van field. It was dry, but it had brought him to East Texas.

By then he was a big, handsome, auburn-haired man of forty-one who smoked cigars continually and had a reputation for keeping his word. Like a lot of other poker players, he wasn't a big talker. "What I learned," he once told a friend, "was by listening." [19]

7

When Hunt approached Dad Joiner, to buy him out—lawsuits and all—the overwhelmed Joiner warned, "Boy, you would be buying a pig in a poke!" Undeterred, Hunt stayed in touch with Joiner, at the same time keeping a close eye on drilling in the area.

Hunt, out of money, tried to interest several companies in a cooperative effort to buy out Joiner. There were no takers. They were afraid of the titles and claims. Then Hunt convinced Pete Lake, his Arkansas friend, to take an interest. Hunt and Lake headed for Dallas, rented rooms in the Baker Hotel, and started dealing with Joiner.

At this point the Arkansas Fuel Company drilled a dry hole a half mile southeast of the Joiner well. Then another dry hole showed up to the northeast. These events sent many an oilman home, but Hunt, closeted with Joiner, continued negotiations. The well Hunt had his eye on was one being drilled by an independent company, the Deep Rock Oil Company, on a small lease almost surrounded by Joiner leases. If the Deep Rock well produced, then Hunt's theory would be confirmed. He kept Joiner in his hotel room much of two days in late November, all the while keeping his own lines of communication open.

Late in the afternoon of the second day one of Hunt's men called from Henderson. The Deep Rock drillers had hit the Woodbine, the same sand from which Joiner's well was producing. It was saturated with oil.

Four hours later Joiner signed his agreement with Hunt.

Basically, there were three contracts: one for the 80-acre lease on which Daisy Bradford No. 3 was situated; another on a separate 500-acre Bradford lease, west and southwest of the well; and the third on the balance of the Joiner leases covering 3,329 acres over several miles in all. The agreement cost $30,000 in cash, which Pete Lake produced, plus four short-term notes totaling $45,000, and $1.26 million, which was payable out of percentages of the production from the leases.

In the depth of the Depression, Hunt had achieved perhaps the biggest business coup of his career—and on borrowed money. Two days after Joiner signed, news of Deep Rock's rich core became public, and the Joiner leases looked golden. One major company offered Joiner a reported $3.5 million for the holdings. They hadn't heard of Hunt's coup. Then the Deep Rock well came in at 3,000 barrels a day. Since the Joiner well, flowing by heads, did not produce nearly as much—a few hundred a day instead of the 6,800 barrels at first gauged—Hunt knew he was right. Before making the deal with Joiner, Hunt had begun construction of his Panola Pipe Line. Soon he was delivering his first runs of East Texas crude oil to Sinclair's tank cars at Friars Switch at 62 cents a barrel.[20]

8

No one, including H. L. Hunt, had any idea of the size of the oil pool that Dad Joiner's well opened up. But others in the region, far from the Daisy Bradford farm, thirsted for oil. More than a dozen miles away in the village of Kilgore, corncob-smoking Malcolm Crim, a general storekeeper, had been told by a fortune-teller, "There is oil on your farm—and someday you'll discover it." Crim never forgot it. He leased thousands of acres but could find no one to drill. Then, when the first news of Joiner's well spread, oilman-promoter Ed Bateman sent a couple of employees down from Fort Worth. They ran into Crim, whose land was too far from the Joiner leases to interest the major companies. However, since it was in the general area of an oil well, money probably could be raised for drilling and—who knows?—it might produce oil. Bateman couldn't afford the money for leases, so his men proposed to Crim the only deal he had had so far: Instead of paying cash for leases, they would put down a real well. Action. If it hit oil, all would profit.

Having no better offer, Crim agreed and rounded up the additional acreage required. Bateman, a former newspaper advertising salesman, began mailing out enticing letters to possible investors. He had a decrepit drilling rig moved in. By the end of October, 1930, Bateman's crew had spudded in the Lou Della Crim No. 1, named after Malcolm Crim's mother.

Amid discouragement and hard times, Bateman's crew drilled steadily down. In the middle of December he had a core taken at 3,629 feet. They had hit the Woodbine sand, and it was soaked with oil. On the Sunday after Christmas—December 28—the well was completed. It flowed more than 22,000 barrels a day, a large well, indeed. Crim drove pell-mell back into town to announce the news to his mother, who had gone to church as usual. In his oil-splashed shirt he met her at the church's steps.

Three days later Kilgore, once an easygoing town of 700, swarmed with 10,000 people.

Bateman needed money to develop the rest of his lease. He was broke and had barely raised enough to hit pay sand. But seeking money during a worldwide depression was disheartening. He decided to sell out, but there were no buyers. Then one day Humble geologist Wallace Pratt got in touch with Bateman. Bateman went to the company's Houston office and discussed the matter in fine detail. He asked $1.5 million cash and $600,000 in oil for his seven-eighths interest. It was a huge price, considering the times. Finally, the Humble officials agreed, and in January, 1931, Bateman had himself a deal.[21]

Crim became rich almost overnight. Known as "the poor man's friend" for his financing of cotton-poor farmers, he canceled every account owed him and mailed receipted bills to his customers. After two successive crop failures and the past season's drought that had forced them to mortgage, many of the farmers had owed him hundreds of dollars.[22]

The Bateman well was thirteen miles north of the Joiner well—too far, it logically seemed, to be in the same field.

9

Among the first observers of the Joiner well were some Fort Worth men who flew down in a small single-engine plane. They included W. A. "Monty" Moncrief and John Farrell.

Moncrief was born in East Texas in 1895. When he was five, his family moved to Oklahoma, where he was later educated at the University of Oklahoma. After serving in France as a machine-gun officer in World War I, he entered the oil business in Oklahoma with the Marland Oil Company. He returned to Texas as vice-president of the new Marland Oil Company of Texas and settled in Fort Worth. But as company founder E. W. Marland became embroiled with the stock market, Moncrief decided to go off on his own. He became an independent oil operator. In 1929 he formed a partnership with Eddie Showers of Houston. They bought three drilling rigs on credit. They drilled about a dozen wells—all dry.

They were drilling for Humble in the Van field in 1930 when a proposition came to Moncrief and his then partner, John E. Farrell, that was to change their lives. The man offering the deal was Barney A. Skipper.

Skipper, a short, stout, bland-faced insurance and real estate salesman, had been pushing the idea of oil in East Texas all the time Dad Joiner had been drilling on Daisy Bradford's farm. Skipper, by then a veteran oil preacher, made his pitch to John Farrell in Fort Worth. Farrell talked it over with Monty Moncrief, under whom he had worked as a landman when they were both with the Marland Oil Company. Moncrief didn't have any geology on the lease block, but he thought it looked promising. The two men bought 5,000 acres of leases for $1 an acre. Then they began trying to sell spreads of acreage to finance a well. They sold one to the Tidewater Oil Company, and Farrell sold a half interest in the rest to the Arkansas Fuel Oil Company. That gave them enough money to drill.

But there were other problems.

"In August of that year," said Moncrief, "we discovered that there were some 'windows' in the block; in other words there was unleased acreage in different parts of our block, well located, which would be near to our location if we drilled where we wanted to drill.

"It so happened there was a Dr. Falvey in Longview, a practicing physician who owned a forty-acre tract on the east side of the block together with some other acreage—but he had kept out the forty acres because that was 'just hog pasture.' I went to Longview and he had an office over the First National Bank on the west front on the second floor, where the afternoon sun shone, and no air-conditioning. His patients were largely colored people.

"I sat in his office from four o'clock till almost six until he was finished with all of his patients and I finally got to see him. I made every argument I could in order to get him to put the acreage in. In order to make it attractive enough to get the lease from him, we even offered to drill him a well on that tract. He refused. He would not have any part of it. He said that was his hog pasture and he didn't want it messed up with any old oil wells!

"So I left there very discouraged about six-thirty in the evening. I went over to the Gregg Hotel to the dining room and there were very few people in there. I had a table by myself and while I was eating my dinner, a man came up to me and said, 'Are you Mr. Moncrief?'

"I said, 'Yes, I am.'

"He said, 'My name is F. K. Lathrop. I work for Kelly Plow Works here in Longview and you have a lease on four hundred acres of my land out there in the middle of this block.'

"And he asked me if we had made a location, and I told him we had not yet. So he said, 'If you will drill on my tract, on the four hundred acres, I will give you a quarter interest in my royalty.'

"So I raised up and I said, 'Mr. Lathrop, you have done gone and made yourself a deal!'" I shook hands with him and next morning we signed up and that is where we drilled the well."

The location was about eleven miles north and to the east of Ed Bateman's well. On the night of January 23, 1931, the rotary bit "fell" into a soft formation slightly more than 3,500 feet deep. Moncrief and Showers had a core sample taken. A little after midnight they packed the core in a gunnysack and stole away to a Longview hotel to scrutinize it.

"The core resembled brown sugar that had been dipped in oil," said Moncrief. "Truly, it was a beautiful sight to behold! By sunrise the next morning we were out buying royalty around the well as fast as we could and as long as the money lasted. The well gauged eighteen thousand barrels a day. If we had drilled in the hog pasture we would have gotten a dry hole, which shows you there was a great element of luck or the Good Lord watching after you that caused you to drill on the Lathrop tract instead of on the Falvey tract."

The Chamber of Commerce in Longview had offered a $10,000 bonus to the discoverer of the first commercial oil well in Gregg County. Farrell and Moncrief qualified. In a burst of generosity they distributed the reward—pocket change in comparison to the profits they anticipated—among the drilling crew that had brought in the well.

As drilling multiplied, the market became flooded with oil. Prices dropped until the pressure was almost too much for Moncrief and his associates. Without sufficient funds to develop the leases further, they looked for a buyer. Harry Sinclair came down from New York in his private railroad car. To impress him with the well's value, they opened it up for a test. "When the stream of oil hit the tank, it sounded like a cannon, shook the earth, and knocked pine cones off the surrounding trees!" reported Moncrief. Sinclair was impressed. But they turned down his offer of $1.75 million.

Later they sold out to the Yount-Lee Oil Company of Beaumont for $2.5 million. The transaction was for the discovery well and about 2,500 acres of leases. When the Yount-Lee subsequently sold out its company to Standard of Indiana, the East Texas property was evaluated at $18 million.

At the time virtually everyone believed the three East Texas wells were tapping three separate oil fields.[23]

10

Some geologists worked out a theory that the East Texas oil was coming from one vast pool. The one-field geologists postulated "an immense stratigraphic trap." The Woodbine sand, they argued, was either the shoreline or the eroded remains of the shoreline of an ancient sea that had once occupied the East Texas basin. The oil had been forced into it and trapped there. The stratigraphic trap idea, which implied a field of colossal size, was almost inconceivable to most oilmen at first. Some companies, convinced by the theory, began investing. A few agreed with the theory but didn't lease—they couldn't see how the market could absorb such a glut of oil that would have to be there. They were in the minority. Thousands poured in to make their fortunes.

Among the big-field theorists was Doc Lloyd, who had been discounted by recognized geologists from the beginning.

"Where he got his information I wouldn't know," said Monty Moncrief, "but anyway he told me at least ten or fifteen times that that field would be at least fifty or sixty miles long and five to fifteen miles wide. Everybody thought he was crazy, including myself. At that time, if we had had any confidence in what he was saying, you could go in between these wells, particularly between our well and the well at Kilgore drilled by Bateman, and buy acreage in there for ten dollars to fifteen dollars an acre that proved to be right in the heart of the field." [24]

Among those early believers was Clint Murchison, who was to become one of Texas' best-known millionaires and wheeler-dealers. He drew a circle on the map and told his landmen to lease everything they could within that circle. "Give them a dollar, two, or five, whatever it takes, but give it to them out of a quarter of their oil." That meant it didn't cost him anything, till later—if he found oil. [25]

Bob Whitehead, a geologist with the Atlantic Refining Company, had tried to interest his company in the huge potential of the East Texas field. Unable to convince others in the company, Whitehead promoted a joint meeting of the Dallas and East Texas Geological societies. At the meeting a poll was taken, in which the geologists estimated the reserves of the field. It was unofficial. No one was asked to sign his assessment.

The consensus was that the field had a billion barrels at least. With that documentation, Whitehead won his point. Atlantic ended up with one of the best positions in the field.

Two geologists from Kentucky, George W. Pirtle and James W. Hudnall, were the first individuals to map out the East Texas field, working out of tents with three field parties in early 1931. They were amazed to learn, in retrospect, how many dry holes had been drilled, very close to the field, before the Joiner discovery. When their map was distributed to their clients that year, there was only a handful of outpost wells drilled within the entire pool. "The big companies hated to see us put out these maps, I'll tell you," said Pirtle, "because our maps were probably just as good as or better than theirs." Within a few years Pirtle and Hudnall were the principal consulting firm in the field. Their maps, accurately delineating the field at an early state, helped hundreds of people make money.[26]

Within three years it was recognized as the largest oilfield in the world—stretching forty-five miles from north to south and five to twelve miles from east to west. There were 140,000 acres of producing oil land, spread over five counties. Because of the early ambiguities connected with the field, independents rushed in and secured leases that set them up for life. A year after the discovery, major companies owned less than 20 percent of the wells and proved acreage. But by 1938 the majors owned an estimated 80 percent. Humble alone acquired 16 percent of the acreage in the whole field and while Joiner's discovery well had been on the edge, and less productive, it turned out that Humble, Gulf, and Ohio leases were in the middle of the field. Geologist-oil historian Edgar W. Owen summed it up: "As had been the case so often in the past, an intrepid individual wildcatter made the discovery, but major oil companies were the largest lease owners." [27]

11

Fattening up his "pig in a poke" kept H. L. Hunt busy on several fronts simultaneously. He had to arrange for financing to develop the leases while fighting off lawsuits and substantiating the titles. When it was over, he had been through about 300 lawsuits, taking about ten years. The old saying, "A producing well clouds a title, a dry hole clears it," was probably more valid in East Texas than anywhere else. Contestants streamed in from everywhere, producing a wilderness of litigation. Sometimes Hunt had 100 cases pending in the courts at a time.[28]

Most of the lawsuits that Hunt assumed were settled out of court, usually for small amounts, thereafter clearing title to the disputed land. Others were fought out in the courtroom. Because he often was a principal in the suits, Dad Joiner became, to quote one reporter, as familiar in court "as the judge's pitcher of ice water." [29]

The sentimental old wildcatter was as susceptible to his lawyer's oratory as were the jurors. "In one case where they sued him over there," said attorney L. L. James, who handled most of the cases, "and I was referring to him in my closing argument, about what he had done for the people of Rusk County and what a godsend he had been to them, he got up and left the courtroom crying like a baby."[30]

Each month Joiner called at Hunt Oil's offices for his monthly check as provided in the original agreement. For a long time he received $30,000 a month, and later he got $15,000 a month. Often Joiner's account with the company was overdrawn. It was believed the old man was depleting his bonanza looking for another field—wildcatting it away. In the depth of the Depression that was about the only way a man could spend money so fast. "But," said Sherman M. Hunt, a nephew of H. L. Hunt, "he got to believing he was Columbus Marion, the great discoverer, and he was going to find another one!"

Then, one day in November, 1932, two years after the discovery, Dad Joiner added to H. L. Hunt's wilderness of litigation. He filed suit against Hunt, his brother Sherman Hunt, Pete Lake, and Hunt Oil Company, charging fraud in Hunt's negotiations with him. By then there were 900 producing wells on the acreage, and Joiner asked the court either to return the property to him or to order the lease owners to pay him $15 million, the presumed market value.

Although the strange suit was, by all accounts, friendly, its defendants had some anxious moments one day after Dad Joiner had several bushel baskets of grapefruit delivered, one to H. L. Hunt, one to Sherman Hunt, one to Pete Lake.

The telephone rang in the Sherman Hunt household. A very excited Pete Lake was on the other end.

"My God, don't eat those grapefruit!" he shouted. "I think they're poisoned—the meat's awful red."

People around East Texas didn't eat much grapefruit in those days, and pink grapefruit was a rarity.[31]

Joiner's suit against the Hunts never went to trial. One day he withdrew it, claiming it was filed "upon a misapprehension of the true facts." He had to ask Hunt for an advance in his oil payments to settle with his attorney.[32] Hunt had as good a record on his other lawsuits. Out of all the litigation he never lost an acre of his leases.

As production continued the Hunt company ranked thirteenth
among the operating companies in the East Texas field, a leader
among the independents. Many majors did not rank so high.[33]

12

Discoveries in the Seminole and Oklahoma City fields, coupled
with the influx of South American oil, had already given the United
States more oil than it could absorb, even though in 1931 a total of
26,690,949 registered automobiles consumed 17 billion gallons of
gasoline a year. The East Texas field was a glut on the market as
supply overwhelmed demand. Oil prices slipped, down to 35 cents a
barrel, then to 20 cents, and in July, 1931, to 10 cents, with large
shipments selling for 5 cents a barrel.[34] At the same time fresh
water, because of the cost of hauling, sold for 10 to 25 cents a
barrel.[35] As the state and federal government sought to regulate
production, in effect repealing the law of capture, many operators
refused to heed the new rules, selling what was called hot oil. This
period of conflict in the oil fields became known as the Hot Oil
War, which will be discussed in Chapter VII. Until the Hot Oil
War was settled, the low prices and instability caused by East Texas
made the oil business as risky as shooting a rapids in a warped
canoe.

Yet in the midst of no money and low prices, many commenced
to build their fortunes. If a man could figure out a way to raise the
money, there were opportunities the like of which had never been
seen before. Because of the scarcity of cash and the desire for oil—
plus the fact that the field's limits were not yet determined—for a
few years after discovery an operator could still make a deal to drill
a well in which the lease owner received one-fourth of the oil in lieu
of money, the oilman getting three-fourths. The problem then
became finding a way to get the well down.[36] One way was through
oil payments, which amounted to futures on an oil well. These
payments came to be a form of money in East Texas.

Many wells were drilled on credit in this fashion. In order to drill
a well, a lease owner or operator would promise the driller a sum to
be paid out of the first oil or a fraction of it, when produced. The
fraction might be an eighth, quarter, or half—whatever they agreed
upon. Once the original amount had been paid off by oil income,

the leaseholder would start pocketing all his oil money. During 1931, 1932, and 1933, oil payments sold for anywhere from 5 to 35 cents on the dollar; those that promised to pay themselves out in six months went higher, maybe for 50 to 75 cents on a dollar. These were excellent investments. Ultimately the holder of an oil payment got his money back and more.

The man frequently given credit for starting the boom in oil payments was Georgia-born Algur H. Meadows, whose small loan business in Shreveport, Louisiana, just across the state line, faced many struggling moments during the Depression. Meadows opened a branch of his loan company in Tyler after the field came in. Next door was the office of Dr. Edgar Vaughn, an ear-eye-nose specialist who had bought stock in Meadows' company.

According to George Pirtle, one day Dr. Vaughn asked Meadows, "Al, why don't you get into the oil business?"

"I don't know anything about it," confessed Meadows.

"Well, there's a young fellow in this bank building who's on the board, named George Pirtle. Tell George to teach you the oil business, and smart as you are, you'll pick it up right quick."

Meadows stayed close to Pirtle, a geologist, for a while, watching him operate. With his background in finance, Meadows soon conceived of the oil payment system. One of his first large deals landed him one of the finest leases in the middle of the field—which still has decades of production left. Meadows had to raise 10 percent of its value with which to drill a well. Pirtle wrote a report on it. Meadows then took the report and borrowed from a New York bank. His company, the General American Oil Company, realized many millions from these transactions. Dr. Vaughn no doubt applauded. He was the company's third largest stockholder.[37]

13

What happened to the men who first opened up the field?

Ed Laster, the driller for the Daisy Bradford No. 3, explained that he never received the leases Dad Joiner had promised as part of his pay, nor, he said, had he expected them. "He didn't give me one single lease," said Laster. "He gave me twenty-five royalty acres on the Bradford farm—was all the acreage that I got from Mr. Joiner at any time. But as the well was going down, Mr. H. C. Miller

[Daisy Bradford's brother] was on the road [as a salesman] and he suggested that we jointly buy leases and he may find a buyer. We bought several leases. Bought three, I believe. And he didn't sell any, but we were caught with them on our hands when the well came in, which was a fortunate thing." [38]

Doc Lloyd, according to one account, had originally wanted Joiner to drill west of the Daisy Bradford No. 3 site, which would have put them in the fairway of the field instead of at its edge. However, another report goes, Lloyd had an agreement with the old wildcatter: If they made a well, he could choose his acreage. While the well was going down, he made his selection. It was to the east of the discovery well. Every acre of it was dry. [39]

Lloyd had his detractors, particularly among the formally trained geologists and representatives of major companies. Lloyd fulminated at the major companies almost every chance he got. One day this practice boomeranged on him. At a mass meeting he made a motion that Humble Oil be run out of the state of Texas. John Suman, a Humble official, promptly stood up and gleefully seconded the motion. Immediately Suman's tongue-in-cheek action triggered laughs from the audience—and ended Lloyd's serious threat. [40]

As the boom grew, Doc Lloyd's massive figure retreated from the stage he had helped build. His picture had appeared in newspapers all over the country. The stationmaster at Overton, one of the little boomtowns, reported a new woman, often with children, stepped off almost every arriving train, asking about Lloyd. If his name had changed, they seemed to have remembered his features. They apparently never found him, and he left the East Texas field without cashing in. He died, at nearly eighty-seven, in a Chicago hotel in 1941, leaving much of his past unrevealed. [41]

Columbus M. Joiner, the Shakespeare-quoting wildcatter, used up the money from his deal with Hunt looking for new oil fields. But like Pattillo Higgins before him, he lived to see the significance of the field he had opened up. For the last several years of his life he lived quietly at his home at 4637 Mockingbird Lane in Dallas. The easy-humored old man at least continued one thing he had done all his life. He read. By the time of his death at eighty-seven in March, 1947, he was reputed to have read 10,000 books. His bones rest today in Dallas, a city that became identified with H. L. Hunt and other oilmen who made their first millions in the East Texas field. [42]

14

Violent death was a familiar event in the oil fields. Men fell from derricks. Fires and gas blowouts engulfed workers and burned them beyond recognition. Some were decapitated; others lost limbs. But the greatest catastrophe of all in East Texas was the explosion of the New London, Texas, school building on March 18, 1937. It took the lives of 296 persons, one of the worst disasters in American history. The large majority of the victims were schoolchildren.

The building was of hollow tile with steel girders on the roof. The school's gas supply was "tapped" from a company line. A gas leak somewhere had built up until the basement and the hollow walls were filled. There was no odor to it, since it apparently was "residue" gas. Suddenly, the whole building was turned into a bomb.

The spark from a light switch set off the bomb. As the building exploded, concrete and bodies scattered everywhere.

A number survived the blast. The tragedy led to new state laws designed to prevent such disasters in the future. One law required that all gas sold to the public be injected with a substance that could be identified by smell as "gas." Unprocessed or "raw" gas may have a "gassy" odor, but the liquid fraction of such gas contributes the smell. Once the liquid has been refined out, as oil or gasoline, the scent goes too, leaving "residue" gas. Then, for safety's sake, the artificial smell is added so that gas leaks can be identified by sensitive human noses.

Had not preventive measures been taken eventually, more tragedies might have followed the New London explosion, for the tapping of gas lines, a common occurrence in those days, presented problems decades later. Geologist John T. Scopes, who while a teacher had been the central figure in the 1925 Tennessee "Monkey Trial," came to have firsthand knowledge of the condition of some of the pipelines.

"United Gas had to lay a new line in the early 1950's to keep from possibly one day blowing up the city of Longview," said Scopes. "Some of the pipes were worn thin. When we finally took up the line, we found more illegal taps on it than you ever saw. I think half the people in East Texas had worked on a pipeline at one time or another, and they knew how to tap it and use the natural gas without charge." [43]

15

Although it had no oil wells of its own, Dallas nudged out Tulsa as the oil capital of the Southwest. The East Texas field made the difference, for it put Dallas in the center of an active oil region, and many of the men made rich by the East Texas field moved to Dallas and made their headquarters there. H. L. Hunt was one of the many to make this move.

A visible symbol of Dallas' new ascendancy became the flying red horse sign atop the Magnolia Building in downtown Dallas. Erected under the supervision of J. B. McMath in 1934 in time for a convention of the National Petroleum Institute, the red stallion Pegasus came to be identified in many minds as synonymous with Dallas. Weighing 6,000 pounds and outlined at night with 1,162 feet of ruby neon tubing, the mythical winged stallion could be seen thirty miles away by motorists driving through the bald blacklands of North Texas or seventy miles away from a plane window. Situated on top of what was then the highest building in the city, it became the largest revolving sign in the world. [44]

In the midst of the Great Depression, more independent oil fortunes came out of the East Texas field than from any other place in the world. This was primarily because of the size of the field. Out of the thousands of tracts and town lots, there was something for almost everyone, at least for those who moved fast enough, boldly enough, and were in the right places at the right times.

The era, symbolized by the East Texas field, also became a point of departure from the old pattern of Texans going, hat in hand, out of the state to solicit funds for expansion and development. It was often still necessary, but more often now there were alternatives. H. L. Hunt became one of the first to grow huge without losing control to eastern capital. Other Texans did the same during this era. Partially this was because Texas bankers were by then knowledge-able enough to back Hunt and others like him. And in East Texas the bankers were further assured because the field was big and proved. The pattern began to change, as Texans accumulated enough from the native wealth to perpetuate local control. Today, even though Texas does not have banks with the immense financial resources of those in New York or Chicago, they are substantial enough to help an oilman grow big without having to go east.

During World War II the oil from the East Texas field was a significant factor in the Allied victory. When the Big Inch pipeline—twenty-four inches in diameter—transported Texas crude oil from Longview to the East Coast refineries, the field supplied more than a half billion barrels of high-grade crude oil during the war years. As H. L. Hunt pointed out, this five-year figure was more than a half dozen major fields would produce in their entire lifetimes.[45]

The field itself became a symbol and had much to do with forming the "Rich Texan" image stamped on the public mind. As World War II, with its shifting about of Americans, helped export the "Texas brag" state of mind, Texans preached the gospel of their great state to the ends of the world. As they explained these natural wonders to "foreigners," precise dimensions were ofttimes overlooked.

Geologist James S. Hudnall observed this phenomenon on Christmas Eve, 1944, while driving home to Tyler. The roads were lined with soldiers, and Hudnall picked up as many as he could take in his car. Most of them had had a few drinks and, on their way home, were feeling good.

As they passed Longview, a corporal from Texas said to an Oklahoman in the car, "You know what this is that we're coming to?"

"No, I don't," replied the Oklahoma youth.

Ahead lay a vista of hundreds of derricks.

"I'll tell you exactly what it is," said the Texan. "I live in Texas, and I know something about this East Texas field. She's seventy-five miles wide, east and west, the direction that we're going. The north end of it—I don't know exactly where that goes, but it extends almost up into Oklahoma. And the south end, now I know something about that. I was down on the Gulf Coast the other day. And they were drilling a well five miles out in the Gulf, and she was still going there!" [46]

That soldier would have made a great promoter.

16

By 1934 all of the Soviet Union produced only 43 percent as much oil as did Texas. In this country, California was the second largest petroleum-producing state. The East Texas field had made certain that Texas would be number one for a long, long time among both states and nations. Eventually almost 30,000 wells were drilled in the field. Although thousands were subsequently abandoned because of water encroachment from the west, forty years after discovery there were still 15,000 active wells. Ironically, of the leases H. L. Hunt had bought from Dad Joiner, all of them had paid out promptly within a few years except one: the eighty-acre lease with the discovery well. Still, it contributed a few dollars toward its purchase price each month, even into the 1970's.[47]

By 1965 more than 3.5 billion barrels had come out of that once-poor earth, with an estimated 1.5 billion barrels left, plus nearly 2 trillion cubic feet of natural gas. The field's total reserves, historian-geologist Edgar W. Owen has said, involved "perhaps half as much as the entire United States had produced to that time."[48]

Not everyone viewed this with jubilation. During a banquet in Tyler commemorating the discovery, at a time when the black giant was going high, wide, and handsome, one speaker after the other extolled the field as the greatest thing in the world, with the greatest number of wells, the greatest everything. Then Henry M. Dawes, head of the Pure Oil Company, stood up. A year before the Joiner well, Pure Oil had found the Van field not far away. It was a rich discovery that insured prosperity for Pure Oil—until the East Texas field. But the East Texas field, with its plethora of oil that disastrously cheapened everybody's oil, everywhere, had nearly ruined Pure Oil.

Dawes acknowledged the accuracy of the extravagant words piled upon the East Texas field. It *was* the greatest thing in the world.

"But as far as I'm concerned, with the Pure," he said, "I feel like the hen that laid the biggest egg. All the other hens in the barnyard cackled and congratulated her. When she could stand it no longer, she told them, 'Well, girls, it may be the biggest egg in the world to you, but to me it was just a pain in the ass!' "[49]

VII

The Hot Oil War

1

Before the fall of 1931 the term "bootleg oil," borrowed from the vocabulary of Prohibition days, was used to denote the illegal production in the East Texas field. But late one dreary night in November of that year a new, catchier term supplanted it. National Guard Sergeant D. W. Johnson, a veteran of both the Army and the Internal Revenue Service, had gained the confidence of a member of a ring of men who were producing oil in excess. As Johnson was checking tanks near Gladewater, a cold, cutting wind blew rain into his numbed face. He complained about the weather to the man watching the lease.

"Just lean up against a tank of that oil," the man said. "It's hot enough to keep you warm."

Several days later, remembering the significance of the remark in underworld parlance, Sergeant Johnson replaced the longer phrase "oil produced in excess of the allowable granted by the Railroad Commission" with the shorter, to-the-point "hot oil." [1]

The East Texas Hot Oil War of the early 1930's changed the industry forever and led to the closing of the "oil frontier." The underlying cause of the Hot Oil War was the rule of capture. Based on English common law, the concept had been clothed in legality since an 1889 decision of the Pennsylvania Supreme Court. He who takes the oil first owns it; all one produces from under his leases is his to do with as he wishes. But since oil moves underground, a hole punched in the midst of a field will flow oil from one's own lease and, given time and opportunity, from surrounding leases as well.[2]

The same philosophy had gutted the fields at Spindletop, Ranger, and others. Not only does an oil glut spoil the market, but all-out production also ruins a field's underground pressure, eventually destroying its productivity entirely.

Unfortunately most oilmen knew little about the technical aspects of a field. "These concepts were just absolutely out of the blue to most of them," said Carl E. Reistle, Jr., a petroleum engineer who became head of the Humble company. "The average man had been producing oil for years and had never heard of this thing of porosity and permeability and gas-oil ratio. All he knew was, you drilled this hole down there, and you started producing, and you'd produce as long as you could and as hard as you could or the other guy'd get your oil." [3]

The 1930's were a transitional period. The overproduction of oil was not one of the recognized crimes of the past. Many oilmen proclaimed that they had the right to do as they pleased with their own property. They had a constitutional right to produce and sell all the oil they could, they contended—or they just did it, without bothering to argue the point.

There were, of course, the pertinent economic factors. If a man was in debt and needed to pay for the wells he had already drilled, the only way out was to run his oil, no matter what newfangled regulations had been dreamed up in Austin or in Washington. Everyone knew that oil traveled and that a man might be flowing oil from beneath his neighbor's lease, too, but at least he sure as hell wasn't losing any of his own.

Twice the size of Manhattan Island, nearly as large as the District of Columbia, the East Texas field was an awesome extravagance in a time of scarcity, an anomaly that forced change on those who touched it—and on many who did not. Too big to be controlled by traditional approaches, it invited chaos. The world was drowning in oil, it seemed, and the prices proved it. At one point the price skidded to 10 cents a barrel, with some going for 5 cents, and one sale of 1 million barrels of East Texas crude netted $25,000—2½ cents a barrel—while a few sales were for 2 cents. Only the motorist found it heaven. Gasoline at the pump went for 7 and 8 cents a gallon, sometimes as low as ½ cent per gallon at the refinery. While the cheap East Texas oil was closing down fields over the nation, there were at one time ninety-five refineries in East Texas, a figure that leveled off at seventy-six, still possibly more than in the rest of the United States.[4] With billions of barrels stored in the East Texas earth, it is no surprise that such an irresistible magnet attracted, as one reporter put it, "the strangest rendezvous of outlaw producers that has existed since the dawn of modern industry." [5]

2

Ross Sterling began his term as governor just as the East Texas story was unfolding in early 1931. Along with the Great Depression, he immediately had an oil problem on his hands. It was May before the Railroad Commission's first proration plan for the field became effective, and despite the plan, drilling was allowed to continue.

By the next month there were 1,000 wells in the field, flowing a half million barrels a day, more than three times the allowable amount. "Teakettle" refineries—which could be built for $10,000 to $25,000 and paid off within a month—proliferated. The low-sulfur, light-gravity East Texas "crude" made gasoline refining relatively simple. Heated to about 500 degrees in a pipe still, the oil then circulated to a bubble tower—a tall steel cylinder—where steam was added. The separated gasoline went off through a vapor line at the top of the tower. Depending on the quality of the crude product, gasoline refining can become increasingly more complex, but in East Texas most refiners sought the cheapest, least complicated means of extracting the fuel. Trucks carried the low-octane gasoline to the larger cities, mainly in Texas. All the while the Railroad Commission fought off injunction suits by the operators, who contended their contracts required them to deliver more oil than the official quota would allow.

Then, in late July, 1931, a three-judge federal court declared invalid the commission's anemic effort to control the field. Constitutionally the Railroad Commission was limited to conservation. Furthermore, the court refused to acknowledge evidence of physical waste which was presented at the hearing.[6] The rule of capture remained unchecked.

This decision left Governor Sterling in a dilemma. He had started out as a farm boy but had become a millionaire and was no stranger to the oil patch. He had been one of the organizers of the Humble Oil Company and had served as its president; in 1925 he had resigned and had sold his interest in the company after Standard of New Jersey took over a majority of the stock. Never a man to court idleness, Sterling entered the newspaper business by purchasing the Houston *Post.* He was chairman of the Texas Highway Commission when he ran for governor in 1930.

Sterling was not the only governor with an oil crisis. In Oklahoma, Governor William "Alfalfa Bill" Murray countered the skidding prices by ordering out the National Guard to shut down the Oklahoma City and Greater Seminole fields until the price rose to $1 a barrel. Yet the East Texas field was ten times larger than either of these. Within a couple of days a delegation of East Texans was clamoring for the same action from Governor Sterling. In mid-August the field was producing 1 million barrels daily, which, according to geologists and Railroad Commission engineers, was more than twice what the reservoir could produce without damage to its underground pressure. Much of the oil might never be recovered.

The critical time had arrived. Sterling declared martial law in East Texas and ordered troops into the field. Every well in the field was shut down by executive order. Brigadier General Jacob F. Wolters led 99 officers and 1,104 enlisted men into the field at 6 A.M. on August 17, 1931. A veteran guardsman who had seen duty in other oil booms at Mexia and Borger, Wolters gave the operators five hours in which to shut in all wells. But the order, ironically, said nothing about new drilling, and while soldiers patrolled on horseback night and day and National Guard planes flew overhead, drilling legally continued, unaffected by the order.

The symbolism attached to Sterling's move, however, was enough to negate its effectiveness in the minds of many. Wolters, in civilian life, was chief counsel for the Texas Company. One of his colonels, Walter Pyron, was a production official for Gulf Oil Company. With Governor Sterling's recent ties to Humble and Standard Oil fresh in people's memories, the damning connections seemed clear: Humble, Standard, Texas, Gulf were behind martial law.[7]

The explanation for this stand by the majors obviously was that of self-interest, but their reasoning was no different from that of many an independent who also wanted the field bridled. If the field were not rigidly controlled, in the long run oil, and its profit, would be lost. But since the majors had more at stake, they were inclined to take the long-range view, and they had the patience and the funds to wait for the slower payout. Many independents recognized the community of interest involved, while others took the stand that if they did not flow their oil now, the majors would rob them of it later on. Additionally, there was the matter of quick returns, too appealing for many to overlook; if the price dropped as a result of a glutted market, why, then they would just produce more oil, to take up the slack in profit.

Violence broke out a few days later, when three men drove into the soldiers' Kilgore camp, exchanged gunshots with the troopers, and roared off.[8] Intermittent violence was to continue for the duration of the Hot Oil War. In the words of one commentator, "The East Texas highways for a time were almost as exciting as a Chicago street during the gang wars." [9]

Most of the time, though, words took the place of bullets. Military occupation was an emotional event. The Gladewater *Gusher,* an afternoon newspaper that lasted only a week, raked its targets with phrases evoking the class struggle. "The governor is guilty of high treason to the state," it charged, "and has shown himself a tyrant and an enemy to constitutional law. These soldiers were not sent here to shut down wells—they were sent here to meet the hungry cry of those unemployed, hungry men. . . ." The *Gusher* was sprinkled with picturesque phrases like "the pompous jelly-bellied representatives of this terrible thing called the oil industry," and virtually every other article ended with: "Sterling must be impeached, and these soldiers must be taken away." [10]

The field was shut down for nineteen days, while, illogically, drilling was allowed to continue. A third of the troops were ordered home in an economy measure. When the wells resumed flowing in September, the overall daily production was limited to 400,000 barrels. At first this meant 225 barrels per well, a break-even point for small independents. The price climbed within a few months to 83 cents, but additional drilling—increasing the number of wells—caused the allowable per well to drop to 165 barrels. Lawsuits soon plagued the Railroad Commission.

Many operators were not content to fight out the issue in the courts. They bootlegged oil out of the field despite the soldiers. A tank truck in those days could carry 500, perhaps 1,000 gallons of gasoline. A man willing to take the risk could earn as much as $100 a night driving a load of bootleg gasoline to Dallas or another city. Elaborate tactics were employed to elude roadblocks and the militia patrols. Decoy trucks headed off troops or Railroad Commission men, while a caravan of filled trucks motored, unmolested, to their destination.[11]

One of the enforcers' toughest adversaries was rugged Tom G. Patten, an independent oilman, who insisted, "It's my oil, and if I want to drink it, that's none of your damned business." His maneuvers to circumvent the Railroad Commission's orders earned him a mention in Robert L. Ripley's "Believe It or Not" column for his "penthouse" over an oil well. Patten had drilled three wells on a one-fourth-acre tract in the middle of the main street in tiny London, Texas. Then he built a one-room house—which he established as his legal homestead under Texas law—over his first well. The structure was held up by four telephone poles. Finally, he obtained an injunction against the soldiers to keep them from entering his "home."

Patten, needing a market for his oil, made a deal with Jack D. Wrather, who owned a refinery at Kilgore. Under cover of darkness he laid an underground pipeline to one of Wrather's refinery lines. Suspicious militiamen soon located the pipe with a metal detector; a bulldozer blade scooped into the earth to sever the line. The persistent Patten secretly dug another ditch into which he placed a quarter mile of fire hose, through which illegal oil flowed once more. After weeks of digging around Patten's tract, the militiamen found it. Patten's next move was to buy a drugstore across the street, tunnel to his "homestead," and, again, using fire hose, connect his wells to Wrather's line. This lasted for a profitable four months. In all, he sold more than 1 million barrels of bootleg oil.

The matter became more than a local tug-of-war in October, when Wrather and his partner, Eugene Constantin, obtained a federal injunction. It prohibited the Railroad Commission, the attorney general, the county attorney, and General Wolters from keeping them from flowing 5,000 barrels daily from each of their wells. The court's ruling ensured legal turmoil just when it appeared order might be returning to the field. General Wolters ignored the injunction and was found in contempt of court. Governor Sterling insisted the injunction applied only to the five wells owned by Constantin and Wrather, and since he was not specifically named in the court's order, he took it upon himself to prorate the field, in the meantime keeping the troops in the field. A long court fight still lay ahead.

As the law lagged woefully behind needs, the most workable enforcement tactics became those such as Railroad Commission engineer E. O. Buck used to shut down Wrather's refinery operations when all else had failed. Buck found a pipeline leading to Wrather's plant. One night, making sure he was not on Wrather's property, Buck had the line tapped, then had cement pumped into it and thence into the refinery; the refinery did not refine anything for many weeks thereafter.[12]

3

In the spring of 1932 the federal courts permanently enjoined Governor Sterling from enforcing proration by martial law, but that was not the end of it. Sterling dutifully returned control of the field to the Railroad Commission and appealed the matter to the United States Supreme Court. Meanwhile, he kept the guardsmen in the field as "peace officers," thereby circumventing the court order.

The major occupation of the "peace officers" continued to be that of pursuing hot oil runners. The results were uneven. In May, 1932, however, eighteen men were charged with 213 separate offenses related to stealing more than 1 million barrels of oil; one of the men was a deputy supervisor of the Railroad Commission. This illustrated the depth of the problem. Times were hard, and temptations were great, for large sums of money were often involved. This made it risky for the force of regulators. One special investigator was peppered with birdshot. A well belonging to one major company was dynamited and set on fire.[13]

That summer Sterling, seeking reelection as governor in the Democratic primary, lost to former Governor Miriam A. "Ma" Ferguson, who had become the nation's second woman governor in 1925—fifteen days after Nellie Tayloe Ross was sworn in as governor of Wyoming. A stand-in for her husband, former Governor James "Pa" Ferguson, who had been impeached in 1919, she had used the double-barreled issues of the Depression and Sterling's handling of the East Texas crisis to win the race. The same year, on the national level, Franklin D. Roosevelt was also to defeat his one-term incumbent opponent.

Then, to make his political doom complete, on December 12, 1932, as Sterling was nearing the end of his only term, the Supreme Court handed down its decision, which invalidated Sterling's enforcement of proration with troops. This time, sixteen months after the Guard had been mobilized, martial law was really over.

General Wolters prepared to send his men home and turn over his headquarters to a young politician—sent up from Austin by his fellow members on the Railroad Commission—who was destined to become one of the central figures in Texas oil.

4

Ernest O. Thompson was dragged into the East Texas picture in early June, 1932, when he received a telephone call from Governor Ross Sterling, asking him to meet him the next day. At the time Thompson was mayor of the city of Amarillo in the Panhandle.

The governor was looking for a strong man to fill a vacancy on the Railroad Commission. Thompson was the only man Sterling knew who had the public respect and the know-how to regulate the East Texas field and curb the illegal distribution of hot oil. Although four years remained on the Railroad Commission term, Sterling could appoint Thompson only for the remainder of the year. That summer an election would have to fill the unexpired portion.

Thompson accepted the appointment and announced for the office the same day.[14] He won the race, in a runoff, while Sterling was losing his bid for a second term.

Thompson, the calmly self-confident "boy mayor" of Amarillo, had made a success of everything he had tackled, whether it required business acumen or political toughness. As a youngster he had built up a paper route and established a newsstand that he eventually sold for $150—a neat sum then—then bought it back and resold it twice more, so that by the time he was in high school he had saved $900. Before he finished high school, he had saved $2,000. After graduation he sold Overland automobiles, attended Virginia Military Institute and Eastman's Business College, and entered law school at the University of Texas. In Austin he established a fortuitous friendship with one of the state's leading lawyers, former Texas Supreme Court Justice Reuben R. Gaines, becoming first his chauffeur, then his secretary. Thompson accompanied the Gaineses on vacation. They were in Vienna during the state funeral for the assassinated Archduke Franz Ferdinand and his wife in 1914, and World War I practically rumbled to a start before their eyes.

When America entered the war, Thompson, commissioned as a captain, was soon promoted to major and landed in France as commander of a machine-gun battalion in the 90th Division. A few days before the Armistice General John J. Pershing promoted him to lieutenant colonel; he was the youngest man of that rank in the United States Army.

After the war Thompson hung out his shingle as a lawyer but soon afterward entered the hotel business by buying Amarillo's largest hotel. The gigantic Panhandle gas field opened up, keeping his hotel full and inspiring him to take over another hotel. He ran for mayor in 1928 and won in a landslide over three opponents.

As mayor Ernest O. Thompson caught the eyes of the rest of the state. He engaged in a fight with the gas and telephone companies as few other mayors have ever done anywhere, anytime. When the gas company threatened to impose what he considered unreasonably high rates, Mayor Thompson counterattacked with a plan to put the city in the gas business. He laid a line into parts of the city—which would serve his hotels—and was about to extend it when the company gave in and reduced rates. With Southwestern Bell it was more difficult. When the company refused to meet the city's terms, Thompson removed all the phones and switchboards from his hotels and urged the citizens to take their phones off the hook. The company still refused, so Thompson served notice he would remove the company's equipment from the city streets and made plans for city crewmen to chop down every telephone pole on the right-of-way granted on city property. Never doubting Thompson would do what he said, the phone company officials reduced rates 15 percent, which was acceptable to Thompson, who had sought 20 percent. After that, reelection was a cinch.[15]

Railroad Commissioner Thompson was to earn an enduring reputation as an advocate of conservation and proration. He was, as oil writer LeRoy Menzing summed him up, "vain, but colorful and effective." Above all, Thompson worked hard. "He was the type that would wake up at three or four o'clock in the morning and read," said Menzing. "And on the airplane he was always writing on his lapboard, writing a speech, something like that."[16]

Thompson, forty years old, was designated by his two colleagues on the commission to supervise the problem field, and in December, 1932, just as General Wolters and his soldiers were leaving, Thompson moved in. He set up headquarters in the general's old tent, calling it Proration Hill, and immediately decided to close down the field for two weeks so engineers could study the field's water drive and bottom hole pressure. In mid-December, after a heavy snow, Thompson, his men, and Texas Rangers systematically shut down all but six wells. The half dozen wells, fenced in, were guarded by armed, bristling operators.

The next day Thompson received a long-distance call from Amarillo. His father was critically ill but insisted on taking the telephone. "Ernest," the old man said, "I see in the Dallas *News* that you have all except six wells closed in. Don't leave there until every well is down. Close them yourself, and then come home." Thompson took Texas Rangers with him to each well and offered to shoot it out. Nobody accepted his dare. But before he could leave Proration Hill, he had another call, that his father was dead.[17]

The shutdown took almost 5 million barrels of oil off the market, but it was a brief respite. Thompson reopened the field on New Year's Day of 1933 with each well allowed twenty-eight barrels daily, and this allotment was increased as more technical data became available. But the hot oil traffic continued unabated, and Thompson, powerless to control it, seemed finally to have bitten off more than he could chew. The Railroad Commission, now fighting alone to enforce its orders, had to spread its undermanned staff over 600 square miles with thousands of wells. Since it could neither fine nor imprison violators, its effectiveness was severely restricted. Months later the state legislature acceded to Thompson's urging and passed a new law making it a felony to produce oil above the commission's allowables.

5

Astonishing though it seems today, most of the nation's oilmen clamored eagerly for federal controls over their industry in the early 1930's. Men in the major companies and most of the independents were alarmed at the chaos. Roosevelt had moved into the White House in March, 1933, and oilmen, despairing of the state of Texas' ever harnessing the field, fixed their hopes on the federal government.

Most of the leaders in the oil industry wanted a federal "oil czar," who could bring all the power of the federal government to bear in prorating the field. The man they wanted for the job, although they were conservative and he was not, was Harold L. Ickes, Roosevelt's secretary of the interior. Men representing major oil companies, as well as many independents, pushed for the Ickes bill, as it came to be called, through which Congress would make the secretary of the interior an oil dictator for two years with the broadest powers.

On May 5, 1933, when East Texas oil was worth 4 cents a barrel, Ickes wrote in his secret diary: "I am being bombarded with long telegrams and even longer letters, many of them urging the appointment of a Federal dictator, and others objecting to such an appointment. Late this afternoon a telegram came in from Governor [Miriam] Ferguson of Texas, admitting that the situation is beyond the control of state authorities, and joining in the plea for stringent Federal legislation." [18] By some accounts, well over 90 percent of oilmen favored the Ickes bill.

Representatives of oil associations from all over the country gathered at the Mayflower Hotel's Chinese Room in Washington. J. R. Parten, for one, was opposed to federal control. President, at the time, of the Independent Petroleum Association of Texas, he swiftly sized up the temper of the oil representatives at the meeting and realized that Wirt Franklin, representing the Independent Petroleum Association of America (IPAA), intended to commit that organization—to which Parten also belonged—to the Ickes bill.

Parten headed for the platform to remonstrate with Franklin, to remind him that the IPAA membership couldn't be committed to a position of federal control without a full vote. Conditions had changed since the last IPAA election, Franklin retorted; matters were now desperate. Franklin committed the IPAA to the Ickes bill. Only Parten and a few others—notably William Keck of the Superior Oil Company—voted against supporting the oil czar legislation.

The Mayflower meeting joined Parten and Keck together in efforts to defeat the bill. Every oil lobbyist in Washington seemed to be working for it. The bill's supporters attempted to direct the bill to the Minerals and Mining Committee of the House of Representatives, where there was no Texan to slow it down. But Parten and other independents like Jim Abercrombie, Hugh Roy Cullen, Dan Harrison, and lawyers Jack and Myron Blalock took the matter up with their congressmen. In the Senate the bill would be handled by the Mining and Minerals Committee, and the situation there looked bleak for the Parten group. Parten and his associates concentrated on the House. They visited Texas Congressman Sam Rayburn to explain why they believed federal control of the oil business would be hazardous for the country. They impressed him with the need for a cautious approach to the bill. Rayburn was chairman of the House Committee on Interstate and Foreign Commerce. They thought the bill should go to his committee.

Rayburn provided the first brake on the headlong flight to pass the federal oil czar bill when he asked Speaker William B. Bankhead to send the bill to his committee. The oil industry as a whole seemed disappointed.

Rayburn also promised Parten and his friends, "I'll not only have the bill in my committee, but you can be assured of the fullest possible hearing. So you can get prepared for it."

The battle lines formed. The antifederal control group had two allies from Texas' government—Railroad Commissioner Thompson and Attorney General James V. Allred. Both were for proration but thought the state could, and should, handle it. But the governor, Mrs. Ferguson, plumped for federal control—a stand which Parten believed, correctly, reflected Standard Oil's position. Then there was support for the Parten group from figures like Clint Murchison, a renowned hot oil operator.

"I knew he was applauding what we were doing," said Parten, "but I didn't have anything to do with Clint, because I knew damned well his hands weren't clean. A fine person—I liked him very much—but Clint was a hot oiler in every respect. Clint didn't want any rules. He had made a fortune by disobeying the rules.

"He showed up in Washington and asked what he could do to help us. Jack Blalock said, 'The thing you could do most to help us is to get on that airplane and get out of town as quick as you can.' And he did."

Many Texans, some of them close personal friends of Parten's, spoke out in favor of such a bill. In addition, said Parten, "All the major oil companies were for it. They'd given up all hope of the state of Texas effectively bridling the East Texas field." [19]

Sam Rayburn's decision to take a long, cool look at the fevered controversy provided the delay the Parten group sought, ensuring the legislation would not be rushed through the House that session. But as 1934 came, the issue of federal control continued to receive energetic backing from a majority in the industry, especially among the major companies. While Rayburn rode herd on the bill in committee, in April, 1934, Interior Secretary Ickes received men who represented 80 percent of the industry. "These oil men are willing to back a bill giving the oil administrator the fullest possible power to regulate the production of crude oil," Ickes wrote in his diary that night. The next afternoon Walter C. Teagle, president of Standard Oil of New Jersey, was ushered into Ickes' office with an idea that astonished the secretary of the interior. "His proposal," wrote Ickes in his diary, "is that the Government make an oil reserve out of the East Texas oil field. He said this is the way, and the only way, to control the production of hot oil. His company (actually, Humble Oil) is the largest producing company in the oil field, but he seemed to think that not only his company but other large producers would readily fall in with the plan, which contemplates the issuance by the Government of bonds for the value of the properties taken over, such bonds to bear interest at 3½ percent. . . . After all, it seemed rather a startling proposition to come from the president of the Standard Oil Company of New Jersey." [20]

Radical though the plan seemed, the government would be footing the bill, with the companies losing nothing, while the government administered the field as it had its reserves on national property in the past. Presumably major companies such as Humble, because of their size and economic strength, would then be in an even better position to produce the field on a much more stable, secure basis. Given the alternatives so threatening at the time, it is not surprising that Teagle considered his suggestion a sound, practical solution, despite any future implications such a government takeover might have presented.

In late May, 1934, the oil czar controversy reached a fever pitch when the Senate Mining Committee approved the Thomas-Disney bill, which would have thrust virtually complete control of oil production into the hands of Ickes. Passage by the Senate was practically assured. Two weeks later, however, Rayburn's House Interstate and Foreign Commerce Committee voted 12 to 5 to table the oil control bill until the next session, in order to "study" it further.

The Rayburn committee's action triggered flaring tempers among the bill's proponents. Congress was near adjournment; all hopes for the bill evaporated for that session. A fellow Texan, Representative Blanton, accused Rayburn of deliberately "chloroforming" the Ickes bill. Rayburn, his face livid with anger, started toward Blanton. It was the third time in days that a fistfight had been threatened in the House. Violence was averted when Congressman Martin Dies, also a Texan and a six-footer, stepped in front of Rayburn and held him back.

Ickes jumped verbally into the battle, publicly criticizing Rayburn.

"Here is a bill that had the support of 95 percent of the oil industry, and is for the benefit of the country. And it cannot pass Congress!" he said bitterly.[21]

The study Rayburn had promised continued. That fall a special House subcommittee, appointed by Rayburn, held hearings that revealed how sharply independents were now divided over the question of federal control. At that time 47 percent of the nation's interstate crude oil shipments originated in Texas. Texas gasoline went to virtually all forty-eight states, and Texas shipped out four times more gasoline than did its closest rival, Oklahoma. Yet this was a state that, by his own admission, Secretary of the Interior Ickes had never visited.[22]

One of the most outspoken advocates of federal control to testify was Frank Phillips, the president of Phillips Petroleum Company, who candidly assessed his industry. Agreements in the oil business, he told the congressmen, meant nothing. "I mean just that," Phillips confirmed. "I am not going to single out any company. I will throw in and say our company is just as crooked as any of them, and I said to my board the other day that we cannot look our grandchildren in the face and be honest about it and continue the way we are doing now. I am frank about things. That is my first name."

Specifically, Phillips referred to the stealing of oil by those who did not adhere to the proration orders, before and after the withdrawal of troops.

"I have employed as large a force of Pinkerton detectives as was ever employed in this state to ferret out information about this field right here," Phillips said, "but I have not got any place. My competitors stole that oil by draining my property when my wells were shut down under the orders of the Governor." [23]

In brief, but pointed, testimony, Bryan W. Payne, an independent producer from Tyler, Texas, offered a specific solution for the problem.

"I want to make it plain that I am for federal control," said Payne, but he wanted to go further, to hurt the hot oilers. "There have been 50 million to 100 million barrels of oil stolen out of East Texas. There has been a profit of probably $25 million. There are 100 hot oil thieves over there that should have their income tax records checked from 1929 to the present time. Those operators have stolen our oil and have turned around and bought surrounding properties and bought their wives and their girls diamonds and homes and automobiles and so forth, and we think the income tax division should send at least fifty agents down there to check their returns. That is all." [24]

The position of the legitimate producer opposed to federal control was represented in the testimony of men like Jake L. Hamon, then in his early thirties, the son of the colorful Oklahoman by the same name. Hamon, later to move to Dallas and become one of the biggest Texas independents, felt that the Federal Tender Board, a mechanism by then operating to monitor interstate shipments, was all the federal control that was needed. The Tender Board regulated the transportation of oil.

"Now, I have never run any hot oil," explained Hamon. "As I say, we have forty wells in East Texas, and we have been badly drained at times by people that have run hot oil, but we have never run any. I say that because I want to justify my position. There is a general attitude that anybody who opposes federal control is a hot oil runner, and I certainly want to disabuse the committee's mind of that fact, because I belong to all of the oil associations and have spent several thousand dollars of my own money trying to help convict these oil thieves. I am on the board of directors of virtually all of the associations in Texas."

"Then you believe that price would control the situation?" one congressman asked. He was referring to the economics of supply and demand as a factor in the prices—not to a governmental structure of price controls.

"Yes, sir," said Hamon. "It always has, and I am sure that it always will." [25]

Hamon's reasoning was that once the hot oilers were restrained and proration orders obeyed, the decreased output would cause prices to rise, as indeed did occur.

A featured witness of the hearings, as he was to be in subsequent appearances, was Colonel Ernest O. Thompson, as chairman of the Texas Railroad Commission. Thompson, of course, opposed any further federal intervention, soft-pedaling the magnitude of the problems. His personal pride was also involved; he had never failed at anything before, and he obviously wanted time to make a success of his greatest challenge. He testified that hot oil was down to 15,000 barrels a day, a large decline from the earlier figures. With the federal manpower already in the field by then, the state could handle it, he thought; were it not for the size of the field, the state could have handled it without help. "It is only when you have an East Texas field that it gives you trouble," he said. "It is the first one we have ever had like it." [26]

The question of price was barely touched on during the inquiry, beyond establishing the fact that the majors set the "posted price," and price controls were not advocated as a solution. Although the way the major companies arrived at the posted price figures for the field was to remain a mystery, a point that was not spelled out was that in the East Texas field, as in few other instances, the posted price was not altogether controlled by the major companies. Because of the seemingly unlimited quantity of crude oil, independents— especially if they were running hot oil—could undercut the majors, forcing the price lower than it otherwise might have been. Although the majors usually controlled price by owning the pipelines, in East Texas many refineries had their own pipelines and could compete very favorably with the largest of companies.

The rule of capture was responsible. On the one hand, it damaged the reservoir by spurring on drilling and production; on the other, it enabled the "little man" to compete with the giants, at the same time providing the consumers gasoline as cheap as they would ever know it. There is little wonder why so many in the industry were nervous over the situation and why they viewed stringent federal controls—an oil dictatorship—as their only hope.

When Rayburn's committee finally released the Ickes bill with the recommendation that it not be passed, it did not.

"They'd like to erase the record and forget, but the API [American Petroleum Institute] and the IPAA [Independent Petroleum Association of America] sponsored that bill!" said Parten. "But ten years later, during World War II, when J. Edgar Pew [of Sun Oil] came around to me at the National Petroleum Council, where we were both members, he put his arm around my neck and said, 'I want to make an apology to you, because at one time I accused you of wrecking the oil industry and now I recognize that you saved it.' That came from J. Edgar Pew." [27]

In retrospect, it is easy to see what a drastic change a successful oil czar bill might have imposed on the industry; one suspects the industry itself, given its predilections during intervening history, would have soon repented of foisting all regulatory authority upon a federal government controlled predominantly by liberal Democrats. The plan, born of desperation, would have vitally reshaped the role of oilmen in society, and it is difficult even now, after the fact, to speculate on what would have been the final result. On the other hand, many liberals and most socialists might look back to that event as a lost opportunity to have achieved stricter social controls over the petroleum industry on a national basis. It was a strange moment in history in which the apparent goals of two disparate groups almost merged, for very different reasons.

The 1934 hearings led to no radical departures in federal legislation, but they did offer insights into the industry's complexities and prepared the Congress for its role in solving the problem in the mid-1930's. It was becoming clear that the industry, though dominated by the majors, was far from being monolithic, and no fast and easy solution was forthcoming. Ultimately the answers to the oil question were to come out of the experience of Department of the Interior personnel in the field, but an enlightened Congress was necessary if those recommendations were to be translated into an enforceable law.

6

While oilmen were pushing in Washington for an "oil dictator," another move was afoot in Austin in the spring of 1933 to strip the Railroad Commission of its regulatory powers. The Railroad Commission was ineffective, and its members were too concerned with popularity with the voters, its critics insisted; the only way the hot oil traffic could be stopped, and prices raised, was by the establishment of a new agency, a state oil and gas conservation commission, which would be appointive rather than elective. H. L. Hunt, by then the largest independent operator in the field, had teamed up with the major companies in support of the proposal.

As soon as it became clear that the federal Ickes bill might be delayed in passage, Texas Governor Miriam Ferguson recommended to the state legislature the passage of a bill to create the new commission. If the bill were approved, she would appoint the members of the new panel—an added reason for her enthusiasm.

Dividing much of his time between Washington and Austin in 1933, J. R. Parten now took up his position in Austin. He and his friends had more allies in Austin than in Washington, but the opposition was formidable. Besides Hunt, there were Humble Oil, the Texas Oil and Gas Conservation Association (composed of influential independent prorationists), and ex-Governor Jim Ferguson, who was calling the shots behind the scenes for his wife, the governor.

The Parten group's strategy was to delay the bill in the State House of Representatives, where they had supporters. "We knew Ferguson could pass it in the Senate," said Parten, "because we knew there were twenty senators out of the thirty-one that were working for the major oil companies. They were on the payroll." But at five o'clock one afternoon Jim Ferguson, growing desperate, put the pressure on key lawmakers and forced the bill through the House by a narrow 71–65 vote. Everyone conceded that the State Senate would pass it the next day.

Railroad Commission Chairman Thompson arrived back in Austin that day and, seeing it was too late to do anything in the House, told a group of senators backing the bill, "Gentlemen, I'm new on this commission. Please give me time to hang up my hat before you take my job away from me. I believe we're doing as much as any other commission could do, particularly an appointed one." He left the State Capitol as the bill's supporters were celebrating its passage by the House. As one group spotted him, someone called him a redheaded son of a bitch. Thompson restrained himself and kept walking.

That evening, as Parten was conferring with his company's attorney in the Stephen F. Austin Hotel downtown, a knock sounded. Parten opened the door to admit Charles F. Roeser, president of the Texas Oil and Gas Conservation Association, accompanied by three other men. They all had been drinking, and flushed by victory and alcohol, they approached Parten with a "good sport" proposition. The bill would pass tomorrow; why not make a statement saying it would be all right after all? Let bygones be bygones.

Cold sober, Parten courteously declined. They talked for several minutes, and Parten offered them drinks. But he had a dinner appointment with a man from Sinclair Oil, to whom he was trying to sell some of his 10-cent oil. As he prepared to leave, Parten told his attorney, "Give 'em all they want to drink and take care of them." Then he left.

What happened after Parten left is not altogether clear. The principals in the incident that followed are now dead. One fragment comes from an eyewitness, Sherman M. Hunt, then a teenager. Young Hunt and his father were having dinner in the coffee shop of the Stephen F. Austin Hotel when they heard the loudest crash of glass they'd ever heard and looked up to see independent oilman Joe Pierson, standing angrily by the cigar stand in the lobby. Pierson had just slammed one of the politicians on the other side—presumably Representative Gordon Burns, a leader in the fight against the new agency bill—onto the glass counter of the cigar stand. "Nobody calls me a son of a bitch!" he shouted. He turned to the manager who had rushed over. "Just put the damages on the bill." Then, just as in the western movies of that day, Pierson turned and walked off.

From contemporary accounts it is possible to reconstruct a somewhat larger view of the affray.

Shortly before midnight Burns entered the hotel. While he was telephoning from the lobby, Roeser and others entered. Roeser accosted Burns and cursed him.

"Go on away," said Burns. "Let me alone. I don't want any trouble with you here."

Roeser accused him of having been "paid off" for his part in opposing the commission. Some of Roeser's companions charged Burns with having verbally abused them from the floor of the House. At this point Burns and Roeser swapped blows and fell fighting to the floor. While they were down, one of the other men kicked Burns. They were pulled apart. Then Roeser hit Burns on the back of the head, and the politician went down again, with more scrambling and kicking. Shouts rang out from the men around them, egging Roeser on.

Finally, a spectator separated the men and led Burns, bruised and bleeding, out of the lobby.

Meanwhile, Parten had talked until midnight with the Sinclair man and, unaware of what had happened at the hotel, returned to his rooms about twelve-thirty. As he entered the lobby, he noticed small knots of men in every corner of the lobby. There was a feeling of electricity in the air.

"What's the matter here?" he asked the room clerk.

"Didn't you see the fight?" said the night clerk.

"What fight?"

"Mr. Charles F. Roeser and a few other fellows just beat up Representative Gordon Burns of Huntsville very badly. They got him on the floor and kicked him. Put him in the hospital."

"This is the first news I've had of it," said Parten. Burns was a friend of Parten's.

Disturbed but seeing that nothing could be done at that hour, Parten went upstairs and to bed. About 3:30 A.M. his phone rang. It was Layton Stanberry, a friend who worked for the Railroad Commission.

"J. R., have you got a gun?"

"Hell, no, Layton, I haven't got a gun. What do you want with a gun?"

Stanberry told him. "I'm going to fix those bastards that beat up my friend Gordon Burns."

Parten attempted to soothe him. "It was tragic, and it was awful, but just go to sleep, and we'll talk about it in the morning."

Early the next morning after breakfast Parten went to the hospital to see Gordon Burns. The representative's mother and father had come from Huntsville and were with him. It was an emotional scene. Burns' face was cut and bruised; one eye was messily blackened. A kick to the kidney had left internal injuries. From the hospital Parten went straight to the third floor of the State Capitol, where he could watch from the galleries what was going on in the House and the Senate, which were on the second floor. In the House of Representatives, orators were aflame over "these rascals that beat up on our colleague." They were almost ranting and raving, they were so furious. Parten then went over to the Senate gallery and found them saying about the same thing. Parten realized that now, suddenly, there was hope of defeating the bill.

As he left the Senate gallery, Parten ran into an old friend on the other side of the issue.

"J. R.," the man said, "everybody's irrational over this awful fight that took place. It was scandalous, but won't you help me quiet this thing down, and let's defer consideration of this bill until things calm down?"

Parten said, "Bob, I want to be utterly candid with you. If there's any way in the world I can get this bill up for a vote before four o'clock this evening, I'm gonna do it!"

The bill didn't come up that quickly, but the emotional atmosphere was not one to evaporate soon. A few days later the Senate committee reported the bill out by an 8 to 6 vote, itself closer than would have been expected earlier. But on the Senate floor it met a hostile majority, now enraged over the Burns incident.

"This bill," said Senator Will Pace of Tyler, leading the opposition, "was conceived in iniquity, and hatched out for the purpose of robbing my people in East Texas. I will do all I can to keep the Standard Oil Company and those allied with it from taking the birthright of my people."

During the debate on the bill Representative Burns was rolled into the Senate chambers in a wheelchair. Burns said nothing. Then he was wheeled out. After a two-and-a-half hour hearing, with the Senate halls thronged with spectators, the Senate defeated the bill by a margin of 20 to 10.

"The lawyers working for the oil companies just couldn't take it," said Parten. "They bunched up and voted against it." [28]

Although the oil czar proposition was still in the works in Washington at this point, the Texas decision relieved some of the pressure on Thompson and his fellow commissioners, and the campaign to subdue the gigantic field continued.

7

The struggle over whether Washington or Austin should predominate in regulating the field extended beyond the oilmen and the politicians to the officials involved on both federal and state levels.

158 A SAGA OF WEALTH

At a time when cooperation between them was urgently needed, all too often there was bickering. This situation was exemplified in the competition between Railroad Commissioner Thompson and Interior Secretary Ickes.

Although the major threats to his authority were now blunted, Thompson's efforts to control the field and halt the flow of hot oil were to fall short. He coaxed the legislature into passing a law making it a felony to produce more oil than the allowable. Then he set up a system whereby producers signed affidavits certifying that their oil had been produced legally.

His ploy didn't work. The affidavits were often signed without a thought to their truthfulness. Some scribbled the names of Thompson or any other persons who entered their minds.

An insight into the difficulty was offered when Tucker Royall, chairman of the Railroad Commission's Tender Committee, approached a flagrant violator.

"To use a slang expression," Royall told the man, "we are separating the sheep from the goats. We sent for you because we want to know who is going to cooperate with us, and we want to know who is against the committee."

The oilman replied, "Well, I know you are nice gentlemen, and I would like to be with you, and I will let you know tomorrow. I will talk with my brothers and my attorney."

The next day he returned, explaining, "I have talked with my attorney and my brothers, and we do not believe in proration. We think that this is a free country. We have bought these leases over here and we own twenty-six wells. We own our refinery. It is our property. We bought it and paid for it and we have got the right to use it any way we see fit."

"Then you refuse to cooperate with us?" said Royall.

"Yes."

"All right. We are going to stop you from flowing hot oil."

"All right. Crack your whip."

Twelve men were put on the twenty-six wells—four in each of three shifts—and for twelve days the oilman did not run a drop of oil over his allowable. But that left only thirty men to police the thousands of other wells in the field, and the oilman was able to go elsewhere in the field to buy cheap hot oil for his refinery. It was hopeless. Even 1,000 men couldn't have done the job.[29]

To make matters worse, Commissioner Thompson spent much of

his time fighting Secretary Ickes, who symbolized to him the concept of federal control. Ickes complained to Vice-President John Nance Garner, a Texan, of the Railroad Commission's lack of full cooperation, and he stated that if things did not improve, he would have to resort to drastic measures of rigidly curbing the whole field's output. Garner replied, according to Ickes, "that the only way to deal with the situation was to take a strong position; that we couldn't appeal to the consciences of those oil people because they didn't have any consciences and he advised me to go after them with a club." [30]

Thompson, for his part, considered Ickes ignorant of the oil industry and its problems. On one occasion he confronted Ickes' seeming ignorance with what must have been a tremendous inner chortle. A "wild" well—spewing forth with such pressure it could not be capped—at the new Conroe field in the Gulf Coast region had frustrated every effort to close it off, and in order to prevent a catastrophe, a moat had been built to contain the blowing oil. Everyone—railroad commissioners and major and independent company men—was doing his damnedest. Ickes fired off a telegram to Thompson, ordering him to shut in the wild well.

A few hours later Thompson, fresh from the scene of the well, called Ickes in Washington.

"Mr. Secretary," said Thompson, "I have read your telegram to the wild well in Conroe and it is still blowing. Do you have any other further suggestions?" [31]

8

In the summer of 1933 Secretary of the Interior Ickes sent to East Texas two young lawyers who were to become key generals in the war against hot oil. J. Howard Marshall and Norman Meyers had written two monographs on *Legal Planning of Petroleum Production,* which had impressed Ickes. The secretary had persuaded them to join his department's effort. Their first assignment was to write a series of rules and regulations under the authority of Section 9-C of the National Industrial Recovery Act (NIRA) that would prohibit the interstate movement of petroleum and its refined products produced in violation of state laws.

Twenty-eight-year-old Marshall, born in Philadelphia of a

Quaker family, was assistant dean of the Yale Law School. In addition to being an attorney, Meyers had a Ph.D. in economics from the Brookings Institute.

Writing regulations to prohibit the transportation of hot oil was relatively simple, a matter of understanding law and legal language. Working out a practical system for carrying out the regulations was another matter. For this they had to study the actual conditions in the field. Although Marshall and Meyers knew how to write regulations, they had little experience with the oil business itself. After they arrived at the Blackstone Hotel in Tyler, they found many willing teachers. A delegation of bankers and oilmen—one of them H. L. Hunt—called on them, offering them an education, primarily in the form of self-serving declarations. Voluntary advice kept coming from lawyers representing every oil company in the field.

The first thing the young eastern lawyers learned was to adjust to the local ways. "I learned when I came down to Texas that if you were any kind of lawyer at all, you were always called Judge regardless of whether you ever had been one or not," said Marshall. "In those days I used to be horribly embarrassed because I still had the title of assistant dean of the Yale Law School, and these fellows would call me Dean and I didn't look very deanish! My colleague, Norman Meyers, happened to have a Ph.D., and they always called him Doctor. None of the rest of us ever thought of calling Norman Doctor. I discovered in Texas you had to have a title whether you earned it or not!"

Their first goal became that of stopping hot oil at the wellhead. They soon acknowledged this to be impractical. The field was so large that every well could not be checked. Many wells were out in the woods, where roads were often impassable. The two Interior lawyers then aimed at ensuring that only "cool" or legal oil was shipped from the field. They worked out a system of federal affidavits, which would certify that oil leaving the field had been produced within the state's allowables. The railroads were required to accept no oil without an affidavit. But the system depended on the producer's truthfulness. Hot oilers signed the federal affidavits as gleefully as they had the state versions, often using fictitious names, and the railroads accepted them without question. With so many oilmen and so much oil, the great challenge for Marshall and

Meyers was that of enforcing the regulations they had so readily drafted.

The Feds soon found themselves in the same undermanned position as were the state regulators. Working closely with Captain E. N. Stanley, the Railroad Commission's enforcement officer, Marshall learned firsthand why it was called a war.

"The only time I got shot at in my life was going into one of those hot oil refineries one night," he said. "We were going in to check where the oil was coming from in this particular refinery, and somebody started blazing away at us. I got behind the biggest tree I could find—but not Captain Stanley. He carried a big six-shooter, and he started shooting over the edge of the refinery, and he went right on in. After he got it quieted down, I think I followed him, but I wasn't anxious to get shot at."

Another reason the new federal regulations lost their punch was the fact that, as Marshall said, "what one group of lawyers invents, other equally smart lawyers can figure out how to circumvent." [32]

The lawyer who became the chief circumventor was F. W. Fischer—Big Fish.

9

"Judge" Fletcher Whitfield Fischer was a formidable country lawyer who represented most of the hot oilers. He was known as Big Fish, the legal terror of the oil patch. Admitted to the Oklahoma bar in 1910 after "reading" law, he had moved to Wichita Falls, Texas, at the height of the oil boom there. He practiced law there until he moved to Tyler in 1931 to get in on the new boom. Despite his looks, he was not a country bumpkin or a buffoon. He was shrewd—some said abusive—and a man with a grandiose view of himself, especially after a series of legal successes, including one at the United States Supreme Court. When Fischer was building a new home in North Texas, modeled on Mount Vernon, he compared himself favorably with George Washington one day in conversation with an acquaintance.[33] Buoyed by his fame in the oil patch, Fischer ran for governor of Texas in 1936, opposing the incumbent James V. Allred. "But the trouble was," Fischer remarked, explaining his defeat, "there wasn't many folks in the state knew I was running, that was the only trouble." [34]

Fischer's country-boy style, with its grammatical lapses, endeared him to East Texas jurors. He liked to talk and tell risqué stories—even in the courtroom.

Fischer acquired some small tracts in the field. His acreage was in the middle of the field, highly productive, but because of its size, his drilling was limited unless the Railroad Commission granted him an "exception"—a special dispensation—to drill another well, closer to the existing wells than official regulations permitted. Fischer represented himself as skillfully as he had any of his clients. Each time he appeared at a hearing he described in vivid terms how the people around him were draining off his oil—"dreening" him.[35]

Fischer's folksy approach to law and his dazzling talent for storytelling made him a formidable foe in the courtrooms or in the hearing rooms of the Railroad Commission. One of the best examples of his flavorsome speech and style is his own account of his cross-examination of a witness testifying for Humble Oil on a proposal to change the proration formula for the East Texas field in the late 1930's. The Humble lawyer had put into evidence the fact that Fischer had already produced 92,000 barrels per acre from one lease he owned. Fischer told it from that point:

"He had a witness on the stand who had qualified himself as being the smartest man in the world. He had graduated from every university that you could count, and he knew all things under the earth, and on the earth, and in the sky, and under the sea. He had him a long slide rule that he run up and down like a bull fiddle. And every time that thing stopped, that answered any question you could ask him.

"Well, when I got around to examine this eminent doctor, I said, 'Doctor, you saw this statement that your lawyer put in evidence about my production of ninety-two thousand barrels per acre, on this lease out at Old London.'

"Said, 'Yes, I saw it.'

"I said, 'How many barrels per acre did I have under that land before I started producing?'

"He worked his bull fiddle a little, and he said, 'Forty thousand barrels per acre.'

" 'Well,' I said, 'let me understand that now. I only had forty thousand to start with; I've done taken out now ninety-two thousand barrels per acre—how much have I got left?'

"He worked his bull fiddle a little again, and he said it was forty thousand barrels per acre.

" 'Well,' I said, 'let me see if I understand you. I had forty thousand to start with, only forty thousand.'

" 'Yeah.'

" 'I took out ninety-two thousand barrels.'

" 'Yeah.'

" 'And I still got forty thousand.'

" 'Yes.'

" 'Well,' I said, 'how come?'

" 'Well,' he says, 'that's because of the hydrostatic pressure on the west side of the field, and every time you take out a barrelful of oil, another one comes in.'

" 'Well,' I says, 'it looks like what old Isaiah said is coming true, ain't it?'

"He said, 'I don't know what Isaiah said.'

"I said, 'You know, Isaiah said he never saw the righteous forsaken or his kinfolks on the WPA.'

" 'Well,' he said, 'I don't know nothing about Isaiah.'

"I said, 'All right, Doctor, tell me why it is that the Lord shoves this oil into me, instead of these other fellows? And every time I take out a barrel of oil He gives me another one?'

" 'Well, it happened because your leases there are high on the structure.'

"I said, 'I see. Did the Humble—did they get up high on the structure like me?'

" 'Oh, yeah, yeah.'

"I said, 'Is the Lord kind to the Humble like He is to me, and every time they take a barrel of oil out, does He shove 'em another one like He does to me? Or is He mad at the Humble about something?'

" 'No, He's kind to the Humble just like He is to you, and every time we take a barrel out He shoves in another one.'

"I said, 'Has the Humble still got under their leases the same amount of oil that they started with, just like me?'

" 'Yes, yes, sir. Got it under there just the same, like you have.'

" 'Well,' I says, 'take that bull fiddle then and work it up and down good, and tell me how many million barrels of oil that they carted away from here that belonged to somebody else.'

"Well, he figured that out at that time, I think, about eighty million barrels that they'd done produced. And according to his testimony, they still had under their line the same amount of oil that they started with before they went to producing, and yet those folks were seriously up there contending that the little man was getting their oil, and that the little man ought to—just for instance in my case, that when I produced forty thousand per acre, that I ought to shut down, and not to be permitted to produce anymore. And leave it there, and they would get it later on themselves." [36]

Big Fish's memory of the hearing scene might bear only a crude approximation to the transcript, but it was bound to be highly entertaining to those not principals in the matter.

The federal lawyers, Howard Marshall and Norman Meyers, came to know Fischer as their number one adversary. When they accepted his dinner invitation one night, they came to know him better. Big, fat Fischer, then in his forties, sat at the head of the table devouring fried chicken with the eagerness of a starving man.

"Fischer didn't throw the bones over his shoulder," said Marshall, "but I expected him to, at any minute! And sitting there washing it down with straight bourbon whiskey by the tumblersfull. This was in Prohibition days, and he had a cellar—he took us down and showed it to us with great pride—with just barrels and barrels of bourbon whiskey. . . .

"And he represented most of these hot oil refiners by every technical or devious device that he could think of. . . . He could figure out more reasons why something was unconstitutional than even I could think of, and I used to *teach* constitutional law.

"But, as with all lawyers, I got to know him, and the first thing I discovered was that he was very quick at getting temporary restraining orders ex parte—'ex parte' means without a hearing. From the federal judge in the area. This was Judge Randolph Bryant.

"Big Fish and the judge were great friends. This was a real judge with all the power of the federal district court, and Big Fish used to make a practice regularly of going out and drinking with Randolph Bryant. The judge liked his toddies. Fischer'd go out there, and he'd get these restraining orders all the time, for what seemed to me no good legal reason at all. And of course, I'd been brought up, as an ancient law professor, under what I thought was the code of legal ethics, that you never talked to the judge about a case pending in his court except in open court or in the presence of the opposing attorney.

"But I found it didn't work that way with Big Fish. I said, well, if this is the way it is practiced in the Eastern District of Texas, I guess I've got to adapt myself, so I used to go out and have drinks with the judge! I think I kept sober, but the judge and I became pretty good friends. And the judge and I finally reached an agreement: He wouldn't grant any more of these ex parte orders without giving me a chance to be heard on behalf of the federal government.

"And I said, 'Judge, I don't care where I am, I'll get a plane or something, and if he wants one of these ex parte orders, don't give it to him until you can hear our side of it.'

"After that I'd get a call from him and maybe I'd be out in Kalamazoo or somewhere and I'd come running to East Texas to argue the case. And once I had this agreement with the judge, I don't think Big Fish ever got another temporary restraining order." [37]

10

The Feds' first major break came one day in August, 1934, when Howard Marshall, in California on a special assignment, received a call from Secretary of the Interior Ickes. On the Texas Gulf Coast, Marshall was informed, the Eastern States Refining Company had sold millions of gallons of illegal gasoline, now bound for the West Coast. Marshall knew the company. The two tankers were already en route to the West Coast through the Panama Canal.

Legal oil, at the time, was selling for from 80 cents to $1 a barrel. Gasoline made from inexpensive hot oil, distributed on the West Coast, would play havoc with that market.

Armed with a temporary restraining order to prohibit unloading, Marshall hurried to an airplane.

One tanker went into Portland, Oregon, and was impounded. The other was headed for Seattle. As it sneaked down the Juan de Fuca Strait and Puget Sound about three o'clock in the morning, Marshall went out on a Coast Guard cutter to intercept the cargo.

When the tanker refused to stop, the Coast Guard cutter's officer ordered grappling irons thrown over, tying his vessel to the tanker. Then he cut the craft's diesel engines.

As the diesels died, flames shot out of the stack, and Marshall— and everyone else on the cutter—heard the anguished tanker captain's scream of horror in reaction to the fire momentarily flaring from the stack.

"Cut that damn thing off—we are carrying gasoline!"

The restraining order prevented the ship from unloading, but Marshall then discovered a nuance that complicated his strategy. The gasoline was consigned to the Fletcher Oil Company. The FBI had assumed this was a corporation qualified to do business in the state of Washington. It was not. It was an Idaho partnership doing business as the Fletcher Oil Company; it would have to be sued under federal rules of procedure in Idaho, its home state. This left the restraining order inoperative, and Marshall deliberately stalled until he could work up the legal papers for a valid order in Idaho. Two hours after the order was released in Seattle and Portland, he had another one in Idaho and left for Boise to argue his case in federal court.

Marshall hadn't the slightest doubt that the gasoline had been produced from hot oil in East Texas, but he had to prove it, at least with prima facie evidence, in Boise, Idaho, thousands of miles from its point of departure.

On the second day of the trial he glanced up to see a big familiar figure lumber into the courtroom. F. W. Fischer! Marshall let loose a greeting loud enough to ensure that the judge would hear him.

"Big Fish, if I ever had any doubt about the heat of this cargo, your presence in this courtroom is proof positive to me!"

Fischer chuckled genially.

Later the judge called Marshall into his chambers and asked, as Marshall had hoped he would, "Mr. Marshall, what did you mean by that?" Marshall was delighted to enlighten him about Fischer's notoriety for representing hot oil runners.

Marshall had a fight on his hands, as Fischer and the other lawyers assailed every scrap of evidence that he introduced. They demanded live witnesses in person and affidavits in the traditional form.

"Well," said Marshall, "if we have to bring the witnesses up here and the actual affidavits, I want to request a two weeks' adjournment, so I can go to Texas and adduce all the proof."

This threw Big Fish and his cohorts into a frenzy of protests. With the company paying $4,000 a day on each of the tankers for tying it up beyond the contracted time, they wanted, above all, to avoid further delay. They were anxious to win the case and move the gasoline out of the ships back in Portland and Seattle. This provided fertile soil for a compromise that Marshall now proposed. "Well," he said, "I've spent a lot of time on the field, and I can testify of my own knowledge as to the way this system works. And that isn't hearsay!"

This time the numerous opposing attorneys huddled in a lengthy conference, but in the end they agreed to Marshall's taking the stand as an expert witness. He testified that he knew, of his own knowledge, that hundreds of thousands of barrels of hot East Texas crude oil had gone into the Eastern States refinery. He even remembered a series of specific leases.

He won the injunction, then proceeded to make the experience so unprofitable for the defendants that nobody involved would try it again. The company paid substantial fines, and after an agreement had been reached, whereby the fuel would be gradually released onto the market according to orders of Interior, the defendants were allowed to unload the gasoline into shore tankage.[38]

11

Finally, at Marshall's recommendation, the Federal Tender Board was established, inaugurating a system of sworn statements on oil leaving Texas, beginning in October, 1934. The idea occurred to Marshall one day as he sat in the Boise courtroom, thousands of miles from the source of the cargo he had tied up. Oilmen now had to apply to the board for a certificate signifying that the oil proposed for shipment was legally produced. They had to stipulate which lease the oil came from, enabling the government to keep a balance sheet on the field as a bank does on money. A hearing then established the facts. A simple operation, it merely reversed the order of proof. Instead of the government's proving the oil was hot, the shipper had to prove it was "cold."

Within thirty days the number of tank cars moving from East Texas dropped by two-thirds; within two months only twenty-nine of its seventy-four refineries were in operation. Shutting off hot oil made the difference.[39]

In desperation, the hot oil traffickers were forced to try more radical, and devious, tactics—some of which Marshall witnessed firsthand. "As one of the members [of the Federal Tender Board] I had authority to sign such certificates," said Marshall.. "This particular man came in and offered me ten cents a barrel on a million barrels of hot oil for my signature on a tender.

"I told him to bring the money the next day in small bills, and he did. And when he laid it on my desk, the FBI was in the next room and picked him up and sent him to jail.

"He was convicted. Somebody who knows said that it went around the field like a cyclone that this had happened, and of course, I didn't get any more offers."[40]

12

A penal code backed up the federal tender system: Fines up to $1,000, imprisonment up to six months, or both were meted out to convicted offenders. Square-jawed Thomas G. Kelliher, a former FBI agent, was named to oversee enforcement of the code for the federal Interior Department. Kelliher had been in East Texas since late 1933, when Louis Glavis, director of Interior's new investigative staff, had hired him away from the FBI. Kelliher and another agent, Joe Cannon, had gone immediately to East Texas, where, under cover, they posed as lease hounds and lived in a house in the oil patch. Ingratiating themselves with the people already there, they soon learned the field, its oilmen, the other federal agents. Then they came into the open.

At twenty-eight, Kelliher was a veteran of some of the FBI's most publicized cases. Before joining the FBI—the United States Bureau of Investigation, as it was then called—in 1931, he had worked his way to a B.A. in physics at Boston College. He had also taught college physics while earning his law degree from the Georgetown Law School. At the FBI he was first assigned to the new criminological laboratory; when the Depression dictated economy cutbacks, the lab was closed, and Kelliher was assigned to a series of headline cases, including the Lindbergh and Urschel kidnappings and the pursuit of public enemies John Dillinger and Pretty Boy Floyd. He helped capture Machine Gun Kelly, who had engineered the Urschel kidnapping. Only a timely transfer kept him from being in the "Kansas City massacre" in which mobsters killed an FBI agent and a policeman and wounded another agent. As agent in charge of the Pittsburgh office, Kelliher helped clean up fraudulent voting and other corruption. While he was working on the election case, a Pittsburgh pimps' "union" called a strike of prostitutes and took their women to Ohio. When they crossed the state line, the FBI entered the case. Kelliher and his associates secured 173 indictments in all, and the veil fell from clandestine operations all over the city. In one instance, it turned out that the wife of one of the top detectives ran two houses of prostitution.

The first thing Kelliher did in East Texas was closely scrutinize the actions of the federal agents, some of them political appointees, already in the field. He exposed one of them for taking bribes and had the man indicted. A short time afterward, as he was attending a March of Dimes birthday ball on President Roosevelt's birthday, Kelliher ran into the man again.

"He came up with a loaded thirty-eight and was about to shoot me through the head," said Kelliher. "I wasn't aware of it. But Bryan Payne, who was an independent operator in Tyler, saw what was going on and got up and hit him in the head with a chair. I mean, it was that close!"

The man pleaded nolo contendere to accepting a bribe and was sentenced, but he was never charged with the assault or attempted murder of Kelliher.

"That wasn't considered a bad thing at the time. We were fair meat. If we'd had an indictment on the gun incident, I don't know if you could have found a jury that would have convicted him. Because the hot oil people were pretty prominent. We weren't particularly welcome."

Kelliher, whose staff was undermanned, had some help from the oilmen for his gigantic task as the chief federal investigator. H. L. Hunt ("I know he never engaged in hot oil traffic; he cooperated in everything I ever asked him") and others paid for several dozen Texas Rangers to be brought in, at a time when the state was cutting every expense it could. But, in general, Kelliher was isolated, and his wife, Dorothy, had two unhappy years because of her husband's unpopular federal position. Added to these pressures were bribery attempts that, in the midst of unemployment and low wages, added to the intensity of the situation. Kelliher himself received numerous anonymous telephone calls in which he was offered cash to relent in his investigations.

His most vivid memory was a silent encounter. "One very prominent fellow came in. Probably suspected I had my office wired, but I didn't. He was an attorney for one of the big refineries and we were about to shut them, and he walked in and opened up his briefcase. He just took out fifty thousand-dollar bills and laid them right across my desk. Those were hard times. He didn't say a word. I just grinned and shook my head."

Reared in a staunch Irish Catholic family, Kelliher hadn't thought twice about his decision. The lawyer left as silently as he had come, his $50,000 roll intact. The man wasn't charged. There was no evidence but Kelliher's say-so. But the word spread as fast as the Joiner discovery had. Soon Kelliher had a new name: "Tough Tom."

Because the federal tender system assured control of the rail shipments, the hot oilers now concentrated on trucking their cargoes out. As many as 250 trucks were running hot oil into a refinery at Shreveport, across the state line in Louisiana. As soon as Kelliher was able to secure the cooperation of the Louisiana State Police, this route was shut off.

Kelliher's relentless efforts against the hot oilers climaxed in 1935. Kelliher and his men moved on a refinery at 2:30 A.M. one Sunday. The plant was going full blast. Kelliher's men had gone to all the leases with lines connected to the refinery and had arrested the switchers. Then he had a pipeline crew trace the lines. There they learned that the hot oil was being bypassed, not into the refinery's tanks, but into a large pipeline that carried the oil to Shreveport, where it went into two 80,000-barrel tanks, which belonged to a major oil company.

"That was my downfall," said Kelliher years later. One of the company's top officials was a powerful man in Washington, on one of the Interior Department's advisory boards. But Kelliher shut down the refinery and filed his report. Then, before formal charges had been filed in the case, Ickes summoned Kelliher to Washington and offered him his choice of two jobs: curator of the Jefferson Memorial in St. Louis or superintendent of the Shenandoah National Park in Virginia. Kelliher suspected the hand of Ebert Keiser Burlew, Ickes' administrative assistant, in the matter. Burlew had sent down agents whom Kelliher classified as political cronies, and Kelliher, finding them of no use, had fired them. Pressure from the major company and Burlew's desire to get even, it seemed, had brought about Ickes' move.

Kelliher made $7,200 a year, then a handsome salary. A short time before, he had declined a job offer from the Tidewater Oil Company at $3,600. Now he reconsidered the Tidewater job. Then about four o'clock on a Saturday afternoon, Sarah McClendon, a Tyler newspaperwoman, came to Kelliher's apartment with an Associated Press story just off the teletype which quoted Ickes to the effect that Kelliher had been fired. With McClendon still in the room, Kelliher called Ickes. Ickes said he hadn't made the statement. Kelliher again suspected it had been Burlew.

"Mr. Secretary," said Kelliher, "if that statement holds, I'm giving a statement to the Associated Press—and you're not going to like it! It will put you in a very embarrassing light, and you know it. You know what I can tell 'em."

"You just hold your horses for about thirty minutes," said Ickes, "and I'll have a retraction on the wire in fifteen."

True to his word, Ickes issued a retraction. John Naylor, oil editor of the Fort Worth *Star-Telegram,* gleefully published both statements side by side.

Kelliher decided to accept the Tidewater job and sent Ickes his resignation. Even though Ickes called him and again offered him a choice of the positions tendered earlier, Kelliher was through. Kelliher moved to Shreveport as a Tidewater landman; in 1970 he retired as vice-president and general manager of the Houston division of Getty Oil.

Which major company was involved in the episode that cut short Kelliher's career in Interior? He wouldn't say for the record. He told his version to James A. Clark when he was working on *The Last Boom,* but when the publisher insisted on an affidavit before printing the company's name, Kelliher declined and, in retirement, decided to let bygones be bygones. After all, it had been nearly four decades.[41]

13

There had been a time when hot oil had flowed twenty-four hours a day, and with as many as 3,000 miles of pipeline over the field there was no way to police it perfectly. Nobody knew where all the pipelines were or where they went. A favorite device was the by-pass that caused the oil to flow directly into a secret pipeline. The maze of pipes was enough to make any investigator dizzy. In one case, an operator had his well's valve rigged up in his house, alongside the toilet. If state or federal inspectors came, he would send his wife to the bathroom. She would lock the door and turn off the valve. In another instance what appeared to be a well was actually a hookup with the Humble company's pipeline; the well's mud pumps were pumping good, stolen Humble oil over to an independent refinery, moving thousands of barrels a day without spudding in a hole. Then there were dummy wells; an operator seemed to have ten wells on a lease when he really had only one which was producing the allowable of ten, thereby saving himself a lot of drilling expenses.

As these examples indicate, there were two kinds of hot oil: that produced over the allowable and that which was stolen. Some oil was both. In any case it was difficult to build evidence and secure a conviction.

Outright thievery of oil was the only way out of poverty for many, and with the confusion in the field this practice was always possible. One oil-theft defendant was accused of stealing from Magnolia, which had a trunk pipeline through the middle of the field. The evidence seemed solid. Magnolia's main line had been tapped, and a line ran off onto the man's lease. There was a cutoff valve on the main high-pressure line, another one at his tank. During the trial the jury was taken to the field to observe the evidence firsthand. They dug out the line, exposing both valve and cutoff.

The defendant steadfastly denied the charge. "I don't know anything about it! How do I know Magnolia's not stealing *my* oil? It's hooked up to my tank."

With that argument he beat the case [42]

When both kinds of hot oil—over the allowable *and* stolen—were combined in one operation, the result was "boiling hot oil." Big Fish, the hot oil lawyer, told of a complaint from one of his clients, who was operating his small refinery on hot oil.

"Judge," the irate oilman said, "I tell you we've got to do something about these illegitimate hot oil runners."

"What's the trouble, Ed?" asked Fischer.

"Well, here I went out yesterday and made a trade with a switcher [the person who looks after the production at the wellhead] on a lease to run me some oil. And I laid a line over and tapped his company's line so I could get some oil. And here some illegitimate fellows come along and then tapped my line and got all of my oil, that I'd paid for. Then to add insult to injury, they meet me down in Kilgore this morning, and they hollered across the street, they say, 'Hey, Ed, do you want some hot oil?' I said, 'No, I do not deal in hot oil. If you want to talk business with me, you come to my office.' "

"Well, Ed," said Fischer, "what do you think we ought to do about it?"

"I think you ought to go down to the Railroad Commission and have the commission make an order against these illegitimate fellows from tapping our lines at night! " [43]

14

Who ran hot oil? From the 1930's to the present, independents and majors alike point accusing fingers at each other. It was not always easy to be certain who was right. Back when Dudley Golden was running the American Liberty Oil Company, there was a saying that "the American Liberty pipeline was so hot you couldn't sit on it." After Golden's death Clint Murchison, who had entered the firm as a partner, came out as the top man.[44] Murchison, who is also dead now, was widely reputed to be a hot oiler—producing over the allowable. His elder son, John D. Murchison, was too young to have personal knowledge of his father's activities at that time. "I can't tell you for sure about that hot oil business," John Murchison said. "Dad was a strong opponent of proration. He made a big issue of that. I think he put it on a, you know, liberty-or-death basis, a matter of principle: 'Nobody is going to tell us what we can do with our oil.' " [45]

Pinning down what oil came from which well and in what quantities invariably proved to be impossible. A high-grade, light-gravity oil with virtually no sulfur, the East Texas product could be readily skimmed into gasoline. Consequently, it was exceedingly difficult to establish the identity of a particular barrel of oil. Even if a man were producing his own leases, so that he would know where his production came from, one of his pumpers might turn dishonest and sell a few hundred—or a few thousand—barrels to a bootlegger in the middle of the night; the pumper would collect the cash, and the owner would never know it. Then there were reclaiming plants that thrived on oil that people deliberately let leak down a creek, simply to be skimmed off and sent through one of the plants.

15

One of the best known, most prominent, and probably the toughest of the hot oilers was Robert J. McMurrey, Sr., a native Texan who ran one of the largest refineries in the field. McMurrey wasn't afraid of the Railroad Commission, the Feds, or the devil.

McMurrey had started out in the sawmill business in East Texas but had gone to Arkansas for the oil boom there in the 1920's. After the Joiner well came in, he sold his rigs in Smackover and headed back to his native state, where he began promoting leases on a tract that contained more than 1,000 acres. He engineered an early promotional coup by persuading a Pathé News crew to film the completion of his first well in the East Texas field. Then he took the movie footage to theaters in cities across Texas to promote interests in the tract. His leases were excellent, but as the market became swamped, he found himself in the same plight as many others.

One day he and a younger brother, Marvin McMurrey, drove to Houston to see the president of Humble Oil, William S. Farish, about selling some of their oil.

"We've all the oil that we can handle," Farish told them, but he had a suggestion. "I personally feel that the best thing an independent can do is to sell his production or leases to the major companies that have the facilities—the pipelines, the refineries, service stations, and everything, an integrated company—and get a good price for it and take stock in the company. You'll make just as much money in the long run."

Rebuffed, the brothers started home. About thirty miles out of Houston, Robert McMurrey, who was driving, pulled over by the side of the highway. "You know," he told Marvin, "Mr. Farish told us something today. We've got to build the pipelines; we've got to build the refineries; we've got to sell gasoline. I think he is right. We can't stay in the oil business unless we're in every phase of the business."[46]

At the little town of Arp, they built a refinery which Robert later bought out from Marvin. Then Robert McMurrey bought another refinery at Tyler. Most of the oil and its products he sold was hot— above the allowable. He didn't think anybody had a right to tell him what to do with his oil.

"He made three types of gasoline," said his son, R. J. McMurrey, Jr., who worked in the refinery as a boy. "There was a white gasoline, an amber gasoline, and a red gasoline. The price was a half a cent on the white, three-quarters of a cent on the amber, and a penny a gallon on the red. The difference in the gasoline was: The white was the natural color, the amber was an amber dye, and the red was a red dye.

"He sold it to the retail customers, and they'd come in on wagons, and that was my first job, working on the loading dock. They'd bring old bath tubs; they'd bring gallon jugs, oil barrels, wooden barrels, any kind of a container that they could bring. Some of them, the old T models had forty- or fifty-gallon tanks strapped to them. They'd get some old barrels, pickle barrels or sugar barrels, anything that would hold any fluid, strap them on these old T models."[47]

Until his death in 1935 while still in his early forties, after surgery for an ulcerated stomach, McMurrey was a leading candidate for the title of King of the Hot Oilers. When Charles Fahy, chairman of the Petroleum Administrative Board for the Interior Department, arrived from Washington to observe conditions in the field, McMurrey's operation was one that was particularly pointed out. That evening, as Fahy, Howard Marshall, and Norman Meyers rested up at the Blackstone Hotel in Tyler, they ran into Robert McMurrey.

Fahy, a soft-spoken fellow from New Mexico, said, "Listen, McMurrey, I've heard a lot about you. I was out with Captain

Stanley in the fields this afternoon, and he showed me one of your hot oil lines. I put my hand on that hot oil line of yours and it was just as *warm-m-m.* That old pump was going *p-u-m-p* . . . *p-u-m-p* . . . *p-u-m-p.* . . ."

"Mr. Fahy, that wasn't my hot oil line," shot back McMurrey, quick as a flash. "Mine goes *pump-pump-pump-pump-pump!*" [48]

16

Over and over lawyers, like F. W. Fischer, claimed that Section 9-C of the NIRA, under which Marshall, Kelliher, and the other Feds operated, was unconstitutional. In 1934 two cases out of the East Texas field were to bring the issue to a head.

The first case was *Panama Refining Company* v. *Ryan,* in which Fischer sought injunctive relief against federal agents—in this case A. D. Ryan, a special agent of Interior's investigative division—seeking to regulate his client. As Fischer explained later, other producers and refiners, such as the McMurrey Refining Company and the General American Oil Company, were also plaintiffs in the case. He represented it as "a conspiracy of the big major companies, such as Standard and Dutch Shell, to shut out the 'little man,' and various other respectable, hard-working independents."

U.S. District Judge Randolph Bryant granted injunctive relief to Fischer's client. He agreed with the lawyer's reasoning that the NIRA regulations did not cover Panama Refining because it was not participating in interstate commerce. The trial judge did not rule on the validity of Section 9-C. But when the case was appealed by the government, the U.S. Court of Appeals in New Orleans ruled against Fischer's client, validating the constitutionality of 9-C. Fischer appealed to the Supreme Court.

It was during this time, while the Panama case slowly wound its way through the courts, that Marshall proposed a legal confrontation to settle the constitutionality of what he was doing.

"Judge," said Marshall to Bryant, "if this act is unconstitutional, I oughtn't to be trying to enforce it against anyone. If it is constitutional, it ought to apply to everybody. And there's a quick way we can get this determined. If I can get a criminal indictment against one of these hot oil operators and persuade his attorney to demur to the indictment on the grounds that it's unconstitutional, we can take this directly to the Supreme Court of the United States. If you will sustain the demurrer. As I say, I can't tell you whether you should or shouldn't, that's your decision. But I have the feeling you think it's unconstitutional."

"Yes," said Judge Bryant, "I do think so."

"Well," said Marshall, "I'll see if I can get an indictment against one of these fellows, and we'll get this thing exact."

With the Amazon Petroleum Corporation as the defendant, they proceeded. Under federal rules at the time, a direct appeal to the U.S. Supreme Court was permitted without going through the Circuit Court of Appeals.

When the Supreme Court agreed to hear the appeal, the Amazon and the Panama cases were consolidated for hearing.

Costumed in a cutaway coat, striped trousers, and wing collar that he seemed squeezed into, Fischer presented his case in December, 1934, to nine men presided over by Chief Justice Charles Evans Hughes. The small courtroom was filled. In his ill-fitting cutaway coat, explaining he was just a country lawyer, Fischer soon had everyone smiling, suppressing chuckles. Even the solemn justices, according to Tom Kelliher's report, were having a hard time holding their grins back.

But as an antagonist Fischer was not to be underestimated. Persuasively he hammered at the constitutionality of Section 9-C in his offhand country-boy style, describing confusing bulletins and executive orders that flooded the field, so that no operator had any idea what a petroleum code meant today or might mean tomorrow. Then he reached into his hip pocket and pulled out a tattered, dirty-looking booklet, the Code of Fair Competition for the Petroleum Industry.

"This heah Section Nine-C is inside some kind of a pamphlet," he said, waving it around. "Nobody really had any notice of it. I had trouble finding this. This is the only place it is! That's the law, Your Honors! It's carried around in the pocket of a deputy administrator. And nobody else knows what it is!"

Fischer maintained there was no law on the case because the original executive order was defective. Howard Marshall, sitting in the audience with Kelliher and other Interior men, was "fit to be tied." Although he was intimately familiar with the case, he had not been asked to participate. The Department of Justice had insisted on handling the case and, because of the interdepartmental rivalry, had not asked for or accepted any advice or assistance from Interior. Actually Fischer misled the court—Marshall called it "a deliberate lie"—with his comments on the obscurity of Section 9-C. It was on the statute books and with regulations issued by the government. Wouldn't the Justice Department lawyers pounce on this?

They did not. Harold M. Stephens, one of the top men in Justice, allowed significant points made by Fischer to go unchallenged. Stephens was generally acknowledged to be the most qualified attorney in Justice, but in Marshall's view he had not adequately prepared his case. After the hearing Secretary Ickes complained to President Roosevelt that Stephens had not taken the precaution to have an Interior lawyer, such as Marshall, at the counsel table with him, one "who could very readily have answered some of the questions that Stephens fumbled, much to the embarrassment of the Government in the trial of the case."

On January 7, 1935, the Supreme Court's decision kicked out Section 9-C, under which the Federal Tender Board had been operating, as an unconstitutional delegation of legislative power to the executive branch. The decision was 8 to 1. The majority opinion of the Court stated that the President had to put Section 9-C into effect by proclamation after having found that there was illegal oil and that the President had not first made the proper fact-finding effort.

The only dissenter was Justice Benjamin N. Cardozo. After the decision was released, Justice Cardozo told his law clerk, who had been one of Howard Marshall's law students at Yale, "Bill, you tell your friends down at the Interior Department that next time they get out one of those orders, to attach 1,500 pages of statistics, tie it up with the blue ribbons of the department, call it a finding of facts, and send it up here and put it on Mr. Justice [James C.] McReynolds' desk with the comment, 'You asked for it; now, goddamn it, read it!' " [49]

17

Fischer's Supreme Court victory was the signal for the hot oilers to flow it freely. The government's legal catastrophe precipitated a crisis like none before. Almost immediately Senator Tom Connally called Howard Marshall.

"Young fellow, can you write a law that's constitutional, that'll stop this racket?"

"I think so, Senator," said Marshall. "How long have I got?"

"How long will it take?"

"Can I have forty-eight hours?"

"Can you do it that quickly?"

"I think Norman Meyers and I can do it in that time."

He and Meyers stayed up most of one night and worked all the day after and most of the next night. In detail they prescribed what should be done to curtail the hot oil traffic and how the system should be operated. They filled in one gap that the old regulation hadn't covered—if the oil was hot, the federal government could confiscate it. They also established an in rem proceeding whereby the government could, if necessary, proceed against the illegal oil itself, rather than the person responsible for it. For instance, the *United States* v. *40,000 barrels of hot oil.* The principle had been used before, but not in fighting hot oil.

The so-called Connally Hot Oil Act went through with only a few minor changes, when it was consolidated with a proposal from Senator Albert Gore of Oklahoma. President Roosevelt signed it into law on February 16, 1935. The whole system of the Federal Tender Board was reinstituted but, with the new law, under specific statutory standing.

Immediately the Connally Act was challenged and ruled constitutional. Right after that Fischer confided to Marshall, "I think you got me, this time."

"Well, Fish," said Marshall, "if I haven't got you, I'm as bad a lawyer as you're supposed to be!" [50]

The Hot Oil War was over.

18

At the cost of an estimated 100 million barrels of hot oil, the law of capture was finally rendered inoperative. The traditional oil frontier of the United States was closed. Governmental control was established. Proration would be the rule for all fields. The profligate waste that had wrecked magnificent fields at Spindletop and Ranger would never terrorize the generations to come.

Whether they liked it or not, the oilmen—some of them—had

forced the issue of governmental control upon themselves. But even their willfulness was not as crucial to the final results as had been the hugeness of the field, which had encouraged the mad scramble that promised plenty for everyone. Although the New Deal had been the instrument that brought about the new controls, the crisis was so monstrous that any government, probably even Herbert Hoover's Republican administration (had he been reelected in 1932), would have had to choose between disaster and drastic action.

Appropriately, the major oil frontier that had opened in Texas was closing in Texas, only a few hundred miles from where Pattillo Higgins had convinced Anthony Lucas to drill. Yet the myriad events since then had been telescoped, within the short time span of thirty-five years. Pattillo Higgins was still very much alive, in San Antonio.

The epitaph for the Hot Oil War came several years later in Madison, Wisconsin, far from the piney woods and court chambers where its battles had been fought. Howard Marshall, by then working for Standard of California, was on a special assignment with William J. "Wild Bill" Donovan, the New York lawyer who was to earn his nickname as a World War II general. For the antitrust suit they were in, Donovan needed an expert witness on hot oil.

"Bill," said Marshall, "I'll tell you who we could get. Big Fish. If there's anybody who ought to know, he would, and he would know of his own knowledge, because he represented so many of these people."

Marshall telephoned the irrepressible Fischer, who accepted with alacrity.

On the stand Fischer testified to the enormous volume of the hot oil during the heyday of East Texas.

The judge peered across the bench at him, his pursed lips reflecting a tinge of doubt.

"Well, now, Mr. Fischer, how do you know that these hot oil refineries ran all this hot oil?"

Fischer beamed back at him.

"Your Honor, I ought to know. *They was all my clients!*" [51]

VIII

Lone Star Sheikhs

1

The image of rich Texans cavorting like Middle Eastern sheikhs was popularized by Edna Ferber's best-selling 1952 novel *Giant* and its movie version. Although ranch society predominated in the book, oil had its moments, and thereafter the stereotype of Texas oilman was that of Jett Rink, the loud, boastful, heavy-drinking, up-from-nothing brawler who drilled gushers and ended up with more money than he could spend.

The image was not new, but Ferber's tale supplied some missing particulars about "the legendary Texas zillionaires." In the popular imagination, there has long been something about wealthy Texans which sets them apart from ordinary rich people. Perhaps the air or the water inside Texas transforms the rich when they cross the state line. Suddenly they are certified Rich Texans, unique in all ways, unlike rich citizens elsewhere. Yet no significant evidence has been unearthed to prove that the Texas rich, oilmen or ranchers, are significantly different from any other rich. All Texans, rich or poor, breathe the same air and drink the same water. Upon reflection, one realizes that the Texas rich are like other rich. They are interesting, even intriguing, but not, alas, unique.

In keeping with the media stereotype, some Texas oilmen have been extremely colorful; others have been ordinary; many have been in between. The dull and ordinary receive little attention because they do not make interesting reading. If some of the overnight rich have been likely to spend lavishly and imaginatively, they have behaved no differently from those of other states who enjoyed sudden windfalls from gold or coal or the stock market.

Yet the legend of the flamboyant Texas oilman continues to grow. When President Gerald Ford began his holiday visits to Vail, Colorado—where he owned a condominium too small for the presidential party—didn't he swap with Dallas oilman Richard Bass, who owned larger facilities? Or consider the time, back in the 1960's, when Houston multimillionaire John W. Mecom threw a cocktail party for King Hussein of Jordan, attended by a cozy group of 700, including some rather famous astronauts. Admittedly an eye-catching instance of large, lavish entertainment—but the largest, or larger than any thrown in New York or California?

Even more symbolic in the popular imagination was the confrontation in 1958 between H. L. Hunt and the sheikh of Kuwait when Hunt made his effort to gain an offshore concession. A splendid picture: two rich sheikhs, dealing for millions, perhaps billions, and one of them, naturally a Texan. But the image is tarnished by the tale's ending. The remarkable concession was awarded to a Japanese syndicate, and Hunt left Kuwait deeply disappointed.[1]

How are Texas oilmen different from the ordinary run of folks? How have accounts become distorted? What has been the reality behind the images? In particular, what have the men been like who have been walking symbols of Texas oil—specifically, Glenn McCarthy, who reportedly was the living prototype of the Jett Rink characterization, and H. L. Hunt, the paterfamilias of the richest oil family in Texas?

To reach the heart of the difference between the rich and the rest of society, one must turn to social observer George G. Kirstein's conclusion that the rich "are different because they alone enjoy total economic freedom."[2] Having total economic freedom does not necessarily lead to liberation in either thought or deed, but it does leave the wealthy, as British author Goronwy Rees expressed it, "at least free to be themselves."[3] To paraphrase Dorothy Parker, Texas oilmen are likely to be just like everybody else, only more so.

Other factors have helped spawn these economically free oilmen.

The depletion allowance is one tax break, shared by oilmen everywhere in the United States, though that has shrunk from a magnificent 27½ percent and vanished altogether for some, while diminishing to 22 percent for others. In addition, the system of private ownership of land—a situation rarely found outside the United States—has been a unique source of wealth in this country, Texas wealth in particular, whereas in most other countries, subsurface mineral rights are government property. U.S. mineral speculators could deal directly with the landowners—often a farmer or rancher. Since many of the holdings were small, a down-and-out oilman had a better opportunity to make a deal, sometimes on credit or against future oil, than he otherwise might. Indeed, a "little man" could hardly have profitably leased five-acre, ten-acre, or forty-acre tracts in the East Texas field if the federal or state government had owned the minerals, simply because he probably would have found it impossible to lease on terms he could afford.

2

The factual basis of the extravagant reports from Texas can be located readily. An oilman does not have to be unique to be colorful, and as Texas has had its share of oil, so has it had its share of fascinating personalities.

With the onset of change in the oil industry, however, it may be that the age of flamboyance has passed. The genuine characters of the oil fields have disappeared with the years. Those who remain are, by comparison, an antiseptic generation. Many of the old-timers were rough and tough and subdued by nothing, not even a long string of dry holes. No one was likely to subdue Ike LaRue, for example.

LaRue and Robert "Slats" Sanders, another operator, were grief-stricken at the death of a close friend. After ingesting some bourbon for medicinal purposes to get their grief in hand, they headed for the funeral home. As the time came to view the remains, Big Ike—his hearing aid turned off as usual—went on ahead, leaving several nice old ladies between him and Sanders. At the casket LaRue took a good long look and bellowed back to his companion, "Slats, the poor little son of a bitch must have suffered something horrible. It don't even look like himself." When Sanders' time came to view the corpse, he realized that LaRue was right. They had gone to the wrong funeral.[4]

How many priceless old fellows like J. A. Bracken are left? Bracken would not lease his land. When the Van oil field was discovered in 1929, his farm turned out to be in the middle of the field, and he soon had an offer of $500,000. Bracken refused. He had no capital, but with a couple of offset wells nearby, he drilled it himself, putting him into the oil business in a big way. He was independent before his windfall, and his millions didn't change him one iota.

On one occasion in his latter years Bracken was accosted by a young man. Arguing while people passed by, they seemed about to escalate their dispute into a fistfight. "Son," said Bracken, "you can look at my old gray white hair and tell that my fighting days are long since gone, and there ain't *no way* I can keep you from hitting me." All the while he had been fishing a well-honed stock knife from his pocket. Now he had it out and poised, and his words danced to a quicker tempo. *"But I'll tell you one thing, young feller: If you do, I'm gonna lay your shit bag right out there on that sidewalk!"* [5]

Tales still circulate about the gregarious, pixie-faced D. Harold Byrd, who used to attend Railroad Commission meetings wearing the full regalia of the Civil Air Patrol, in which he was a colonel. During the 1940's he threw a yearly shindig at his Dallas home after the Texas-Oklahoma football game, traditionally played in Dallas each October. Initially an open house for friends who dropped in after the football game, the October party became institutionalized into an annual affair attended by 1,000 or more. According to one writer, Byrd once left the Texas-OU game early, standing up to invite everyone in his section to the party. To this day Byrd insists that he had merely yelled to some guests seated nearby, "Y'all come on to the house after the game!"

Bryd's assistant, Bess Bond, had to start calling the invitations as early as August. Once a newcomer from the East called to see if she could be invited. "If she's got that much gall, let's just invite her!" roared Byrd. Guests came from all over the country, consuming thousands of dollars' worth of barbecued game and liquor. Finally, the crowds got too unmanageable, and the famous parties had to be discontinued.[6]

Billy Byars, a drilling contractor, expressed his economic freedom when he held a reception for 105-TT, his prize bull, in the governor's suite of Tyler's Blackstone Hotel—with the guest of honor present. It was all in fun, of course, down to the gold-plated shovel that an employee wielded for any emergencies. 105-TT was too large to wedge into the bathroom.[7]

Many Texans have manufactured material for the mythmakers by acting out roles inspired by the consuming interest in Texas "color." The big eye-catchers have been those like J. M. "Silver Dollar" West, Jr., a second-generation Houston oilman who kept eighty silver dollars in each of two specially lined pockets. Although he carried his own butter when he dined out—and had telephones by the dozens in his home—silver dollars became his trademark. He threw them away like confetti, tipping twenty to twenty-five at a time. Paunchy, usually carelessly dressed, he arrived at the Neiman-Marcus store in Dallas one day, followed by companions lugging canvas bags filled with silver dollars. He was shopping for a decanter that would hold a whole case of bourbon he intended to give his attorney for Christmas. Stanley Marcus, running the store, happened to remember a huge one in storage that had been originally used as a display piece. He showed it to West.

"That won't hold twelve quarts!" bellowed West.

"Ten bucks, it will," retorted Marcus.

West summoned an aide to empty the case of booze he had with him into the decanter. It held three gallons exactly. West paid off the bet immediately, but the price, which was $2,500, exceeded his remaining silver. For the emergency, he whipped out a roll of $100 bills.[8]

Flamboyance, in many instances, is an almost bankable asset—when it helps promote drilling. Investment capital comes from many sources outside the industry. "It takes a certain flair to attract this kind of money," said Ralph Spence, a churchgoing family man who eschews the boisterous life, "and some of these boys have had it. They get criticized for throwing a champagne party or coming up in a big car and getting out in a white suit and a big hat and white boots, but it's just business. Because, doing that, boy, he inspires those people to turn loose of their money! They think, 'He's successful!' Fellow comes around in coveralls that are beat up, they say, 'Hell, I don't think he can find oil.' The show of success may be backed up by a big bank loan, but it's necessary to get the capital to carry on a program to drill the wells. And success attracts success." 9

3

Outsiders have had their troubles interpreting Texas to their readers and viewers, often fumbling their facts and inflicting mental pain and suffering on the subjects of their published results.

Oddly enough, the literary event which created the most controversy within Texas—Ferber's *Giant*—seems to have bothered few oilmen. Today the book has a certain quaintness to it, and the narrator comes across as a self-conscious outsider writing for an information-starved audience. A finicky reader with any degree of familiarity with Texas would probably be mildly irritated as Ferber glides over occasional geographical and other gaucheries—for example, mistaking "The Eyes of Texas" for the state song (which is "Texas, Our Texas"). Many Texans still laugh about the name for the central setting of the novel, the million-acre Reata Ranch. In Spanish, *reata* means rope. In Mexican slang, where double entendres abound to entrap the unwary, *reata* also means penis.

Among oilmen the general reaction to the movie *Giant* was muted. Nancy Toudouze, who used to have drinks with Edna Ferber when the novelist was staying in Corpus Christi while researching her book at the King Ranch and other locales, remembers that everyone seemed to love Ferber and like her book. "Mainly, I don't think it hurt the ranchers' feelings," said Toudouze. "I think anybody in the oil business paid much attention to it." 10

According to Dallas oil writer Jay Hall, oil people did become concerned about one small detail of the movie version. "That was when they were sitting around a swimming pool and the subject of the depletion allowance came up," said Hall. "Well, of course, to the oil people that's like attacking motherhood and God and the flag and everything else. Particularly in those days. And there was considerable effort made to get that part deleted. Because it had no bearing on the story. Even the American Petroleum Institute (API) went to try to get the thing pulled out. It could have been left out.

And that's the only thing I ever heard. Nobody particularly thought much of it." [11]

Giant is about a landed ranching family in South Texas, along the order of the Klebergs of the King Ranch. Oil is almost an intruder, a kind of counterpoint in which Jett Rink is something of a farcical heavy. Portrayed quite unsympathetically, Rink is "a living legend" and "a twentieth-century Paul Bunyan striding the oil-soaked earth in hundred-dollar boots." [12] But most of his actions, usually under the influence of alcohol, are those of a crude, raw, brash man—much less of a "character" than many of the real oilmen have been. And the word traveled fast that Rink was modeled after Houston's Glenn McCarthy, the one Texas oilman known to everyone in America at that time.

4

In 1975 Glenn McCarthy sat in his office in Houston, where he had once been king. He recalled his only meeting with Edna Ferber and discussed the events which followed. His broad shoulders were still evident on his somewhat heavy six-foot frame, and McCarthy seemed mellowed but with his toughness still intact. Behind his dark-shaded glasses was a shyness, and his manners were those of an old-style southern gentleman. There was an intensity about him that probably had not changed much over the years; his jaws frequently flexed, his fingers tapped, and at times his feet kept beat to the rhythm of his words as he spoke of subjects close to his heart, especially the oil industry.

"I didn't even know she was a writer," said McCarthy. "I was introduced to her, but I didn't pay any attention, you know. And it was the only one time that I talked to her. . . . I got many calls later on, after the movie *Giant,* from very prominent attorneys in Los Angeles, who wanted me to sue her. . . . Most everyone thought she was trying to portray me, and the attorneys said they'd take the case for nothing. I told them I didn't want to because, in the first place, I didn't think that she'd given my life, and therefore I wasn't perturbed about it. . . . If she did, she tried to portray me in two parts ... one of them a family man and the other a blustering, heavy drinker.... I could see very easily how she would do that 'cause the only time I ever met her was at a cocktail party. I think that's how she got her version.... And it's true, I drank. I drink now, when I want a drink. But not like she put it." [13]

While Ferber was researching *Giant, Time* magazine ran a cover story on McCarthy, labeling him the "king of the wildcatters." "At 42," the piece ran, "he looks like nothing so much as a Hollywood version of a Mississippi River gambler—a moody and monolithic male with a dark Civil War mustache, a cold and acquisitive eye, and a brawler's shoulder-swinging walk." [14] A quarter century later McCarthy saw the *Time* article as an early act in a series of gut shots against the oil industry from the news media. "*Life* and *Time* magazines tried to brand the oil operator as a rambunctious spendthrift, too-heavy drinker," he said. "They smeared ... everybody, including me. *Life* magazine reporters came down to see me, and I was nice enough to take them out to my ranch, and some of the things they printed on me were"—his voice dropped low— "pitiful.... For instance, I had a ranch, and at one time there had been a lot of goats on it before I bought it. I didn't want goats. I wanted cattle." He sold his goats, ordering his ranch foreman to kill the few which had been overlooked and butcher them for meat. There were about a dozen left when he took the *Life* staffer for the tour. "I rode up on the hill and saw these goats. I didn't say anything. I just reached down, pulled the gun out, and shot five of 'em. Then we went over and picked the goats up and took 'em back. I had a freezer. But according to this woman, I was the most merciless man that ever lived. You should have read those articles! They tried to do everything they could to me, I guess." [15]

Even in retrospect, McCarthy's was a dramatic career. Born on the Spindletop field in 1907, several years after the boom had faded, McCarthy excelled in physical competition from an early age. He started in the oil fields as a day laborer and later operated a filling station in Houston for a major company. After failing in his first few attempts as an oil operator, he produced a well at Conroe. He became a millionaire at the tender age of twenty-six, when he hit at Anahuac in the Gulf region on a drilling site condemned by other companies. One success followed another, and he built a refinery. On March 17, St. Patrick's Day, 1949, he opened the most publicized of all his investments, the sprawling Shamrock Hotel in Houston, which cost him $21 million and took three years to build. He entered newspaper publishing, broadcasting, and the motion-picture business, but he kept finding oil. He lived well and hard, becoming the talk of Houston and, finally, a legend around the world. New York and Hollywood celebrities mingled with all sorts of Texans as a mob of 37,000 gathered to see his Shamrock on opening day.

At his peak McCarthy owned the McCarthy Oil and Gas Corporation, a $700,000 mansion, a chain of neighborhood news-papers, the Beaumont Natural Gas Company, the twenty-two-story Shell Building in Houston, a steel plant in Detroit, a 15,000-acre ranch, a chemical company, and numerous other interests. Being millions in debt was no worry to him, but as he began extending his credit more and more, he was turned down for a $70 million Reconstruction Finance Corporation loan. Then his creditors, the Equitable Life Insurance Company and Metropolitan Life Insur-ance Company, began to get cold feet. Finally, with his empire threatening to collapse around him, McCarthy began selling off his investments to satisfy his nervous creditors. He sold the Shamrock to Conrad Hilton, then unloaded his $15 million chemical plant and other investments. In the 1950's he ventured into foreign oil in the Middle East and South America but got out because of the risks of foreign ownership. The McCarthy tide was ebbing. Today he doesn't borrow anymore. "You've got to be a gambler to be an oilman," he told Houston newspaperman Lynn Ashby, "but only gamble with your own money"—advice that many an oilman would eschew. A few years ago he sold his Houston mansion for $1.5 million and began dividing his time between Houston and his West Texas ranch. His became a different life-style, and the rough reflection of Jett Rink was replaced by the sturdy mien of Bick Benedict, the ranching hero of *Giant.*[16]

In his office he has maintained mementos of the earlier days: an immensely enlarged color photograph of him with a rifle on a craggy hill of his ranch, taken by a *Life* photographer; another one of him and his family. On his desk there is a picture of his mother, and in the front office the *Time* cover of 1950 is displayed.

If he regretted the way the press had handled him, the one thing he did not regret was the Shamrock. "It was a good, profitable venture, and it didn't cause me any trouble at all. . . . I got twenty-two million two hundred and fifty thousand dollars for the Shamrock, all to pay debts. I sold all of Sharpstown. I owned the land that the domed stadium [the Astrodome] is on. I owned three hundred and fifty-four acres out there; part of it was oil land and the other part was real valuable real estate. So I sold off all that. I had to pay off approximately fifty-two million dollars, and I sold the things that were readily able to turn into cash." [17]

Jim Clark, who often worked for McCarthy as a public relations man, believes that none of the stories captures the colorful old operator's true character. Citing the *Time* cover story, Clark recalls, "In the story it said—old Red Johnson, he was the reporter—that Glenn was the kind of man who would drive a car with one hand one hundred miles per hour with a bottle of whiskey setting at his side. So one of his friends, when he read that, called Glenn up and he said, 'Glenn, you ought to sue that guy. You ought to sue him for that!' Glenn said, 'How in the hell am I going to sue him? The son of a bitch was sitting with me when I did it!'

"But," Clark continued, "he had more native intelligence about oil than any other man I ever knew. He was remarkable. He could find oil where nobody else would even look! . . . People had confidence in him. He had more deals offered to him than anybody else. He could drill a well cheaper than anybody else, though he wasn't an engineer. . . . Hell, the Gulf Oil Company got into every deal they could with him, just for that reason."

At one point famed oilman Harry Sinclair offered McCarthy $50 million to sell out to Sinclair. Although the sale would have simplified McCarthy's financial problems, he turned Sinclair down. "He couldn't consider selling out," said Clark. "He had created something. It was his baby. He was the man that would run it. Although he loved Mr. Sinclair—they were close friends—he didn't want Mr. Sinclair for a boss. Or anybody else.

"Nobody will ever write the real story of Glenn McCarthy. That guy in that show *Giant* was a sissy [by comparison]. He didn't have any flamboyance; he didn't fight; he didn't do anything compared to what Glenn did. . . .

"Glenn has always been basically shy, except around people with whom he was thoroughly acquainted, but if you came into his office to talk with him, he was the greatest salesman that ever lived. . . .

The oil industry failed to take advantage of him the way it should have, and I was very critical of them. I still am." Clark's voice rose with evangelistic fervor. "The oil business should have taken Glenn McCarthy over and used him as a salesman, because he was it: the *only* man in the forties and the fifties who had captured the imagination of the people!"

As Clark sees it, McCarthy's natural sense of promotion should have been channeled to benefit the entire industry, and the men in the major companies, especially, should have publicly embraced him and recognized his valuable qualities, perhaps helping him over the pitfalls that threaten a man with a high public profile. McCarthy and his colorful career became a symbol of the American dream: the self-made man who hadn't lost the common touch, who promoted charities, who was still interested in the public good. The public identified McCarthy as the prototype of all oilmen, so that the publicity that he received also shone on the rest of the oil business, independents and majors. Instead, Clark recalls, many oil people, especially those in major companies, privately condemned McCarthy and other colorful oilmen, grumbling, "They're gonna lose us the depletion." But the majors have always dominated the industry, simply because they were larger and more powerful, and the implication is that the policies of the majors, not the antics of a handful of colorful independents, in the end cost the industry its depletion allowance.

Other forces also were at work. Corporations have maintained low public profiles of their executives, as if afraid they might be caught being themselves. Even top executives have to answer to a board of directors and stockholders. McCarthy, in contrast, was his own boss and acted like it. Dr. Frank L. King, who made his money in real estate, once said, "I never worked a day of my life for another man." This same independent spirit seemed to shape McCarthy and many others like him, and the colorful qualities—a certain lack of inhibition or a knack for doing things with a flourish—that endeared them to people generally may have been the very ones that made more sedate men grimace.

Clark's view is that McCarthy's public relations—the man himself—had a substance which the campaigns of the major companies lacked. Although McCarthy may have been open to valid criticism at times, Clark continued, he had been the genuine article, not a charlatan, and the public realized this. At the same time the majors were formulating oil policies as if they were of no concern to the public. In time, Clark believes, this corporative attitude alienated the people and boomeranged upon the majors and independents alike. *That*, not the colorful men like McCarthy, insists Clark, cost the industry its depletion allowance and lowered it in the public's esteem—indirectly a self-inflicted wound that will always scar oilmen.

"Glenn didn't lose touch with the people," said Clark. "He never did anything to hurt the oil industry. Anywhere in the country or anywhere in the world you went, after this Shamrock opened, everybody asked me about Glenn McCarthy. They didn't give a damn about anybody else." [18]

5

While Glenn McCarthy was the object of cover stories and having his financial ups and downs in Houston, another man, in Dallas, was accruing his hundreds of millions quietly but steadily. In fact, Haroldson Lafayette Hunt was practically a billionaire before anyone ever took much note of him. From the day in 1930 when he had bought out Dad Joiner in the East Texas field, Hunt had developed his leases there and had consistently expanded his operations elsewhere. At the time of his death, in 1974, Hunt's was the only billion-dollar fortune in Texas. Former Texan Howard Hughes had begun as heir to the Hughes Tool Company, a business directly related to oil, but while Hughes took his money out of Texas, Hunt stayed there with his money to the end.

As the largest independent operator in the world during World War II, Hunt claimed to have held more oil reserves than all the Axis nations put together. It was his eldest son, Hassie (H. L., Jr.), who called his attention to this.

"What about Rumania's oil?" asked the elder Hunt, thinking of the giant Ploesti field.

"Including Rumania," replied Hassie.[19]

Although this claim seems inflated and open to serious question, no one appears to have challenged it, despite its having been published a number of times.

How much was H. L. Hunt and his family worth at his death in 1974? In 1967 a sum of $2 billion seemed to be a fair guess. By the mid-seventies some estimates of the family assets were as high as $5 billion. But as the family's businesses have no outside stockholders and publish no reports or balance sheets, only family members and the Internal Revenue Service have accurate figures, and neither is talking. Hunt himself once modestly said, "We've never really tallied it up."

The network of money-making machinery during Hunt's lifetime included three oil companies, Hunt Oil, Placid Oil, and Hunt International, which operated in many states and overseas. A refinery in Alabama produced asphalt and Parade brand gasoline, which was sold at 300 filling stations in the South. Finally, among the visible components of the fortune, there was H. L. H. Products, a food company.

He used the profits, estimated at $1 million a week, to invest in real estate—ranches in Wyoming, Montana, and Texas, cotton plantations in Mississippi, Arkansas, and Louisiana, timberlands all over the South, grazing lands and citrus groves in Florida, vast pecan orchards, and other land in Dallas, Atlanta, and other cities.[20]

Hunt was a tall, unpretentious man with shrewd, crackling blue eyes, easily overlooked in a crowd. In 1948 he was practically unknown, even in Dallas, where he tended his fortune. When a photographer snapped Hunt's picture on a busy Dallas street, the quiet operator commented, "I thought he was one of those street photographers who give you cards." The photo, fuzzy and candid, changed everything when it ran full page in *Life* magazine. The caption called Hunt "the richest single individual in the United States."

In a way the *Life* picture was a turning point for Hunt, who subsequently gave his first press interview in fifty-nine years to a "friendly" local newspaperman, Frank X. Tolbert of the Dallas *Morning News*. In the interview Hunt derided the idea that he was the richest man in the country, saying, "Money as money is nothing. It is just something to make bookkeeping convenient."[21]

Afterward, though, he accepted publicity more easily. Over the years he gave a number of other interviews, one to an *Esquire* reporter, another to *Playboy* magazine. At eighty, in 1969, he was interviewed by newsman Mike Wallace for CBS's *60 Minutes*. He remembered the *Playboy* interview as "pleasant," "fairer than I expected." [22] Welch Wright, his longtime secretary, said the *Playboy* piece summed up his philosophy better than any other inverview. [23]

H. L. Hunt was a man of many images. Though he was the bete noire of the liberals, interviewers, liberals included, found him surprisingly mild. Tom Buckley, who conducted the 1967 *Esquire* interview, concluded that Hunt was "an amiable old devil, mildly eccentric perhaps." In a way, Hunt caught people off guard. "He had a quality of making you want to do things for him," said Art Brenton, who once handled public relations for Hunt. Brenton called him the best one-to-one dealer there ever was. [24] One suspects Dad Joiner would have agreed.

Although fellow oil billionaire J. Paul Getty has been widely quoted as saying, "In terms of extraordinary, independent wealth, there is only one man—H. L. Hunt," Hunt intimated the remark was designed to take the spotlight off Getty himself, who realized that people resent great wealth. Hunt commented: "A man with $200,000 is about as well off, for practical purposes, as I am." [25] When accused of having a home—his Mount Vernon on White Rock Lake in Dallas—that was several times larger than George Washington's home, Hunt countered that his was only a very little larger.

Bunker, H. L. Hunt's second oldest son, believed his father's acquisitiveness was exaggerated and that making money didn't interest him as much as "doing a good job." He probably didn't spend more than $3,000 a year on himself, Bunker said with a laugh, "and that includes vitamin pills." [26]

Bunker Hunt's estimate of his father's expenditures may have been understated for dramatic effect, but the point was valid. H. L. Hunt kept a low profile, as the following anecdote amply demonstrates. Once when Hunt Oil employees were ordered to keep everybody else away from a "tight" well—on which no information is given out—a new man reported to the tool pusher that the only person he had seen was "a curious farmer in wrinkled and baggy khakis who wanted to go up and examine the well." But, the new man reported proudly, he had not let the farmer in.

The tool pusher laughed. "Yes, I know all about it. You did exactly right in turning a stranger away from a tight well—even if that old farmer was H. L. Hunt." [27]

Not everyone accepted the "old farmer" image. Devin Garrity, a publisher whose conservative leanings brought him into contact with Hunt after World War II, remembers Hunt's satisfaction over the power and status his money gave him. In the 1950's, Garrity said, Hunt, planning to fly from Dallas to New York, called the Waldorf-Astoria to have his regular suite ready. The call came on short notice, the day of the flight, and the king and queen of Greece were at the time ensconced in the suite. The royal couple had to be hurriedly moved. So swift was the departure that their flowers were still there when Hunt and his entourage arrived. In a tone which left no doubt that he knew he had caused their hasty flight, Hunt said, "Oh, wasn't that nice of the king and queen to leave their flowers for us?" [28]

Others saw a variety of personality features in the Dallas billionaire. Karl Hess, who was later to become the chief writer of the 1960 and 1964 Republican national platforms, went to Texas in the 1950's to design and edit Hunt's *Facts Forum* magazine. "I honestly liked Mr. Hunt—found him commendable in some ways, simply wrongheaded in others," said Hess. "Some claim he was also devious and vicious. I don't know about that. He never appeared that way to me in our personal relationships.

"He had a droll sense of humor. At least I found it to be so. I actually thought he was rather like Will Rogers. Honestly. My impressions of him are all very warm."

Hess observed, though, that Hunt's ways were sometimes trying to those around him. One day, while Hess was in Dallas, Hunt announced that he needed a new car and casually assigned an employee to purchase him one. The employee bought a Cadillac. The next day Hunt informed him that he didn't want "one of those big cars," since he always drove a smaller make.

"He said he wanted a car like he had," said Hess. "So they got him that kind of car, and then somebody asked him where he had put the Cadillac. And I really seem to recall that he said he didn't remember.

"He liked to drive himself. He was very funny about automobiles. There was one brand he absolutely didn't like. One time a geologist got to an appointment late, and Hunt asked what kind of car he was driving, and the geologist mentioned the hated brand. So Hunt assumed that was a reflection on the man's character and fired him. He was pretty good about things like that. Kind of idiosyncratic.

"But also I remember being out with him on one of his ranches one day while he patiently explained to a machinery operator the proper way to pull the stumps. He had a lot of practical knowledge, and he could express it very well.

"If he hadn't become so intensely ideological, he would have been an absolutely remarkable man." Hess offered as an example an idea that Hunt had proposed to him: "Had real estate all over the place. And he thought it'd be nice to set up a number of five hundred-acre farms, with dormitories, around the country where young people could come and learn practical farming. And what a difference that could have made! That could have been a major attack against agribusiness. Could have been a major way of preserving family farms, to have someone like Hunt interested in practical, small-scale agriculture. He seemed to have a good instinct for natural things. And one of his daughters talked him out of that by saying that it didn't make any difference whether people grew food or not if the dread atheistic Communists took over. So he abandoned what could have been a historically important thing and then became just another anti-Communist. I think he was much better than that. I didn't think so at the time, but I do in retrospect."

Hess' association with Hunt proved to be brief because they clashed over how Hess should perform his task.

"I couldn't imagine continuing to work for a man who, as a conclusive end to any argument, would remind you that he was rich and therefore right. That was always disconcerting, but it's also unanswerable. After a while it was quite clear that we were going to end up enemies or separated, and I really liked the old guy."

Hess left, concluding that "it would be better to clear out than to sit there and get angry." [29]

Hunt's widely quoted statment "Everything I do, I do for a profit" and a favorite saying, "Given the choice between luck and intelligence, always take luck," both applied equally to his gambling. There is, however, a strong indication that he liked to bolster his luck with precise knowledge. Les True recalled an occasion when a large group of Texas oilmen rode the train together to an American Petroleum Institute convention. There was a poker game all the way from Dallas to Chicago. Though the players kept badgering H. L. Hunt to get into the game, he refused. "No," he said firmly, "you're all like babies. I know too much about the game. I know how cards run, and I remember cards." They wouldn't give up, and finally, he gave in. "Well, all right—when you play with me, you play for keeps." Upon arrival in Chicago, True saw one of the men present Hunt with a check for $24,000—and that was only a fraction of his winnings.[30]

Hunt's favorite card game was gin rummy. He liked to play for $1 a point, a stake which many oilmen refused. One of the few who ever won much from Hunt was Glenn McCarthy, who had never played for $1 a point before. He won $3,000 the only time they ever played together.[31]

In gin rummy, as in the oil business, the information one picks up as the game progresses is all-important. As with oil drilling speculation, information is the best thing you can have, outside of unmitigated luck. Discards are like drilled wells—dry or otherwise. And H. L. Hunt's memory was like a flytrap for exquisite details.

Hunt once asked Dr. J. Clarence Karcher to play a "nice pleasant game" of gin with him at the Dallas Petroleum Club. "Well," recalled Karcher, "I could see that I could go down with less than ten or gin. Of course, I was trying to go pretty quickly because I thought I could catch him with a few points in his hand. I said, 'I meld,' and I turned my discard face down, to stop the play. He reached down, put his hand on my cards, and said, 'Don't show me your hand and I'll tell you what you've got.' I held them up, and he called off every damned card in my hand! I hadn't discarded more than four or five times, but he had a terrific memory. If I picked up one of the cards that he played, he'd remember that one. Then he'd watch my discards. And that's all the cards he'd seen of mine. I mean, he was really sharp." [32]

On at least one occasion Hunt's cardplaying became integrated with an oil transaction. Jake Hamon was planning to drill a shallow wildcat well in Louisiana in an area where he had 2,500 acres and Hunt's company had 2,500 acres. It was customary for one company to contribute dry hole money—a contribution to drilling expenses in the event the well is dry—to the other's drilling in such a situation, but the Hunt people wouldn't give Hamon the $2,500 he wanted. Finally, he marched indignantly into Hunt's office.

"Now, look here, Haroldson," said Hamon, probably the only person to call Hunt by that name, "this isn't right, I'm going to drill this well, and I want some dry hole money!"

"Well," said Hunt, "I saw you playing gin over at the club the other day with Ed Landreth, and you were playing for a dollar a point."

"Yes," admitted Hamon reluctantly. "I didn't want to, and I just played him one game. I normally play for a penny a point, maybe a nickel."

Hunt said, "You've got to play me a couple of games of gin at a dollar a point."

"I've played poker with you, and I know better."

Hamon finally acceded. Hunt won $800 the first game, $1,100 the next. Then he reached into his pocket and handed Hamon $600.

"Here's the rest of the twenty-five hundred." [33]

Aside from his ultraconservative politics, Hunt's most publicized interests were probably his nutrition and health concepts. In his early years he chain-smoked cigars, ate what he could, and often went without sleep. During his interview with Frank Tolbert in 1948, he filled the room with cigar smoke. He liked to pay anonymous visits—Tolbert later dubbed him "the Caliph of Cash"— to backcountry general stores, play checkers, and eat crackers with sardines or cheese. As he grew older, he became more interested in his health, stopped smoking, and turned to more wholesome food. Because he bought much of his food from health food stores, avoiding white bread and white sugar, he was frequently called a food faddist or health food nut. In retrospect it appears that he was an early spokesman for what has become a widespread suspicion of overrefined food and additives.

One of the health mentors most admired by Hunt was Dr. Joe D. Nichols, an exuberant M.D. in Atlanta, Texas, who served for years as the national president of Natural Food Associates. In his later years Hunt seemed determined to follow Dr. Nichols' admonition to "eat natural, poison-free food grown on fertile soil, eaten fresh and not overcooked." Hunt began growing most of his vegetables in a garden near his home and ate much of his food raw, along with whole-grain bread, nuts, and fruit, with honey as a sweetener. Despite these personal preferences, though, his own H.L.H. Products food—not to be confused with the Hunt Food Company, with which he never had any connection—produced *not* health food but ordinary canned vegetables.

There were no cocktails or wine in the Hunt home, and he told

Tolbert that he had tried to maintain a nonalcoholic and non-Communist business organization—which he did. Into his last years he was still active, though his activities were more often political than business-related. In his eighties he began to decline. He was stooped, down from his former six feet, his skin pale like parchment, and his white hair thinning, though his grip remained firm. By the summer of 1974, when he appeared to testify before a federal grand jury in a wiretap investigation involving two of his sons, he had to be pushed in a wheelchair. Later that summer he went into the hospital, his condition grave. In November, at the age of eighty-five, he died. His funeral was marked by simple ceremonies at Dallas' huge First Baptist Church.

His will gave his widow all his stock in Hunt Oil and distributed to his ten children and their families the rest of the estate. Ray Hunt, his son by his second marriage, was named the sole executor. Although his lifetime accumulation and its yield had been pegged as at somewhere between $2 billion and $5 billion—enough leeway, if divided up, to make thousands of people millionaires—it was generally accepted that before death Hunt had passed on hundreds of millions of dollars to his survivors through arrangements such as trust funds. He was not one to relinquish his wealth needlessly to the IRS.

After his death Americans finally learned of the circumstances of Hunt's two families when the salient details of his marital record appeared in *Newsweek* and other publications. He had six children by his first wife, the former Lyda Bunker—four male, two female. The sons are H. L. "Hassie," Jr., Bunker, Herbert, and Lamar; his two daughters are Margaret Hill and Caroline Schoellkopf. The first Mrs. Hunt died in 1955. Two years later Hunt married a Hunt Oil secretary, Ruth Ray Wright, by whom he had already fathered children: a son, Ray Lee, and daughters—two now married—Helen Kreiling, Swanee Meeks, and June Hunt. Hunt formally adopted these four offspring after the second marriage, and Mrs. Hunt revealed that he was their father. Rumors floated that a power struggle was going on between the first and second families, but the charges were staunchly denied amid demonstrations of solidarity.[34]

6

Of H. L. Hunt's five sons, Bunker and Herbert have taken—somewhat reluctantly, it would seem—the center stage. H. L., Jr., or Hassie, withdrew from active participation in the oil business in the 1940's, although at one time he was reputedly worth $250 million. Lamar is more interested in the sports world than in oil. Ray Hunt, the only son of the second marriage, is president of Hunt Oil, chairman of both the Hunt Investment Corporation and the Woodbine Development Corporation, and very active, though apparently on a smaller scale than his older half brothers. There is still speculation that he will wind up one of the most influential men in Dallas, if not the state.

Unlike his father and his half brothers, Ray Hunt, now in his middle thirties, has been active in civic and community projects. A trustee of Southern Methodist University, of which he is a graduate, he has also served as president of SMU's alumni association and is a director of the Dallas United Way and the Dallas Chamber of Commerce. A quiet man like his father, Ray Hunt seems to accept any publicity that comes his way as a form of necessary evil. He explained to a Dallas *News* reporter, "If I had my own way I would prefer that my name never appeared in print again. I'm just that way."

Bunker and Herbert Hunt, like the other Hunts, have offices on the twenty-ninth floor of Dallas' First National Bank Building. Like many other affluent men, they work long, ten-hour days, drive two-year-old automobiles, prefer baseball games or Boy Scout meetings to high society, eschew flashy jewelry and high-fashion clothes, and have trouble staying on a diet. But unlike other men, they faced going to prison during the middle 1970's.

On the eve of their trial for wiretap conspiracy in late September, 1975, their business empire included Placid Oil Company, a thirty-eight-year-old firm with production in Texas and Louisiana, believed to be worth $400 million (twice that of Hunt Oil, according to Dallas newspaper estimates); Penrod Drilling Company, a partnership which included Lamar and another of the nation's biggest drilling companies; Hunt International Petroleum Company, for overseas activities; and the Great Western United Corporation, the Denver sugar beet refining company that also owns Shakey's Pizza Parlor chain. In addition, Bunker Hunt had one of the finest racing stables in the world, along with cattle ranches in Mississippi, Oklahoma, North Texas, Montana, and New Zealand. He purchased the Montana ranch and cattle in 1973 for $7.5 million. His was the first filly in history to win $1 million in stakes.

Born in El Dorado, Arkansas—Bunker in 1927, Herbert in 1929—they worked on family farms as youngsters and on oil rigs when they were students. "As a kid," said Herbert, "I lived on the outskirts of town and my family had about ten acres, so I got most of my spending money by raising fryers. I also had layers at the time, so I was in the egg business. I experimented with all kinds of livestock and crops, including pigs. I gave up the pigs because people complained about the smell. The turkeys almost broke me when I lost fifty at one time!"

Herbert was eventually graduated from Washington and Lee University with a degree in geology. Bunker attended the University of Texas at Austin, left to join the Navy, and after the war attended SMU one semester before going into the family business.[35]

In 1968 *Fortune* magazine listed Bunker Hunt as one of America's leading centimillionaires, his wealth assessed somewhere between $300 million and a half billion.[36] He had drilled $11.5 million worth of dry holes in Pakistan, but he kept drilling in Libya until he found the mind-boggling Sarir field in which he became a fifty-fifty partner with British Petroleum.

In 1973 Bunker Hunt soared into the headlines when Libyan leader Colonel Muammar el Qaddafi nationalized Hunt's oil properties in that country. A Hunt spokesman estimated the loss at 5.5 billion recoverable barrels of oil, worth about $23 billion. There is little doubt that this field alone would have enabled him to have eclipsed his father's fortune several times over. Some admirers still think he will wind up richer than his father.[37]

But like most other oilmen, Bunker Hunt also turned to other business ventures. By 1974, when oil prices soared, he had bought up a fortune in silver. When the price of silver jumped to $6.24 an ounce, doubling in two months, insiders blamed Bunker Hunt's buying; he was said to have owned or contracted for 50 million ounces worth a paper profit of $200 million.[38]

The commodities market was an enticing one for the brothers Bunker and Herbert Hunt in the 1970's. Their major target became sugar in late 1974, when they made a tender offer for controlling stock in the Denver-based Great Western United Corporation. After a stormy contest the Hunts won control of Great Western by buying up about 55 percent of the outstanding stock. The climax came about a month after their father's death.[39]

In 1975 the brothers Hunt were about to go on trial, and they had a great need to establish a definite, beneficial public image. Both Bunker and Herbert Hunt submitted to interviews for the first time in their lives, first with *Newsweek* and then with the Dallas *Morning News*. The Dallas paper devoted a full page to them.

Their problems started in 1969 and 1970, when the telephones of six Hunt organization employees were tapped. H.L.H. Products was losing money hand over fist, more than $50 million, according to Bunker Hunt, and the brothers suspected much or all of the loss might have been embezzled. The Hunt brothers hired two investigators to tap the phones of the suspected employees, and the police entered the picture when bugging equipment was found in the investigators' car. The two investigators were convicted, sentenced to prison, and later paroled. For the next several years the matter smoldered. Charges and countercharges flew among the Hunts, the suspected former employees, the investigators, the federal government, and the contending lawyers. Two former aides of H. L. Hunt were found guilty of mail fraud. Herbert and Bunker Hunt were indicted on wiretap charges and faced trial. A Hunt lawyer said he believed one of the Hunt employees had been a CIA agent. The Hunts contended that they were being pursued by the government "because of our conservative political beliefs" and that the government had asked them to provide a cover for their agents in Libya, which they had refused three times. At the trial, moved to Lubbock out on the high plains, in the latter part of 1975, Mrs. H. L. Hunt and a dozen Hunt family members attended to dispel rumors of internecine family strife over the Hunt interests. "I'd do anything for them," testified their stepmother.

The brothers could have received up to thirty years in prison and a $60,000 fine if convicted on the six counts of wiretapping. Herbert Hunt admitted authorizing the six wiretaps to protect their aging father, afraid embezzlement would bring on the collapse of H.L.H.

Food Products and its parent company, Hunt Oil. Finally, the jury believed that the Hunts had not willfully violated the law, and they were acquitted.[40]

Lamar Hunt, the sixth child and youngest son of H. L. Hunt's first marriage, is considered a founding father of the American Football League. He kept the fledgling league alive in the early days until the National Football League accepted it. Behind his determination were millions. He lost heavily at first. After three seasons he pulled his franchise out of Dallas and moved it to Kansas City, where he found success with the championship Chiefs.

Associated Press sports editor Will Grimsley described Lamar Hunt as more like a bank clerk than a multimillionaire. At the time Hunt was an owner of five professional sports teams, of which the Chiefs were best known. His interests also spread into baseball, basketball, soccer, and tennis. A spearhead in the movement to introduce professional soccer to the United States in the 1960's, he became a co-owner of the Dallas Tornado team in the North American Soccer League, and he financed the operations of World Championship Tennis, a touring pro troupe run by Hunt's nephew, Al Hill, Jr., with eighteen leading pros in his stable. Sportswriter Grimsley noted, "Someone remarked facetiously that his next move would be to buy Wimbledon and stage his own tournament.[41]

IX

LONE STAR SHEIKHS (CONT'D)

1

After 1930, when supremacy in oil production had emphatically shifted from Oklahoma and California to Texas, thousands of experienced operators flocked to the state, and inevitably, native Texans, as well as new residents, began to swell the ranks of the Big Rich in the oil industry.

Who are the Big Rich in Texas? Obviously, their wealth far exceeds the garden-variety millionaire, but by how much? Certain fortunes rear up like icebergs; they are above the waterline, but how much more lies below? To corral others in a Big Rich roundup may prove a difficult assignment. Even a centimillionaire's fortune may elude public notice. H. L. Hunt and his family clearly have long been Big Rich, as have the inheritors of Sid Richardson, Clint Murchison, Sr., Hugh Roy Cullen, and R. E. "Bob" Smith.

Among other famous operators, now dead, certain other names appear as prime candidates. James A. Abercrombie, who once ran a dairy and started in business as a dredging contractor, used to call himself "just a dumb clam digger." Before his death he was ranked a centimillionaire by *Fortune*. In addition to his own production company, he had founded the Cameron Iron Works. The late

George W. Strake, Sr., one of Houston's leading oilmen, was well on his way up the multimillion-dollar ladder.

There are also some survivors from that older generation of operators, among them Toddie Lee Wynne, a lawyer-oilman who was Clint Murchison's partner; Algur H. Meadows, the majordomo of the General American Oil Company; Jake L. Hamon; H. B. Zachry, also a construction mogul; Claud B. Hamill; Michel T. Halbouty, and George (his brother Herman is dead) Brown. To these and to descendants of the deceased Texas sheikhs one may add the oil magnates of the new generation, including Edwin L. Cox, Frank Pitts, brothers J. Hugh and William T. Liedtke, and Robert A. Mosbacher. Still, the list is probably incomplete, and many aspirants to the "big money" will exclaim, "Why, I'm worth as much as he is!"

Most oilmen who have made it big have not limited themselves to the petroleum industry, a trend exemplified by George and Herman Brown. Herman Brown is dead now, but George Brown carries on as "one of the most powerful businessmen in Houston—and the nation." According to one writer, his holdings are "probably the most extensive in Houston's monied establishment." George Brown's domain is vast. He presides over banks, holding companies, and huge concerns within and outside the oil industry.[1] Yet his identified wealth and power, one assumes, are only the tip of the iceberg. His case illustrates the difficulty of assessing accurately the economic stature of many such men, who are often scarcely known to the public despite far-reaching power and unmeasured wealth.

After amassing an immense fortune in construction and having it fattened by government contracts during World War II, the Browns invested in oil-related businesses. After World War II they, and others, bought the Big and Little Inch pipelines—built during the war to transport Texas oil to the East Coast—from the U.S. government to form Texas Eastern Transmission Corporation. Thus they were Big Rich but not, in the beginning, primarily oilmen. Many oilmen branch out into other businesses after achieving success with oil. The Browns did the opposite; their fortune was established before they branched out into oil and gas enterprises. Yet for the investigator their case poses the same problem: How does one know when oil money is still oil money?

2

Oklahoma-born Jake L. Hamon of Dallas is now an "old" Texan by virtue of his having resided in the state for about forty years. Usually overlooked in the published rankings of the Big Rich, Hamon has spent more than half a century in the oil business and is one of the most successful independent operators.

His father was a power in Republican politics in Oklahoma. By 1920 his influence was felt throughout the Southwest. In 1920 Hamon, Sr., provided the crucial switch of delegates that led to Senator Warren G. Harding's nomination. During the campaign that followed, according to a Harding biographer, he arranged "the most tumultuous demonstration Harding was to find on his tour." [2] By the time of his death shortly after the election, Hamon, Sr., had become so overextended in building a railroad through Ranger and Breckenridge in West Texas that when the economy changed, he lost it all. His son explained, "He borrowed so much money to build the railroad; then oil dropped in price from three dollars and fifty cents to a dollar, and it just broke him. So I didn't inherit any money, unfortunately."

He did, however, inherit friendships through his father, a cherished asset in a world where information and contacts are so valuable. He knew some of the leading oilmen of the time. When his father died, young Hamon was a sophomore at the University of Chicago, studying geology. At eighteen he had to drop out and go to work. In order to transact business for himself, he went to court in Oklahoma and had his minor's restrictions removed. He began in the oil fields as a "nipple chaser"—carrying out the orders of the tool pusher—and then graduated to tool pusher. Later he gained a working interest in a drilling company, which he sold when he left for Ranger to buy old wells. When he had enough money to drill on his own, he returned to Oklahoma, where he brought in a wildcat north of Chickasha. But by the early 1930's, when he went to East Texas, he was nearly broke because of the Depression. Within a short time he had remedied that by drilling productive wells in the East Texas field, and by increments he grew to his present comfortable position.

In 1975 Hamon was still going strong—drilling and producing in eight states. He seems to have won every award that is given in the oil industry. His list of directorships, honors, and various offices fill a respectable space in *Who's Who in America*. A fast reader with an incisive mind, Hamon's well-stocked office library of histories, biographies, and business volumes related to oil complement the novels, histories, biographies, classics, and detective stories in his home library.

"I once wrote a profile on Jake in which I called him probably the most intellectual man in the oil business," said Jay Hall, a long-time observer of oilmen. "Yet he is a hardheaded businessman, and he watches the buck like he didn't have any." Les True, who has known both Hamon *père* and *fils,* said, "Jake's a gentleman" and "sharp as a tack." He recalled the time Hamon repaid a loan by personally taking the money each month to his creditor, instead of mailing it, just to show his appreciation.

Probably Hamon's most notable quality is what Jay Hall describes as a feeling for the other side. Though he refuses to comment on the matter, Hamon has reportedly sponsored several Jewish oilmen for membership in the Dallas Petroleum Club—unsuccessfully—and is dedicated to the principle of equal economic opportunity for minorities. Hall remembered when blacks were picketing a café across from Hamon's offices. Other businessmen suggested that a counterpicket be set up. "And Jake thought that was a little bit horrifying," said Hall. "He didn't particularly get upset about it, but I mean, he didn't think that was quite fair, and his remark was, 'Well, if we send those colored people over there to fight, then they do have some rights and we ought to recognize them.' Now that was kind of the way he put it, and I suspect that's when he began to get his consciousness about these things, because I don't remember back in the years, way back, about Jake being a great patron of the underdog." [3]

3

In Houston two of the most publicized Big Rich figures of the past few decades have been John W. Mecom and R. E. "Bob"

Smith, both native Texans. Smith is now dead. Mecom, in his sixties, is still flourishing.

John Whitfield Mecom has been on top, has known what it is to decline, and is now reasserting his claims to the upper rungs. With interests in the Middle East and South America he was once classified by *Time* as "Texas' third biggest independent oil producer (after H. L. Hunt and J. Paul Getty)."[4] Getty, of course, was a non-Texan. Mecom has come a long way from the college dropout who started out with $700 borrowed from his father. Within two years he had $100,000, and he kept expanding. About hunting oil, he once said, "There's no thrill like it. Every time you hit, it's like making a touchdown." After his early successes Mecom kept oil as his base while diversifying into industry, hotels, and ranching. An only child who likes to run his own show, the restless Mecom owned a controlling interest in the Reed Roller Bit Company, a prime competitor to Hughes Tool. At one time, his assets were estimated at $500 million—an exaggerated figure perhaps, but his centimillionaire status was undoubted. At one point, according to *Fortune* magazine, his holdings were sufficient to pay his debts and taxes and still leave more than $100 million cash.

"John gambles like a pro," a fellow oilman said. "He takes a long, careful look at the odds, but once he's made his play, he'll back it until your eyes bug out."

One of Mecom's biggest deals was a package plan that didn't come off. He was negotiating with Houston Endowment to take over the Houston *Chronicle,* the Rice Hotel, a controlling interest in the Texas National Bank of Commerce, a garage, and a laundry—a matter of $84 million in all. The deal was off and on during 1966, but finally it fell through owing to Mecom's unwillingness to sell off his oil properties in order to raise cash, along with the foundation's equal unwillingness to accept a smaller down payment. Whatever the reasons, Mecom didn't brood over it unduly. Over the past decade he has kept busy trading and building his properties—and searching for oil.[5]

Another only child, just as independent and one of the richest of the Big Rich, was Robert Everett "Bob" Smith, who died at seventy-nine in 1973. Born in the Northeast Texas blacklands at Greenville, Smith was worth hundreds of millions at his death. As early as 1957 *Fortune* magazine ranked him in the $110 to $200 million category. Several years later a fellow businessman estimated his wealth at $500 million. Smith himself never did say, nor have those who work for his estate said. He did not like to talk about how rich he was.

Smith's father, a railroader, had hunted gold and later had some shallow oil production at Batson on the Gulf Coast—the first such operation which young Bob observed firsthand. After finishing high school in 1911, he roughnecked in the oil fields for a couple of years and then went into clerical work for oil companies—Texas Company, Gulf, Humble, and others. "I figure I was fired from at least five jobs besides the ones I quit," Smith said. "The trouble was I couldn't take orders unless they were properly given." When the United States entered World War I, Smith left his clerical job with Gulf in Tampico and entered the Army. He had played semipro baseball, and now he became an amateur boxer, fighting for several years. After the war he worked for Humble for a while, then took a job selling oil field equipment. Fired from that job after he was a district manager, he promptly found another job in Tonkawa, Oklahoma, where, when he was twenty-seven years old, he actually became an oilman.

It was 1922. A norther had slashed into Oklahoma. Texas oilman Bob Graves shivered under the norther's blast and wished he was home, farther south. "If I could sell my two rigs today, I would do it, just so I could get out of this cold country and go home." Smith heard him and walked up to him to say, "I'd like to buy your rigs, if the price is right." They agreed on $25,000 for the two rigs. Smith did not have any money, but the next morning he presented himself to a local banker. Even though Smith wasn't putting in any of his own money, he convinced the conservative banker it was a good deal. He drilled wells, earned money, and paid off the loan. When he sold his interest in the oil rigs, he was $4,500 ahead.

He headed back to Texas, bought a rig on credit, paid for it, and with his extra money bought royalties and leases. In 1925 he moved to Houston, where he eventually entered a partnership with Claud B. Hamill, son of the Curt Hamill who had helped drill the discovery well at Spindletop. In the East Texas field and elsewhere, Smith and Hamill leased land and drilled wells on their acreage.

Over the years they made a great deal of money. In 1939 Smith bought out Hamill and continued on his own as an oil operator. After World War II he began to buy up Houston real estate.

One who prided himself on his physical conditioning—he lifted weights into his seventies—Smith in his younger days always acquitted himself well with his fists. He told Jake Hamon he had been bested in a fistfight but once. At the Mardi Gras in New Orleans a masked celebrant had "whipped the devil out of him," according to Hamon. Analyzing it later, Smith confided, "I think it was Jack Dempsey, because I learned later that he was there at the Mardi Gras. It's bound to have been Jack Dempsey!"

In later years, as he became wealthier and wealthier, Smith eschewed such roughness and channeled his leisure energies into church and civic activities. His fighting took a different, less physical direction. He was strongly opposed to anti-Semitism and was a supporter of the Latin American community in Texas. He served for six years as chairman of the Texas Good Neighbor Commission in the 1940's, organized to soothe Anglo and Chicano feelings; later it was an agency to further relations between Texas and Mexico. The Mexican government awarded him its highest honor for foreigners, the Order of the Aztec, and in 1954 the National Conference of Christians and Jews named him to receive their Brotherhood Award.

Smith and Roy Hofheinz were responsible for the Houston Astrodome, through a county bond issue. Shortly after the domed stadium opened, the two partners ran into a serious disagreement over its operation. In a buy-or-sell situation, Hofheinz bought out Smith except for a 10 percent interest, which Smith probably retained because he was an inveterate baseball fan. He never missed a game of the Astros when they were in town.

His business acumen was legendary, and until 1968, when he began to slow down because of a neurological disorder similar to Parkinson's disease, he was a dominant force in Houston's business and civic world. "He had the greatest intuition of anybody I've ever known," said Hamill. "He just knew what to do at the right time." For example, Smith was probably the largest individual owner of choice holdings in Harris County, in which Houston is situated. "He told me—twenty years ago—that he was gonna buy land to hedge against inflation, because there was going to be a huge inflation years ahead," said Dooley Dawson, a bank executive in charge of agricultural loans. "Turned out he was right."

Tenacious, hardworking, fast-thinking, Smith went at full throttle. His office attorney, William N. Finnegan, remembers, "He was a person who made quick decisions and was a very good delegator of authority. He could carry on a full day's work in about four hours. . . . He wasn't really bothered with details. He was looking at the results. But he never was a halfway man. If he agreed to do something, he went all the way. He sort of liked to lead the pack." In the words of one friend, "Bob could never have been a Roman Catholic. He couldn't be Pope." [6]

4

In his time Hugh Roy Cullen of Houston was perhaps the biggest of the Big Rich. Cullen was a self-tutored man who used "creekology"—knowledge of the course of rivers and creek beds and other surface clues—to work out underground formations for oil finding.[7] But underneath all his millions, many perceived him as, basically, a workman-turned-entrepreneur. "He was like an old early pioneer that rode across the plains of West Texas in the early, early days," said Tom Kelliher. "He was just that type. A rugged individualist with a deeply lined face—he looked like an oil field hand, and that's what he was!" [8]

Cullen was the oldest of his mother's children by her second husband. He was much younger than his five half siblings, so that his first born status in the second family brought him responsibility at an early age. Born in 1881 on a farm near Dallas, he was young when his parents separated. After the separation Roy and his brother were briefly abducted by their father. As a result, Roy was kept out of school until he was eight to prevent his father from trying to take off with him again. Because of his late start in school, he was only in the fifth grade when he was twelve, and school ended abruptly one day when he refused to let the principal whip him for fighting. He quit, despite everything his mother could say, and took a $3-a-week job in a candy factory.

His was a lonely childhood without playmates. His half brothers were much older than he, his classmates had been younger, and at twelve he was the oldest boy at home and, by the customs of the time, the man of the house. By day he worked sacking candy, and at night he took to his room and studied maps and devoured books—history, Sir Walter Scott's *Waverley* novels, Greek myths, Carlyle, Shakespeare, Dickens, and Blackstone on English common law.

While still very young, he went to work as a cotton buyer, and he later moved to Mangum, Oklahoma, where he continued his cotton business and helped build up his father's farm. One night, when rustlers drove off his horses and mules, his reaction presaged his response to later situations. He buckled on a Colt pistol, borrowed a neighbor's horse, and tracked down his stolen stock. When he found them in a valley, with the thieves absent, he rounded up his animals and took them home.

When he was twenty-two, already established in both Oklahoma and Texas as a cotton buyer, he married Lillie Cranz, from a Texas German community, and took her to frontier Oklahoma. One day he rode in from town and announced to his wife, "I'm going in business for myself. I don't ever expect to work for anyone but myself again."

And that was the way it was. He went to a banker he'd dealt with before and borrowed $50,000 to buy cotton. Within two months his credit was up to a quarter million, and he seemed on his way.

Cullen entered the oil business after the Ranger field opened in 1917, leasing far from the boom, in central Texas. A friend persuaded him to join him in a venture in which Cullen would have his expenses, plus one-fourth of what the leases brought.[9] Characteristically, Cullen read every book on geology he could find in the library.[10]

His heyday was in the 1920's, when he established himself as one of the top oilmen in Texas, with as much money as he could ever want. After scoring at Pierce Junction, he was approached by Jim West, a cattleman and lumberman who wanted to go into the oil business. West had an offer he didn't think Cullen could refuse: He'd put $4 million into the West Production Company, make Cullen president of it with a quarter interest. After thinking it over, Cullen told him, "I'm not interested." West couldn't believe it.

Instead, Cullen proposed a fifty-fifty deal with each putting up $5,000. They flipped a coin to see which one's name would come first, and they were in business as "Cullen and West." The partners' first hit was at Blue Ridge in the Gulf Coast area, near where others had found dry holes. Cullen had drilled Pierce Junction against geological opinion, and at Rabb's Ridge, also in the Gulf Coast region, he again overruled the engineers' report, saying, "I've studied the ground myself and I've got the gravity meter reports. They bear out the 'creekology' of the place. I'm going to drill on top of the ridge." He brought in the field.

The partnership with West broke up in 1932, when Humble offered them $20 million for the field. West wanted to sell. Cullen didn't. He thought it was worth at least $100 million, maybe even twice that. After they had argued it out, Cullen went along. "It's your company as much as mine, and if you want to sell, we'll sell," he said. "But after this deal is closed, we're through as partners. I'm not going to find any more oil fields for you to give away!"

In the 1930's Cullen kept finding oil. He brought in the large Tom O'Connor field, which he shared fifty-fifty with Humble, with 500 million barrels of reserves. While others were struggling through the Depression, Cullen was sitting atop a fortune whose buying power would be difficult to measure today. But he didn't stop. While many others joined breadlines, he built an immense white house in Houston's exclusive River Oaks section. Finished in 1933, the Cullens' dream castle was a huge stone baronial mansion with white columns facing a huge courtyard.[11] That same year a man he was to fight strenuously in the years ahead, Franklin D. Roosevelt, moved into another white house in the nation's capital.

The remainder of Cullen's life was to be devoted largely to conservative politics and philanthropies, mainly in Houston. Probably no other oilman, especially from Texas, has given away as much money directly as did Cullen. Most of it went to hospitals and education, but one small item, amounting to more than $216,000, may have been as close to his heart as any of his gifts. When a biography of him was published in 1954, he sent—through the Texas Medical Center, a beneficiary of his philanthropy—individuals, newspapers, and libraries over the country 108,000 copies.[12]

5

Two of Texas' biggest millionaires came from the same little town. Just a short drive west of what was to become the East Texas field, Athens has been called "the cradle of Texas millionaires." Sid Richardson, five years the elder, and Clint Murchinson, Sr., remained close friends all their lives. They both are dead now, but their fortunes remain.

Murchison, whose family owned the local bank, could have stayed in Athens with an assured future. But he was guided into the oil business by Richardson and made his first oil money near Wichita Falls. By 1925 he had about $5 million, enough to "retire" on. But after his wife died in 1927, he went back into business and entered the East Texas boom in the 1930's. As he grew older and wealthier, he became known for a number of folksy clichés which were representative of his style, such as "I figure a man is worth about twice what he owes." Another one was: "Money is like manure. If you spread it around, it does a lot of good. But if you pile it up in one place, it stinks like hell." [13] A trader from the word go, Murchison became a model of the Texas wheeler-dealer, diversifying beyond oil and gas into insurance, publishing, and transportation, displaying everywhere his golden touch.

Like Richardson, Murchison was a top-rate horse trader of the old East Texas school; he could evaluate properties accurately, he had a fine grasp of economic trends, and people liked him whether they agreed with him or not. "He had a very charming personality," said his elder son, John D. Murchison. "He had the ability to make people like him. He had a good sense of humor. He wrote very humorous letters. He was not formally educated especially well—he never finished college—but he was quite literate." [14]

Murchison's foray into New York publishing came as a result both of his forecasting postwar economic trends and his personal interest in his sons' future. While his sons, John and Clint, Jr., were in college, Clint, Sr., began scouting around for something for them in the publishing business. At first he considered a chain of Texas newspapers, but finding no good buys there, he looked into New

York publishing houses. He bought 40 percent of Henry Holt and Company stock, which later merged to become Holt, Rinehart & Winston.[15]

"He was a good trader," said his son John, "and could anticipate trends. I think the Henry Holt purchase was a perfect example. Here was a little company that was dormant, that was doing very poorly, and he saw that there would be a hell of a lot more college students and high school students in the next twenty years than there had been. Holt was primarily a trade book publisher, and with the new management that he and his group brought in, the emphasis went into textbooks, and that's where the real growth was. But they continued the trade book side for prestige and general business purposes, too.

"He had a good feel about that sort of thing. That's why he went into the insurance business. He saw that it was going to be a growing industry, and it was. And he foresaw the inflation. You know, 'Cash makes a man careless.' 'Money is like manure,' all these clichés. Of course, he always borrowed money, and he worked on leveraged ventures [i.e., using equity as collateral and lots of credit to make a large gain—the "high roller" approach]. He felt that the political realities were that wages would keep increasing, labor unions would press for higher wages, and this would have an inflationary impact. Of course, he was right about that. The trick is to know when to get off the merry-go-round." [16]

The enduring bond between Murchison and his friend Sid Richardson was their love of trading. In fact, the only thing that made Richardson stand out as a boy in Athens was his trading ability. Richardson's first business coup, he told Dallas newspaperman Frank X. Tolbert years later, came when he was sixteen, after he was laid off his $1-a-day job at the cotton compress in Athens. With money he had saved from trading and working, he left to see Louisiana, where he found some "pretty, fat, red calves in high grass." Bright-faced, always smiling or laughing, Richardson beguiled the farmers into taking him for a hapless city slicker with more money than he needed. Soon they found themselves bidding against each other to sell him their calves. He bought several hundred head of calves below the market price, shipped them to Texas, and pocketed three times what he had paid. [17]

Richardson's charm as a conversationalist became a major factor in his success, as it had been in his transactions with the Louisiana farmers. Above all, he delighted in gulling the sophisticated. At a California party he passed himself off to a *Look* magazine writer as Clint Murchison's chauffeur, succeeding—to the embarrassment of the writer—until Murchison laughed and set her straight.[18]

"There's no way you can exaggerate Sid's colorful personality," said Ed Owen, who knew him well. "The only thing is, you must not underrate his intelligence. Sid was born to be a trader. He loved to trade, and he wasn't much interested in anything except trading. That's why he and Clint Murchison were such close friends, because both of them loved to trade."

Like Murchison, Richardson was open about his fondness for credit. "He described very carefully what his concept was," said Owen. "He said, 'We are starting on a long, continued course of inflation, and I'm going to borrow all the money that I can borrow, and I'm never going to pay it back. If I ever pay any of it back, it will be in ten-cent dollars. There's only one way to operate and that is to borrow to the hilt and use it to get things done.'

"I remember one time he was in so damned deep to the Fort Worth National Bank that they were just worried to death. It had reached the point where the Federal Reserve Bank was giving them hell about having Sid's paper. They said, 'Well, we've tried to get him to stay off, but we haven't had any luck.' Sid was one of the most skillful conversationalists I have ever known. The guy really had charm. The bank told the Federal Reserve guy, 'You go talk to him and see what you can do.' So this guy came over with fire in his eyes and went to work on Sid, and he wound up by agreeing that it'd be all right for the bank to extend some more credit to him!"

Richardson's big strike came in the Keystone field, one of the big ones in West Texas. In his early forties, he apparently knew exactly what he had at the outset, and he knew what he was going to do with it, even if his hints to his friends may have been elliptical, as when he was approached by Jay Adams, an executive in Gulf Oil's leasing operations.

"Sid got the damned thing on a farm-out," said Owen. "It had some stinking shallow production, and he drilled the deep wells and got a magnificent field. Gulf wanted to buy it. Sid and Jay Adams were very close friends. Jay'd come over every day and dicker with Sid about buying the leases for the whole property.

"Leigh Taliaferro [general manager for independent Lew H. Wentz, for whom Owen also worked] would sit there with them. This one day Taliaferro was up there in the room and told me about it. And Jay put on his talk again.

"Sid said, 'Godammit, Jay, I've told you a dozen times I'm not going to sell it!'

"Jay said, 'Well, the company authorized me to pay eighty million dollars for it. Sid, that's more money than you'll ever know what to do with!'

"Sid said, 'No, I want to be *big* rich!'

"Jay said, 'That's big rich as *shit!* You wouldn't know what to do with any more money.'

"Sid said, 'Oh, yes. I'd just be like the rest of these rich bastards and have me some foundations.'

"Well, Jay decided right then it was no more use talking to Sid. So he just gave up. Sid never seemed to take anything seriously. But he *always* knew what he was doing. He handled his business extremely well, and after he got going a little bit, he had some *damned* good men working for him." [19]

Two frequent partners in various ventures with Richardson were Murchison and Fort Worth publisher-oilman Amon Carter. Richardson and Murchison lent a helping hand to another native Texan, Robert Young, in his proxy fight for control of the New York Central Railroad in the late 1950's. They bought 800,000 shares of New York Central stock for $20 million, which made the difference for Young and eventually made them a profit. With Carter, Richardson bought the Texas Hotel in Fort Worth and refurbished it into a leading hotel. Carter, a showman and the number one booster of his city, had heard that Dallas real estate magnate Leo Corrigan was planning to buy the hotel, a Fort Worth landmark. Carter didn't want Dallas money in it; he had used the Dallas-Fort Worth rivalry to sharpen his own city's pride, even to the point of carrying his own Fort Worth water over to banquets he attended in Dallas, and he called Richardson to go halves with him in the purchase.

They hired H. H. "Andy" Anderson to run the hotel and to

upgrade its accommodations. Anderson was soon in a position to observe closely the workings of Richardson's mind firsthand. He recalled the time a watchman at a Richardson-owned carbon black plant in the Texas Panhandle had unwittingly tampered with the boom on a crane, causing it to ram into a section of the plant. There was extensive costly damage.

"You mean you didn't fire him?" asked a surprised Anderson later.

"Fire him? Hell, he's not going to do that again!"

How much was Richardson worth? "I was told once—by one of the loan men in the Chase Manhattan Bank in New York, and they should have known—that he was the first billionaire west of the Mississippi," said Anderson. "They used to come down and try to lend him money. They damned sure wanted him to know he could have it if he wanted it, and they'd come by to see him and spend a day or two or three or whatever was necessary to get to see Sid and ask him if there was anything they could do."

Above all, Anderson observed, Richardson had the rare ability to put people at ease—"He knew how to be a human being"—and enjoyed being with people. In fact, it may be said that he craved companionship; he was never seen alone. A billion dollars seems to have been inadequate to the task of inoculating him against the loneliness of bachelorhood.

"He loved to go to a Mexican café or some out-of-the-way place where they had kind of soul food," said Anderson. "And he never would have any money in his pocket. He'd get lonesome, and he'd call me up. He'd want me to come and get him. That meant his chauffeur wasn't there, and he knew that Andy liked him and enjoyed going out and having a quiet dinner in some Mexican café or some rib joint. And he always expected me to pay for it. He knew, of course, that I would charge it to the company. But I never did see any money on him. People would talk to him about money. He would discuss it very freely, but I would never see him handle any. Isn't that funny?" [20]

6

Jim West the younger was a great big old fat fellow, the one they called Silver Dollar West because of his propensity to toss cartwheels around the way John D. Rockefeller used to give away dimes. And he loved painting cars; he would paint anyone's car free—but one had to accept West's choice of colors, which were wilder than most people wanted. He liked good cigars and would buy out all the expensive cigars at a counter. One day someone asked his father, old Jim West, why his son bought expensive cigars like that when he, the father, smoked ten-cent stogies.

"Well," drawled the old man, "young Jim has something that I never had—a wealthy father.[21]

Starting out with an inherited fortune of a few million dollars is very characteristic of many contemporary oilmen; a large number of Texas families have remained in the business and built on what the founding fathers started. Some have branched off into other businesses or pursuits and added greatly to their original fortunes. "Really," said Sherman M. Hunt, himself a second-generation oilman, "it is amazing to me the number of the second generation in the oil business that, by God, have worked like the devil. They aren't just sitting back, doing nothing. Sure, you have got some of them that do—that's all they do, they're just sitting back, taking life easy—but there is a whole bunch of them that really get out with 'em!" Hunt's younger brother, Stuart Hunt, and John Murchison, old Clint's elder boy, used to play together as kids; today the sons of both families are among the hardest-working businessmen to be found in Dallas.

Nephews of H. L. Hunt, Sherman and Stuart Hunt are the sons of the older Sherman Hunt, who was a middle child in the large old family. Now in his late fifties, Sherman Hunt bears the Hunt family resemblance which one sees in pictures of H. L. Hunt—"Uncle June"—or Bunker Hunt. Very popular in the industry, Sherman Hunt has served as president of the Texas Mid-Continent Oil and Gas Association and, therefore, as an industry spokesman. He started out in the East Texas field as a roustabout and roughneck for his uncle's company, later worked as a scout, and then went in for himself when the Tinsley boom came in Mississippi in 1939, buying and trading leases, picking up daywork when necessary. His first oil field work, while he was still in high school, consisted of "swamping" on a truck—that is, unloading a gondola of gravel with a scoop shovel.

The family oil company, the Headwater, was formed in the late 1930's. When the elder Sherman Hunt suffered a heart attack and was not physically able to carry on, the two sons took over. Sherman and Stuart Hunt still operate the company and have a ranch in Montana, one in Texas, and a big farm in the Louisiana delta country, where they grow soybeans and rice. The brothers are in business together on everything.[22]

The educational opportunities open to second-generation oil families have led some of them into other endeavors. Fred LaRue, son of the colorful Ike LaRue, was Attorney General John Mitchell's top assistant during the Nixon administration's Watergate scandals of the 1970's and is one of many who have gone into law. Many oil families have sent their children to private schools in the East. One young scion complained when he returned to Texas after his first term at an eastern school, "I know you wanted me to see other parts of the country, but I never thought you'd send me where I couldn't even understand what they were saying." [23]

Bachelor Sid Richardson had no children to leave his legacy, but his nephew, Perry R. Bass, was his great favorite and took over after his uncle's death. Others who may be considered second-generation oilmen, though indirectly, are sons-in-law of oilmen, who have continued in the business. Corbin Robertson, head of Quintana Petroleum, is the late Hugh Roy Cullen's son-in-law.

One of the small independents, Ralph Spence, was the son of a minister. Spence, who grew up in Presbyterian manses scattered over South Texas, worked his way through a B.B.A. degree at the University of Texas at Austin just as World War II broke out. He married Mary John Grelling, the daughter of Tyler oilman Louis Grelling, and after the war, was about to become a bank examiner for the Federal Reserve Bank when Grelling, who had made his money buying and selling leases in the East Texas field, prevailed on him to learn the oil business instead.

Spence talked it over with Henry Bell, Sr., a banker with vast experience in financing oil deals. "If you don't go into the oil

business, you're dumb," said Bell. "I don't believe you're dumb."
Spence followed this advice and in 1949 went out on his own,
trading leases and drilling wildcat wells. He named one of the fields
he discovered after his wife, whom he had nicknamed Pokey.[24]

7

Next to the Hunts, the best known of Dallas' second generation
are the eastern-educated Murchison brothers, John D. and Clint W.,
Jr., whose offices are on the twenty-third floor of the First National
Bank Building, a few floors down from the Hunts.

The brothers' mother died of yellow jaundice in 1927, when they
were both young. For some time thereafter the boys lived with an
aunt in San Antonio. About 1930 Clint, Sr., bought a few hundred
acres out in what was then the countryside north of Dallas, and the
boys rejoined him. "During all this period of the thirties we saw an
awful lot of the old-timers in the oil business," said John Murchison. "There was always something going on, a poker game or a
bridge game or a party, and my father was very thoughtful about
the kids participating in all this. I mean, we knew all these people,
and they were really characters, too!

"It was a real experience. I can remember Oswald Jacoby coming
out there and playing bridge and poker. I saw him once put on a
demonstration of backgammon, blindfolded. Someone would throw
the dice for him and tell him what the dice were, and he would tell
him what to move. Kept it all right in his head."

John Murchison later attended the Hotchkiss School in Connecticut and from there went to Yale until World War II intervened. As
a combat pilot he flew both the P-39 and later the P-47, with the
Army Air Corps first in North Africa and Italy and toward the end
of the war in India and China. After the war he returned to Yale,
where he had been studying economics, and ended up taking his
degree in political science.

Stocky, aggressive Clint Murchison, Jr., attended the Lawrence-
ville School, and during the war served in the Marine Corps. He
graduated from Duke University as top man in his engineering
class. After the war he earned a master's degree in mathematics at
M.I.T.

After graduation from Yale, John, plagued with an asthmatic condition that had been aggravated in China, headed for the dry climate of Santa Fe and worked in a bank for a couple of years. During the postwar period his father bought, as part owner, the Henry Holt and Company publishing house. Young John became a member of the Holt board. "Gee, it's hard to realize how *small* things were in those days," said Murchison. "I think, hell, the total sales of that company was probably four or five million dollars a year. I went on the board, really, just as a learner. My father's pattern was that he very rarely took a formal position in these companies. He would have a nominee serving as a director, either an associate or a costockholder or employee—somebody whose judgment he trusted. He never attempted to exert very direct control. It was generally a very loose and informal process."

John eventually moved back to Dallas to work for an insurance company his father controlled, where he learned about the stocks and bonds of the business. By the time the elder Murchison died his sons were deeply involved in the business of venture capital.

In 1961 the two Murchison brothers took over the Allegheny Corporation, which included the New York Central Railroad, and the Investors Diversified Services up in Minneapolis, through what *Time* described as the "biggest and bitterest proxy fight in U.S. history." They defeated Woolworth heir and Wall Street titan Allan P. Kirby on his own ground. John Murchison recalls, "We won the proxy fight, we won the battle, and I guess you might say we lost the war, because old man Kirby held thirty-five percent of the stock. We beat him. Even with that thirty-five percent we still beat him, and then we sat there for two or three years at an absolute impasse. I mean, he was a very bitter, vindictive guy. He was in his sixties late sixties, and he, you know—by God, nobody was going to do anything to his company. He thought it was his company. So everything that we would try to accomplish he would block, because he had sufficient stockholdings to sort of exercise a veto power over recapitalization, merger, spinoff, anything of that nature, and so we finally sold out."

At the time they acquired Allegheny, the two brothers had doubled the original stake built by Clint, Sr., to an estimated $150 million, with interest in at least 100 companies. Before the Allegheny shoot-out they owned parts of or directed enterprises worth more than $1 billion. The Allegheny, a vast Manhattan holding company, had assets of about $122 million with controlling interests involving something like $3.4 billion.

Today they operate as Murchison Brothers, individual entrepreneurs in partnership, and are involved in a variety of businessess that include oil, insurance, banking, minerals, real estate, and professional sports. Although John is a co-owner of the Dallas Cowboys, Clint, Jr., does most of the ownership work. They are continuing the family interest in oil.

"We are increasing our activity, have been the last two or three years," said John Murchison. "Percentage wise, I don't know how to characterize it. We're the largest stockholders—I hesitate to say control—in Delhi International, which is in the oil business in Australia and Canada, and we're gonna get active in the U.S. We're also in Kirby Petroleum down in Houston. But you certainly wouldn't put us in the same category as the Hunts or Richardson's outfit or Jake Hamon or any of the big independents. I mean, we're just not in that category."

When he was interviewed in 1975, John Murchison had just returned from Europe, where he had seen the F-16 and the Mirage in the Paris Air Show. He is a director of Ling-Temco-Vought and retains an active interest in aircraft. (LTV is the Dallas aerospace corporation built by James J. Ling into a conglomerate that once controlled billions before Ling's fall as a result of federal antitrust action and debts. Murchison was one of the "new blood" directors who began rebuilding LTV after Ling's ouster.) While in Europe he had gone to Bordeaux, near where the brothers have an interest in a vineyard with Toddie Lee Wynne, Jr., and others. As a director of the Denver-based Hamilton Brothers Petroleum Company, he flew to Britain for ceremonies related to the delivery of oil from the United Kingdom sector of the North Sea Field.

What are John Murchison's goals in the years ahead?

"Well, I think I would like to continue to develop some of these companies we're involved in, Delhi, Kirby—see 'em grow. They're not big companies. I'd like to phase down my own personal activity in business and get my affairs to a point where I didn't have to have any crises that I have to attend to, so I could come and go as I pleased. I'd really say that my aims are rather modest. I want to continue to play an active role in business and civic affairs and have

John D. Rockefeller, Sr.

Pattillo Higgins.
API

James McClurg Guffey.
API

Captain Anthony Lucas.
API

John W. Gates.
API

Walter B. Sharp.
API

Governor James S. Hogg.
University of Texas Archives

Senator Joseph W. Bailey.
University of Texas Archives

Walter Cline.
Mrs. Henry W. Barton, Collection

Joseph S. Cullinan.
API

The Lucas gusher at Spindletop, January 10, 1901. This is the discovery well that heralded the age of liquid fuel and made Texas an oil state.

Texas Mid-Continent Oil & Gas Assn.

Corsicana in 1898. This was the first important refinery in Texas.
Texas Mid-Continent Oil & Gas Assn.

"Boiler Avenue" at Spindletop in 1903.
API

Fannin Street in Sour Lake on the Gulf Coast, 1902.
Texaco, Inc.

Main Street in the oil town of Ranger, Texas, 1919.
Mobil Oil Corp.

The famous Northwest Pool at Burkburnett Field, 1919.
Exxon Corp.

Teamsters at the Breckenridge Field, 1920.
API

Where the gigantic East Texas field began, 1930. C.M. "Dad" Joiner, third from left, shakes hands with his geologist, A.D. "Doc" Lloyd, in front of the Daisy Bradford No. 3, the discovery well.

Texas Mid-Continent Oil & Gas Assn.

Joe Zeppa, near Longview, Texas, in 1934.

Glenn H. McCarthy at Bailey's Prairie, Texas,
in 1940.

Forty years after the Lucas well gushed in at Spindletop, the Hamill Brothers—Al, Curt and Jim—gather in 1941 at dedication of monument at Beaumont, Texas.
Texas Mid-Continent Oil & Gas Assn.

Happy partners after Wise County strike in the 1950s. Left to right: George Mitchell, John A. Jackson, Merlin Christie, Johnny Mitchell, Ellison Miles.
John A. Jackson Collection

W.A. "Monty" Moncrief with Bob Hope in the Scurry County oil field, Texas, 1949.

Oliver W. Killam, the "Kit Carson of Oil" on the rig floor of a wildcat well near Laredo, with oil writer Nancy Heard Toudouze, 1957.

Nancy Heard Toudouze Collection

D. Harold Byrd in Cape Royds, Antarctica, 1963.
M.W. Huntley Official U.S. Navy photograph

J.K. Wadley (foreground) with oilman Leland Fikes at a groundbreaking ceremony in Dallas, Texas.
Texarkana Gazette

Thomas G. Kelliher (far left) at a signing ceremony between Iran and the Tidewater Oil Co. for leases in the Persian Gulf, 1962.

Oilwoman Catherine Terrell Smith with painting of her father, Dr. Truman Terrell.

Oil writer Leroy A. Menzing (left) at Gulf Oil's first offshore drilling test off the Texas Coast in 1947.

Leroy A. Menzing Collection

Jay Hall, oil editor of the *Dallas Morning News* during the 1960s.

Geologist–oilman Michel T. Halbouty (left) with oil writer James A. Clark, 1972.
Gittings

Ralph and Mary John Spence at ceremonies at the University of Texas in 1976 honoring him with a distinguished Alumni Award.

R.E. (Bob) Smith.

J.R. Parten, "that liberal Texas oilman.".
Blackstone—Shelburne, N.Y.

some time for hunting and skiing. I don't want to goof off, but I'm not consumed with ambition. And it's about as simple as that." [25]

8

The decision of how to deal with his father's footsteps was not so simple for another second-generation oilman, George W. Strake, Jr., of Houston.

His father, the elder George Strake, discovered the fabulous Conroe field after geologists had condemned it. In 1932 the Conroe field was the third biggest in the nation, and Strake, Sr., held a third of the acreage. In the depths of the Depression he was among the richest men in the nation. It was a massive heritage that George Strake, Jr., born in 1935, began to grapple with very early in life.

Educated in Catholic schools in Houston, Strake took a degree in economics at Notre Dame, where he served as president of his senior class. After naval service as the executive officer of an LST he entered Harvard Business School and earned an M.B.A.

"Hardest two years of my life," he said of the Harvard days, when he and his wife, Annette, lived in a small apartment and pinched pennies. "I worked so hard—I thought I was going to flunk out of business school. We went out for dinner three times in my first year, I was so petrified. I had been in the Navy two years, floating around on the ocean, and hadn't cracked a book. It was one of the best things I ever did. You can lose everything you have in life, but you know, I'll always have that education.

"Everyone thought I was so tight. Well, the reason I was so tight was I didn't have any money. I had saved two thousand dollars from my Navy salary, which was what got me through business school. And I worked in the summers for Dad, in the oil fields. I was scraping through on nothing. To live with the name and not have any money was an achievement. Because I had made a deal with my dad that I would go to the business school, he would give me a job in the summer, and I would have no obligation to come back to work for him. He paid me three hundred dollars a month.

"At first I thought the challenge would be overcoming the image of being the son of a wealthy person. . . . In fact, every fight I ever had in grade school was over that issue. I don't care whether you were ten feet tall, I'd take a swing at you on that. And I ran for class president at Notre Dame. My dad was on the board at Notre Dame, and I lived in mortal fear that [the students] were gonna find out about it. Two months before I got out of the graduate school, [I finally solved the problem.] 'Look,' [I said to myself] 'it's there, I can't change it, and I might as well capitalize on it. I might as well not apologize for it and move on from here.' "

After receiving his master's at Harvard Business School, he declined other offers and went to work for his father at $500 a month. "The thing that finally tipped me to come back to work for Dad was not the money that was available or that he might leave me someday; it was the reputation he had left me. To my knowledge I had *never* heard anybody say he was dishonest. I am satisfied that he never did anything [about which he] wasn't a thousand percent sure it was absolutely the right thing to do. He got that lodged in his mind; he would buck presidents or bishops or cardinals or whatever. When he gave you his word on anything, it was as good as something in concrete."

Strake, Sr., died in 1969. Today Strake divides his time among the oil business, real estate and stocks, and civic matters. "I always threaten that I'm gonna move to Butte, Montana, and tell everybody I'm not interested in anything civic or charitable," he said, "but if I were there on Monday and if by Friday nobody had asked me to do anything I'd probably go crazy." During the winter of 1974–75 he served a five-month tour as foreman of the Harris County grand jury. He is on about twenty boards in the city.

Memories of his boyhood with a busy father seem to have impressed on him the importance of spending time with his family. He and his wife take a vacation each year with friends, then another with their six children—three boys, three girls, in 1977 ranging in age from three years to 17. He coaches Little League baseball and finds time for hunting. "I love to hunt," he said. "One of the reasons I like hunting ... the best times I remember with Dad were the hunting trips. 'Cause there were no phones, there was no outside competition for his time. I could never forget those.

"My goal is to be a good father and to be the best citizen in the city," he asserted without hesitation. "I think the biggest compliment anybody could give me is for people to say that I'm recognized for what I can accomplish on my own, not because my name happens to be Strake. The worst thing I would want you to think is that, you know, Strake doesn't do anything but spend his time at the country club. I'd rather work as a roughneck in the oil field than do that." [26]

9

The two leading oil cities in Texas are Dallas and Houston. Houston, despite the Middle East's much vaster reserves, is the oil capital of the world—because it is still the technological headquarters. What is the difference between the oilmen of the two cities?

According to Houston oilman Johnny Mitchell, the difference is obvious. "The Dallas oilmen, they're really opera-minded—you follow me? That's the way I classify 'em. And down here one of them wouldn't know how to find an opera house. That's it. It's very simple."

The key to his assessment is the East Texas field, where many of the Dallas oilmen made their fortunes. "They had it made about '35. They had time to do something different. The oilmen here—they're still fighting the same battles. See, when you make it in one big puddle, you've got cash. In East Texas they made it on a ten-thousand-dollar well and a prolific boom. About '35, they were all rich, and they became richer as the price of oil went up. In the forties here, hell, there weren't but a dozen oilmen that would walk the streets. Smith, Hamill, Grubbs—a few people like that." [27]

After the East Texas field came in, both oilmen and newly rich landowners flocked into Dallas. At first the old guard "cotton families," who had long ago made their money from Texas's agricultural products, gave them a cold shoulder, despite their fine houses, clothes, and automobiles. But within a few years the best clubs began to accept them, and finally they, as has been the pattern elsewhere, were an accepted part of the local environment. Then, as Stanley Marcus put it, "the descriptive phrase of 'new oil rich' was changed to the simpler and less patronizing 'oil wealth.' " [28]

The Dallas Petroleum Club started in 1933 with fifty members. After several decades on the first floor of the Adolphus Hotel, it is now at the top of the First National Bank Building, where, among other things, the food is as good as can be found anywhere. Several such clubs followed in Midland, San Antonio, and Houston. The Houston Petroleum Club was organized in 1946 under the aegis of R. E. "Bob" Smith, and its glass-and-chrome quarters opened in 1951.[29] It is now situated in the new Exxon Building.

Dallas, though still growing, was more settled when Houston embarked on a sustained boomlike period after World War II. In 1945 the area in Houston that now holds the sprawling Texas Medical Center was open country, except for the Hermann Hospital, the College Inn, Rice Institute, and Bill Williams' Chicken Shack. "The first job I ever did was to appraise some cattle out where the Shamrock Hotel is now," said banker Dooley Dawson. By 1975 there were 147 banks in Houston.[30]

John Mecom once unwittingly corroborated Johnny Mitchell's analysis by saying of the Houston Symphony, "I don't like their program. I'd rather watch television."[31] During World War II Houston sportswriters came up with what they considered a crackerjack scheme to sell war bonds. Hugh Roy Cullen, president of the symphony society at the time, was persuaded to sponsor a wrestling match to occur while the Houston Symphony Orchestra played. Admission was through the purchase of war bonds. A funeral march provided background music for the main event. At one point a bloodied 230-pound wrestler leaped onstage and began conducting the orchestra. Houston's image as a cultural center was a long time changing, and the smirks must have stretched all the way from Dallas.[32] Today Houston's cultural life, if lacking Dallas' tradition, is nonetheless lively and energetic, one of the few American cities with its own professional opera, ballet, theater, and symphony companies. But in many minds the distinction between established cultivation and boomtown remains.

10

A native oil sheikh who cannot cite the names of several famous persons he has known just hasn't moved around very much at all. Walter Cline might have become mayor of Wichita Falls and a prominent leader in Rotary International if he had never heard of oil, but the chances are that his oil money helped make it possible—

by providing him with the leisure time, if nothing else. Cline once handled the International Rotary convention at Ostend—"and did it to the entire satisfaction, I assume, of Albert, king of the Belgians." In Brussels the king awarded Cline "the same decoration he gave Lindbergh for flying the ocean—the Knight Commander of the Order of Leopold, whatever that is. It is about half as big as a pound sack of coffee. The bank won't loan me a damn cent of money on it, I can tell you that much about it. But it's a nice compliment." He and his wife were also presented at Buckingham Palace.[33]

Knowing one celebrity was a factor in D. Harold Byrd's getting to know a celebrity-to-be. Byrd was visiting in the Dallas Hotel room of his friend pianist José Iturbi when a knock came on the door. Since Iturbi was in the bathroom shaving, Byrd opened the door to a boy with a head of curly light hair who wanted an audition with Iturbi. Byrd invited him in.

At Byrd's request, the boy began playing "Clair de Lune" on Iturbi's piano. Byrd went to the bathroom door.

"José, there's an old man in here playing 'Clair de Lune' better than you do."

"Who is he?" asked Iturbi.

"I don't know—some old man."

Iturbi came out, saw the boy, and laughed. Then he listened carefully. He soon concluded that the boy had great possibilites. The boy's name was Van Cliburn, up from Kilgore, and the meeting was the beginning of a long relationship between Byrd and the Cliburns.[34]

Jake Hamon's stature in the oil industry and the leisure time his wealth provided brought him into contact with Calouste Gulbenkian, the legendary Armenian oilman known as Mr. Five Percent because he owned 5 percent of the vast Middle Eastern concessions. Hamon, between marriages and footloose at the time, had letters of introduction from officials of Standard of New Jersey and Shell. Gulbenkian was a lively eighty years old and residing at the Hotel Aviz in Lisbon.

Because Hamon had presented letters from the major oil companies, the wily old Gulbenkian suspected Hamon wanted to buy him out. This suspicion was confirmed one day when he asked Hamon what his daily production was. Hamon, unaware that

Gulbenkian, like most Europeans, computed prodution in terms of tons, not barrels, gave a figure that staggered the Armenian. Gulbenkian had multiplied Hamon's figure by seven, because there are seven barrels to a ton. Thereafter, Gulbenkian treated Hamon with the deepest respect. ("I was surprised that he was so impressed with my modest production," said Hamon.)[35]

11

One of the most intriguing associations has been that of Texas oil money and Hollywood. As one Los Angeles newspaperman phrased it, "The Texas jillionaires seem to gravitate toward the motion pictures like moths to a candle." Howard Hughes may have been the first one to blaze a trail from Texas to Hollywood. Since then the road has been well traveled in a variety of ways. Jack Wrather, whose family hit in the East Texas field, went into movie production in the 1940's, marrying actress Bonita Granville in the process. After TV came along, he formed Wrather Television Productions and paid a reported $3 million for rights to the *Lone Ranger* radio and TV programs.[36] In recent years Caruth Byrd, son of oilman D. H. Byrd, has produced several movies.

The most enduring symbol of the Texas oil-Hollywood relationship has been Dallas oilman E. E. "Buddy" Fogelson's marriage to red-haired actress Greer Garson—a union which remains intact to this day. Most such marriages have not been so stable, and many have been stormy. There are, for instance, the two marriages of actress-singer Ann Miller—herself Texas-born—to William Moss and Arthur Cameron respectively. According to her memoirs, *Miller's High Life,* Miss Miller's introduction to the oil-rich world came with her marriage to Moss, who had come from Odessa and had previously been married to movie star Jane Withers. The marriage with Moss did not work out. "I simply couldn't keep up the pace with Willie and his wild and wooly Texas millionaire friends and their drinking parties," she said. "Hollywood has always been known for its wild parties, but they're tame compared with these Texas binges that last for days." They married in 1958, and after three years of marriage, they were separated. It was then that Midland-born Arthur Cameron entered her life. He was handsome, youthful-looking and sixty; she was thirty-eight. Smitten by his charm she started dating him while awaiting her divorce. The scenes that followed were like those of a Mack Sennett comedy. Moss had detectives following her; Cameron hired sleuths to tail Moss' operatives. "So every time I left the house," she said, "I would always look back to see if everyone was ready to go before I took off—with two cars full of detectives following me." She decided to marry Cameron, but there was the matter of their divorces' not being final. Cameron asserted they could obtain Mexican divorces and be married there. They held the ceremony in Mexico City.

Life with the unpredictable Cameron, reputed to be worth $100 million in oil and real estate, led her to some of the most fashionable spots of Europe with gifts that included a $125,000 20-karat-blue-white diamond ring. But life with Cameron grew decidedly stickly. She'd been warned about his weakness for pretty women, and she soon realized he had "a whole swarm of sweeties on the string." The marriage was annulled, one day before her divorce from Bill Moss became final.[37]

Some Texas oilmen—and their employees—have seen so many movie stars up close that it is a routine experience. During World War II D. Harold Byrd was entertaining a group of movie stars after a war benefit in Dallas. He had provisions to take care of fifty people at what was then his "country home." Among the stars were Maureen O'Hara, Dinah Shore, Errol Flynn, and Bruce Cabot. Handsome, swashbuckling Flynn wandered back into the kitchen, where a black woman was washing dishes.

"Say, I'm hungry!" Flynn announced.

She kept on washing dishes.

He said, "Well, listen, I'm hungry. Do you know who I am?"

"No, sir."

"I'm Errol Flynn. the movie star."

"So what?" She kept on washing dishes.

Byrd and actor Bruce Cabot happened along at the denouement of the scene. "And if we didn't kid that son of a buck!" Byrd laughed in retelling it thirty years later. "I'll tell you, she took him down—that movie actor stuff didn't mean anything to her."[38]

On occasion the Texas-Hollywood axis has proved profitable to both sides, as it did when W. A. "Monty" Moncrief got together on a deal with Bob Hope and Bing Crosby. For some time when the

Fort Worth oilman played golf with the two stars, they would chide him, "Get us an oil deal. Why don't you get us an oil deal?" Moncrief remembered them the day after he ran into Paul Teas, a Dallas geologist, at the Santa Anita racetrack. Teas had some oil and gas leases in Scurry County in West Texas, where a discovery well had been drilled. The next morning Moncrief agreed to pay for the leases already bought and to enlarge the play by buying additional leases, carrying Teas for an eighth interest. Then he thought of Hope and Crosby. Both were enthusiastic.

By the time they had finished buying more acreage they had invested about $160,000 in the play. Then they drilled their first well—a dry hole which cost more than $80,000.

"Naturally," said Moncrief, "they were a little bit discouraged, and I wasn't jumping up and down myself. You could tell by talking to them over the telephone that they thought this oil business was a cinch. Everything that you touch ought to be productive and come in. They didn't know the hazards of the business.

"Shortly after that we decided to go up to the north end and drill another one of our leases, and it proved to be a good big well. Then we drilled twenty-seven straight producers after that and subsequently sold out along with some other acreage, which some other people had in there, for a little over twenty million dollars. That made Bob and Bing five million dollars each after we got through with the whole business." [39]

Ann Miller, no doubt, would have settled for as pleasant a memory of her relationships with Texas oilmen.

X

OF ETHNICS AND WOMEN

1

From the beginning the oil business was dominated by native white Americans. There were a handful of oilmen with ethnic backgrounds of Irish or German descent, but blacks, except for some in low-status jobs in the early years, were excluded from the oil field labor force entirely. In later years, after the discovery of the East Texas field, a few ethnic Americans began to promote and drill wells themselves. Some of them—Jews, Italians, Lebanese, and Greeks—have forged highly lucrative careers. Even a few women have carved out niches for themselves in the male-dominated world of petroleum.

Anyone possessing the money and information could have drilled or leased his way to a Texas sheikhdom, even in the early years. But these simple requirements were not readily acquired, by either white Anglo-Saxon Protestants or ethnics. Access to both money and reliable information was reserved to those who "fitted in" among the oil fraternity, who had a record of previous successes, or who were known and trusted already. This eliminated most men. "Belonging" and "connections" had different meanings in the oil business from those in the upper-crust social world, but they were just as crucial. And having the right connections was only the first step in amassing an oil fortune.

According to veteran oil watcher James Clark, personality was the essential complement to connections for the prospective oil hunter. "I don't know what to call it except for a sort of sixth sense," he said. "First, you've got to be a gambler. No question about that. Second, you've got to be a promoter. Also, it takes someone who can work day and night. He can't lose his concentration on what he's doing. He's got to be focused on that one thing, and that concentration is absolutely necessary. And he has to be able to take setbacks— constantly. Every day, with things that happen at the well and deals that are being made. He has to be somebody that can take that. Now *that* is what kept me out of it! There are fifty thousand things that can happen every day to a drilling oil well. And they're all bad. The one thing that can happen good is to hit that oil sand. It just takes a special type to do that." [1]

2

Joe Zeppa was the first successful Italo-American oilman in Texas. Being foreign-born, he was a rarity. Ironically, his knowledge of Italian was a factor in his becoming an oilman. He had friends who helped him raise money. Most important, he exhibited a combination of native intelligence and patience required to work out the knottiest problems.

In 1975, a few months before his death at eighty-two, Zeppa looked back on his career in an interview at his Tyler office. Though a little hard of hearing, Zeppa was still working and had been living in Tyler since 1933—the height of the East Texas boom. From time to time he would pause to light a cigarette, as carefully as he chose his words.

In 1906, when he was thirteen, Zeppa left northern Italy to join his older brother in New York. He started school in the fifth grade, learning English as he went along, and he was graduated from the eighth grade two years later.

After he left school, Zeppa recalled, he started looking for work. "My brother was working for a living, and he couldn't afford to send me to high school. So I scanned the papers to find work of one kind or another. Sometimes lasted very long, sometimes didn't. I came across an ad in the paper, the New Englander Beds, and I remember that I worked in that factory. I worked in the oldest library in New York, the New York Society Library, for a while. Then I got a job on Wall Street as an office boy, and I worked there until 1917, and I went to high school at night."

Though not yet a citizen, Zeppa joined the Army when the United States declared war on Germany in April, 1917. Months later he was at the front in France with the First Engineer Corps. After the war he returned to his Wall Street job briefly, until a former captain in his company invited him to lunch. Someone who spoke Italian was needed for a project involved in converting Italian trains to burn Mexican oil and the old commander immediately thought of Zeppa.

He was in Italy for six months, working with that nation's largest bank. But as the lira dropped in value, postwar elections changed the political situation, and strikes disrupted train, telegraph, and postal services. Zeppa returned to New York until the situation improved, and almost simultaneously oil was discovered in El Dorado. The former captain sent Zeppa to Arkansas to oversee some interests he had acquired there. The Italian immigrant found himself in oil country, and his entrée into the oil business was around the corner.

His first employer went bankrupt when the price of oil dropped sharply, and Zeppa accepted an offer from a prominent El Dorado oilman. Later he went to work for a California oil company with properties in Texas. Then the Depression changed everything. Zeppa gained valuable experience as he worked to help the company weather a financial storm, but the firm was going into receivership. He had just married in March and was renting a furnished house when his job caved in. In desperation, he decided to work for himself.

"This was in 1931, the very worst part of the Depression," said Zeppa. "You couldn't get any money any place. Well, I had an old friend by name of Bob Stacey, who was working for United Gas Company, and another chap by name of Sam Dorfman, a second-hand dealer, you know. He bought old pipe and sold it and so forth. And Bob had the idea of getting in the drilling business. Well, we didn't have any money. In fact, I just barely had enough to pay the rent and grocery bills. Bob didn't have anything, though he had a job, and Sam Dorfman was well fixed, because he was in a partnership with Sam Schlar and Sam Gold—the three Sams.

"Bob Stacey said, 'We can get Dr. Falvey.' Falvey was an old friend of ours from El Dorado who had moved to Longview. He had a lease that he wanted developed. He had two or three wells on it and was selling oil, getting paid. Sam Dorfman had a secondhand yard in Longview, and he had a lot of junk, just piles of junk. Draw works [the heavy steel equipment that lowers and raises drill pipe and casing and rotates the drill pipe] and pumps and just everything—you couldn't tell what condition they were in. We bought two drilling rigs from him, for twenty thousand dollars, complete.

"We formed this company without a dime. Bob had a job. Sam Dorfman was well fixed. I was broke, but I borrowed money from a friend. We gave him a note for the twenty thousand dollars, then we borrowed from Dorfman about two or three thousand dollars to put in the bank. He was the only one that had any money. We signed a contract with Falvey, so we had to get pipe for these wells."

Zeppa's friends now proved to be his capital. The friends he had made in Arkansas and Louisiana were the ones he sought out in his time of need. He bought two strings of pipe from a supply company on credit, although the representative told him, "Joe, I'm not supposed to do it. But I'm going to do it, if I have to lose my job. You say you can pay for it in thirty to sixty days?" Zeppa thought he could.

He called his fledgling company the Delta Drilling Company because the triangular Greek letter *D* would designate the three partners in it—Zeppa, Stacey, and Dorfman. Thus, Zeppa, a native of Italy, was in business by virtue of his own talents, friendships he had developed over the years, and the good credit furnished by Sam Dorfman.

After several years of struggle the company began to stabilize. About 1940 Zeppa bought out Stacey, thereby increasing his share of the company to 58 percent. Then, in the mid-fifties Delta took over the properties—and problems—of J. C. Hawkins, an individual operator about to go into receivership. "He had a jillion leases, and royalties, scattered all over God's kingdom," said Zeppa. "He had got in such bad shape that nobody wanted to touch him. It turned out to be a good deal. Within two or three years we had the company worked out of debt."

In 1975 Zeppa characterized his company as moderate-sized drilling contractors with a "fair" amount of production. Delta companies were also operating in Venezuela, Brazil, Argentina, Mexico, and Italy. Delta had six rigs in Italy and were shipping in a new one. In Mexico two barge units were working for Pemex, the government company. But the foreign operations were not without headaches. During their first year in Argentina, Delta lost almost $1 million because of changes in the rate of exchange.

As an Italian immigrant, had Zeppa experienced any animosity or discrimination in East Texas? "I couldn't tell any," he said. "You know, I'm one of these people that never notice these things. I try to behave like I should, most of the time, and it never occurs to me that people might have some animosity against me. I'm sure there are people who do, but they never showed it to me, or indicated it to me, face to face."

Why did he succeed? "I don't know," he said. "I haven't tried to be successful. I've tried to run my business like I would in any other business. Try to be honest, try to run the thing like it ought to be run, try to always have some regard for the other fellow." [2]

3

Beaumont-born Michel T. "Mike" Halbouty is of Lebanese ancestry—"*Ab*solutely!" he says emphatically. The only other Lebanese-American oilman to operate in Texas was the late Bobby Manziel.

Like many another immigrant's son, Halbouty selected education as his pathway to fortune. A 1930 graduate of Texas A&M, he remained another year to earn a master's degree in geology and petroleum engineering. Twenty-five years later, in 1956, he returned to earn the Professional Degree in Geological Engineering, the first one conferred by A&M. He probably is the only oilman in the country to have resumed his formal education so long after graduation.

He has packed so much into his life that the outline of his

personal history runs to twelve single-spaced pages. His list of publications alone is as long as that of a professor who has devoted his life entirely to research and teaching—far from the hurly-burly atmosphere of the oil business. In addition to technical works, he collaborated with Houston writer James A. Clark to write *Spindletop* and *The Last Boom*—both histories of the Texas oil phenomenon. Industry awards have been heaped on him, and he has served as president of the American Association of Petroleum Geologists (AAPG). Along with such side duties, he is president and chairman of the board of the Halbouty Alaska Oil Company (Halasko), the first independent company to discover gas in Alaska.

Halbouty, according to Jim Clark, who grew up with him in Beaumont, was "a brilliant kid" from the beginning and was allowed to skip grades in school. Early in life he knew what he wanted.

"I was a water boy at Spindletop in 1925, during the second boom," said Halbouty. "They paid me twenty-five cents an hour, and I'd go from one rig to the other." But before that his curiosity had shaped his future. "When I was a child, I wondered about how the mountains were formed and why a river was there and why there was ice in one place and no ice in other places. And I went to my favorite teacher and I said, 'Now I'm interested in how these things are formed,' and she said, 'What you ought to do is probably study geology.' And she interpreted what the meaning of geology was. She said, *'Geo,* from the Greek meaning the earth, and *ology,* Greek meaning the science. So it's science of the earth.' I told her, 'That's what I want to do. I want to study the science of the earth.'

"Father was a groceryman," said Halbouty. "We considered ourselves to be very poor people. But my daddy was a *very* hardworking man, and he'd get up in the morning, four o'clock, three o'clock, go buy himself ten dollars', fifteen dollars' worth of vegetables, trying to make a dollar out of 'em."

After college in the early 1930's Halbouty went to work for the Yount-Lee Oil Company in Beaumont as a geologist and petroleum engineer. Less than two years later he was chief geologist and petroleum engineer—a position he occupied until Yount-Lee was sold to Stanolind in 1935. Through the offices of W. E. Lee (the "Lee" of Yount-Lee), Halbouty then joined Glenn McCarthy as his chief geologist and petroleum engineer, vice-president and general manager. A couple of years later Halbouty went on his own as a consultant. By the time he entered the Army as a captain in 1942 he had been responsible for discovering nine new fields and extensions. He was clearly on his way to the big time.

During much of the war he served on the Army-Navy Petroleum Board. At the war's end he was a lieutenant colonel. He returned to the consulting business in Houston and shortly afterward began to drill his own wells with great success.

"One thing that it's very important that you should know about me," he said. "In no time in any of my speeches or public appearances have I ever gotten up and extolled my self-serving features. I have never asked for anything. I have never adopted a self-interest, self-centered attitude—what's good for Mike Halbouty. When one of the senators called me not long ago—I'm not going to mention his name, but it may be obvious to you who he was*—and he wanted to know what I thought of what he was doing about putting in depletion for independents and leaving it out for the majors. Two or three days before he called, I made a speech in Dallas, and I strongly, strongly stated that under no circumstances should the depletion allowance be segregated and that even though it might benefit a lot of independents, I felt like in the long run it would hurt the nation. The independent and the major companies' exploration segment should suffer together or enjoy the consequences together. So this senator heard about my views, and he tried to convince me of what he was trying to do, and I said, 'Look, let me tell you something. You just said that what you are doing is good for me. I don't want anything good for me. You shouldn't be thinking what's good for me! You should be thinking of '—my voice rose to a rasping shout—'*what's good for the people of this country!*' And I said, 'I supported you, but I'm not supporting you anymore.'"

He documents his concern for the country with a case from the mid 1950's when he became involved in a fight over drilling in a Gulf Coast county. "It had a lot of small tracts that weren't any bigger than this room. Yet people were locating and drilling on them. They were damaging the reservoir. So I filed suit against the

* U.S. Senator Lloyd Bentsen (Democrat, Texas) had a depletion plan in the Congress about that time. Halbouty, however, is a Republican. The Republican senator from Texas is John Tower.

Railroad Commission for permitting those wells to be drilled. I lost. So I filed it in the appellate court. I lost. I filed it in the higher appellate court, and I lost. It went into the Supreme Court and I won.

"I lost two million six hundred and fifty thousand dollars by winning that case! I bring that out to you to indicate to you that I'm *not here trying to do something for Mike Halbouty.* All my life [I] have done something for the people of this state, my industry, and the people of this nation. And my speeches will verify it." [3]

It does not detract from Halbouty's successful legal struggle to note that such a public-minded stand is easier for one who can afford the luxury of losing millions to win a point of principle and that altruism was not the foundation of his fortune. Probably few men would have carried the matter so far, with the stakes as they were.

4

Halbouty and Zeppa are contrasts that are often found in the oil business: Zeppa, the quiet, methodical, low-keyed entrepreneur, and Halbouty, the quick-moving, voluble, highly educated, outspoken public figure. An equally striking contrast can be seen, for example, in two Houston brothers with ethnic backgrounds.

One can't tell it by their names, but the Mitchell brothers— Johnny and George—are the sons of Greek immigrants.

For a number of years they worked as a team, with other partners—an often effective operation in an industry that has known a great many brother acts. While they were active as a team, their personalities complemented each other: Johnny Mitchell, the gregarious, fun-loving older brother and promoter; George P. Mitchell, the serious, calculating trader with an eye for the future. Today George Mitchell is president and the major stockholder of Mitchell Energy and Development Corporation, one of the leading petroleum and real estate development operations in Houston.

Their father came from Greece as a twenty-year-old youth.

"He worked on the railroad," said George Mitchell, "and an Irish timekeeper the first payday said, 'What is your name?' and he said, 'Savva Paraskivopoulis.' The timekeeper said, 'Hell, you're Mike

Mitchell from now on. That's it.' That's how we got our name. My mother came to this country, too, as a Greek immigrant, and they were married in 1911 and settled in Galveston.

"She came to Florida, and he noticed her picture in the paper, and he sought her out and found her in Florida and married her. It took three years, trying to find her. It was a Greek paper saying this young immigrant was coming in, and she was a very pretty woman, and he had this picture in his wallet for three years, and he finally found where she was, so he went over there and talked her into marrying him.

"He was really the rebel of the family too—as a twenty-year-old boy he left a mother and four brothers and sisters in Greece and never saw them again. He died here about three years ago at ninety-one, and he had a fascinating life. He never had a day of education in his life. They had no schools in the rugged Peloponnesus, where he came from. He tended sheep and goats in the mountains.

"He corresponded with his family very meagerly because when he came to this country, he not only couldn't read and write English but couldn't read and write Greek either. But he had a good mind on him, so some Greek foreman on the railroad taught him about six months so he could write his mother. Saw this young man crying; he said, 'Why you crying?' He said, 'I'd write my mother, but I don't know how to write.' He had such courage to get over here. But he had to, he had no opportunity in Greece."

Like their father, the Mitchell brothers—now in their sixties—can remember days when they grabbed at the faintest glimmer of opportunity. In the early 1930's Johnny Mitchell worked in the East Texas field as a student engineer for Humble. His career as a wildcatter began in 1936, while he was on vacation in Galveston and ran into some other Greek-Americans who had abandoned a well in Louisiana. They offered him $1,000 cash and stock in their company to work over the old wooden derrick well with its vintage draw works.

Although his boss at Humble warned him, "Johnny, you're gonna starve to death," he quit his job and called himself an oilman. Decades later Mitchell acknowledged that his boss had been right.

"By the time I got back to Louisiana the Greeks had started fighting, because they can't stand prosperity. They started suing each other. And I wound up with one lousy well and a lawsuit—and busted.

"I formed my own little company from that time, and I called it the Katina Oil Company, after my mother, and I went over to Vinton, Louisiana, and I sold stock. I didn't know anything about the security laws, I guess they didn't have them in those days, but I sold stock to every Greek in Texas. I built my wooden derrick. I bought a rig from a company here, used fi' thousand dollars.

"So I made that first well. The Greeks heard about it. There was a solid traffic line from Orange, Texas, to Vinton— just ten miles apart—of just Greeks who'd come to look at the well. So I drillt the second well, and it was dry; then I was busted again."

His bad luck was solid for the next several years. First his crew sued him for their wages. Later his rig went on sale at a sheriff's auction on the courthouse steps. Mitchell rushed to Houston, raised enough money to buy back the rig, pay his men, and resume drilling with the same crew.

"And my luck was always bad. I don't think I made a well from 1937 to 1942. I tried everything. I went to Galveston and got my Greek preacher. He blessed all four corners of my derrick before I started. I figured that if I had a little 'church' with me, I might make a well, you understand. I put the derrick in and made a dry hole there, too."

He had no car, ate on credit, bounced hot checks "all over Vinton," and wore a wrinkled $15 suit until World War II. In the process he drilled fifteen wells—all dry. When the war came, he went into the Army as a reserve officer. He stacked his drill pipe and left his rig in Vinton while he served in Patton's Third Army in Europe for three years.

"All I could dream about was my little rig," he said. "To get back to Texas and my rig—all I could think about, see. I got back, and the first thing I did, I borrowed a car and I drove to Vinton, to look at my rig. That rig was a mass of rust! I had to be the sickest man you ever saw. I'd dreamed about it for almost forty months, and I'd dreamed about the wells I was gonna drill, the things I'd missed. I had it in my mind here.

"I came back and found a different world. The oil business was a promoter's world then. It wasn't the time to go into the field with my fi'-barrel well. I mean, it was a new ball game, in '46. You have to raise money, you got to drill wells with capital. So I remained in Galveston about two years and formed my first syndicate. I called it the Big Nine after the nine Jewish people in it, nine successful Jewish people."

After the war there was little room in Texas for small-time oil hunters. Huge amounts of capital were essential to finance drilling, although, fortunately, in addition to the Big Nine, Johnny Mitchell had a friend in Galveston with plenty of capital, unorthodox capital. Johnny recalls, "I had Mr. Sam Maceo, who owned the gambling area of Galveston. He'd turned oil-minded. So he invested with us."

Sam Maceo, who operated the Balinese Room on Galveston Island, was a suave Italian-American who began his career in a barbershop; he had cut the little boy Johnny Mitchell's hair. A reputed Mafioso in later years, Maceo was the gambling kingpin in wide-open Galveston during the war years and afterward, and the Balinese Room was the showplace that brought in both glittering entertainers and big spenders. Although the Balinese Room had facilities in the back for customers with a yen for games of chance, the big gambling that Maceo controlled was elsewhere, in the horse race parlor downtown and a bookie operation.

Maceo was a master of public relations. According to William Kugle, an attorney who represented the district in the Texas legislature in the early 1950's (and, as a reformer, lost his reelection bid), the popular Maceo made generous contributions to "every church, Catholic and Protestant, in the county" and after Maceo's death even many citizens fighting the gambling interests were opposed to closing the famed Balinese Room. Finally, in 1956, a special task force from the Texas attorney general's office shut down Galveston's gambling activities, reported to be a $5-million-a-year operation. By then Maceo had been dead several years.

Johnny Mitchell noted that Maceo's backing—like that of other investors with more conventional backgrounds—was limited to financial involvement in the drilling enterprises.

"He was always kind to me," said Johnny. "Right before the war Sam bought stock in my little oil company, and he became an oilman, and that's all he would talk about. Right after the war he'd made lots of money and would take part of everything I drilled here in Houston.

"Sam could be classified as a member of the gambling society, which he was, you understand. But he was a high-classed gentleman. I'll tell you one thing: He was the nicest partner I ever had. He'd come out in a station wagon with his spaghetti machine and cook spaghetti and sweat out every well. He had a special station wagon with a stove in it. If Sam had lived, he would have been a hell of a good oilman. Everybody loved him. People who knew him were crazy about him.

"Before Las Vegas, he was it. Sophie Tucker, all of them played the Balinese Room. I guess Sam was welcome in every house in America—except Galveston. His own hometown. Sam tried to get in that fifteen-cent country club, and they wouldn't let him in, and it almost broke his heart. He did more for Galveston than anybody I ever knew. But that's the kind of town Galveston is. It's a two-class town, all poor and a half dozen snobs. They're still wearing high button shoes down there. The old-timers, they never had a bit of fun; they never been nowhere; they ain't going nowhere."

Today the Mitchell brothers own Pelican Island, a subdivision, and a country club in Galveston, all symbolic of power and status in a city where they suffered as the offspring of poor immigrant parents.

Johnny Mitchell's luck changed after the war, when he teamed up with others who were specialists or had contacts and equipment. A key man was H. Merlyn Christie, whom Mitchell had known from his high school days, when Mitchell worked as a lifeguard and Christie visited Galveston's beach. Christie became a successful broker for Bob Smith and knew the people who had money. Another partner, Roxie Wright, had drilling rigs. George Mitchell handled the geology. Under the banner of CM&M—Christie, Mitchell, and Mitchell—they formed a syndicate, and money began to pour in. Through Christie's contacts they acquired heiress Barbara Hutton as a partner and obtained money from the Singer Sewing Machine fortune. Bob Smith often provided necessary capital. In the 1950's a big turning point was the Wise County gas field in North Texas, which turned out to be hugely successful. Gradually the Mitchells bought out the other investors, and eventually George assumed the dominant economic and administrative position in what became Mitchell Energy.

"Georgie wanted to have a bigger part than me because he

wanted to work harder," said Johnny Mitchell. "And I didn't care." He indicated he had enough to keep him content. One of his flashy symbols of success today is a large house on five acres in Houston's Memorial area— "a Taj Mahal," one person called it. Displaying a photograph of a portion of its columned grandeur, he said, "I guess you'd call it Grecian—it was designed by a couple of Greek boys."

Mitchell clearly thinks that members of other minority groups helped him achieve the comfort which he enjoys today. Aside from Sam Maceo, the Italian, he cites the pivotal contribution of Jewish backers, not only to his career, but also to the success of other oilmen.

"Every supply house that was secondhand was the oilman's best friend," he said. "And they were all Jewish-owned. And every oilman, as hungry as we were, we'd go see Mr. Rauch, Morris Rauch, who helped me like a father. And I'd walk in there, and I'd say, 'Mr. Rauch, I need a hundred dollars to get back to Louisiana,' or 'I want a hundred foot of surface casing.' It wasn't only me; it was every oilman who ever operated that'd go to a Jewish supplier and never got turned down. You see, this is what made them—if there was any prejudice, they overcame it. They made more money. You know, in those days it meant a lot because you were busted. Busted, see. They took chances. I mean, Mr. Rauch could have furnished George Strake the pipe for Conroe, could have owned part of Conroe, but he just give it to him on credit. He could have swapped pipe for acreage. This happened all the time, and the oilman never forgets it."

Johnny Mitchell misses the up-and-down life of the old days. The industry has changed in almost every way. Yet, as he sees it, his brother is equipped for this new era. "When you gamble with nature, really, it's like a love affair. The way I look at it. It's not anymore. The relation between oilmen and oilmen is not what it used to be. It's a cold business; it's all business.

"George has been very successful. He's a hell of an oilman. He envisions the future. He doesn't scare. He's a new type of breed we didn't have in the old days, see. What he likes, he gets. He's an optimist, understand. And he dudn't have any fun, you see. I've had more fun in five years than George's had in ten, see."

Less outspoken than his brother, George Mitchell is circumspect in describing how it was to grow up in a poor immigrant's family in

Galveston. "There was prejudice against the Greek-American of poor parents. We didn't associate much with what you call the upper class. I would say this: It made us strive harder. Being poor with any other heritage might have been the same."

At Texas A&M he helped support himself with part-time work and summer jobs. In the late 1930's room, board, and laundry cost $450 a year at A&M. He was graduated in 1940 with a degree in petroleum engineering, at the head of the engineering class, and went to work for Amoco in southern Louisiana until he was called up as a reserve officer during the mobilization a few months before Pearl Harbor. He served for four years in the Army Corps of Engineers in the Houston-Galveston area, gaining a great deal of management experience that would prove helpful later on.

At the war's end he lined up six modest accounts and became a consulting geologist/petroleum engineer. When CM&M was formed with his brother and Christie, George Mitchell provided the geological surveys for the firm. In the 1950's, after the Wise County field began to produce, George Mitchell began buying out his partners. When the dust settled, he owned almost 80 percent of the company. Although oil and gas still account for two-thirds of his company's activity, he has expanded into real estate; since 1964 he has acquired thousands of acres in the Houston area. Mitchell Energy, which earned $12.5 million in 1974, went public in the early 1970's and is listed on the American Stock Exchange.

Mitchell is currently engrossed in his real estate operations. The Woodlands, a suburban development project planned for 150,000 residents, has been financed with the assistance of the Housing and Urban Development Department which has given a $50 million guarantee on bonds. Mitchell believes that The Woodlands will ultimately be worth $3 billion. There will be 47,000 residential dwelling units.

In emphasizing this real estate project, Mitchell differs from the vast majority of his fellow oilmen. He has no doubts that the nation's energy crisis will be solved within fifteen years, but he expresses deeper concerns about the urbanization crisis. His new town, he believes, will be a microcosm of what can be done to counter the devastating results of white flight from the central city. His economic interests have obviously guided him into this area of concern, but he has been influenced by "limited growth" experts, including Buckminster Fuller and Dennis Meadows et al., the latter of whose Club of Rome report, *The Limits to Growth,* provided a chilling elaboration of the consequences of continued growth.

Mitchell helped set up ten-year studies to identify the specific problems of the limits to growth. Held at The Woodlands near Houston, the sessions are cosponsored by the University of Houston, Dennis Meadows, and the Club of Rome.

"After I read Meadows' book, I decided we had to do something, so I got hold of the University of Houston. I convinced them that if [the university became directly involved], I would get the Club of Rome and Meadows to join. Meadows was very enthused about it. . . . And after ten years of study we'll have a handle on the problems so that the world can . . . do something about [them]. And in the next fifty years maybe we can come to grips with it and see what should be done."

George Mitchell laments nearsighted thinking. "I find that nine thousand nine hundred and ninety-nine out of ten thousand of my counterparts do not get concerned. They don't know what I'm talking about. . . . So I guess my ten-year exposure to Buckminster Fuller got my thinking reoriented to the problems of the finite world and resource recycling. Then *The Limits to Growth* is really a monumental work. Although the data bank used in the Club of Rome study probably is very off, I think that the concept of the interdependency of everything is so important that we *must* start working on this. This is what we *have* to do, if we're going to come to grips with problems. . . . If Meadows stays with me and the Club of Rome stays with us and the University of Houston—if we do have the opportunity, we'll put up the funds for it—I think we'll make a contribution to understanding.

"The limits to growth have a very deep concern to me. Now, I have ten children [ranging in ages from the mid-teens to the mid-thirties]. I'm glad we had them before all this talk about population explosion. But we're very fortunate, and they're very wonderful. I would agree on it [limiting populations] with our new families and our children. I'll bet that we had more children than all ten of 'em will, put together. And I think I'll win." [4]

5

Although Jewish capital has been instrumental in drilling a great many wells, Jewish wildcatters are relatively rare. But bearded M. B. "Bill" Rudman of Dallas, who is the son of an immigrant Jewish tailor and is as colorful as any old-timer, learned about oil in the flamboyant boomtown atmosphere of the fields. What has motivated him?

"Well, I wanted recognition, and I feel I was considerably handicapped because I was a Jew. It's a Christian business, and very few Jews have succeeded in the business. It's made me realize I had to have more integrity. My word had to be my bond. I had to be *fair* in my dealings—a little better. Try a little harder. I had it come back to me a couple of times, when I'd make a strike: 'Why did that have to happen to a Jew? Why didn't it happen to somebody else?' "

Born in Bonham, Texas, in 1909, Mayer Billy Rudman moved with his family to Drumright, Oklahoma, an oil boomtown, before he started to school. His father, a clothier, went into the machine shop business and followed the booms as a supplier. Young Bill grew up in oil towns in Oklahoma. Invariably he was the only Jewish boy in school. A sickly youngster, he once suffered from tuberculosis and had double pneumonia twice. Other boys picked on him. As he grew, though, Bill Rudman learned how to fight, and more important, he learned how to fit in.

"I was a DeMolay as a young man, and my dad was a Mason, and the two guys who were big shots in the Ku Klux Klan were Masons. Without knowing it, I went to them, and they endorsed my application. They liked me, see. It was just one of those things. I was a 'nice guy.' And they'd seen me fight a guy in front of about six thousand people one time. He'd jumped on me at a football game."

After high school he tried college, stayed one year at Oklahoma University, and dropped out. "I was bored with formal education," he said. "Really bored." When he was about twenty-one, his father moved to East Texas after the discovery there. Soon afterward, despite his father's anemic interest, young Bill Rudman started promoting wells.

"My father and I didn't get along. He told a man one time, 'All he does is, he changes clothes twice a day, he goes to the gymnasium and works out—YMCA—and combs his hair all the time.' But he taught me a lot. He was a great man. Born in Russia, came to this country when he was sixteen, learned English on his own, and wrote. He could dictate a contract by the time he was thirty years old as good as a lawyer. I've seen him many times tell an attorney how to write a contract. Self-educated. Came through Galveston. That's where his ship landed.

"My mother is Jewish, she was born in St. Louis, and a brilliant woman, absolutely brilliant. Great intuition, very deep, philosophical. Great heart, just great. She gave me strength."

He moved to Dallas in 1942, when a Tyler bank would not let him have $40,000 that he believed would have made him a million. "I just couldn't make the loan," he said. "I decided it was time to leave." He participated in the drilling of twenty-nine dry holes before the tide started turning in his favor.

"Being just a little jerk in the business," he said, "I didn't have access to very good information, and this is a scientific business more than anything else. So I'd say the highlight of my life was in 1951. I had an interest in over one hundred seventy-five wells, but I only had five thousand dollars a month income. And in the oil business when you have a family and a lot of traveling expenses and you're trying to drill wells, that's just like being a pauper. But in 1951 I kicked off the Williston Basin, and I sold Amerada ten thousand acres through there. I retained some leases and some overrides. From that I had substantial income. I don't remember changing my life-style. I liked luxuries. I borrowed five thousand dollars to go to Europe when I had all my money in North Dakota then. I was afraid I would never get to go."

Rudman now participates in about fifty wells a year and never goes to the drilling rig. "I have complete confidence in my men. I don't want them around me if I can't delegate the authority. We run a very tight organization. We make decisions quickly, and we act quickly. That's the advantage independents as a whole have over big companies. A lot of people can say no in the big companies, but there are not many people can say yes. I have an operation where a lot of people can say yes.

"And I belong to all petroleum clubs, almost, in the mid-continent of the country and also London and belong in Cuba and Rome, but not in the city of Dallas. . . . I imagine there's a secret committee. There have been some very good Jews that haven't been able to get in. I never tried. I know better. I have been asked to join, and I said, 'You get this man and that man and *that* man to endorse my application, and I'll make one.' I knew they wouldn't. I don't know how anti-Semitic they were. But I imagine I wouldn't be accepted. Might not be because I'm Jewish. You know, I'm very outspoken. I'm controversial, see. Everybody doesn't like me. I don't try to please everybody. I do the best I can, but apparently I *don't* please everybody. A lot of people don't like my loud dress. So I don't know which it would be.

"Did you ever hear that story about the guy walking down the street, waving the knife? A guy said, 'Where you going?' and he said, 'I'm gonna kill every Jew I see.' Other guy said, 'Why?' Said, 'Well, didn't you know they killed Christ?' He said, 'Man, that happened two thousand years ago!' He said, 'I don't give a damn, I just heard it!' But it's amazing that the people who profess to be such good Christians, they worship one Jew and hate all the rest of them. It's unbelievable. And how do you practice Christianity by practicing hate? I don't understand that. Can you imagine being a founder of the All-American Wildcatters and having found as much oil as I have and not belonging to a club in the city that I live in?"

Ironically, one month Rudman made four speeches at the Dallas Petroleum Club, as a guest speaker, although he was not a member.

Despite his religion and his flashy wardrobe, the thing that most of all sets Rudman off from his fellow oilmen is his uncompromising opposition to smoking. Once a three-pack-a-day smoker, he quit when he was twenty-five, and a number of years ago he founded the Anti-Smoking League to educate people on the harmful effects of tobacco and to motivate them to quit. In the 1970's he helped finance antismoking campaigns in Texas that have led to state and local laws prohibiting smoking in specified public places. In Dallas he spoke before the city council and told the cigar-puffing mayor pro tem, "You're the worst offender in this room."

His activism grew out of his frustration at realizing how smokers were contaminating the air of nonsmokers of all ages. "I began to see how people were becoming abusive, and it wasn't that they were just destroying themselves—which I agree they have a right to do—but they *don't* have the right to make you smoke and to kill you. But you realize there are seventy percent of the people that *don't* smoke. The whole idea is to get smokers to realize that they are the *minority*—they are not the majority, and they just can't run rampant over people. I have signs in my house: 'Please Don't Smoke' and 'Thank You for Not Smoking.' And I don't let my wife have parties anymore. I just put an end to it. I'd rather pay the cost of a luncheon somewhere than have my house permeated with smoke."

Although he doesn't require his employees not to smoke ("not any of my business"), no one—employee or visiting millionaire—smokes around him. For those who have not yet got the word he hands a card with a brief request duplicated in English, Japanese, French, Italian, Chinese, and Spanish: "As a personal favor, please refrain from smoking in my presence. The smoke gives me headaches."

Without a doubt Rudman qualifies as being one of the healthiest of oilmen, despite his sickly childhood.

"I work out every day, two or three hours a day, and I don't drink, and I don't smoke. I mean, I drink a *little* bit. I eat proper food, I eat very little meat. Chicken, veal, fish—that sort. Some fish, you see, will live three hundred years. That's where you get long life—from the trace minerals, zinc, potassium. I eat fish ten times a week.

"Give a man all the gold, oil, or wealth in the world," said Rudman, "and unless he is well—in body, mind, and soul—he is truly the poorest of the lot." [5]

6

The oil business, by and large, is a man's world. Although some women occupy positions as oil industry lawyers and geologists—there *are* even a few female speculator-operators—women are noticeably absent from all levels of the business.

Elizabeth Kathryn Martin's Ph.D. dissertation at East Texas State University, "Lexicon of the Texas Oil Fields," documents in detail the maleness of the environment as reflected in the workers'

252 A SAGA OF WEALTH

language. "In the oil field," writes Dr. Martin, "around the drilling rig or the pipeline, women are as scarce as they are on most battlefronts [and] profanity makes its appearance as meaningless epithets and as socially taboo terms to describe equipment. . . . Women around the drilling rig are usually met with frowns. There is no place for them in a situation which requires male strength and durability to perform the difficult tasks. Nor does the worker want any pressures or restrictions placed upon his language by the 'presence of a lady.' " [6] Language of the oil fields, often permeated with sexuality and obscenity, expresses the "dominant male aggressiveness" that is characteristic of the work scene, and it would be surprising if this did not extend to other aspects of the industry as well.

Even in the field of oil writing, women are enormously outnumbered by men. Nancy Heard Toudouze was probably the first female oil editor in the United States—a pioneer in the truest sense. She reported on oil and gas in Corpus Christi and San Antonio for years, a colleague of top men in the field like James A. Clark of Houston, LeRoy A. Menzing of Fort Worth, and Jay Hall of Dallas.

Born into a New Mexico ranching family, Toudouze grew up 100 miles from a doctor. El Paso was the metropolis, and oilmen were thought to be undesirables by the people who influenced her childhood. "My daddy used to say, 'Show me two men from Oklahoma, and I'll show you two oilmen, and I'll show you two sons of bitches,' " said Toudouze. "He really thought they were just nothing! They left your gates open. They drank a lot. We never had seen any people like 'em." In those days a man could get shot for leaving a gate open too many times.

Nancy's first exposure to the boom atmosphere came when her family gradually lost their ranch to hard times in the 1920's and moved to Hobbs, New Mexico, where oil wells were just coming in. The elder Heard went to work as a cattle inspector, and young Nancy went to work on the local newspaper for $6.50 a week. One of her first assignments was an oil story. Despite her reluctance, her career as an oil writer had been launched.[7]

Like Nancy Toudouze, most oilwomen have entered the business through special circumstances. Most women operators and drilling contractors were widows of oilmen, inheriting their husbands' responsibilities. But Catherine Terrell Smith—Mrs. George Thomas

Smith of Fort Worth—was in business before she ever married, and her husband is in another business. Her special circumstance was the untimely death of her brother, who would have handled the family's oil interests had he lived.

Her father, Dr. Truman G. Terrell, devoted his primary attention to the practice of medicine. He pioneered in allergy research, used liver extract to combat anemia, and improved Pasteur's treatment for rabies. While he concentrated on medicine, a business manager ran his other business interests, which eventually included an oil company. The Trumter Petroleum Corporation was named for the doctor: *Trum* for Truman, *ter* for Terrell.

Catherine, who began her college training in the East, had returned to the University of Texas, where she graduated in 1942. Her brother, eighteen months younger, went to the war at about the same time.

"My brother was killed in World War Two. As a result, my father thought I should know something about business. I was the only surviving child. He had a friend who was well acquainted with stocks and bonds, so I spent two years studying stocks and bonds. I worked in the laboratory—Terrell Laboratory—to find out what made it tick. Did various things, so someone in the family would know about the business investments."

Her parents, she said, "didn't know how to spell *'can't.'* " When managerial problems arose with the oil company, her father suggested that she take over.

"I told him I didn't know anything about the oil business," she said. "He said it was time that I learned. I said it would cost him money. He said he'd be willing to pay. That was the beginning of my learning the oil business, which of course I had to do on my own. There was no one to help me. I went to the public library. I thought I would look for *any*thing on oil. I found one book on accounting. And that was all at that stage of the game. So I had to slowly collect textbooks to find out what was going on.

"If the war had not started, I don't know that I would have been in business at all. We don't know these things, of course, but I ended up with a bear by the tail, and I still have that bear by the tail, and I don't know how to let it go. Matter of fact, I sort of enjoy having it around!"

Today Mrs. Smith's base of operation is in the downtown Fort

Worth Club Building. She chooses her words carefully, whether she's talking about business or her personal life. She seems to take her responsibilities as wife, mother, and oilwoman in stride. Her company's field operations are concentrated in the area north of Fort Worth, close to the Oklahoma boundary.

"We drill shallow wells, as shallow as we can find them," she said. "Most of them are under fifteen hundred feet, and a lot of them are less than a thousand feet. We do a lot of secondary recovery, water flooding [injection of water to raise the reservoir pressure in order to produce more oil], so we get a shallow lease and start flooding it. Or sometimes we pick up leases that other companies drilled years ago, and we go back in and water-flood them. I would say we have been successful in our way. We are not a large company. We are a small company. We keep our head above water."

In 1952 oilwoman Catherine Terrell married George Thomas Smith. Now they have a grown daughter and a grown son. How has she been able to run an oil company while raising two children?

"I have very, very good people associated with me," she said. "And they knew that my children were gonna come first. When they were little, I took 'em to school and I took 'em to their birthday parties. I just managed. It doesn't take too long to do those things, really, if you know ahead of time that you're going to do them. But they went to school early in the morning, so by the time I dropped them, why, I came on here. And I ran car pools just like all the other mothers."

Significantly, Catherine Terrell Smith took no lengthy maternity leaves. "Catherine Ann was born on a Sunday, so I just worked through Friday. Truman was born on a Saturday, so I was working Friday when the doctor sent me to the hospital." She chuckled. After the birth of both children she was back to work in about two weeks.

"My husband likes to tell people how backwards he and I have done things. He studied geology in college, and he's in the feed ingredients business. I studied history, and I'm in the oil business. But he and I are good friends, in addition to being husband and wife, so we have a good time together. Very rarely does a day go by that we don't talk to each other several times during the day. I mean, he calls me about as often as I call him. See what's going on in the world.

"We enjoy a lot of things together—business, hobbies. We used to play a lot of golf, and we still hunt together. Whatever comes up. Not pheasants so much, and I don't care for big game. We have done a lot of quail and duck and geese in the Louisiana marshes. It's more fun to go than it is to shoot. . . . Running around out in the bayous and riding marsh buggies and that sort of thing."

Has the oil business been a greater challenge because she is a woman?

"I'm quite sure, indirectly, that it probably has been," she said. "However, I've found that if you do whatever it is that you're doing, and you do it well, you don't have too much trouble. People have been very nice to me; the men that I've met in the banking part of the oil business and the drilling part—they've all been very nice to me. I don't know whether they've treated me differently, but they didn't laugh me out of the picture or anything like that. I find that I wanted to be sure I knew what I was talking about before I would talk to any one of them about drilling a well. Or if I happened to run into my banker, I wanted to be sure I knew what I was talking about. So perhaps I studied a little bit more than a man in my position might have done. Possibly.

"I've never had time to be bored. Life is very exciting." [8]

XI

On the Trail of a Dream

1

Achieving success in the Texas oil fields is one version of the American dream that has attracted thousands from all over the nation and the world. The overwhelming majority of these candidates quit—or died—long before realizing their goals. The handful of individuals who won the long shot represent a heterogeneous mix of backgrounds, personalities, and experiences. A brief examination of a number of randomly chosen cases immediately demonstrates that though the oil success stories all seem to have certain characteristics in common, there is no universal prerequisite for oil wealth.

A large proportion of the oil rich have had some family background in oil and were guided into the business by relatives. John G. "Jack" Pew, the retired vice-president of Sun Oil, was born in Beaumont in 1902, at the height of the Spindletop boom. He comments that the oil business "was born in my veins." Others, like independents Glenn H. McCarthy and Claud B. Hamill, feel the same way. Lesley H. "Les" True saw his first well at Desdemona when he was a boy. He started as a timekeeper and gang laborer when Magnolia was laying an eight-inch pipeline from Corsicana to Beaumont, and forty-six years later he retired as president of the Magnolia Pipeline Company. Carrol M. Bennett, chairman of the board of Texas Pacific Oil Company, was born in the old oil province of West Virginia; his father was a graduate geologist from the University of West Virginia, and young Carrol studied petroleum engineering at the University of Texas.

Many who acquired university degrees in geology had no oil in their backgrounds at all. D. Harold Byrd, whose father was a small-town businessman, was a top amateur wrestler at the University of Texas while earning a degree in geology. George W. Pirtle, a Kentucky farm boy, milked cows and grew tobacco. His uncle taught him the rudiments of astronomy and introduced the boy to geology during visits to nearby caves. Later Pirtle took a master's degree in geology at the University of Kentucky.

For those who had no family heritage in oil, the career choice came at varying ages. Carl E. Reistle, Jr., whose grandparents were wood engravers from Switzerland, moved with his family from Denver to Oklahoma City—in the oil country—while he was in grade school. He took a degree at the University of Oklahoma and worked for the Bureau of Mines as a petroleum engineer until he joined Humble in the 1930's. Eventually he became president and chairman of the board. Frank Phillips, whose huge Oklahoma-based Phillips Petroleum Company was worth $350 million by the time he was in his early sixties, started out in Iowa, selling an antibaldness hair tonic made from rainwater. Eric Schroeder, armed with a journalism degree from the University of Missouri, took his first newspaper job at little Vernon, Texas. He entered the oil business years later when his father-in-law, an inventor of oil field equipment, died; Schroeder was forced to take over the company, and his oil career was under way. J. R. Parten, who passed the Texas bar in 1917, decided to go into the oil drilling business instead of the law after World War I.

George W. Strake, Sr., orphaned by the time he was nine, worked his way through St. Louis University with a major in economics before taking a job with Gulf Oil in Mexico. Algur H. Meadows, son of a Georgia doctor, wandered throughout the South. In the course of his travels, he was a security guard, a traveling salesman, a movie stunt man, a member of the Louisiana bar, and a partner in a loan company. Hugh and Bill Liedtke, whose father was a lawyer for Gulf Oil, opened a law firm in Midland, a boomtown in the Permian Basin of West Texas. After they began successfully trading in oil, they joined George Bush, from Connecticut, and organized the Zapata Petroleum Corporation, which subsequently diversified into offshore drilling. After the Liedtkes and Bush split up, Bush retained the offshore company and eventually entered politics. The Liedtkes ended up with control of Pennzoil, a huge corporation whose headquarters is one of the landmarks of downtown Houston.[1]

2

Turn-of-the-century Chicago newspaper publisher Herman Kohlsaat had nothing to do with oil, but most oilmen would probably whisper a fervent *amen!* to his comment on the occasion of a severe illness. When his wife asked him whom he wanted as pallbearers if he should die, he responded, "Six bankers. They have carried me all my life and it is only fair that they should carry me when I am dead." [2]

Raising money is at the heart of success in the oil business, and the appeasement of creditors at crucial moments has been a major preoccupation of many oilmen. Edward F. Simms, admittedly an eccentric figure, vowed to pay his bills only once a year and assigned one employee to the almost full-time task of insulating him from his more persistent creditors.[3] Few have been so assiduous; most have paid their debts as best they could.

In fact, paying his debts earned South Texas entrepreneur Larry A. McNeil a special inquiry from the Internal Revenue Service. McNeil, who had quit his executive position with Texas Eastern in order to develop a field with some associates, was making $15,000 a year with his new company—and paying $8,400-a-year interest. After he filed his 1961 tax return, an IRS agent called on McNeil to see if there was a decimal point mistake. The agent didn't see how McNeil could make the payments, nor could he understand why a bank would lend him so much money. But McNeil had mortgaged everything he could, and his unlikely gamble proved extremely profitable in the end. Eddie Chiles, president and chairman of the board of The Western Company of North America, a multimillion-dollar Fort Worth firm that started out as an oil well acidizing service, can trace back to an equally shaky beginning. Acidizing refers to the process of introducing acid into the drill flow; it is a safer and cleaner alternative to "shooting" a well with nitroglycerin. In August, 1939, Chiles and a partner were ready for their first job, the Texas Railroad Commission, responding to a flood of oil from the Illinois basin, shut down all the state's oil fields for two weeks, to enable prices to creep back up. The partners had already invested their personal savings and bank loans and "were operating on the very ragged edge of our finances." The two weeks' hiatus, during which they would owe their employees, was a heavy blow. "It was like another Great Depression coming along." The only possessions Chiles hadn't mortgaged were his wife's car and their household furnishings. With these as collateral he borrowed from a small bank in Seagraves, where they were headquartered, and weathered the storm for a happy ending.[4]

There are times when paying off obligations may become the consuming motivation in a decision. Glenn McCarthy brought in a gas well which Humble, with offset acreage, had helped finance with $40,000 in bottom-hole money (paid when the total depth is reached, whatever the results)—quite a lot at the time. McCarthy offered the well, which produced gas and several hundred barrels of oil a day, to Humble's Morgan J. Davis for $100,000. Davis made a counteroffer, but McCarthy wouldn't budge from his original figure. Finally, Davis reluctantly agreed, and Humble paid McCarthy $100,000. At lunch the same day Davis saw a friend who operated an oil field supply company. "Do you know," the man said, "that Glenn McCarthy, as of yesterday, owes us *one hundred thousand dollars?*" Davis laughed as he realized the cause of McCarthy's stubbornness. "As of today," he told the supplier, "he owes you *zero* dollars." [5]

Many oilmen, even the most successful, have slipped deeper into debt before they have climbed out and flourished. When D. Harold Byrd was drilling in East Texas, his long-faced accountant confronted him one day. "Colonel Byrd," he said, "we're spending *too much money*—faster than we can bring it in." "You just tend to the books and I'll run the company," Byrd chastised him, "because I'm gonna make a million-dollar company out of Byrd-Frost." The next year the accountant returned, unhappier than ever. "Well, you've done it. Today we owe one million six hundred and eighty thousand dollars!" [6]

Bankers have loomed large in the life of nearly every oilman, and each one seems to adopt a different attitude toward his creditors. Jake Hamon, restrained, gentlemanly, and more likely to express gratitude, remembered one old-timer whose emotions were memorably negative. "These bankers!" the old wildcatter grumbled to Hamon one day in Tulsa. "I just treat them like prostitutes. I don't speak to them in the street, I just acknowledge them in their places of business." [7]

Dissatisfied with Dallas banking services in the aftermath of the Ranger-Desdemona boom, feisty Tom Dees proclaimed to his partner, Oscar True, "I'm going to Austin and get me a charter and start me a bank. You can't get a check cashed in this town before nine o'clock in the morning!" His new bank, named the Day-Night Bank, opened on Main Street with a large sign proclaiming: "Day-Night Bank, Open from 7 o'clock in the Morning till 9 o'clock at Night." Dees' bank, which maintained the unorthodox hours several years, finally evolved into the Republic National Bank. [8]

Securing bank loans for oil development has always been a crucial matter. Ed Owen recalls, "Texas banks were big enough to finance the local oil producers from the earliest days of the industry." But no bank, in or out of Texas, would finance oil operations before the era of proration. Before those controls were effected, producing properties "were subject to such wide fluctuations in crude oil prices that they did not serve as satisfactory collateral." Producers were forced to obtain credit from supply companies and, sometimes, from banks on a personal basis. "It was the stabilization resulting from controlled production—proration—and establishment of tangible reserves which made native capital plentifully available at the banks." Eastern financing, according to Owen, was never of much use to independent producers. The eastern capital came from investment bankers and stockholders, who were far removed from day-to-day fluctuations in the field and who made their profits underwriting equity issues, largely for integrated companies. [9]

Although some men, such as Hugo Anderson of Chicago, built reputations as oil bankers far from the Texas fields, local bankers began to finance Texans with enthusiasm after the East Texas boom. With the advent of proration, which provided engineering data as proof of a well's anticipated productivity, the bankers accepted the estimated reserves—oil in place—as collateral on loans.

While the East Texas field was gushing handsomely, Henry Bell, Sr., a pioneer oil banker in Tyler, often granted loans from a phone booth in Kilgore. He also kept a long pistol to protect the safe at his home, which he kept well stocked for emergency loans requiring immediate cash.[10]

Fred Florence, the generalissimo at the Republic National, was proud of his motto, "The last thing we say is no." His bank was a favorite among the hustling entrepreneurs. A Jew from a small town who made good in Dallas, a city not especially noted for its casual acceptance of Jews, Florence was described by merchant Stanley Marcus as "a banker of extraordinary ability and perception [who] possessed a calculator type of mind, an ability to read people as well as figures, and a positive approach to all problems." Florence once said to Bill Rudman, "I want your business, and I want you to be part of our bank." Rudman did not change banks, though, and a few years later Florence asked, "How much money do you owe?" Rudman rattled off an enormous figure. Florence picked up the phone and ordered the entire amount to be deposited in Rudman's name. "This is your bank from now on," he said. "Pay that bank off. You can have anything you want over here."

Other oilmen remember Fred Florence with gratitude, Harold Byrd among them.

"I never went to him one time that he didn't go along with me," said Byrd. He confided to friends once, "Old Fred Florence is just as solicitous about my health as he can be. If I get sick, he sends flowers over. And you know, Fred got sick the other day, and I sent him flowers and took 'em to him." Years later, when Byrd repaid Florence and his Republic National Bank, the tab came to $8 million.[11]

Not all bankers were so generous with oilmen. They had seen cavorting oilmen loudly promoting gushers that fizzled overnight. Particularly before proration, some bankers were reluctant to invest in speculative drilling on even the most promising sites. After making the Joiner deal in 1930, H. L. Hunt began looking for a large bank to provide the funding necessary for drilling and transporting oil from his leases. He approached the head of a large bank in Shreveport, Louisiana, presented a well-prepared financial statement to the aristocratic old banker, and asked for a modest $50,000 loan.

To Hunt's surprise, the banker was unimpressed.

"You are broke and your statement shows you are broke," the banker brusquely concluded.

Hunt tried to explain that oil in place was a bankable asset.

"I have seen you oil fellows," the banker said. "You drill a well and it begins to flow. Then you take a trip to Europe and buy one or two automobiles, and when it quits flowing you are broke! I will not lend you $50,000, and I do not wish for you to open an account in this bank."

The stiff-necked Louisiana banker missed out on the biggest opportunity in his life. Hunt next called on Nathan Adams, president of the First National Bank in Dallas, who signed over the money that same afternoon. The millions which both men made during the long years that followed can be traced to Nathan Adams' quick decision on that fateful afternoon in 1930.[12]

3

"I suppose I'm not a hard trader," said Eric Schroeder of Dallas, a newspaperman turned oilman, now in his seventies. "I know I'm not. I was never brought up that way. You get along best in this business if you can pinch the other fellow." [13]

Trading is a way of life in the oil business, and many a good trader has used his skills as a ticket to the multimillionaire class. As Schroeder indicated, the character of a trader seems to develop at an early age. Old-timer John H. Wynne thought that a trader was born to his calling. But an analysis of Wynne's personal experience would suggest that, like a good bird dog, a wily trader must be schooled in his craft from an early age. Wynne once recalled his father's lectures on the subject of shrewd trading. "He said, 'Well, you could start down the road here, and you'd be leading a horse that you paid a hundred dollars for. Somebody would come up and offer you a hundred and fifty dollars for it. You wouldn't know whether to sell your hundred-dollar horse for a hundred and fifty or not. Well, it's just as simple as this. All you have to do is . . . learn to analyze whether you would pay one hundred fifty dollars for the horse or not. If you wouldn't pay one hundred fifty dollars, you're darn sure you ought to sell him.' I never forgot that." [14]

Simply stated, Wynne's rule is a sound tenet for any businessman: Appraise a property for its true value, and buy it for less than one can sell it, sell it for more than one would pay for it. But as Sherman M. Hunt has pointed out, shrewd trading—in oil and other industries—is largely dependent on complex psychological factors. "There is one piece of advice my dad gave my brother Stuart and me, and I think it must be the secret to being a good trader," said Hunt. "He said, 'Don't ever try to make the last penny out of a trade.' Make sure the other man is satisfied with his trade and that he has made a profit, too. Because you want to make another trade. You don't want to be the last man to get a chance at something. You want somebody to come to you first. If you treat them right and they feel that they have made a good deal, then both sides are happy, and that is the sign of a good trade." [15]

The criterion of value in the oil business is not always simply determined, for one is forced to assess the worth of something hidden under the ground. J. K. Hughes, a native Texan, arrived in Mexia soon after the first well was drilled in 1920. According to the legends, Hughes parlayed a meager investment into a royalty that netted him $100,000—enough to form a company and start drilling. While he was drilling a fifty-acre lease, two gushers came in nearby. He declined an immediate offer of $100,000 for the lease. His partners were astounded; after all, the property had cost only $7,500—why hadn't he accepted? Then Hughes revealed that the same fellow had made a second offer of $250,000, which he had also declined. Hughes and his associates agreed to keep the lease, even though offers later soared to $1.5 million. Hughes became one of Texas' richest men. [16]

4

An affinity for hard work and long hours is usually a prerequisite for success in the oil game. Oklahoman Tom Slick, Sr., whose family later moved to Texas, literally died from overwork at the age of forty-six. At his death he was worth more than $35 million, and he admitted long before that he had all the money he would ever need. [17] Most have been more fortunate than Slick. Curt Hamill, one of the drillers at Spindletop, lived to drill a well when he was ninety-five.[18]

The "business" of the oil industry is not exceptionally time-consuming—no more than any other enterprise. But an oilman usually supervises the drilling on several sites concurrently. D. H. Byrd, who once drilled fifty-six straight dry holes, thereby earning the nickname Dry Hole to fit his initials, remembered the hectic pace of his earlier days. "I had a colored chauffeur and a Pierce Arrow and I would keep five wells drilling, and I would drive while he slept and he would drive while I slept, and I covered three hundred and fifty miles a day for several years. I don't know anybody else who ever worked that hard or drove that far." [19] J. K. Wadley, asked why he kept working although he was extremely wealthy, gave an answer that most oilmen probably would have endorsed: "If I don't work, I'd die." [20]

George G. Kirstein, pondering the lives of the successful entrepreneurs, has concluded that hard work and sacrifice are mere external manifestations of inner compulsions. "They spend long hours of focused, narrowly concentrated and unremitting attention on the object of their interest not because hard work is virtuous or is rewarded for its own sake, but because their drive compels this behavior," he wrote.[21] The inner drive, of course, may spring from more than one source: a variety of insecurities, the need for power, status, or recognition, or a striving for perfection or excellence. Johnny Mitchell said, "If you happen to be successful and you own a few million dollars' worth of property, that's all a person needs; you don't have to be the richest man in town," but the truth is that some *do* have a need to be the richest or most successful man in town.

A powerful competitive spirit seems common among oilmen, even in moments of recreation. In his youth, Sherman M. Hunt played golf with J. K. Wadley, who took great pride in his game. Although he was playing in heavy boots that he'd worn to inspect a gold mine, Hunt was leading after nine holes, and he asked to quit. Wadley insisted on continuing to eighteen. Sure enough, he caught up and won. Years later Hunt chuckled. "I guess if I hadn't lost, we would still be playing. He wasn't going to let any darn kid beat him!" [22]

For most of the self-enriched, work is a way of life which becomes more important than the goal to which it is directed. Getting there is more than half the fun, especially for the independent operators. During a casual moment Dr. Joseph E. Pogue, a prominent Chase Manhattan oil economist, asked E. L. DeGolyer to estimate the value of his corporation. DeGolyer, who had left the presidency of Amerada Corporation to become an independent operator, was unprepared for the question "De, what are you worth?"

"Oh, hell, Joe, I don't know," said DeGolyer. "I never think about it."

"Just make a guess."

DeGolyer took an envelope from his coat and began multiplying barrels of oil in the ground times a dollar, plus his gas at a nickel per thousand cubic feet—strictly rule of thumb.

Finally, DeGolyer announced, "Oh, I don't know, Joe. Somewhere between ninety and one hundred million."

"I thought that's about what it was," said Pogue. "Now, do you know what you'd be worth today if on the day that you left Amerada you had done absolutely nothing but keep your Amerada stock and the dividends?"

"No, I never thought of it."

"Ninety-two million," said Pogue, "and I don't want to know what the hell you've been doing the last twenty years!"

"Maybe so, Joe," said DeGolyer, "but think of the fun I've had." 23

5

Under the best of circumstances, the oil business is a game of chance. Before achieving any lasting success, most of the wildcatters had to sit out agonizing periods of uncertainty, waiting to pounce when the golden moment arrived. And once the daring move is made, even the most promising investment can fail miserably. The breaks can go either way.

One tale of unexpected good luck is told by Ed Owen, who was appraising the estate of Lou Wentz, a large independent he'd worked for over the years. When Owen evaluated some West Texas leases at $5 an acre, Wentz's general manager exploded at the high figure. Owen countered that anything in West Texas was worth at least $5. After an argument Owen offered to buy the leases himself at $5 per acre. The manager accepted on the spot.

Today Owen admits that he was taking a tremendous chance. "I suppose he was right, that they weren't worth five dollars," he recalls. "But it just happened that some damned fool drilled a wildcat well offsetting one section of them and opened a new shallow field. I could tell that it wasn't going to do an awful lot of good, so when prices went up, I didn't even wait out my six months for long-term capital gains. I unloaded a good big batch of that stuff immediately. I came out of it very nicely." In Owen's case, contrariness, rather than shrewdness, resulted in an unexpected windfall.[24]

For others the bad breaks have seemed like an endless plague. Ralph Spence watched Morris Coates drill his one hundredth dry hole. Like Dad Joiner, Coates was an old-timer, but his lean years were even leaner than Joiner's worst. With his credibility all but gone, Coates managed to finance a desperation deal to drill one more well.

"I've always thought that the Lord takes care of wildcatters," said oilman Spence, a minister's son who is a prominent Episcopalian layman. "This old boy—they all but gave up on him, but he got his deal across and produced, found Prewitt Ranch field, a real fine field, and he had a part of it. He started making money like he'd never made in all his life. And just in time, because then he had cancer in his eye. His eye was removed, and he was down a long time. I thought it was nice that the Lord had stepped in when that old boy needed Him. If he'd missed that deal—no way for him to pay for it. He had nothing. He had nothing!"[25]

Pete Lake, who had backed H. L. Hunt early in the East Texas field and understood all too well the behavior of the breaks, grew wary of oil promoters in his later years. When offered a "sure thing" by some young wildcatter, he would cheerfully fire back, "Fellow, I'm too old to go broke now."[26] Ralph Spence, who joyfully recounted Morris Coates' eleventh-hour redemption, had firsthand evidence to verify Pete Lake's maxim. Spence leased a block of 1,000 acres at $10 each, right across a road from a Humble drilling site. Humble attempted to buy him out, offering a small, but profitable, payment and an overriding royalty. Spence declined, convinced that his acres would soon make him rich. Humble drilled three producers on its tract, while Spence, who could see them drilling from across the road, sank three dry holes. If his leases had produced, he would have been rich, but somewhere between their boundaries the oil ended. So close, but not near enough, Spence clearly recalls his feelings at the time.

"Sick! Sick! Ill! Just couldn't believe it. I was going to get *in* the oil business, instead of fighting it on the edges. That thousand acres, it would have really set me up, and I would have been young enough to enjoy it." [27]

Even with a successful strike, the oilman's fortunes are still at the mercy of chance; a producing well can become a dry hole overnight. When Arthur Cameron made a drill-stem test of a wildcat west of Fort Worth, the oil spouted over the derrick majestically, just like in the movies. With the flow cut off and pipeline installed, Cameron still faced a lawsuit from a major company which contended that he had acquired his geological data for the well illegally. Hoping to build a favorable climate for his lawsuit, Cameron planned a grandiose celebration. Through the influence of his partner, western movie star Randolph Scott, the world premiere of *Abilene* was held in the area. There was a street dance, featuring the world's champion square dancers; football hero Sammy Baugh, who had a ranch nearby, was to make an appearance. A *Time-Life* writer arrived to record the festive event for posterity. As an excited mob swarmed around, the tap was turned on the well, but not a drop of oil came out. Subsequent test drillings around Cameron's well have resulted in a string of dry holes. Geologists speculate that a "wad" of oil and gas was trapped under Cameron's well and that once the drill-stem test released the "wad," there was nothing left.[28]

There is no rule that works for everyone. The "contrariness" that made money for Ed Owen has proved disastrous for others. Barney Skipper, who made a fortune on the East Texas field, blocked up 2,500 acres around the Hawkins field. He was already worth $3 million when Mobil offered him $5 million for his holdings. But, as he confided to a friend on the day of Mobil's offer, "I've always wanted ten million dollars before I died. I told 'em I'd sell it for seven million."

"Barney," remonstrated his friend, "I can't believe you'd turn it down!"

"I'll get seven," Skipper doggedly replied.

At the time another man was drilling near the edge of Skipper's block. That night he drilled into the formation that should have produced oil—and it was dry. The next morning Skipper's leases weren't worth $1 an acre. When he saw his friend, he laughed.

"Well, at least I had it—in my own mind!" [29]

Finally, many oilmen with shares in reliably productive wells have seen their vast fortunes transformed into massive debts overnight. In order to collect on his investment, an oilman must sell his product. And the oil market is notorious for sudden and unexpected changes. There have been times when barrels in the ground became next to worthless because of overproduction. But the riskiest move of all is when the oilman, using funds from one profitable strike, seeks to discover a new field by drilling wildcat wells, a high-stakes gamble.

Sherman Hunt tells the story of an old man who turned up in his Dallas office one day, with a long cardboard box under his arm. Thirty years before, the old-timer had been an "extremely well-to-do" oilman in East Texas.

"I'm broke, Sherman," he announced. "I'm selling neckties. I don't have a dime."

Hunt said, "I guess I'll have about half a dozen."

"No, I don't want you to buy any. I just want to come around and see everybody I know."

"Well, I want to buy half a dozen anyway," insisted Hunt, and he made the purchase.

After they had visited for a while, the old man said, "You know, everybody has sure been so nice to me, I don't have a regret in this world." He had made his fortune, lost it, and before he could recoup, his time had run out. He accepted his lot as one of the hazards of the business.[30]

6

Oilmen consciously acknowledge that luck and the gambling spirit are as intimately a part of the oil business as derricks and slush pits. "After all," Ed Owen said, "a pound of luck may outweigh a ton of brains." [31] Though some oilmen assert that luck can be enhanced by other factors, they never discount the importance of blind know-how. "The more efficient you are, the more luck you have," as Claud Hamill expressed it. Bill Rudman voiced a similar view when he said, "The better informed you are, and the harder you work, the luckier you get." [32] Sherman Hunt is convinced that luck is *the* essential ingredient. "You can have all of the geology, science known to man, but you're still taking a big risk when you start drilling. We're dealing with something we can't see. And I think everybody in the oil business *is* a gambler. Without exception. I don't care how pious they are. Even J. K. Wadley, who never played a hand of blackjack in his life, was a gambler!" [33]

Probably because most oilmen believe in luck—especially their own—cards and dice have been as much a part of oil field life as drill pipe. In one of the booms that followed Spindletop, Jim Sharp—the hot-tempered brother of Walter B. Sharp—was drinking with some cronies when Howard Hughes, Sr., drove up in a spiffy new automobile. As Hughes entered with duster, goggles, and cap, Sharp asked the bartender for a blank check, then hollered at Hughes at the other end of the bar, "Howard, how much did you pay for that automobile?" "Three thousand dollars," replied Hughes. Sharp wrote the check for that amount to "Cash" and said, "Howard, I'll match you for the automobile and let the bartender pitch the dollar." They flipped. Sharp won the car, dressed up a roughneck in Hughes' driving regalia, and took a joyride.[34]

One instance of a major dispute's being settled by the toss of a coin—a common practice among some oilmen—occurred when M. D. Bryant and Fred Turner were at loggerheads in a lawsuit concerning a tract of West Texas land in the 1940's. One day they had lunch together during the court's noon recess in Austin. As they were returning for the afternoon session, Turner said, "M. D., these damned lawsuits are going to break us."

"Yeah," agreed Bryant, "let's just flip for the thing, and we'll split it. Heads will be the north end, and tails will be on the south end." Well dressed as they were, their rough-and-tumble competitiveness took over, and they sat down on the curb of an Austin street and flipped a coin. Turner won the south end, Bryant the north end, thus settling a six-month legal battle. They returned to the courtroom and announced they had settled the case out of court.[35]

The most publicized coin toss settled a dispute between Clint

Murchison and Toddie Lee Wynne during a trade of oil and insurance properties in the 1950's. The two Lone Star sheikhs were stalemated; their respective "final" offers were $498,000 apart. They flipped a coin, and Wynne won.[36] A less publicized contractual misunderstanding with even higher stakes was settled by Glenn McCarthy and an associate by flipping a nickel. McCarthy won. The difference came to more than $1 million.[37]

Not only among oilmen is coin flipping accepted as a perfectly rational solution to an impasse, for Texas cow traders do the same thing on a much smaller scale, after bargaining down to a $10 or $5 difference. A cow trader, like an oilman, submits to chance's final verdict when nothing else works. Usually neither man loses, and the winner gains. A man is not likely to settle an issue in this manner unless he is already confident about the deal. Take the example of a cow trade. The buyer realizes he could afford to pay $160 for a cow but wants to pay less if he can; the seller can profit by pocketing $150 but thinks he just might get more. On a flip, the winner gains the disputed $10 both are striving for. No one necessarily loses.[38] Coin tossing also provides an additional psychological benefit. A man may feel he is "giving in" if he pays more or accepts less than his last offer. But when he flips, win or lose, fate takes over, freeing both traders from loss of face. The only basic difference between a cow trade and an oil deal is the scale and the complexities of the properties.

Chance figures in the oil business in more ways than in obvious gambles. Even the most distinguished of geologists have recognized the crucial role that luck sometimes plays. Howard Marshall once asked his old friend Everette L. DeGolyer how he had chosen the location for the Potrero del Llano No. 4, a well drilled in Mexico in 1910. That famous well had flowed wild for two months, and oil had run down the river and into the Gulf of Mexico before the well was controlled. After capping, a twenty-one-day test gauged 100,000 to 110,000 barrels per day. By 1934 Potrero de Llano No. 4 had produced 93 million barrels, notwithstanding losses and a 1914 fire. Kansas-born DeGolyer had chosen the drilling site before he completed his undergraduate work at the University of Oklahoma. His reputation was established at a tender age.

"You want the truth?" DeGolyer replied to Marshall's question.

"You know damned well I do," said Marshall.

"Well," said DeGolyer, "Lord Cowdray [Sir Weetman Pearson, of London, the principal owner of the Mexican Eagle Oil Company] had issued orders to the people in Mexico, because the stock was kind of weak, that we'd better start drilling a well somewhere. My boss got hold of me and said, 'Lord Cowdray says we got to start a well somewhere. Where'll we start it?'

"I said, 'I don't know. Let me think about it.' I got in a boat and went up the river, and the first big bend in the river, you know, maybe there was a high place there one time that made the river turn at this point and there might be an anticline [an arch or "hill" in the underground structure] there, so I just went out there and drove a stake. I had no more idea that I was going to run into cavernous limestone than the man in the moon!"

His decision was not entirely unreasonable, of course. The bend in the river did mean that sometime in the river's history there probably had been a high point there. But while an anticline in which oil is trapped is often found in the bend of a river, it does not necessarily mean that one will be. An element of luck was obviously involved.

DeGolyer's discovery made him a favorite of Lord Cowdray's and started him on a fast climb to prosperity. By 1919 he was vice-president and general manager of Amerada Corporation. Ten years later he was president of Amerada, and in 1930 he was named chairman of the board. In 1932, at the age of forty-six, DeGolyer was a multimillionaire, thanks to Amerada, but he left his secure executive job and struck out for Texas.

Howard Marshall wondered about that, and one day he asked, "De, how did you ever come to leave Amerada?"

"Well, Howard," said DeGolyer, "I was sitting in my big office in New York, and I was badly hung over. And I said, 'DeGolyer, if you keep moving these papers from this side of the desk to this side of the desk, and you do it long enough, you'll begin to think it's important!' So I said, 'DeGolyer, if you can make all that money for Amerada, why don't you go out and see if you can make some for DeGolyer?'

"So I resigned, and it took me sixty days to make the resignation stick. And I sold the Amerada stock and I started out with an original stake of about four hundred thousand dollars and went into the exploration business. The first big prospect that I developed, and I did the geophysics myself, I found Old Ocean." Old Ocean is one of the great fields on the Gulf Coast. Jim Abercrombie was involved in it through his association with DeGolyer. Seismographic "shooting," in which sound waves from explosive charges are plotted, was used to detect the geological features of the underground structure. A problem is that the pattern of the sound waves can be misinterpreted so that the structure may seem to "shift," and the deeper the structure is, the greater the chance for error. "I shot it and, hell, the anticline stuck up like a pecker on a honeymoon night! I leased everything but fifteen hundred acres which was in an estate and I couldn't lease it. I tried and I tried and I tried. I knew my shooting could be off. I didn't figure I dared drill that well without that fifteen hundred acres, and the only thing I could do was to buy it in fee simple. And I paid two hundred sixty thousand dollars for it. So that took a big bite out of that four hundred."

He drilled the first well. As he had suspected, the structure did "shift" (i.e., it was not exactly where it was first believed to have been), and every acre of the 1,500 was right on top of the field. That meant he owned it in fee simple: no lease, no royalty, nothing to share with a landowner.

With a twinkle in his eye, he said, "Howard, remember something simple: in the finding of oil, it's good to be good, but *it's better to be lucky!*" [39]

7

Journalist Stewart Alsop, in a study of America's Big Rich, concluded that Mr. Big uses money to make money, works like hell, has a good idea and gambles on it, hires good brains but runs a one-man show, doesn't throw his money around—at least not until he has reached the pinnacle—and shuns highly taxable income as if it were poison.[40] Yet this neatly fitting formula does not come to grips with many of the personal factors which underlie the qualities necessary for success in the oil business: the special instinct for trading, the patience to suffer through setbacks, the knack for grabbing at that golden opportunity, and that almost fanatical fondness for risk taking. These qualities, which are manifested in adults as a flair for business, are usually the result of personality factors developed long before maturity. Patience and confidence, for example, usually imply a fierce independence of spirit which has been common among wildcatters as well as top-ranking corporation executives. Many of the uniquely independent men have been school or college dropouts in earlier years and have evidenced a certain impatience, a reluctance to operate in any social environment which resisted their domination. These men feel uncomfortable when they are not calling the shots; many of them have struggled to "take charge" since childhood.

Many of the men whose lives have been examined in this book have enjoyed a favored place in the family: an only child, the firstborn, the only boy, the first son, or the youngest of the family. The place in the family, of itself, does not ensure special handling by parents or by siblings. But if a pattern of favoritism is established and reinforced, the favored child often internalizes a positive self-image which remains as an intangible asset through the rest of the favored individual's life. Many would agree with Eddie Chiles, the firstborn of four siblings, when he remarks, "Guess I was lucky to draw the first spot." [41] Bob Smith, an only child, always liked to run a one-man show. Of the two billionaires connected in some way to Texas oil—H. L. Hunt and Howard Hughes—Hughes was an only child, and Hunt was the "baby" of a large family, a factor which some psychiatrists relate to the "only child" pattern of development. Because he was the youngest child, his parents, especially his mother, probably spent more time with him during his early childhood than they had with his older siblings. There was no younger baby to come along and dethrone him. In Hunt's case, special attention from parents who valued self-reliance very highly seems to have prepared their son for supersuccess.

These early family experiences and the formative associations which follow during later childhood might provide the social education which is necessary for business success. Many of the oilmen who grew up in an atmosphere of favoritism where self-reliance was a cardinal virtue chafed at the restrictions imposed by formal education. They were self-educated, largely, and learned by experience.

Even though he was a dropout, Hugh Roy Cullen learned all he could about geology by reading every book on the subject available to him. Having dropped out of school, some of the men might have been goaded to "catch up" with those who enjoyed the advantage of higher education. This sense of being "left behind" might also result in the subconscious drive that causes a woman, a Jew, or a black to put out that necessary extra effort.

For many of the older oilmen, dropping out of school was a sign of impatience; their true school was the world of entrepreneurs. By dropping out, they often gained a jump on the ones who remained in school to learn facts that were of little value in the oil business. Referring to the older giants of the industry, Ralph Spence said, "Most of them were men without education. They didn't have a whole lot of education to stand in the way of the possible. Far as they were concerned, everything was possible. They didn't know better, a lot of 'em." [42] Frank Yount, who was responsible for the second boom at Spindletop (two decades after the first had petered out), was one of these. "I don't think he went through the third grade," said Mike Halbouty, "but he knew about natural geology, what it meant, how to drill wells—he was just a genius. The man died when he was fifty-two years old. My God, that's young! If he hadn't died, if he had lived to be seventy-five years old, the Yount-Lee Oil Company would be comparable to one of the big majors today." [43]

Whether they attended school much or not, most successful oilmen seem to share a common striving for perfection. Bob Smith made decisions very fast, had a fantastic memory, and was a perfectionist.[44] Banker Dooley Dawson, who specialized in agricultural property, said of the oilmen, "If they built a fence, it had to be straight, and every post had to be the same height." [45] This tendency to perfectionism is usually accompanied by reliability: The perfectionist attends to details or holds underlings strictly responsible for the details; he insists on careful planning and precise execution of plans.

But these virtues are of little use in a vacuum. Sherman Hunt once described the most important factor in his success: "Being in the right place at the right time." [46] W. A. "Monty" Moncrief called it "being where lightning might strike," and he illustrated his assertion with an event from his life. He was at Meigs Field in Chicago when a friend from Fort Worth arrived from Michigan in a small private plane. The friend told him of new wells in Michigan that were producing 400 to 500 barrels an *hour*. A few days later

Moncrief made an agreement with his friend on some leases—and every acre proved to be productive.[47] He had happened to be in the right place at the right time. Yet it may be more to the point that he knew what to do with the information when he got it.

Carrol Bennett, chairman of the board at Texas Pacific Oil Company, thinks the key to success can be expressed in two words: "Timing and guts!"[48] Ed Owen agrees. He illustrates his point with a story about Morgan Davis, a leading executive for Humble/Exxon.

"Now the reason Morgan Davis got to the top is that he had a very great talent for [making critical, timely decisions]. He could almost always tell where a decision had to be made, and if he had enough information, he made it; if he didn't, he waited until he did have enough.

"One time, while Morgan Davis was president, Humble had been doing some work in the Bahamas and Florida, and Morgan couldn't quite make up his mind what to think about it. One day he asked me to come sit with him in the office. [He] said we'd be interrupted a lot of times, but we could discuss this and see if we could make any sense out of it. As a matter of fact, I spent the day in the office, and I didn't get to talk to him about this thing more than ten or fifteen minutes. That phone was ringing all the time. But to sit there and watch that guy make these decisions, sort out what he could act on immediately from what he should tell someone to do further on—boy, that was really a fascinating performance!"

Davis later put together the merger of all the Standard-linked companies into today's Exxon. Owen quoted Wallace Pratt, Humble's retired distinguished chief geologist, as saying that no one else could have done it.[49]

The ability to make instant decisions is dependent on self-confidence. Each of the successful oilmen enjoyed an abiding faith in his ability to make a correct decision and achieve his individual goal. With some, like J. K. Wadley, strong religious faith was the personal foundation for unshakable self-confidence. A Baptist who attended church twice every Sunday, Wadley was a sharp trader who didn't drink and didn't gamble—except on oil wells. "He had the greatest faith of any man I've ever, ever known," said his friend J. Q. Mahaffey. "He just thought that the Lord did everything and shaped his life and was responsible for his success—all of that."[50]

Considering the millions that Wadley accumulated, it would have been difficult for him not to believe that he was among the chosen.

George W. Strake, Sr., who became one of the nation's most prominent Catholic laymen, was another whose religious faith seemed to be an important factor in his success. "I sincerely believe and try to live the philosophy that all good comes from God." [51] He was once quoted, referring to his Conroe field discovery, "I didn't even know what I was doing, but the Lord did." His son, George W. Strake, Jr., asserts that the remark was often misunderstood. According to the younger Strake, his father had done everything humanly possible to achieve a successful well, but he had left the final outcome in God's hands. " 'Lord,' he said, 'you gotta take it from here.' That oil's either under there or it's not." Strake, Sr., who had used his $20,000 insurance policy as backup in the depths of the Depression, could very well have missed the field, for he had drilled near its edge. As things turned out, he believed in himself enough to have one-third of the productive acreage under lease. Strake was an orphan at nine when his mother died, his father having died seven years earlier, yet those few years of contact with his mother proved to be crucial. "His mother was a very religious person and instilled it in him that when he thought he was right, not to let anything in the world dissuade him," said Strake, Jr. "He was very close to his mother. When he felt he was right, I'll tell you, he was really a bulldozer!" [52]

Strake and others like him seem to be what we might call psychic winners. Whatever the hardships, whatever the barriers, they intended to win, and usually they did. As Ed Owen said, "Pessimists discover very little oil." [53] Les H. True's optimism carried him to the presidency of the Magnolia Pipeline Company. "There were a lot of people who could have done the job I did, as good as or better than I did," he said. "But I always believed I could. I could always make decisions. They weren't all right, but most of them were. I didn't believe there was anything I couldn't do. My mother always told me that I could do anything I wanted to do if I wanted to do it bad enough. If I wanted to do something, she'd say, 'How bad you want to do it? You can do it if you want to bad enough.' She said, 'You can do anything—you can *fly* if you want to bad enough.' I believed that." [54]

As almost any psychiatrist would agree, words like that from one's mother, at an early age, make a permanent impression.

One of Texas' most colorful and most successful wildcatters was a living example of the early-instilled self-confidence to which True referred. Born in 1874, Oliver Winfield Killam based his oil hunting operation in Laredo during the 1920's. He found millions' worth of oil where everybody else knew it wasn't. His mother, he told University of Texas Professor Mody Boatright in the 1950's, was a major influence in his success.

"My mother was a rather outstanding woman with a great deal of ambition for her family and especially for her boys," said Killam. "And many things that she taught us have stuck with me all through life. One of the things that Mother always told us boys was that we could be the kind of men we wanted to be. Whatever we made up our minds to do, we could just do if we wanted to do it bad enough. Well, when I was about sixteen years old, eighteen, about 1890, I began to think of what I wanted to do in life. . . . So along about that time the first crop of millionaires out of New York, the Vanderbilts and Morgans and Gates and some of the steel magnates, were getting a good deal of prominence in the newspapers. Their pictures appeared and there was a write-up every Sunday in the St. Louis *Republic.* I was then living about forty miles north of St. Louis. And after having read those stories, I decided, well, I am going to make a million dollars. And Mother said I could do it and I just started out to do it, believing in Mother's teaching that I just couldn't fail.

"Of course, it didn't work out like I planned it all. . . . But it never occurred to me that I couldn't do it. I just had such explicit faith in Mother that I just thought that there was no question about it."

He started out with a law degree from the University of Missouri, then went into business. In the 1890's he promoted lead and zinc mines in Missouri; at one point he worked in an Arkansas lumberyard for $10 a week. Then he moved on to the Indian Territory, where he borrowed $500 to purchase a small store and lumberyard. After eight years in Oklahoma, during which he served in the legislature, he moved to Texas on the Mexican border and went into the oil business.

"It was a very foolish move to make," he admitted. "I had a wife and three children. I didn't know anything about the oil business, and I could have gotten myself into pretty deep water."

He helped organize the Mirando Oil Company and opened up the rich Schott field. Five years after going to Texas, Magnolia paid Killam $1.175 million in cash for some of his production. And he was still climbing.[55]

Killam carried his self-confidence with him into every venture, however slight. He owned some property near Laredo, including an old building and a lake stocked with bass. Les True recalls an occasion when he visited the old wildcatter.

"I came into Laredo one evening, and he was in the hotel lobby," said True. "He said, 'Hey, check in and come with me. I'm going to have some people for dinner tonight, and I want you to join me. I got to go catch some fish for supper.' So I went out there with him. Got in the boat. I paddled the boat while the old man fished. He had twelve people, counting myself and him. He caught twelve bass, and then we quit and come on in, took them to the kitchen, cleaned 'em, and had 'em for supper that night. Wasn't no question in his mind about catching those fish. He knew he could." [56]

Influences, of course, extend beyond the family. Inspiration for some has come from early reading. When Jake Hamon was growing up, he recalls, "Why, you just figured that you were either going to be President of the United States or you were going to be a millionaire. There was an author in those days—I've always been a great reader—Horatio Alger, and there was another one named [Nat] Henty, not as well known, but they were both similar. They wrote stories for boys. The poor boy always got to be head of the business, and things like that. In those days, why, hell, you just knew you were going to knock the ball over the fence in some department." He read all of the Horatio Alger books, with their rags-to-riches plots. "When you reread one just for curiosity, you wonder why they had such fascination. It's rather juvenile writing, really, and stereotyped, but ... it's odd, when I was a boy, why, a new one would come out, you just had to read it, you know." [57]

Many of the oilmen were influenced by adults, aside from their parents, who made a lasting impression. One learns from others in many ways, a form of education that is intangible and invaluable. John G. "Jack" Pew of Dallas, retired vice-president in charge of production at Sun Oil, got to know most of the oil industry's leading lights during his childhood, when his father, J. Edgar Pew, was in charge of Sun's production. "My father's friends in those days, you know, were rugged individualists," said Pew. "And they'd get mad and leave a meeting and come get me by the hand and tell me what they were mad about. And I learned a lot from presidents of other companies as well as I did from officials of Sun Oil." His father was president of the American Petroleum Institute in 1924 and 1925.[58]

Most oilmen, certainly early in their careers, have known what it is like to absorb the shocks of dry holes and sustain themselves emotionally through streaks of bad luck. The experience of misfortune is likely to influence a person thereafter. "What makes luck is to get to the end of that rope and hang on, isn't it?" said Bill Rudman. "People ask me, 'How do you find so many wells?' I say, 'Because I drill so many dry holes!' That's how I find 'em, that's how most of the guys find them." [59]

But dry holes cost as much to drill as gushers. After a string of losers the money can run out. Then what? "After you've been broke a time or two and faced bankers who want their money when you haven't got it," said Jake Hamon, who has not been confronted with that kind of problem for a long, long time, "why you get a little cagey. You decide, 'I ain't going to do that anymore, I'm just not going to get out on a limb,' or 'I'll just stay closer to shore.' " [60] Of course, the oil hunters who succeeded got cagey, but they never quit.

Once the tide has turned, and a lifetime of wealth seems guaranteed, most of the oil hunters seem to keep right on drilling as if they were still trying to make a start. Sherman Hunt offers one explanation for this puzzling phenomenon. "I think everybody in the oil business, every independent, is always looking to make that big one," said Hunt. "I believe if a man is ninety years old, if he'd made ten of them, he'd still be looking for that next big one. I have tried to analyze it, and I know if I had had all the money in the world, I would try to find another oil field. It is beyond money. There is a fascination to it that's just unbelievable." [61]

Jake Hamon, with offices in Dallas, Houston, Midland, Denver, Amarillo, and Ardmore, Oklahoma, is one of the biggest independent operators in the country. In 1965 he drilled a 21,000-foot well

in West Texas—the world's deepest. His record lasted for three
months. The project, which cost him and his partners $2.8 million
and took more than a year to drill, was still producing as of 1975.
And Hamon, in his seventies, was still going strong. Why?

"I'm independent because I've made enough money," he said,
"but I still want to find that big field! That's my whole ambition.
I've never had a big discovery. That's why I keep staying in the
business. It isn't to make money. It's hard to explain. You just . . .
goddamn, you want to find an East Texas field! You want to find a
Smackover; you want to find a Spindletop. All I've ever found are
small fields." [62]

8

H. L. Hunt spoke of "creating" great wealth. A. H. Meadows
dreamed of "creating" a great art collection in Dallas. In conversa-
tions and in published interviews with oilmen, as well as other
businessmen, the word "creative" keeps popping up. Yet none of
them seems to be creative in the traditional sense of artistic creation.
Why, then, are they so obsessed with the word?

One is inclined to discount a businessman's pretensions to
creativity as the frustrated claims of a person who, instead of
creating something of lasting value, has only *acquired*, usually as a
direct result of having exploited the earth's resources or, sometimes,
his fellowman. A flourishing company is not a book or a sculpture.
An oil well is not a poem or a painting but a metallic welt upon the
face of the earth. There seems nothing creative about it.

To find meaning in a businessman's claims to creativity, one must
seek to fathom the thinking behind the words. The key to this
puzzle lies in the feeling of magic engendered by the discovery of
oil. For some, oil seems to come from nowhere just as a magician
plucks cards and coins from the naked air. To discover an oil sand is
a magical thing; where there was nothing, suddenly there is
something valuable which has been "created" by "magic."

Then there is another explanation for the notion of creativity in
the oil business. One must have ideas and must execute them in
order to find oil, make money, and build a financial empire. The
same qualities are required for artistic production. Intuition may

shape either endeavor, but the outcome depends on the individual's orientation—whether toward acquisition of wealth or artistic communication. Is creativity—or the energy that springs from the creative urge—like electricity, useful for many purposes? A psychiatrist told George G. Kirstein, during his study of the rich, that he was convinced that artistic creation springs from the same source as the driving force which compels the self-enriched, though the objectives vary. "You and I would agree that the artist's goals are higher," he told Kirstein. "But the quality you seek, the drive you discuss, the energy you observe, is of the same nature in the winning politician, the brilliant scientist, the great novelist, and the self-enriched businessman. What it is I don't know any more than I know why some babies are active and others are lethargic. But when the self-enriched describe their own careers as 'creative' in a way they are correct."[63]

Finally, there is the argument that the rich are economically creative. Ralph Spence cited the example of his Pokey field discovery and demonstrated how it, indeed, did create wealth. All the production, of course, was new wealth, which came out of the ground and did not exist as wealth before. Landowners received one-eighth of this. A considerable amount of money was spent around the county in the process of finding and developing the field, thereby enhancing the local economic picture. In addition, Spence's property there went onto the local tax rolls—a new source of income for local government and schools. The discovery made new wealth—created it, perhaps—and distributed it.[64] Spence—and others like him—could be certified as economically creative.

9

Economic creativity, of course, has many pathways. Many, perhaps most, independent oilmen have eventually sold their production and discoveries to major companies. Some have even merged their companies and become a part of a major company, while others would not consider it. Many, though, have held onto what they had, remaining with their own companies.

Personality—matters of identity and ambition, perhaps even quirks—partially explains the directions their behavior has taken, but economic realities have also played an equally crucial role. Sid Richardson and H. L. Hunt held tightly to their hugely rewarding leases once they realized the magnitude of their potential. Both men had goals that stretched far beyond what was visible to others at the time. Power and ambition are probably the major motivations of every man striving for wealth, but a strong sense of personal identity—or need for it—also guides the man who concentrates on growth of his personal business empire. A man running his own company, small or huge, can shape his world. In the analogy of the family, he is the patriarch of his business, the head of the household. When the chips are down, he is, or can be, an autocrat.

The importance of personal identity also helps explain the independence of many oilmen. Glenn McCarthy, turning down a large purchase price from Sinclair, valued his independence more than profit, but his company, bearing his name, also was a symbol he did not care to have submerged in a larger corporate entity.

Frequently an oilman may find it necessary to risk loss of identity in order to grow economically. In a business where high expenditures are almost routinely required, "new" money can become essential to expansion; the alternative often is that of grow or die. The founders of the Humble company, facing this dilemma, resolved it by selling control to Standard Oil of New Jersey. The Texans continued to run the company as they liked, some of them eventually becoming managers of Jersey Standard. It may have been the only way of expanding on the scale they had in mind. They were able to maintain their corporate identity, but they had to accept a compromise, ultimately losing control. Decades later the Humble identity was erased by the merger into present-day Exxon.

If he is lucky, the growing oilman reaches a point where he must choose between building a much larger company with outside money (by "going public" or perhaps by merging with a major) or continuing with a large but limited operation. Which way the scales dip will depend on the personality and the goals of the individual. It takes a staggering outlay of funds to put together an integrated oil company with production, pipelines, refineries, and sales outlets, and even then it may remain a "small independent company" that will scarcely trouble the majors except, perhaps, in a regional market. H. L. Hunt's Parade gasoline was never a serious competitor to giants like Texaco and Exxon.

Developing one's oil properties, all the while expanding one's business empire, may in the end produce the epitome of the American economic dream. But it also carries the seeds of antithesis. Most decisions to keep or sell are based on the oilman's perceptions of the current economic realities. One selling his production to a major company may do so for a variety of reasons. If it will take years for the leases to "pay out," he may find it preferable to accept a hefty profit now and let the major firm develop the property. If one has partners in a field, they are likely to influence what one does. Selling out, for instance, may be the wisest solution to a tangled relationship. Others, with no thought of identity, have sold their companies to the majors with little more concern than if it had been just another profitable trade, which is what it probably represented to them. In those cases, the oilman himself did not remain with the company, further evidence that he was selling a property with which he did not personally identify. In any event, selling out for a profit is usually the surest way to make money in the oil business. Hanging onto a lease or a field invariably courts risks which could cause one to lose everything after all.

That this economic creativity has influenced the economy of Texas goes without saying. It might be impossible, however, to trace every dollar to its ultimate destination. Money makes money, brings in other industries. Cheap energy in the form of natural gas lures in manufacturers. Population growth follows closely upon economic expansion. Inevitably everyone benefiting from petroleum income will spend most of it—for labor, services, goods. It is difficult for the wealth not to touch thousands who are totally unrelated to oil. Whether the money is filtering down or percolating up, it is on the move.

But the new wealth has made itself felt in other, vital areas. As individual oilmen have painted the details of this collective American economic dream in bold strokes, sometimes with garish colors, they have brought vicarious thrills—and sometimes resentment—to those who could never attain such heights of success. This psychological influence is the most difficult to measure with any degree of precision, but it may be as significant as the wealth itself. The fact of Texas' being the number one oil producing state has provided bountiful substance to any preexisting reasons for pride, so that even those with no share in the grandiose wealth could bolster their sagging egos by identifying themselves as Texans.

During World War II Texas contributed 2.3 billion barrels of petroleum toward the defeat of the Axis Powers. This fact was still fresh in the memories of those attending a Senate committee hearing in 1946, when Senator E. H. Moore of Oklahoma, himself an oilman, commented on Texas' role in the global conflict.

"I think we won the war," volunteered J. D. Sandefer, Jr., an independent producer from Breckenridge, Texas.

"I knew you would feel that way about it," said Moore.

"May I say we had a little help from Oklahoma," Sandefer acknowledged graciously.[65]

Many of Sandefer's fellow Texans, whether they had ever pursued this particular American dream or had even seen an oil well, knew how he felt.

XII

MILLION-DOLLAR IDEAS

1

Ideas in the oil business can be worth fortunes. Inventions, innovations, the promotions of wildcat acreages, geological concepts, or any useful, practical idea can provide the swiftest entrée to the world of success and money.

Geologist John A. "Jack" Jackson was well acquainted with oil fields. After working his way through junior college during the Depression as a 50-cents-a-day early-morning radio announcer, he had labored summers in the oil fields while pursuing a degree in geology at the University of Texas. He worked for Arkansas Fuel Oil Company after graduation, then helped locate desperately needed bauxite deposits in Arkansas during World War II.

After the war Jackson hired on as a geologist with Dallas oilman Jay Simmons. A month later Simmons introduced Jackson to his flamboyant friend Arthur Cameron, then living in Hollywood, who also hired Jackson. Simmons paid him $450; Cameron raised it to $750 a month, an excellent salary for 1948. A month before he had been making $375 a month with Arkansas Fuel Oil.

Simmons asked Jackson to examine a ranch in Wise County, north of Fort Worth. Its owner, Jimmie Hughes, thought there was oil on the land. Jackson discussed it with a geophysicist, who stoutly disagreed with Hughes. But landowner Hughes kept pestering Jackson, showing him logs of old dry holes in the area. They indicated showings of oil and gas—enough to excite a nonoilman but not enough to justify drilling another well.

Jackson, however, was intrigued with Hughes' beliefs. Gradually he began to see a geological picture that reminded him of the one in Arkansas where he had helped explore for bauxite during the war.

At his home in Dallas' Oak Cliff section, Jackson frequently worked until two or three in the morning. He kept thinking of the pattern he'd found in Arkansas. "Everything I did kept pointing toward this theory, that instead of these deposits being on the highs or the lows they were on the shelfs, where we found the bauxite in Arkansas," he said. "They were weathered deposits. They had holes in them. And the holes contained gas. [This was based on the theories of deposition of weathered granite masses.] The same geological processes that occurred in Little Rock took place in the Fort Worth Basin to form the Wise County conglomerates. The only difference between a bauxite deposit and a porous conglomerate is that the weathering of the bauxite reduced silica and increased the alumina content. The weathering of the conglomerates formed holes which were ultimately filled with oil or gas. It was that simple, for wherever you found bauxite in Arkansas, you would find weathered conglomerate lenses in the Fort Worth Basin. The trick was to learn the pattern of deposition."

This technical data might have little meaning for someone ignorant of geology, but Jackson concluded by 1948 that a huge gas field was in the basin area and that the Jimmie Hughes ranch was sitting right on top of it. But having a theory was one thing. Proving it and selling it to others were something else.

There had been drilling in the area. One dry hole showed some gas and oil; another produced gas, for which there was no significant market at the time, and it was abandoned. Jackson became more and more convinced that he was right. He tried to persuade his employers, Jay Simmons and Arthur Cameron, to go into it, without success. Eventually he left the security of the Simmons-Cameron payrolls and went off on his own as a consultant.

Discouraged with his reception on Wise County, he confided to Hughes that there seemed to be nothing more he could do, and he couldn't afford to continue without some remuneration for the work he was doing. Hughes responded by giving him the lease on his 2,800-acre ranch, which Jackson could then sell—if he would drill three wells on it. He went to all the well-known contractors and drillers. None was interested. Then one day he ran into an acquaintance, Ellison Miles, who operated a drilling company with his father-in-law. Jackson approached him with a fifty-fifty proposition. Miles accepted. They sold a quarter interest to a friend of Miles for $15,000, then raised another $15,000. The $30,000, plus a quarter interest, went to a contractor for drilling the well.

The well, the D. J. Hughes No. 1, its site located by Jackson, was a producer, with 132 feet of effective gas conglomerates, further documenting his theory that the Hughes Ranch was the most prolific area in Wise County. But by the time they had set pipe on the well their costs had soared to nearly $55,000. They tried to sell the well. There were no takers. No one wanted gas or believed Jackson's theory of the magnitude of the field.

"I went to everybody in the county," Jackson said. "I just went up and down the streets, trying to get somebody to buy that well. They were beginning to call me 'Wise County Jackson, the Dry Hole Kid'—a kind of guy who'd gone overboard on Wise County and on gas.

"While I was out on a well in Lubbock in West Texas one day, I ran into an oil lease buyer in a coffee shop. This man was on his way to Canada. There were lots of plays up in Canada and in Wyoming. So I told him all about this story, and I told him about this gas and about what it someday was gonna be worth. That was all."

The following Sunday, Jackson had a long-distance call from a man in Houston who was interested in the lease. Discouraged by now, Jackson reluctantly agreed to send him a report and a log of the well.

"Well, it wasn't very long until I got a telephone call. It came from the Mitchell organization. The man said, 'This is Mitchell in Houston, and we want to talk to you about testing and purchasing the Hughes well and acreage. Can we send a man up?'" [1]

Suddenly, after the darkest moment, a break had come. It had started with Jackson's conversation with the lease buyer in the Lubbock coffee shop, who had talked to a friend in Denver, who in turn had called an acquaintance in Tulsa, who had called a

Chicago man who was interested in Texas oil and gas. That was the man who had called Jackson. The Chicagoan, who was well acquainted at the Balinese Room in Galveston, had discussed the deal with a casino dealer whose son worked for the Mitchells, Eventually, it came to George Mitchell's attention. The Chicagoan was soon out of it, with a profit. Mitchell decided the concept had geological merit and bought the deal. It was 1952.

Jackson and Miles sold the well to the CM&M group for $55,000, which paid their debts and left them with $1,000 and an overriding royalty on the leases—a one-sixteenth for each.

As the second well was drilled, it further documented Jackson's theory of the Fort Worth Basin's being a large stratigraphic trap. Stratigraphic traps involve those reservoirs of oil or gas formed by a "pinch-out" of the formation, such as one sees in ancient shorelines, sandbars, and erosion surfaces. The East Texas field, for instance, is a huge stratigraphic trap. In this particular case in Wise County, Jackson theorized, there was an ancient erosion of a granite mass to the east (the Muenster Arch) and as the sea washed in, the shoreline would recede and deposit numerous conglomerate lenses over a wide area over a very long period of time, building up the section. As the water came in and out, the exposed section weathered, while the tides continued to deposit shales containing carbonaceous matter. The same thing had happened in geologic time in Arkansas, except that there the deposits had been silica and had produced aluminum instead of gas and oil conglomerates.

Jackson and Miles leased thousands of additional acres, and drilling continued. When the third well was drilled, the leasing agreement terms to Hughes had been met. However, there was no market for the gas, and each well added to the mounting costs. Lone Star Gas, which provided Dallas with its fuel, offered less than the Mitchell group was willing to accept.

Miles and Jackson went on the road, trying to sell the gas they knew was in Wise County. Some days they would fly to several cities. At one point they obtained an interview with N. C. Mac-Gowan, the top man at United Gas in Shreveport. They showed MacGowan the data; he called in his geologist, John T. Scopes, who had been the central figure in the 1925 Dayton, Tennessee. anti-evolution trial.

"First time I ever saw John Scopes," said Jackson. "John was quiet and was rather unusual in that he didn't mince words—what he said was pretty much the summary of the whole of his thinking. I got the map out and some logs. He kept looking at it, never said a word. I asked him if he wanted to check this, he said yes; everything I asked him, he said yes. When we got through he said, 'Let's go into Mr. MacGowan's office.'

"MacGowan said, 'John, how much gas have they got up there?'

"John said, 'Oh, Mr. MacGowan, I think they've got at least a hundred million and probably a half trillion.'

"He said, 'Well, give 'em an if-and-when contract.' "

The contract, though not legally binding, created leverage with which to raise the price. Lone Star Gas, in whose backyard the field was situated, had had no competition for residential customers. United Gas, however, did have industrial customers in Dallas and intended to use the Wise County production as reserves. But when United's contracts expired in the early 1950's, Lone Star stepped in and negotiated to supply that industrial market as well. This left United with less need for the Dallas-area gas. Lone Star again was top dog; the leverage had evaporated. Lone Star, now the only market in the area, offered Mitchell 10 cents per thousand cubic feet of gas, a low price, and refused to let Mitchell handle the processing of the gasoline, a major point in the negotiations. Essentially the Mitchell group was back where it had started.

By now Mitchell had 270,000 acres under lease in the area. It had drilled seventeen wells but had to shut them in because there was no decent market. Money was scarce, and the Mitchell group's regular backers soon felt the strain. Then Mitchell associate Merlyn Christie brought in centimillionaire Bob Smith. The magic of his name was a boon to the operation. The operation became known as Christie, Mitchell, and Mitchell (CM&M).

It was an exciting time for those in on the day-to-day development of the acreage. One block of leases, which was to become the Miles-Jackson field because they drilled it for themselves, provided the basis for one of those pleasant interludes that any oilman welcomes.

"We went through a formation seventy-five or eighty feet thick and assumed it was productive, from the cuttings," said Jackson. "Then we went through another zone that was ten to twelve feet thick. And then we went through the third zone which was ten to twelve feet thick. We took a drill-stem test, and boy, it hit the ceiling, and it just blew oil all over everything."

Although the production still was not sold, there was cause for a minor celebration. George Mitchell had acreage all around the Miles-Jackson oil well, so he was extremely pleased by the news. Despite the absence of a market for gas, this was another solid sign that the breaks were steadily accumulating. Bob Smith's hefty investment had helped keep the operation solvent in what could have been a very desperate lean period. As drilling continued, producing both gas and oil, the substance of Jackson's original projections began to appear evident. Success still was not in sight, but the odds seemed remarkably better.

As more wells were drilled and the reserves began to grow, the size of the field began to attract others. Natural Gas Pipe Line Corporation, suppliers of gas to the city of Chicago, outbid its competitors with 15 cents per thousand cubic feet and executed a $100 million contract. Natural Gas promised to build a $30 million pipeline from its line in the Texas Panhandle. CM&M would have control over the gasoline refinery, a big, profitable point worth millions.

The drilling by then had been a smashing success—163 producers. Of the first eighty-five wells drilled, only two had been dry. CM&M had spent $10 million in drilling and leasing, but the record was excellent: 106 good gas completions, 57 oil completions, and at least 150 proved locations yet to be drilled.

After a long wait for the Federal Power Commission's approval of Natural Gas' Pipeline application, in late 1956 the gamble paid off, and the dream became reality.

Almost overnight dried-up, sun-blasted Wise County boomed. As the pipeline linked up, the wells began sending gas to Chicago—and money to Texas. It was the opening of a highly profitable operation, eventually covering about 500,000 acres that CM&M had leased for $2 to $3 an acre on an average. George Mitchell—today operating as president of Mitchell Energy and Development—ended up in the commanding position in the field that spread into adjoining counties.

Today Mitchell Energy owns about 65 percent of the entire field and by partnerships owns about 90 percent, having bought out Bob

Smith, Waterford Oil Company, and some of the others. It is a large field, on which Mitchell Energy has about 1,100 wells, with more locations to drill. George Mitchell estimated in 1975 that there was about 250 billion cubic feet of gas left—a large reserve. When one adds to the Mitchell holdings those held by Phillips Petroleum, Sunray, Lone Star, and others, which would include many fields in adjoining counties, the field is huge, indeed, though not in the same category as the gigantic gas field discovered near Amarillo in 1921.

A conservative figure of the total gas originally in the field has been established at 3 trillion cubic feet. With the oil added to that, the total value—including the years during which the price was very low—will be, Mitchell says, "at least a billion dollars for the life of the field." In addition, new pockets of gas are still being found. Although in 1976 the field's interstate gas was selling for only 30 cents per 1,000 cubic feet (mcf) because of FPC controls, prices were clearly on the rise. As the twenty-year contract with Natural Gas Pipe Line expired in December, 1977, a new agreement raised the price to $2.02 per mcf, with an annual built-in hike of 8 cents per mcf. This, however, had not been approved by the FPC, which meanwhile was holding the price of "old" (or previously discovered) gas in that particular area at 54 cents per mcf. If the top negotiable price is ever allowed, the value of the remaining gas would rise geometrically. "When the last mcf or the last barrel is produced," said George Mitchell, "I think the one-billion-dollar value will be on the low side."

Unlike many who have promoted lucrative fields in the past and ended up with little or nothing, geologist Jackson held onto a share of the action until he was assured of being well-off. He had had to find others to finance the idea—and the best market had been one that piped the gas 1,000 miles on a three-and-a-half-day journey to Chicago—but he was insured a minimum income of about $200,000 a year from 500 wells in which he had an interest.[2]

2

A slender, reticent Missouri native, Carroll Deely borrowed an idea used in another field of mineral exploration—diamond bit coring—and transferred it, profitably, to the oil business.

Forced to drop out of college during the early Depression, Deely started out as a roustabout in the Kansas oil fields. He worked his way into the exploration department of the old Midwest Oil Company in core drilling. Cores provide detailed information on what the earth looks like below the surface. At times it is essential to finding oil.

After the war Deely and some partners organized an independent drilling company. The U.S. Bureau of Mines wanted more reservoir information on a field in Oklahoma. Conventional equipment had failed. One man with the bureau who had had experience with industrial diamonds in potash mining suggested using diamonds to cut a core in the Oklahoma field. Deely, who had done coring for the bureau during World War II, was called, and he applied the principle of diamond bit coring to the oil business. Diamonds had been used before in oil well coring, but not successfully. Theoretically, coring with diamonds should have been popular because of the diamonds' ability to cut harder material than the standard coring equipment. However, the use of diamonds was in the pioneer stage, and the cost was high.

In that first experiment Deely demonstrated, to his satisfaction, that diamond bit coring was *the* way to do it, but the market seemed nonexistent. Then he found his greatest opportunity to prove it to the world in what looked like the graveyard of all opportunity—the Rangely, Colorado, field where Stanolind hired him to core a well.

The Rangely job was in rugged country, fifty miles from any town. It was also the coldest time of year. And right off the bat, Deely ran into trouble. The diamonds were cutting beautifully when one of the diamond crowns twisted off. "Boy, this is the end of it!" he told himself. It meant a "fishing" job—fishing out the crown, a dreary bit of business for anyone looking for oil. As he sat there, the picture of gloom, the tool pusher came in and slapped him on the back.

"Hell," the man said, "don't look so glum! We ain't mad at you. We want you to get a basketful of those things!"

Deely perked up. When it was over, his operation had cut Stanolind's expenses by one-third. It had also saved time by coring a total of about 500 feet in less than thirty days. This meant the company was able to put the well on production sixty days quicker.

It saved time and money. This marked the beginning of a new industry.

"So every place we would go after that," said Deely, "when we had trouble selling them on diamond bits, all we had to do was say, 'It worked in Rangely!' They would say, 'If it worked in Rangely, it will work here,' and that is the way it went from then on."

The company expanded and went into diamond bit coring entirely for a period of time, until others saw how profitable it was and swarmed into the field. At its height, Drilling and Services, Inc., had about ninety engineers in twenty-five offices over the United States and in foreign cities like Milan, London, Paris, and Munich, as well as in the Middle East and South America.[3]

3

Indiana-born J. Clarence Karcher's family moved to the Indian Territory when he was five. His father was a mechanical engineer. Clarence went to the University of Oklahoma, where he studied physics and electrical engineering. As an honor graduate in 1916 he accepted a fellowship in physics at the University of Pennsylvania to begin graduate study.

While he was still a student, he was invited to spend three weeks at Thomas A. Edison's laboratory at West Orange, New Jersey. The brief association with Edison was to prove valuable to Karcher. Edison often dropped in at the laboratory to examine young Karcher's data. They would talk about some of Edison's inventions. Karcher gained insight into Edison's character that was to serve him in future years.

"'Without perseverance and persistence little can be accomplished in any endeavor,'" quoted Karcher. "I consider this admonition from Edison to be the most useful advice that I have received during my entire lifetime."

Edison also offered him an insight that was to prove helpful later in Karcher's work on the seismograph. In one of his experiments Karcher had experienced anomalous effects that he considered a nuisance. He mentioned this to Edison, who asked him if he had maintained a daily log of these in his research. Karcher had not. Edison admonished him to do so thereafter, impressing on him that such "nuisance" events are often clues to new useful information. He told how he had ignored such an incident once and continued with his experiment as planned. By doing so, he had overlooked an invention that later became the Nernst glower, discovered by a German scientist. Karcher never forgot the story.

When World War I broke out, Karcher accepted a wartime position as an assistant physicist with the Bureau of Standards, working on locating enemy artillery by sound ranging. Karcher's assignment was to design and construct an acoustic device to detect and record the blast from a field artillery piece by using sound waves through the air.

He began investigating the possibility of using seismic waves through the ground instead of air waves. Using geophones to monitor the sound waves, Karcher found that the shock wave would travel through deeper and deeper rock layers as the distance increased between the gun and the geophone.

Back at the University of Pennsylvania after the war, Karcher realized that the idea had value in measuring the depth of hard subsurface layers of limestone in exploring for oil and gas. He discussed the idea with geologists from Texas and Oklahoma, and in the summer of 1919 he conducted weekend tests in a rock quarry. In 1920 a group of Oklahoma men interested in the oil business formed a company, Geological Engineering Company, in which Karcher was offered an interest. He accepted and undertook more experimental work that resulted in the development of the reflective seismograph. Karcher and his associates tested the device at locations where there were enough known geological data to confirm the results.

They were ready to set up business when oil dropped in price from $3.50 to 50 cents a barrel within a two-month period. Oil companies lost interest in Karcher's instrument, thinking it too expensive to find such cheap oil. Karcher returned to Washington and the Bureau of Standards.

By 1925 oil was back up to $3 a barrel, and several companies were interested in the reflective seismograph. One of the companies was the Amerada Corporation, headquartered in New York but operating in Oklahoma, where Karcher had done his early experiments. One day Karcher had lunch with Everette L. DeGolyer, vice-president of Amerada, at the New York Bankers Club. DeGolyer was fascinated by the possibilities of Karcher's methods.

Three weeks later DeGolyer and Karcher worked out an arrangement to form the Geophysical Research Corporation of New Jersey with offices in New York. Karcher, with a 30 percent interest, was elected vice-president and general manager. The rest of the company was owned by Amerada. After some refinements in their devices and the organizing of field crews, the first crew was leased to Gulf in September, 1925. Within a year and a half, the first discovery was made, at Pawnee, Oklahoma.

In 1930, as policies changed at Amerada, a new president offered to buy Karcher's stock for the company. Karcher sold his interest for $300,000—which left him free, economically, to do as he wished—though he remained on for a few months at his $20,000-a-year salary. But with his $300,000 grubstake, it was only a matter of time till he resigned and organized Geophysical Service, Inc. (GSI), with, Karcher later revealed, DeGolyer as a sub rosa partner.

Karcher headed for Houston, where he began contracting seismograph crews to major oil companies. As their successes in exploring the subsurface to depths of 10,000 feet became known, business grew rapidly. For the first few years GSI had the entire United States virtually to itself; by the end of 1933 it had forty crews in the field and had crews overseas as well. Its success in finding oil was spectacular, and some of the company's own oil properties were soon worth several times the value of the geophysical firm itself.

Karcher eventually sold out GSI for $10 million to Stanolind, but that was far from the end for Karcher. He then organized the Comanche Corporation, which he ran up to a $10 million company, and then the Concho Company. In 1975, well into his eighties, he was at long last making plans to sell some of his properties and retire.[4]

4

Even more revolutionary than the seismograph, in its day, was the development of the rock bit. It led indirectly to the amassing of one of the leading fortunes in the world.

The early rotary bits were steel-tempered and wore out quickly. The rock bit that was to change this came from machinist John S. Wynn and Howard R. Hughes, Sr., who improved on the original idea.

One day at Sour Lake, one of the wild boom fields on the Gulf Coast that followed Spindletop, Wynn sat idly at his lathe, spinning a piece of machinery with metal cones on the floor, just as another person might pass the time by whittling. As the cones meshed and turned, an idea came to Wynn: Why not put those cones on a body attached to a drill stem that would go through rock?

Wynn worked out a model, but nothing came of it until a Sun Oil foreman, stuck with a section of rock he could not bore through, remembered the drill in Wynn's shop and borrowed it. The bit cut through 134 feet of rock and made believers out of all who witnessed it.

One day Sun Oil's J. Edgar Pew mentioned the incident to Walter B. Sharp. Sharp instantly realized the bit's great value. He discussed it with his friend Howard Hughes, Sr.

"Wynn's got a rock drill," Sharp told Hughes. "I want you to get it and not come back without it." [5]

Hughes appeared at Wynn's shop and told the foreman he had a hard rock to drill in Shreveport, according to Wynn's version, and the foreman let him have the bit. But instead of going to Louisiana, Hughes took the bit to Houston and went to work on it with mechanics and engineers, remodeling it into a more effective roller bit. Later Hughes returned to Beaumont and offered to buy Wynn's interest. Wynn sold out for $6,000. This was in 1909. Decades later, when he was in his eighties, Wynn still considered it a fair enough price. More work had had to be done on it, and he had wanted to help the industry.[6]

The rotating cones that ground away at hard formations eventually became the Sharp-Hughes rock bit. Sharp financed it, Hughes worked out the ultimate improved design, and they formed the Sharp-Hughes Tool Company to handle the business the revolutionary new tool would generate. Almost immediately its popularity soared. Even the old cable tool bit, which pounded heavily up and down in the hole and went through rock, was not as fast as the new bit. To prevent competitors from copying its features, Sharp-Hughes only rented its services and took it to a drilling site in a gunnysack under great secrecy. The company's employees fitted it on the drill stem away from the eyes of the drillers, then removed it in privacy when the rock had been penetrated and its services were no longer needed.

After Walter Sharp died, his widow retained the family's half interest, while Hughes managed the company. But Hughes as president often spent more than he made and drove her to distraction. He indulged in such extravagances as shipping his fifty-foot yacht overland to California via two flatcars, not to mention his fast, flashy automobiles. Each year Mrs. Sharp made up the company's deficit. In this state of frustration, acting on the advice of Joe Cullinan, among her principal advisers, she decided to sell out before Hughes' flamboyant, almost irresponsible ways siphoned off the comfortable fortune her husband had left her.[7] As it turned out, the clever, likable Hughes transformed the Hughes Tool Company, as it thereafter was known, into a highly profitable enterprise that was inherited by his only child, Howard Robard Hughes, Jr., and became the foundation for the mysterious billionaire's immense wealth and widespread operations.

XIII

POLITICS AMONG THE PETRO-RICH

1

As Senator Joseph W. Bailey no doubt would have agreed early in the century, politics flavored with oil may produce a concoction that is more complex than meets the eye. Since the days of Spindletop, oilmen and politicians have often enjoyed a cozy and, some of the time, symbiotic relationship that has benefited both sides.

If today oil does not have the effect it has had on previous elections, it remains one of the dominant forces in the political life of Texas. As oil money has often lost its identity through multifarious investments that include banking, manufacturing, real estate, and construction, it has become more and more difficult to trace its impact—which was difficult enough in the past. Although the subtle, quiet links between oil and politics may remain unearthed forever, evidences of the connection have festered to public notice over the years, and recent signs are as fresh as yesterday's headlines. One of the political names brought out in the investigation of the wiretap conspiracy charges against the brothers Herbert and Bunker Hunt, for instance, was former Governor and former Secretary of the Treasury John B. Connally. The Hunts were acquitted in 1975, but in the process news reports brought out relationships that, however legitimate, only confirmed in the public mind the coziness already suspected between oil and politics. The Dallas *Morning News* reported that Bunker Hunt had paid Connally a hefty retainer to "arbitrate" disputes between Hunt and the Libyan government over properties there worth as much as $23 billion.[1] Of the living Texas politicians, tall, handsome, silver-haired Connally is the one with the most visible oil connections. He seems to be almost uniformly appreciated by oilmen ("John Connally could turn this country around," said Claud Hamill), and his ties reach back at least to the time he was on the payroll of Fort Worth oilman Sid Richardson's organization. Starting out as Lyndon Johnson's protégé, Connally also enjoyed the friendship of House Speaker Sam Rayburn—all built-in assets to an employer like Richardson, who was interested in a man with the proper political connections to help maintain the depletion allowance and other industry-related legislation.

"I'll pay you enough so Nellie and the kids won't go hungry," Richardson is said to have told Connally during a long night's conference in Fort Worth decades ago, "and I'll put you in the way to make some money." Connally became Richardson's man for politics and general operating, serving as chief administrator and working in Washington on legislation to discontinue federal regulation of natural gas prices. When Richardson died in 1959, Connally became one of the three independent coexecutors of the estate.[2]

Connally held his first public office as secretary of the navy during the Kennedy administration, a position he used as a stepping stone to the Texas governor's office, which he won in 1962. The next year he came to national notice when he was wounded in the Kennedy assassination in Dallas, and after that he became unbeatable in state politics. His return to Washington power came as secretary of the treasury under Nixon and, subsequently, as his special adviser. Connally's presidential aspirations were never well concealed as, with poor timing, he turned Republican in time to suffer the buffetings of Watergate. In 1975, while the Hunt brothers faced trial in Texas, Connally faced criminal charges of a payoff—of which he was acquitted by a Washington, D.C., jury—that were redolent of Senator Joseph W. Bailey's ordeal about seven decades before. Ironically, the allegations against Connally involved not oil, but milk.

Better than any other relationship, Connally's employment with Sid Richardson symbolizes the intense interest oilmen have displayed in the political system. At the same time most Texas politicians have been as interested in the well-being of the petroleum industry, an interest as logical as a Wisconsin politician's interest in the dairy industry or a North Carolinian's in tobacco growing.

"Throughout most of history," wrote Robert L. Heilbroner, "wealth and power have gone hand in hand." The alliance, an obvious one, has grown with but occasional public outcries. Working together, possessors of wealth and power may achieve a stability of their own. Over most of history, wealth has been a vassal to power, for as Heilbroner explained, "it was easier for the ruler to become a rich man than the rich man a ruler." [3] Despite the examples of the Kennedys, the Rockefellers, and a spate of wealthy senators and governors, Heilbroner's insight holds generally true. Lyndon Johnson became a millionaire after he succeeded in politics, while billionaire H. L. Hunt, for all his money, could not have been elected governor or senator if he had run. Acquiring wealth and attaining political power demand different talents; the wealthy men who have succeeded at politics have more often been from the second generations, who did not have to devote their time and energies to building the family fortune. The notable exceptions, though, do exist.

Slim, athletic, witty George Bush has had both wealth and power. An oilman before he became a politician, he enjoyed a family heritage that few oilmen have had. His father, Prescott Bush, had served as Republican senator from Connecticut, where George had grown up. It was more unusual for Bush to take his background (Yale, '48; Phi Beta Kappa in economics) to the oil fields of West Texas' vast Permian Basin than it was later for him to enter politics. The fortune he made in oil, in West Texas and in offshore drilling, gave him the financial security and time to pursue his political ambitions. Bush began his rise in the Republican party in Houston when he won the Harris County party chairmanship. Not long afterward, in 1964, he ran for the U.S. Senate, a giant leap but not an illogical one considering the structure of the Texas Republican party of that time. Defeated that year by incumbent Senator Ralph W. Yarborough, a liberal, in the LBJ rout of Goldwater, Bush two years later won a congressional seat in his silk-stocking Houston district. Again he tried for Yarborough's Senate seat in 1970 but was deprived of having the liberal incumbent as a foe when conservative, well-financed Lloyd Bentsen, Jr., upset Yarborough in the Democratic primary and then, with the help of John Connally, rolled over Bush in the fall. Since then Bush's offices have been appointive: ambassador to the United Nations, Republican national chairman, ambassador to China, director of the Central Intelligence Agency. Now in his fifties, Bush may not be through with running for office, however; in 1974 he seriously considered a candidacy for governor of Texas before deciding to remain as GOP national chairman. [4]

Unlike Bush and a number of others, most Texas oilmen over the years have tended to limit their interests in politics to the areas of government vitally affecting them. The state, for all its conservatism, has been less conservative than the majority of its rich oilmen. Most of its life Texas has been, and basically remains, a Democratic state. Part of the reason is that Texas, a land of natural wealth and multitudes of rich folks, is also a land of poor people. Poor people vote too—more so in recent decades as change has been forced on the state's conservatives. Ironically, oil has helped industrialize the state; this has led to the growth of unionization and the growing political power of labor which has been a counterforce to the ultraconservatism of wealth.

Oilmen have exerted influence upon politicians in two basic ways: publicly through direct lobbying as a member of an industry group and privately through personal friendships formed in various ways. There seems to be no way to compute the number of oilmen who played golf with President Dwight D. Eisenhower. Former Humble chief Carl Reistle has known all of Texas' governors for the past several decades and knew LBJ closely, as well as senators like Hubert Humphrey, Henry Jackson, and Everett Dirksen.[5] It seems safe to assume that M. A. "Mike" Wright, the present head of Exxon, U.S.A., headquartered in Houston, is equally familiar with the leaders of Texas and of the country.

The roll call of oilmen who have politicians for friends would produce a lengthy scroll. Almost all oilmen's offices feature framed letters or autographed photographs from leading politicians, frequently presidents. One encounters Eisenhower, Johnson, and Nixon over and over. Practically every Texas oilman voted for Richard Nixon in 1972, if not in 1968, and Nixon must have dispatched his photograph or a letter of appreciation to every oilman who contributed a substantial sum; judging by the evidence displayed on oilmen's walls, almost everyone did. But in the aftermath of Watergate and the impeachment hearings, a large majority of the oilmen seem to have regretted it. "We gave money to Nixon, and lived to regret it," John Murchison said. "Sorry we did that." [6]

It goes beyond saying that an oilman enjoying a personal friendship with a public official may influence the official in a way usually beyond the reach of the ordinary citizen. Wealth, status, and mutual interests are factors that gain entrée almost anywhere.

The direct participation of Texas oilmen in the machinery of government has not been uncommon, but it has not been at the same level as the industry's economic value to the state. Ross Sterling and Beauford Jester both served as governor, Sterling in the 1930's and Jester right after World War II. Other Texas oilmen have filled important posts in national politics and federal government, but a sampling suggests a pattern of key positions in specialized areas. Robert A. Mosbacher's job as President Ford's campaign finance chairman falls into this category. Dudley C. Sharp served as Eisenhower's secretary of the air force. More frequently, the positions have been in administrative or advisory capacities, related to the petroleum industry. Howard Marshall and J. R. Parten served on important petroleum boards during World War II. Carrol M. Bennett of Dallas, chairman of the advisory Committee on Emergency Preparedness of the National Petroleum Council, which reports to the secretary of the interior, estimates that Texans make up about 25 percent of his group. The committee's mission is to decide what the United States should do in an energy crisis; it was assigned them before the Arab embargo. In 1975 it was working on the problem of emergency storage, in the event of another embargo. [7]

Powerful Texans in national government have been a tradition since the state's early days, indicating that the responsible factors predated the rise of the oil industry. At one point in the 1970's, for instance, both parties' national chairmen—Republican George Bush and Democrat Robert Strauss—were Texans. The fact that relatively few officeholders have been oilmen is not surprising. On the whole,

Texans in Washington have defended the oil industry, and this, one concludes, is the most important point of all. Exerting one's influence at crucial political turns is the only kind of power most oilmen have been interested in anyway.

The obvious role oilmen as a class have played has been as voters, and here the pattern can be clearly seen. Political preferences seem to follow closely that of "Texanized" oilman-entrepreneur John W. "Bet-a-Million" Gates in the first decade of the century. "I'm a fighting Republican," he said. "I will always be a fighting Republican. But I will prove my loyalty by my contribution to the party for the national and state campaign." [8] Things haven't changed much. If one substitutes the word "conservative" for "Republican" in Gates' statement, he could have been speaking for practically all of today's oilmen—with, as will be seen, a few notable exceptions. The overwhelming majority today tend to characterize themselves as "Texas Democrats," with the implication that they are not just regular Democrats, but "independents" who vote in the Democratic primary and in the fall support the Republican nominee for President. The most noticeable number of exceptions came during the LBJ candidacies.

Dallas oil writer Jay Hall, who has seen his share of nouveau riche, chuckled. "I always used to say that the first thing an oilman did after hitting it rich was buy a Cadillac, start cussing the government and voting Republican! I've seen that happen time after time." [9]

When it comes to funding political candidates, these views translate into contributions for Republicans and conservative Democrats. A few have backed George Wallace in the past. Yet, surprisingly, some independents have made contributions to liberal candidates. At least one, to be met later in this chapter, has been a consistent supporter, and others have been occasional backers. The occasional support can be traced primarily to the fact that in the past even liberal candidates in Texas have been sympathetic to the independent segment of the oil industry.

"I know of one man who is a staunch Republican, whose whole family is Republican, who contributed to [liberal former U.S. Senator] Ralph Yarborough," said Jay Hall. "But he did it for a purpose, because Ralph Yarborough was going down the line for the oil business, the depletion allowance, and maybe the other guy wasn't. They'll play both sides—that's not unusual. Wherever their interest is." [10]

The basic political conservatism among oilmen probably goes beyond the fact of their wealth. Although, as Jay Hall suggested, once a man enters the moneyed class he has something to conserve, other factors also enter into it. During the days when the law of capture was in force, the rugged individualism of the frontier undoubtedly helped shape the thinking of many. But even today, as Ed Owen reminds us, there remain built-in factors that make oilmen conservative. It is a high-risk enterprise; in order to attract capital, there must be either the lure of steady profits or the chance to make a bonanza. "You have to be conservative," he said. "You have to have some assurance that there is going to be a future. So it is inevitable that they have the same general point of view about it." [11]

2

In 1925 the Austin *American,* commenting on the reentry of Standard Oil into Texas during Governor Miriam A. "Ma" Ferguson's first term, noted that a corporation lawyer had lobbied through the legislature a bill which allowed Standard to obtain controlling stock in Humble Oil and that the state's Supreme Court had permitted it.

"These gentlemen did not use brass bands while they were hunting legislative ducks," asserted the *American.* "They stated their mission briefly and they were given what they asked." [12]

As the years wore on, old Jim Hogg's thundering fulminations against Standard Oil and other large companies were largely forgotten. By then, for one thing, the structure of such corporations had changed. But as the chore of raising tax money grew onerous, suspicious eyes from time to time have darted toward some of the state's corporative guests. In 1959, as the Texas legislature seemed headed inexorably toward a sales tax—which did not come for a few more years—the crusading *Texas Observer* in a front-page editorial backed a graduated tax on the sixteen major oil companies in Texas. State Representative (now Congressman) Robert Eckhardt of Houston had such a bill prepared that would levy a tax yielding, at that time, about $17 million. In an attempt to warn Texans "of the sales taxers' sellout of their fellow citizens to Eastern business octopi," the *Observer* presented a rundown on companies that were the special target.

"Sixteen oil companies produce half the oil in Texas," said the *Observer*. "They are headquartered in New Jersey, New York, Delaware, Pennsylvania, Ohio, Indiana, and Maine—none of them in Texas. One of them, Standard Oil of New Jersey, only last year completed its digestion of a company which had played a historic role in Texas economic history, Humble Oil & Refining Co. Jersey Standard is one of the three most massive corporations on the round, round world."

The *Observer* listed these sixteen as Standard Oil, New Jersey (with Humble its operating company), Gulf, Standard of Indiana, the Texas Company, Socony-Mobil (with Magnolia, Texas, its operating company), Shell, Atlantic, Sun, Phillips, Sinclair, Continental, Skelly, Tidewater, Amerada, Standard of California (with its operating company, Standard Oil Company of Texas, Delaware), and Cities Service. The liberal newspaper suggested that the state legislature could tax every one of these without any of the other 6,600 Texas oil producers paying another penny, thereby eliminating the need for a sales tax.

"We repeat: not one of these companies is headquartered in Texas," the editorial concluded. "Yet they take half our oil." [13]

A general sales tax was supported not only by oil and gas people, but also by industry and business in general. Carl E. Reistle, Jr., a Humble executive, formed the Citizens for a Sales Tax and within three legislative sessions saw the sales tax become law. Reistle was careful to make clear he took on the sales tax campaign as an individual, not as an official of Humble.[14]

Aside from businessmen pushing for the sales tax, there were other, subtle influences, especially that brought to bear by the teachers in the state. "The teachers' pay raises are intimately connected with oil taxation," said Ronnie Dugger, longtime editor and now publisher of the *Texas Observer*. "It's a very subtle question. The teachers want more money, more salaries—where are they going to get the money? Do they advocate natural resources taxes? Hardly! One reason: The leadership of the Texas State Teachers Association is conservative, always has been. But another is just the pragmatics of it. If teachers came charging in for pay raises on the basis of taxation that would offend the major economic interests, the major economic interests would redouble their opposition to the teachers' pay raise. I mean, it is the liberals who are for raising the teachers' pay, and I guess the teachers' lobbyists figure, 'Well, the liberals are going to vote for us anyhow, so let's not offend the conservatives on where we get the money. Let's offend the liberals because they've got to vote for pay raises.' "

Dugger admits that oil does not control newspapers, education, and culture, but he insists it has a pervasive influence that ramifies down into individuals and royalty owners and independents, thereby affecting all.

"This textural political culture that we have is simply honeycombed with the influences of private economic power finding its way into the political mind," said Dugger. "Everything is interrelated. Insurance, oil, banking, steel, all of it—you get into a complicated system of nexus that one should not simplify. It was, I think, logical and correct for people in the late thirties and fifties and perhaps even into the early sixties to think about oil really being *the* dominant force in Texas. Now we are really a part of an integrated corporate system that is national and increasingly international." [15]

In 1974 the *Texas Observer,* still crusading, noted that the chances of reforming the state's "illogical and unjust property taxes" rested largely with the Texas Research League, a tax-exempt foundation funded by business interests over the state. The league provided the research on which the legislature based its tax recommendations. As documentation of Dugger's contention, an examination of the league's board members indicated that they were chief executives representing interests in oil and gas, banks, utilities, insurance, cotton, retail business, construction, and similar activities.

The *Observer* noted, "It is an honor roll of real biggies, Exxon, Tenneco, Brown & Root—the total net worth of the corporations represented by the men on the board of directors of the Texas Research League is astronomical." [16]

Yet everything has not gone smoothly for some of the biggies. In 1976 a small echo of the Jim Hogg days was heard in a legal matter that hinted of the influence of large oil companies on Texas political life. The state's attorney general, John Hill, sued Gulf Oil for $1.05

million and Phillips Petroleum for $375,000 in civil penalties for illegal corporate contributions to political candidates. The maximum possible penalty would mean revocation of their charters to do business in Texas, if convicted, but Hill did not ask that. Among Texas politicians to whom Gulf allegedly made donations, channeled through attorneys and lobbyists, were former Texas Attorney General Crawford Martin, Senator Lloyd Bentsen, Senator John Tower, Lyndon Johnson when he was Vice-President, and former Congressman George Bush.[17]

3

If the industry has been at ease with state government, its relationship with the federal behemoth has been something else. The career of Joseph S. Cullinan, a founder of the Texas Company, is symbolic of the changing political stances of many an oilman over the years. In a 1916 article in the Houston *Chronicle* that was later published in the *Oil and Gas Journal,* Cullinan argued that federal control of the nation's oil business was necessary. He contended that Congress had the power and authority to condemn and take over all pipelines and to exercise the right of eminent domain over petroleum deposits. Federal legislation, he believed, might determine a "reasonable price" for consumers, royalty owners, producers, and all others.

Such thoughts from an oilman today would likely invite accusations of heresy. What brought "Buckskin Joe" to this pass was his deep concern over the wasteful drilling and production then being practiced. A conservationist, Cullinan saw no solution short of federal control. As Cullinan grew older, however, and as the Texas Railroad Commission took more and more responsibility for control of production, he changed his views, noting that state agencies would be better qualified for the task of regulation.[18]

The issue of federal control became the focus of one of the historic oil fights in the 1950's. In the *Phillips Petroleum Co.* v. *Wisconsin et al.* case, the United States Supreme Court ruled in 1954 that the Federal Power Commission should regulate the wellhead price of natural gas sold in interstate commerce. Justice William O. Douglas, frequently an industry critic, was one of the three dissenters, contending that sales price and profits have significant effect on the rate and methods of production. (In 1974 Frank Ikard, a former Texas congressman who had become president of the American Petroleum Institute, said Douglas' view had been proved accurate; while demand for gas had doubled, he cited, gas wells and reserves had declined.)

To counteract the High Court's decision, Congress in 1956 passed the Harris-Fulbright bill to exempt natural gas from federal price control. But just as all seemed to be moving smoothly for the industry, a bombshell burst. A Texas lawyer for Superior Oil Company was accused of offering a $2,500 contribution to Senator Francis Case to influence his vote for the bill.

"I couldn't *believe* it," said Nancy Heard Toudouze, a liberal who, like Justice Douglas, favored the legislation. "You know, you didn't need to bribe anybody. Everybody was falling all over themselves to do the oil industry favors. This backwoods, backwards 1800 way of doing things. Texas got the blame, naturally, because Texas is capital O-I-L and G-A-S." [19] The furor that followed climaxed in President Eisenhower's vetoing the Harris-Fulbright bill.

Today the question of federal control weighs more heavily on the minds of oilmen than ever before. Probably 100 percent of oilmen—independents and major companies—are fearful of what the next move by Congress will be. "We are constantly under threat that national political action—not state political action—will control the future of the industry," said independent Michel T. Halbouty. "If this happens, the big will get bigger and the small will get smaller, which would mean the eventual elimination of the independent. If that happens, who will drill the wildcat wells in this country, and especially the dry holes?" [20] Nor are the independents concerned only with their own fate. They view, correctly it would seem, their future as ultimately tied to that of the majors. Glenn McCarthy, once the best-known independent in the country, expressed horror at the trends. "With higher taxes on major companies," he said, "how are they going to get money to build hundred-and-fifty-million-dollar refineries or billion-dollar pipelines? I don't understand why they would want to cripple it like that, make it nearly impossible to operate. They're not going to get any new people in the business. Why is any young man with brains going to go into the oil business when he can see there is no possibility of success?

The only thing I can see is that if it gets worse and worse and worse
... the government themselves will try to take it over—and, God,
what a mess that would be!" [21]

There was, indeed, talk of the federal government's assuming a
more active role in oil and gas production, even to the extent of
forming a national company similar to Pemex in Mexico and
nationalized operations in other countries. As horrific as this
sounded to veteran oilmen, many oil critics were not convinced it
would result in a "mess," while others believed that controls less
than nationalization might lead to clarification of the energy crisis.
More than anything else, the expressed fears of nationalization
represented to oilmen a symbol of what further federal controls
might ultimately bring.

4

The single greatest explosion of patriotic fervor over federal
control has been Texas' tidelands issue. It fanned far beyond its
economic origins into a flaming political conflagration that paved
the way for successful Republican entry into the once stoutly
Democratic state. When the issue was finally resolved, oilmen had
experienced two victories: vindication of the position of state control
and statewide acceptance of the national party to which they felt
closer.

The tidelands issue erupted in 1949, when federal officials first
asserted claims to submerged lands off the Gulf Coast. Texas' claims
traced back to its entering the Union by treaty in 1845, the only
state so annexed. As an independent republic after gaining its
freedom from Mexico in 1836, Texas had claimed jurisdiction over
three leagues into the sea, instead of the traditional three miles; this
amounted to slightly more than ten miles, a substantial difference.
The treaty of annexation stipulated that Texas was to retain all its
public lands. However, the state also was admitted on "equal
footing" with other states, a clause that was to be emphasized by
federal lawyers. Although there were other states with oil properties
beyond their shores, notably Louisiana and California, the Texas
tidelands issue was unique by virtue of the state's history. "In some
respects," Ernest R. Bartley, a scholar of the controversy, has

written, "its claims are stronger than those of the thirteen original states." [22]

In 1948 Texas' submerged lands had brought in $25 million in income, including some not affected by the federal claims. But the three-league limit involved 2,608,774 acres beyond the traditional three-mile limit. Potentially considerable wealth was involved, for there are 380 miles of coast line.

The United States Supreme Court heard the case in June, 1950. Justices Robert Jackson and Tom Clark both disqualified themselves because each had been a U.S. attorney general before going to the bench. Seven members of the Court were left to decide the case, and in December, 1950, they handed down a four-to-three decision for the federal government—a one-vote margin determined by a minority of the court. Justice William O. Douglas wrote the majority opinion, an action that inspired an impeachment resolution from the Texas House of Representatives.[23]

Attorneys for Texas filed a motion for rehearing, arguing that the "equal footing" was not pertinent to the state's treaty with the United States. When the High Court turned down the motion, the howls could be heard all over Texas. The next stage of the battle was in Congress, where legislators sympathetic to Texas and other coastal states passed bills to establish ownership by the states. President Harry Truman vetoed such bills twice.

As the election year of 1952 appeared, the issue had become a dominant one in Texas. Oilmen such as multimillionaire Sid Richardson were active in making General Dwight D. Eisenhower the next President; Eisenhower was pledged to support the tidelands states' claims, as well as Texas' three-league limit. Texas Governor Allan Shivers, a handsome, dark-haired conservative Democrat, approached Democratic nominee Adlai Stevenson, who indicated he would veto a quitclaim bill. The die was cast. Shivers returned to Texas and helped arrange the machinery of a "Democrats for Eisenhower" campaign to deliver the state to the GOP in the fall. Practically all the Democratic state officeholders from Shivers down were cross-filed on the Republican ballot in the general election, ensuring Shivers and others freedom from opposition as they helped elect Republican Eisenhower.

Obscured by the rhetoric that followed was the fact that the state had required producers to pay the usual one-eighth, or 12½ percent, royalty, while the federal government might require a 37½ percent royalty, as on other federal property. The difference could amount to a considerable sum for an oil company. It was explanation enough of oilmen's preference for doing business with the state.

Tied to the state ownership of the submerged lands was the fact that income from public land is dedicated to the permanent school fund, which is shared by all public schools in the state. This became the public issue that eclipsed all else. The liberals in Texas, feisty and on the way up when this issue hit them, roared at the "sellout" by the "Shivercrats," but they were outshouted by a battle cry of "Save the Tidelands for Our Children." Shivers soundly defeated liberal (though the word was less used in those days) Ralph Yarborough in the Democratic primary and led an all-out fight for Eisenhower in the fall.

Advertising whipped voters into a frenzy. A campaign newspaper financed by Clint Murchison showed a beaked Stevenson sneering at a classroom of Texas children, "Tideland funds for THOSE KIDS? Aw, let them pick cotton." TV, still new, became part of the highly effective saturation campaign. One parent reported his children came to him with tears in their eyes, crying that "they're trying to take our tidelands away!" Political writer Theodore H. White reported that the Eisenhower-Shivers campaign used an estimate $6 million in all, while Stevenson forces in Texas raised only $180,000.[24] Part of the reason for the low figure for the Democrats was that Lyndon Johnson, then in the Senate, did not push with much vigor Stevenson's cause and fund raising for the national party.

Looking back on it, Ronnie Dugger, publisher of the *Texas Observer,* said, "Texas probably, given the way the election turned out, would have gone for Eisenhower anyway, but Shivers simply rhetoricized the tidelands issue into whether you were for or against the schoolchildren! The vital interest of the oil companies in keeping the state the administrator of the tidelands was completely lost. The people had no real idea the issue was the protection of the public patrimony. They thought it was the protection of public schoolchildren! It terrorized the politicians, apparently. Johnson in endorsing Adlai [Stevenson] that year made an absolutely tidelands-saturated statement that just because Stevenson is wrong on tidelands doesn't mean that Eisenhower is necessarily right on everything else. And of course, the press was almost symphonic in its orchestration of the hysteria. Certainly it increased Eisenhower's lead, and it gave Shivers the cause or the pretext he needed to do what he wanted to do, which was to endorse Eisenhower even though he was a Democratic governor." [25]

In 1952 the Eisenhower-Nixon ticket, with the help of Shivers and oil money, put Texas in the GOP column for the first time since Hoover had defeated Al Smith in 1928. Attention turned to the White House, whose new occupant had promised to sign a quitclaim bill. Pushed through Congress, the bill went to Eisenhower's desk, and he signed it on May 22, 1953; this, despite a few other lawsuits, essentially ended the matter.[26]

In recent years the state land commissioner, Bob Armstrong, has exacted more than the old 12½ percent royalty from the oilmen leasing in the Gulf, thereby increasing the take on a par with what it might have been with federal control, but the productivity of the lands has not approached the rhetoric of the 1952 campaign promises. Looking back on it, oil writer Jay Hall thinks Texas might have made a gigantic mistake in the 1950's.

"During all this hassle," Hall said, "Sam Rayburn was speaker of the house and he came up with the Sam Rayburn compromise, that there'd be a sixty-forty deal between the states on these offshore lands. Allan Shivers, the governor at the time, and Price Daniel, the attorney general—they couldn't see it. That was a bad deal—the big ol' federal government up there was robbing Texas, see. Well, as I understand it, the best stuff that has been found off of Texas has been out [beyond the three-league limit] in federal lands! It's kind of ironic." [27]

5

For years the depletion allowance has ranked, with oilmen, alongside God, mother, and the flag. At the same time typical of its opposition is the *New Republic,* which once called it "the vicious depletion allowance which gives a special tax benefit to oil and gas producers." [28]

The 27½ percent depletion allowance, which was in effect for most of the taxable years of the old timers, offered the entrepreneur a protective cushion in the event he struck it rich. If, for example, he was lucky enough to make $1 million a year from his discovery, the depletion allowance assured him of $275,000 tax-free. The remaining $725,000 would be taxable, but before turning over a high percentage of it to the Internal Revenue Service, he had the opportunity to keep drilling and charge off his expenses, up to a limit—which he could have done, without the depletion allowance. If he missed finding another field, he could write off his expenses, just as any other businessman does, thereby sliding into a lower income tax bracket. If he did hit oil again, he would have 27½ percent of the new wealth free of taxes. If he found another $1-million-a-year field, then of his $2 million he would have $550,000 charged off to depletion.

Most critics of the tax write-off say that the oil industry used its political brawn to secure the legislation back in 1913. The familiar formula was established in 1926, when the 27½ percent figure was approved as a compromise between the 30 percent advocated by the Senate and the 25 percent in the House.[29] Signed into law by President Calvin Coolidge, the figure was in effect until 1969, when it was lowered to 22 percent; in 1975 the 22 percent depletion allowance was eliminated for the majors, while small producers retained it in a scaled formula whereby it was to decline to 16 percent in 1983 and a permanent rate of 15 percent in 1984.

The original depletion allowance came about during a crisis in the industry when new capital was needed, insists oil historian James A. Clark; the new law created an attractive tax shelter for eastern money, thereby bringing infusions of capital. The men behind it, he insists, were primarily easterners interested in making more money.

"The oil industry didn't have a damned thing to do with depletion," said Clark. "But oil organizations have taken credit for it—and are blamed for it. One of the associations said it was the father of depletion, and one of my witnesses who was there at the time said they were against it!"

Clark interprets moves in recent years to cut or abolish the depletion allowance as political revenge. "It's simply something to get even with the oil industry for promoting Nixon. Well, I think if the oil industry's entitled to being stepped on for something, it ought to be for promoting Nixon, because he didn't turn out as good as he should have. They should have had better judgment. Well, anyway, we're all suffering." [30]

Because of the increased costs of drilling, oilmen unanimously argue, the industry can't continue without a depletion allowance or other such tax break. Glenn McCarthy cites offshore wells that cost $85,000 a day to drill. If it takes thirty days, that's $2.5 million. "It's gonna take a hell of a well to pay back that cost, let alone the dry holes," he said. "If they're going to take all your money away from you when you make one well, and you're not going to recoup those other nine that you drilled and were dry holes, how can you continue to operate? That one well may not produce but for a few years. It may not produce long enough to pay you back for itself, let alone all the other explorations.

"Right now you pay five hundred thousand dollars to drill a well to eleven thousand five hundred feet. That's an awful gamble, and the chances are not great to get it. I can live on five hundred thousand dollars. I don't need five hundred million dollars to live on. I could live on less than five hundred thousand dollars. Why should I go in and invest the hard-earned capital that I have now in trying to make it when I know the possibilities?" [31]

By the mid-1970's beleaguered oilmen were chafing under what they considered a double bind—federal price controls and attacks on the depletion allowance—that had left most of them exuding an air of frustration and even futility. A crowning blow came in 1975, when U.S. Senator Lloyd Bentsen, a conservative Texas Democrat, planning a large-scale campaign for President, broke ranks and supported cuts in depletion. While oilmen experienced feelings of betrayal, Bentsen's tactics rewarded him poorly. His campaign fizzled nationally, and then his favorite-son strategy caved in as Texas Democrats stampeded to Jimmy Carter.

Some oilmen admit that most of their problems have involved a failure to communicate accurately their plight to the public and to Congress. "We've never bothered to talk to consumers," said outspoken Johnny Mitchell, a former president of Texas Independent Producers and Royalty Owners (TIPRO). "We've never bothered to talk to the Chamber of Commerce in New England, and here and here and here, to explain the situation. We've always gone to Washington when the house was burning down, looking for a fire extinguisher. Too goddamned late. I blame myself more than I do anybody else. I've preached these things, that we are to blame for most of our problems." [32]

The oilman's image is itself a barrier to presenting the industry's case in a realistic light, believes Bill Rudman, the Dallas independent.

"There's such a black name that we have," he said. "It's a shame that our country will have a catastrophe and that the price of oil will be impossible to buy. You know, you buy a quart of almost any kind of booze, it'll cost you from four dollars to ten dollars or twelve dollars a bottle. If you buy a gallon of water that's distilled, it costs you a dollar. There's no liquid that can be bought as cheap as gasoline, and that's the energy of our country. The public have got to be made to realize that they have been buying energy *too cheap* for a number of years, and that's because the Middle East let oil come to this country that only cost five cents to fifteen cents a barrel to find and produce. You take a gallon of gasoline, you take a four- to five-thousand-pound automobile, and you drive it with five people ten, twelve, fifteen miles—compare that with the cost of other liquids. It's ridiculous. You've got no right to buy energy that cheap, as hard as it is to find." [33]

6

Most people perceive Lyndon Johnson and Sam Rayburn as having been closely aligned to oil interests. The implication is that they, along with other congressmen from Texas, were as cozy with oilmen as peas in a pod. On a closer examination, the truth has been less simple. Although Johnson and Rayburn were friendly with individual oilmen and customarily led their colleagues in defending the industry, on the whole it was a strange relationship. Both had fierce opposition from the forces of oildom, and Johnson at times used his own considerable power in the Senate as majority leader to protect his own flanks against oilmen's attacks.

The most frequently cited example of Johnson's coziness is that with Houston's George and Herman Brown. During World War II the most conspicuous instrument of the Browns' financial arm was Brown and Root, which made untold millions on wartime construction projects for the federal government; more recent coups in

government contracting have been the building of the NASA
Manned Spacecraft Center, drilling the Mohole Project, and under-
taking a $900 million cost-plus agreement on U.S. facilities in
Vietnam. The Browns entered the oil industry in a big way after
World War II, when they and partners bought the Big and Little
Inch pipelines from the government and founded Texas Eastern
Transmission Corporation. The closeness between the Browns and
the two most powerful Texans in Washington apparently never
faded, and over the years the Browns represented a telling source of
campaign funds and backing that could open other purses.[34]

Johnson and Rayburn were probably the most effective defenders
in Congress of the depletion allowance for oil and gas. Senate
Majority Leader Johnson determined who sat on the powerful
Senate Finance Committee, and House Speaker Rayburn did the
same for the House Rules and Ways and Means Committees—all
committees likely to consider any proposed change in the depletion
formula. Twice Johnson and Rayburn were instrumental in guiding
price decontrol bills through Congress, and both times they were
vetoed, once by a Democratic President, once by a Republican.

Ronnie Dugger, a liberal journalist and Johnson observer, traced
what he considers a gradual metamorphosis by Johnson, who, he
said, antagonized oilmen early in his political career. "He began
with some votes that were out of character for a Texas congressman," said Dugger. "Hostile to the oil interests during World War
Two. In 1946 he engaged in active anti-oil-company rhetoric.
Talking about Standard Oil attorneys running against him and
things like that. In 1948 [when he was elected to the Senate over
former Governor Coke Stevenson, a conservative, by 87 votes] he
engaged in what I would call vestigial anti-oil-company rhetoric
because he was in the course of 'getting right' with the major oil
companies. Then, of course, he went to Congress and took up the
Leland Olds case in 1949 and the oil depletion allowance and
tidelands oil. He was for state ownership of the tidelands in 1948, so
you see, he was beginning to 'get right,' in the language of the
industry. After that he was certainly understandable as a senator
from Oil." [35]

Historian Clark, looking at the performance through lenses of a
different color, agreed that Johnson had been helpful to the industry
but he did not believe he was usually rewarded by gratitude. "The

oil people in Texas generally always fought Mr. Sam and always fought Lyndon Johnson," said Clark. "That's how idiotic they were. They fought the only real friends that the oilman had!" [36] Rayburn had said the same thing earlier, and a year before his death, in the presence of his biographer-to-be, he had almost sobbed as he spoke of how ingrate oilmen had sought to destroy both him and Johnson politically.[37] Once when the conservative Dallas *Morning News* seemed to have joined forces with oilmen in an attempt to jolt Rayburn out of his congressional seat, Rayburn buttonholed Dallas merchant Stanley Marcus and pleaded, "They claim that I'm against the 27½ percent depletion allowance, but singlehanded I've saved it for them, using my own methods to do it. Get them off my back!" [38]

As his power grew in the Senate, Johnson had his own means of keeping recalcitrant segments of the industry in line. In order to run unopposed for the Senate in 1960, while he was also seeking the Democratic nomination for President, Johnson had to ensure that any substantial funding for a foe was eliminated. He had his enemies in Texas, and several itched to oppose him. The story is that one Houston man was poised to run, but the majority leader sent the word back from Washington: "The minute he announces, I'll let 'em bring up the Proxmire amendment to abolish the twenty-seven and a half percent depletion allowance!" With a threat like that, from a man who could make it come true, the oil money ready to fight Johnson suddenly dried up.[39]

7

While politicians have invariably exercised the ultimate levers of power, oilmen have just as consistently interested themselves, both openly and behind the scenes, in the political processes. Of these, Hugh Roy Cullen was probably the most visible and influential.

Cullen, the Houston supersheikh, was a prime funder of the right long before much was known about H. L. Hunt's political philosophy. Centimillionaire—or perhaps billionaire—Cullen, probably then the richest man in Texas, was a crusty, outspoken rugged individualist of the old school. Cullen's introduction into politics can be traced back to an embroilment in Oklahoma over moving the county seat. During an argument Cullen shoved a screen door against his opponent's neck. When the town marshal sought to arrest Cullen, the future oilman slugged it out with him in the town square, for which he was fined $9.25. Cullen, barely twenty, vowed vengeance at the polls, made speeches against the town's incumbents, and saw his candidates defeat the mayor and both the day and night marshals.[40]

As he grew older and richer, Cullen tackled larger game and looked on himself as a powerful figure in national politics. In 1932, thinking it might be better to elect Democrat Franklin D. Roosevelt than reelect Republican President Hoover with a hostile Congress, Cullen went east to see what FDR was like. He returned with the opinion that the New York governor was not only "bigmouthed," but also dangerous, and set out to fight him, which he relentlessly did thereafter.

Cullen's political activities seemed to have consumed as much time, in season, as did his oil business. He was active always in Houston's politics and sometimes in state politics. In 1940 Cullen helped bankroll W. Lee "Pappy" O'Daniel, a flour salesman who had been elected governor of Texas first in 1938 promising old-age pensions, with the Ten Commandments and the Golden Rule as his platform. After consistently fighting the New Deal, in 1948 Cullen supported Dixiecrats J. Strom Thurmond and Fielding Wright for the presidency. He attacked "creeping socialism" and defended "free enterprise" in a one-man battle of publications, telegrams, and letters over the next several years, as he poured material from his offices on the seventeenth floor of the City National Bank Building in Houston. He bombarded congressmen with letters and telegrams. When *I Chose Freedom* by Soviet refugee Victor Kravchenko was published, Cullen mailed a $25,000 check to Charles Scribner's Sons, the publishers, asking that copies be distributed to libraries and schools at his expense. On another occasion he bought 10,000 copies of John T. Flynn's book *The Decline of the American Republic* from the Devin-Adair Company, whose publisher, Devin Garrity, remembers Cullen as "a very generous man." After the Korean war erupted, he wrote his old friend Texas Governor Allan Shivers, "Our country is in a hell of a boat, and I don't know how we can get out of it—unless we impeach Truman and throw out Dean Acheson and General Marshall!"[41]

One of his most publicized misadventures occurred in 1954, when Cullen, through the Sons of the Republic of Texas, invited Senator Joseph McCarthy, the hero of the right, to speak at San Jacinto Day ceremonies in Houston. April 21 commemorates the day in 1836 when the Texas revolutionary army routed Mexican President Antonio López de Santa Anna's army at the Battle of San Jacinto. President Eisenhower had been invited but had had to decline.

The invitation to McCarthy was so galling to many that it stirred campus action. "That kind of ticked me off because McCarthy didn't strike me as the type of person who ought to be celebrating Sam Houston in Texas!" said Ronnie Dugger. "A few of us started a petition at the University of Texas, where I was at that time a student. I remember it was forty feet long and had fifteen hundred names on it. Bob Kenney was the student editor, and he and I were designated to present the petition to Cullen in Houston. We went in, and Bob and I sat down, and Cullen was across his desk. Cullen looked at Bob and said, 'Are you a Communist?' Bob is the essence of the quiet, soft-spoken sort of Texas type and he said, 'No.' And Cullen looked at me and said, 'Are you a Communist?' I said, 'No.' And he said, 'All right, let's talk about this thing!' So we talked about it, and he said he couldn't withdraw the invitation, that it was too late, but he saw our point, and we left on pretty good terms. After he got his blood question out of the way, he was a southern gentleman. He was very polite." [42]

Even though schools turned out and businesses closed, with fine weather, only 3,000 to 4,000 people attended the ceremonies. Ten times that had been expected. A few months earlier pianist Liberace had drawn more people to a concert. [43]

8

The Texas oilman who attracted more attention than any other for his political views was probably H. L. Hunt, who in turn must have felt himself to be one of the most misunderstood of men. His fellow oilmen, conservative themselves, usually took great care to dissociate themselves from the stigma of his stance. Some called his views "too severe for me" or "too far-right" or "not typical of Dallas." A consensus is probably represented by Hunt's old friend

Jake Hamon, who first knew him in the East Texas field during the 1930's, when they were working together for conservation laws.

"He called me Jake, and I'd use his name, Haroldson, which very few people ever used," said Hamon. "But of course, he was too far to the right for me. I used to tell him he ought to spend some of his money on civic things or give it away to charities or some worthy cause, instead of spending it on some silly far-right organizations. But he had his hearing aid off when I talked to him about that. He was a hard worker, and after he had gotten way up in the purple, why, he completely lost interest in the oil business. He branched off into these right-wing things, trying to save the world from communism." [44]

Despite the far-right labels that others bestowed on him, Hunt shunned the label "conservative." He called himself a "constructive," embodying "the best of conservative, independent, and middle-class measures." He made it a point to correct interviewers who called him a conservative.

"I always stress to them that there is not a conservative hair in my head," he said. "I believe in action, and I like positive and *constructive* action." [45]

The threat of communism was real to Hunt, and he clearly believed that its threat to the United States was strong. Yet he suspected the United States might follow the example of England faster than that of Russia; at that point, the socialists being weak, he reasoned, the Communists would take over. He judged fascism to be as bad as communism. "Hitler promised much to the Germans for a time," he said; "then he carried them into total destruction—as any totalitarian leader can be depended upon to do." [46]

His most durable vehicle for disseminating his anticommunism beliefs was a series of radio and television broadcasts, beginning in the early 1950's and financed by foundations he had established. The first was *Facts Forum*, which was within a few years aired on 246 stations from Portland, Maine, to Portland, Oregon. A television version was carried on 67 stations. Attacked in Congress for its tax-exempt status, *Facts Forum* was called "neither fact nor forum" by Senator Mike Monroney, while Representative Wayne Hays of Ohio said it gave "both sides of one side" and was "no more meriting tax-exemption than the A&P." Hunt disbanded *Facts Forum* in 1957 and succeeded it with *Life Line,* which continued to go strong for years; at its peak it was carried by 531 radio stations with an audience of 5 million.[47] Eventually *Life Line*'s tax-exempt standing was canceled, following an energetic investigation by Congressman Wright Patman, an East Texan ,who had caused many a secrecy-shrouded, hitherto tax-free foundation to quake.

Karl Hess, who worked for Hunt on the early *Facts Forum* magazine, came to see the billionaire's political side up close. "I remember when I first got to Dallas, one of the funniest things was when he introduced me around at the office. He obviously meant to introduce me as being a prominent anti-Communist from New York, but he kept saying 'a prominent anti-Semite from New York.' And I kept saying, 'I don't think that's right.' He realized his goof, and one of the things he did, I think, because he was embarrassed by it, he had a huge dinner for a big anti-Communist rabbi from the East.

"I also have the strong recollection that Hunt was one of the easiest people in the world to con—on an ideological basis. There were more people preying on him, while I was there and later on; anybody who'd say they were anti-Communist could get him [to contribute money]. The magic word. And he supported, I think, a lot of people who were not up to him. But then ideology makes fools out of everybody.

"*Life Line* was his big hobby apparently. *Facts Forum* was. He put a lot of money into those things.

"I remember some of the oil people said that every day he spent on politics they lost a million dollars." [48]

Hunt's views frequently presented surprises, when examined closely. He called the Peace Corps helpful in some countries, and he seemed to have genuine admiration for President John F. Kennedy. He cited the Kennedy family's fiscal responsibility and Kennedy's support of anti-Castro Cubans. He called the assassination of the young President "the greatest blow ever suffered by the cause of liberty." Kennedy's murder also brought some uneasy moments for Hunt. To many Americans, Hunt symbolized the anti-Kennedy sentiment in the country, primarily because of the *Life Line*-type broadcasts, and being in Dallas, he found himself to be a special target. He received threatening calls that he and his wife would be shot, and he and his wife were rushed out of town to spend most of the time at the Mayflower Hotel in Washington. Both the Dallas police and the FBI would not hear of their returning to Dallas until a few days before Christmas, 1963. When he refused to hire bodyguards, Dallas policemen watched over him until he finally insisted that they leave.[49]

As early as 1952 Hunt exerted himself actively in support of favorite candidates. That year he backed General Douglas MacArthur, perhaps his all-time favorite, for President. At the Republican national convention two contested delegations arrived in Chicago from Texas—one pledged to Taft, one to Eisenhower—and Hunt was a delegate on both slates. Behind the scenes he worked for MacArthur's candidacy, and as a result, reported Hunt, the general came within a hair's breadth of being elected President in 1952.

The night before the first ballot was taken, Hunt learned at two o'clock that morning that the Ohio senator, seeing the trend toward Eisenhower, was willing to transfer his delegates to MacArthur. Hunt, delighted, called his MacArthur for President committee into action. But at six o'clock the same morning, Hunt said, he was informed that Taft had changed his mind and would wait until after the first ballot. At that point, Hunt believed, MacArthur and Eisenhower were equally matched, and the switch by Taft would have turned the tide MacArthur's way, ensuring nomination and victory that fall. Instead, the shift went Eisenhower's way, and MacArthur faded from the center stage of history.[50]

One suspects Hunt fancied himself a kingmaker from that day on. Certainly he interested himself in the electoral process, often with frustrating results. At the 1960 Democratic national convention he supported Lyndon Johnson for President; when Kennedy was nominated, Hunt said he personally urged Johnson to accept second place. Johnson was never to acknowledge the influence. Four days before the 1960 election Hunt publicly announced his support of the Kennedy-Johnson ticket, barely in time for Senator Henry Jackson, then Democratic national chairman, to repudiate the endorsement.[51] In 1964 Hunt was observed working for Senator Barry Goldwater's nomination behind the scenes of the Republican national convention.[52] Four years later he supported an attempt to defeat Arkansas' dove, Senator J. William Fulbright, then chairman of the Senate Foreign Affairs Committee. Hunt acknowledged giving financial aid to Fulbright's conservative opponent in the Democratic primary, and then he backed Fulbright's Republican foe in the fall.[53] In the sixties Hunt was reported to be a strong supporter of Gerald Ford, "lobbying very much" for Ford to be nominated for President or vice-president. He was said to have been still actively supporting Ford when the House minority leader became vice-president following the fall of Spiro T. Agnew.[54]

Hunt attained the pinnacle of his political philosophizing with the publication, by his own companies, of two books, *Alpaca* (1959) and *Alpaca Revisited* (1967). *Alpaca* might be characterized as a political romance. It conveyed his concept of an ideal government in which graduated suffrage was a focal point. But, he insisted, he had never intended that the United States adopt his model constitution. He had in mind the emerging countries of the sixties, which he hoped would find it an alternative to dictatorship. It was a means of enticing the landed gentry and other powerful representatives of the status quo into a republican form of government and a possible method of interesting a nation's top achievers in taking part in government.[55]

Alpaca Revisited (1967) contained the up-to-date version of Hunt's political theory, for by then he had had eight years in which to rethink, polish, and revise his first offering. Among his tax provisions the severance tax on natural resources would range from zero to 30 percent, with a 15 percent limit on gift taxes, 25 percent on inheritance and income taxes. Manufacturing and sales taxes might reach as high as 100 percent on "luxury items" such as alcoholic beverages and tobacco, while "necessity items" were limited to a 4 percent tax. Tax exemptions were restricted to philanthropies "advancing medical science, care of the sick, and public enlightenment to promote personal initiative and individual liberty," which, one suspects, would have included *Life Line*. Withholding taxes were banned.[56] In his system of graduated suffrage, everyone from eighteen on was entitled to two votes. Then there were bonus votes, provided no citizen had more than five, that could be earned by ranking in the upper percentile of taxpayers or one's graduating class or voluntarily paying a poll tax.[57] Despite his model government's being labeled a "cashocracy" by many, he insisted that achievement and contribution, not money, were the measuring rods of citizenship in Alpaca. And there were surprises. An Alpacan form of Social Security cared for those over sixty-five (half pay) and the indigent and infirm ("only to cover their necessities").[58] The eighteen-year-old vote was slightly ahead of the times, but the most intriguing facet of his dream probably was the requirement that legislation be valid only for a period of twelve years after which laws must be either reapproved or discarded.[59] It was something that some old-line liberals, say of the Clarence Darrow persuasion, might have swallowed and relished, as a vehicle of continual legislative review to eliminate the clutter of old laws and to make law relevant to the needs of the present.

Despite his exertions, there is no evidence that Hunt made anywhere near the impact on American thought that he intended. Politically he was a figure of the frontier that had vanished forever with the Hot Oil War that he had toiled to end. His America had changed, and somehow, sharp-eyed old trader that he was, he had failed to realize it, in the process losing touch with the mass America that he sought to influence. His standing with both left and right must have left him disappointed. Liberals saw him as the Daddy Warbucks of the far right, funding indiscriminately every antidemocratic cause that came along. A survey of the known facts reflects that this wasn't true; he seemed to be as close with his political spending as with everything else. On the right, William Buckley, Jr., carefully dissociated himself from any semblance of accepting Hunt's behavior and thinking. In 1967 Buckley charged that Hunt's "eccentric understanding of public affairs" gave "capitalism a bad name." [60] In a column written after Hunt's death Buckley noted that Hunt had taken offense at the column and had written newspapers suggesting Buckley was surrounded by Communists. Admitting that Hunt had "led a most useful life," Buckley concluded: "Life would on the whole have been easier for thoughtful advocates of the free market if Mr. Hunt had been a socialist rather than a conservative." [61]

9

One oilman who has truly got things done for the industry is Jake L. Hamon, although he has never run for public office. Hamon, in his own quiet way, has exerted as much influence as has any of his colleagues, usually lobbying in Washington as an official representative of various petroleum organizations. Now in his seventies and an oilman since he was nineteen, Hamon has probably done as much for the industry as any other living man. "Jake could open any door in Washington, you see," said Johnny Mitchell. "Jake knew the top echelon." [62]

Respected by all sides, very wealthy, and a winner of most of the industry's accolades, Hamon has known practically all the Presidents—though not necessarily on intimate terms—back to William Howard Taft. Like his father before him, Hamon is a Republican all the way, but he also knew Harry Truman and "admired him a great deal." Both Hamons, father and son, were close friends of Sam Rayburn, and the younger Hamon said, "I could always get Sam, if we had something hurting in the business, to arrange an appointment."

Influential as he had been in Washington over the years, his impact back home, where he is a member of the Dallas Establishment, ironically has been limited. "Sure," he acknowledged, "I've sat in on all the meetings and all that, but truthfully I don't think that I would say I made much of a dent on the thinking of the Establishment. They're fine people and all that, but the Establishment's largely the newspapers and the utilities and the banks and the department stores. The oilmen are a minor part in the overall economy of Dallas. They're fragmented, and their business does not depend on Dallas. They're really like guests in a hotel, as Everette DeGolyer used to say. He'd say, 'Hell, I can move to one hotel or another, and I could just as well have moved to Houston as Dallas.' And he said, 'People can't understand why an oilman isn't more civic-minded than he is, but really, what he's interested in is schools and orchestras and things where his children and family will have a pleasant life. . . .'

"I'm sometimes suspected of being too liberal by my associates," says Hamon, who subscribes to the principle of racial economic opportunity. "But I don't think that's necessarily entirely true. There are a lot of oilmen that, you know, are liberal and aware of the social problems." [63]

To classify Hamon as a liberal for these beliefs would be elevating him higher into liberalism, probably, than he is or wishes to be. His views, however, do illustrate a pattern shared by other, scattered oilmen who have taken what might be termed "liberal" stands on specific issues, without forfeiting their conservative status. George

Mitchell, for instance, is concerned about the limits to growth on our finite planet. Bill Rudman expresses compassion for blacks. And Joseph S. Cullinan, a Democrat of the pre-New Deal old school, opposed the Ku Klux Klan during its heyday in the volatile 1920's.

Cullinan, proud of his Irish heritage, always flew the national Irish flag on St. Patrick's Day at his family home, Shadyside, at South Main and Montrose in Houston. But beginning in 1922, when he was deeply troubled by the KKK's strength in Texas Democratic politics, he began flying another flag, the black skull and crossbones, on top of his downtown Petroleum Building head-quarters. When anyone asked him why, he replied, "The display of the Jolly Roger is intended as a warning to privilege and oppression within or without the law—the latter including witch-burners, fanatics, and the like who fail to realize or ignore the fact that liberty is a right and not a privilege." [64]

If Cullinan's chosen symbol baffled those not privy to the workings of his mind, his words seemed clear enough.

More to the point, and a brass-collar Democrat to the end, was one of the most noted recipients of oil wealth, the inimitable Miss Ima Hogg, the only daughter of Governor Jim Hogg. Although few may have remembered her as an oil heiress, she was the beneficiary of oil found on family property after her father's death. She never married, and she never left the Democratic party of her father. As one writer put it, she "could never really adjust to the fact that Texans of above-average intelligence could be Republicans." During the 1972 presidential election, when Senator George McGovern was running against President Richard Nixon, driving many Democrats into Nixon's fold, Miss Ima was honored at a museum dinner. Although it was strictly a nonpolitical affair, she opened her speech with: "I am so glad to see so many of my friends here, and to know that you are all Texans and all Democrats." The reaction was considerable. The next day various members of the audience sought to clarify to her their presidential preferences. After several hours of phone calls like this, she called one of her hosts from the evening before and said, "Listen, *you're* a Democrat, aren't you?"

Her models for political morality were noble Texas Democrats she had known in the distant past, such as John Reagan, whom her father had persuaded to give up his U.S. Senate seat to become the first Railroad Commission chairman. Lonn Taylor, director of a museum she had blessed with her support, said, "She measured men like Richard Nixon and Gus Mutscher * against John Reagan and found them wanting and told people about it." To the end she was her own boss and said what she thought about politics as about other topics. She once scandalized those attending a sedate sherry party in River Oaks, the posh Houston enclave, by stating that she considered Vladimir Lenin the greatest man of the twentieth century. The response was predictable and instantaneous: "Oh, Miss Ima, you're not a *Communist!*" Compounding their horror, she then told of a trip she and her brothers had taken to the Soviet Union in the 1920's.

"I've been in jails in the United States and I've been in jails in Russia," she snapped, "and the ones in Russia were better!" [65]

10

Through little clues, from time to time one finds small evidences of oilmen participating in what may be called liberal causes. A 1975 perusal of a printed list of large contributors to Common Cause, the so-called people's lobby, turned up the names of two Texas oilmen. John D. Murchison had given $500. J. R. Parten contributed $2,000.[66]

To the average Texan, the name J. R. (for Jubal Richard, which he does not use) Parten may not mean much, but he is well known among oilmen and in Democratic circles, where he has taken an active part in state and national politics for more than four decades.

He is referred to as "that liberal Texas oilman."

He contributed to liberal candidates Senator Ralph Yarborough and Don Yarborough (a candidate for governor in the 1960's, not related to the former senator) and has supported a large number of liberal enterprises for many years. He may well have been the only Texas oilman who voted for, and actively helped, George McGovern in his 1972 campaign against Nixon. Even Howard Marshall, a Democrat all his life and an old friend of Parten's, admitted that he could not go for McGovern. Not only did Parten stay, but he did so enthusiastically.

---

* A speaker of the Texas House who became embroiled in a scandal.

In 1975 the tall, erect, white-haired Parten, almost eighty, was still tending his office in Houston, still concerning himself with the politics of the country. A man of deliberate speech with solid, unwavering blue eyes and the craggy features that one expects of a Texas pioneer, Parten's public service goes back to the 1930's, when Governor James V. Allred named him to the board of regents of the University of Texas, where Parten had earned a law degree years before. During World War II Parten was director of transportation for the Petroleum Administration for War and became responsible for construction of the Big Inch pipeline. Fellow oilman Howard Marshall said Parten was the only man respected enough by both majors and independents to get the job done. He also was a longtime member of the National Petroleum Council, chief of staff of the U.S. delegation to the German Reparations Commission at Potsdam and Moscow in 1945, and for eight years chairman of the board of the Federal Reserve Bank in Dallas.

Parten's initiation into the controversial issues of his state came while he was chairman of the University of Texas's board of regents. During Parten's second year on the board, university president Harry Y. Benedict asked him to meet some of his friends one day. They were three black college presidents, who wanted Benedict and Parten to help them secure a modest appropriation from the state legislature for graduate education at Prairie View Normal, the segregated state school for blacks. At the time a black student had to leave Texas to earn a graduate degree.

Since efforts had been unproductive with the board of Texas A&M College, which controlled Prairie View, Parten took the A&M board's chairman, an old friend, to lunch one day and gained ermission to advocate the matter to the legislature. To Parten it became a challenge. "It was unthinkable that Texas had done nothing," he said. He went before the Appropriations Committee of the State House of Representatives, requesting a $150,000 appropriation per year for graduate education at Prairie View Normal. The legislature gave $75,000, which, while insufficient, became the first appropriation on record for black graduate training in Texas.

The more one analyzes the lives of oilmen, the stronger the impression grows that the social and family environment that produced such rich men placed relatively little value on many of the issues that have stirred society for the past few decades—or rather that the emphasis was placed, rather sternly, on the side of the status quo. The rare exceptions, such as Parten, seem to be those in whom the family instilled a feeling for the underdogs of society at an early age or those who, like Bill Rudman, because he was a Jew, found themselves cast in the role of an underdog. In most other families the desire to get ahead, through acquisition or finding the windfall that oil represents, seems to have been fertilized all the more strongly.

It is all the more remarkable that Parten, in a state that has traditionally been conservative, has not concealed his views. "I've always identified myself as a liberal quite openly," he said, "because my philosophy is that the only way that this republic can be maintained is through liberal means. I don't think you can maintain our form of government and our free society with anything except liberal means."

Parten was one of the early bankrollers of the liberal *Texas Observer*. What were his original motivations? "In order to permit the other sides of the stories to be told," he said. "The trouble about journalism in Texas today is that the editorial policies of every one of our large metropolitan dailies are exactly the same. And that's unfortunate. I'm a great believer in the value of the dialogue. For that reason I've devoted a lot of time and a lot of effort to further the activities of, and to preserve and maintain, the Fund for the Republic, which was established by the Ford Foundation in 1952 for the purpose of surveying the whole question of the feasibility of the preservation of the Bill of Rights of the Constitution in this day when we are in competition with communism and fascism.

"I know it shocked a lot of people when the Fund for the Republic came out and said even the Fifth Amendment should be maintained. I have a deep conviction that all the amendments should be maintained—if we are going to continue to have a free society, if we are going to continue to have our form of government. After all, it is just a thin line between a fascist dictatorship and a republic such as we have today, and if it hadn't been for Watergate, we might have one right now. I think contributions should be strictly limited. It can get close to buying office, just as Nixon was buying office. I believe very firmly that if it hadn't been for Watergate, we might not have had any more elections. We were getting very close to a police state."

The *Texas Observer,* which he helped start and has since supported, has frequently published editorials he did not agree with. What has been his reaction?

"I learned a long time ago that you can't expect everybody that you admire to agree with you on everything," he said. "I've helped the *Observer,* I think, every time they have asked me to, and still do. A lot of things they have published I don't endorse. But it's the only newspaper in Texas that you can depend upon for the other side of the news."

Why is he a liberal?

"Well, the only way in the world you are going to preserve our form of government is by liberal means," he said. His family background may have been part of the reason for his views; for one thing, he has been a habitual reader since childhood. When interviewed he was reading Fawn Brodie's biography of Thomas Jefferson and other historical works; history is his major field of interest. "I think everybody ought to read a lot," he said. "My family encouraged all of us children to read."

Parten's three favorite governors in Texas history have been Sam Houston, Jim Hogg, and James V. Allred, the latter one a personal friend until his death. "They were the three great governors of Texas, in my book. My family and I were great admirers of Houston for stands he took—first, for winning the independence of Texas and, second, for his giving up the governor's office rather than change his mind on the question of secession. The Texas legislature should take a leaf from Jim Hogg's book and come up with a bill to regulate monopoly utility rates in Texas now. I don't believe in regulation of any business unless it's a monopoly, but when a monopoly is granted, it has got to be regulated."

The 1972 election was one in which Parten not only backed the Democratic nominee, as few, if any, other oilmen seem to have done, but did so in anything but a lukewarm way. The issue with Parten was the Vietnam war.

"I had a great admiration for George McGovern," said Parten, "and I admired him particularly for his stand against the war in Vietnam. He had guts enough to come out early and say so. He made quite an impression on me.

"I was trying to be silent. My friend Fagan Dickson told them at the *Texas Observer* that I was foursquare against the Vietnam war and I was doing everything I could to get it ended. But I was playing a quiet game, trying to have some influence on the Johnson administration. But I finally just gave up. In 1966 I just gave up all hope. I went to the White House several times prior to June, '66, and in June, '66, we had dinner there.

"I told Johnson, 'If you don't stop the war, the people aren't going to stay with you. It doesn't make any sense.' I told him furthermore, 'If you don't stop it, you are going to be responsible for perpetrating a great tragedy upon this nation.'

"Johnson said, 'What's that?'

"I said, 'You're going to be responsible for electing Dick Nixon President of the United States, if you don't stop this war.'

"He said,"—Parten growled out the words, in imitation of LBJ— " 'Well, there's nobody I'd rather run against than Tricky Dick.'

"But he never got the chance.

"I never went back after June, '66. We turned down all invitations. Johnson had one great weakness. He would not look at the other side of the coin on every issue. He would not tolerate the devil's advocate. One of the things that made Franklin Delano Roosevelt great as a President, in my opinion, was that he wanted all shades of opinion around him and he wanted them all aired before he made a decision. It's a sound policy. Any business at any time, the chief executive officer had better listen to the devil's advocate. The devil's advocate is essential to sound thinking. Johnson wanted everyone to agree with him.

"This idea of 'Oh, don't rock the boat and don't indulge in controversy'—I like to go back to old Jim Hogg's statement, which I think is classic. He said, 'Let's have unity, but for God's sake let's not smother in harmony!' " [67]

XIV

WHAT DID THEY DO WITH IT?

1

There is a delightful *New Yorker* cartoon by Richter which depicts a huge gusher spewing oil until it resembles the overstimulated fronds of a gigantic palm tree. The landscape is a flat, cheerless, desertlike country that makes one think of some parts of West Texas. In the foreground stands a shack, with an old flivver beside it, and a woman, her hair bedraggled, washing dishes in a tub. Her man, already blackened by the spurting liquid, is streaking toward her, yelling and pointing wildly at the fantastic tower of oil.

The work-worn woman is smiling from ear to ear, as she says, "It's wonderful, Harry! How late does Neiman-Marcus stay open?"[1]

This amusing cartoon provides a clue to the question of how oilmen often spent their money, once they had made it. All of them lived better than before, and some consumed very conspicuously, contributing to the Texan image of movie fame and popular stereotype. The stereotype lingers. He is brash and loud, especially loud, in all the ways that "loud" has meaning—voice, dress, sensitivity, style. "Dollar" Bill Texasmouth, the oil king, spends like Coal Oil Johnny, tools around town in his monogrammed Cadillac, throws lavish parties for hundreds or thousands at his twenty-five-room mansion, jets to New York or Paris on a whim for a wild,

boisterous weekend of nightclubbing, wears ornate, handmade cowboy boots and a fifteen-gallon Stetson, and brags, brags, brags. He
is filthy rich, colorful, and obnoxious.

On the whole, the image is exaggerated. Parts of it have applied
to some oilmen, and more so in the past than the present. Generally,
Dollar Bill Texasmouth's characterization is a fantasy that doesn't
exist much today, if at all. The lavish parties can still be found,
high-stakes gamblers do exist, big homes and cars remain in sight,
but today oilmen are, on the average, quieter, muted to the point of
being almost invisible to public gaze. For one thing, as the IRS
raised the tax rates, accountants began to play a larger role and in
the process calmed down many a rambunctious spender. And others
learned that the ways of power and status more often are subdued.

Whereas at one time the embellished anecdotes about our old
friend Texasmouth were parallel to those of the turn-of-the-century
Chicago rich, San Francisco rich, or New York rich—enhanced by
cowboy boots, hats, and oil wells—today the wealthy oilman may
not be readily detected from any other highly successful businessman. And in our era of diversification the oilman may have as
much of his money in other businesses as he does in oil. He has
merged into the economic mainstream.

As with other wealthy people, some oilmen keep their money for
themselves and their families, in the process extending their financial empires, while others give it—or part of it—away. Still others
dispense with it in both strange and ordinary ways. But in the past,
more than now, oilmen did not always swim in the mainstream.

2

The eye-catchers, in disposing of their money, have been people
like Houston's Jim "Silver Dollar" West. In addition to his pen-
chant for paying bills with silver dollars that he carried by the
sackfuls, he displayed a mania for communication. West's fleet of
thirty automobiles was so equipped that every car was tuned in to
the Houston police wavelength and to the sheriff's office. He was
informed up to the minute on any crime news, which often enabled
him to outrace the police to the scene, day or night. In his house he
had twenty-four telephones; there were twelve more in his garage.[2]

Probably few people have ever chosen to act out their fantasies, like a child dreaming of being a policeman or a Texas Ranger, in such a persistent fashion. Although bounteous wealth may make virtually anything possible, most oilmen are likely to insist that their money hasn't changed them any. In most cases this may be true. None has been known to build a tiny house after hitting it rich, but it is possible to own a splendid residence without being ostentatious. The castles that many an oilman of an earlier era called home are still being built but are rarer today. Bill Rudman keeps a Rolls-Royce but considers his life-style relatively simple, though comfortable. "I'm living in the same house I lived in twenty-five years ago," he said. "My wife wouldn't move out of it; she's in love with the house. And the home has actually cost me about two hundred million because I had to borrow the money and I sold leases up in North Dakota to pay for it—and the leases would have produced. I live in a very simple house. Three bedrooms. Of course, it has a small gymnasium so I can work out when the weather's bad." [3]

Many have bought summer homes in the cool mountains where they can escape the simmering Texas heat. W. A. "Monty" Moncrief has a ranch on the Gunnison River in Colorado; J. Clarence Karcher had one in Wyoming while his children were growing up. John D. Murchison, a member of the group that originally started Vail, Colorado, has a house there that he visits in both summer and winter. So does Herbert Hunt. Morgan Davis, the former head of Humble, has owned a home in the Virgin Islands. [4]

An affinity for the land seems prevalent among oilmen, and not only because of tax benefits. Dooley Dawson, who for years was the Bank of the Southwest's vice-president in charge of agricultural loans, explained it: "Usually those boys come from small towns and have farm or ranching backgrounds. They never get away from it. They're always wanting a piece of land of their own." [5] Jake Hamon offered an additional explanation: "An oilman always figures he's taken a lot out of the earth, and the first thing he does, when he gets a ranch, he fixes it all up, with fertilizer and every other thing." [6] Replenishing the earth may be part of it, but economics also lurks near the surface in most ranching and farming operations; the goal may not be further enrichment, necessarily, but the habits of a successful businessman are not likely to change for even a sideline. The Murchison farm near Athens, Texas, today is run by the second-generation brothers, John and Clint, Jr. In 1975, as they faced a depressed cattle market, the farm's manager was quoted as saying they were cutting corners until things got better. "I can assure you the owners expect the cattle to pay a profit," he said. "We are not running a showplace." [7]

Most oil money has gone into investments, not necessarily oil-related. With the gigantic King Ranch in South Texas, it was oil money that not only bankrolled its expansion, but was responsible for its weathering the Depression. A timely leasing came in 1933, when the old King estate owed about $3 million after paying inheritance taxes and other expenses. Humble, for a cash loan of more than $3 million to clear up the ranch's debts and an annual bonus of 13 cents an acre, secured exclusive drilling rights on 1,133,156 acres. It proved to be a bonanza for both Humble and the King Ranch, with gas reserves alone estimated at 25 trillion cubic feet. As the royalties began gushing in, ranch manager Robert J. Kleberg, Jr., and his relatives had a continuing problem in reinvesting the money. The King scion until his death in 1975, "Mr. Bob" Kleberg devoted most of the income to developing his livestock and property and amassing additional ranching lands in foreign countries. At one time the ranch's holdings sprawled over six Texas counties and several foreign nations including Cuba, Australia, Brazil, Argentina, Venezuela, Morocco, and Spain. The largest holdings were in Australia, about 12 million acres.[8] Many another landowner has used his oil money similarly, but never before on such a grand scale.

Hunting, travel, sports—all the leisure-time activities that other Americans enjoy have also filled the never-idle hours and days of those with oil money. The heyday of the big game safari seems to be over, but the trophies linger on. By the age of twenty-five John Mecom, Jr., had taken all the big African animals but the rhinoceros and the bongo, a striped antelope. As he grew older, his interests turned more toward conserving wildlife than killing it, and he stocked the Mecom ranch in the Laredo area with exotic game such as zebras, oryxes, llamas, impalas, wildebeests, and lesser kudus.[9] (Exotic game, especially deer, is popular on other Texas ranches. Les H. True is one of several who have game such as as mouflon, fallow sika, and black buck antelope.) In Dallas, Harold Byrd's trophy room contains the proof of three safaris to

Africa, three to Alaska, and other hunting trips in the United States and South America. "I've got twenty-eight of the top animals of the world," said Byrd, "and I have some mounted—polar bear, grizzly, tiger, mountain lion—but for the most part I have the horns." In his International Room at his home, situated atop his six-place garage, he keeps antiques and museum pieces he has collected in thirty-five years of globe-trotting. He has lots of jade and "one of the finest collections of ivory anywhere." [10]

Travel becomes second nature to an oilman because he often has to fly to distant foreign countries on business. Leisure travel is just as common. Jake Hamon always spends New Year's in Paris. He and several of his friends, from the United States, Britain, Switzerland, and France, have been getting together for a party there annually for the past ten years. "We just entertain each other, and our wives shop, and we just have a good time," said Hamon. "I've spent a lot of time traveling all over the world. I'm going to Peking Friday. I'm going through the museums. You know, the only thing is I don't have a camera hung on me; otherwise, I'm a typical American tourist. I've spent a lot of time in Spain and England. Last year we spent a good deal of time in northern Italy." [11]

Most oilmen, as befits highly competitive men, follow sports avidly, and a number of them have involved themselves directly as financial backers of sports ventures. With some, such as Clint Murchison, Jr., and Lamar Hunt, professional sports have become more of a business than a hobby. Bob Smith was involved early in the Houston Astrodome, that spacious temple to pro sports, because of his lifelong interest in baseball. John Mecom, Jr., while still in his twenties, put together an automobile racing team that won three tops events in Nassau's Speed Week and built a flashy race car named the Hussein, after the king of Jordan. To Mecom, sports was as grimly serious as business. Referring to his racing entries, he said, "Second or third is not what we came after. We're not in it for the romance and we're not in it for the money. We're in it to win." [12]

Others have chosen quieter pursuits. Clint Murchison, Sr., once out of the hustle-bustle, became an expert on migratory birds. Eloquent, handsome Walter Cline filled his library with rare volumes and served as mayor of Wichita Falls. In the 1930's he was mentioned as a candidate for governor.[13] Everette L. DeGolyer, while amassing his fortune, played a central role in the formation of

Amerada Corporation, Texas Instruments, and Texas Eastern Transmission but also enjoyed an active life in bookish, educational pursuits. He and others were the main financial backers of the Texas Country Day School, which grew into St. Mark's School of Texas, a Dallas prep school for boys comparable to those of the East. At the urging of oilman J. R. Parten, then a regent, DeGolyer accepted a distinguished professorship in geology at the University of Texas for the 1939–40 term and later lectured at Princeton. In the 1950's, when a wave of self-anointed censors swept over Texas, as chairman of the Dallas Public Library trustees DeGolyer stood up for controversial books. "We are not going to block free access to ideas and to thought," he said.

Possibly DeGolyer's most shining act was his saving the *Saturday Review* from economic shipwreck, becoming its publisher and subsidizing it until it was on its feet again. He was a rare book collector to his death, and his final disposition of his lifetime collection ranks along with his resuscitation of the *Saturday Review*. He gave his science library to the University of Oklahoma, which left it one of the best collections in this hemisphere. His geological library went to hometown Southern Methodist University, with his trans-Mississippi or western collection of the DeGolyer Foundation going on loan to SMU's Fondren Library. In all, 89,000 volumes were involved.[14]

3

A man with a few million dollars will have no problem finding a project to support. Some have found the unusual. Harold Byrd backed an Antarctic expedition of his cousin Admiral Richard E. Byrd in the 1930's and has a mountain range named for him. A fellow oilman told him, "I've known you to drill in some out-of-the-way places, but I never thought you'd go to the South Pole!" [15]

Nobody, though, has approached Edgar B. Davis' doggedness in disposing of money. He not only gave it away, but found ways of spending it that no other oilman seems to have duplicated. Idealistic, rosy-cheeked Davis, an erect, six-foot-three giant of a man who weighed around 350 pounds, was born about 1873 in Brockton, Massachusetts, to an old New England family. Instead of going to

Harvard to play football, as he first intended, he took a $6-a-week job in a shoe firm, where he worked his way to the position of treasurer and a comfortable bank account. Then, in 1908, he suffered a nervous breakdown that changed the course of his life and career. Many believed his hunches and attitude toward money later in life stemmed from this event. Recovering after he left the sanitarium, he traveled around the world for a year or more. In the Far East he became intrigued with the British and Dutch rubber plantations in Malaya, Java, and Ceylon. When he returned to the States, he managed to interest officials of the General Rubber Company, later part of the United States Rubber Company, to invest, and he was sent back to buy several large plantations. Named the general manager of the rubber plantations, he became a director in U.S. Rubber and gained a large block of the company's stock. For the next decade, which he spent in Asia, his outlook came to be shaped by what he saw and learned there; for one thing, he concluded that his life was directed by God.

He left the rubber business worth $3.5 million. He then initiated what was to become a pattern of his life. He started giving his money away. A million went to friends and former employees. Then he bought land at Buzzards Bay, Massachusetts, where he built a $100,000 home on the sands.

By now he was more than fifty years of age and had never been in the oil business, nor had he ever had anything to do with Texas. But his older brother, Oscar, and some friends had some oil leases near Luling, Texas, about forty miles south of Austin. They asked Edgar to check on the leases. At Luling Edgar Davis learned the geologists didn't believe there was any oil in the entire county. Well, Davis had a hunch that there was oil, but his brother and friends, accepting the geological verdict, wanted out. Edgar Davis bought them out and formed his own company, the North and South Oil Development Company, and started drilling, even though he knew absolutely nothing about the business.

Luling, a town of 1,500, became Davis' headquarters. Ignoring geology and playing his hunches, he drilled six dry wildcat holes, one after the other, and started a seventh. By the summer of 1922 he was broke and at rock bottom, his phone disconnected, his office furniture sold, his drilling crew unpaid, his bank account overdrawn. A local bank refused to cash his check for $7.40. Then one hot, dry August afternoon Davis and two friends drove out to see the seventh well. Still no oil. As they left, one of them glanced back and uttered a cry of surprise.

Oil was shooting out of the derrick.

Although it was only a 150-barrel-a-day well, it was what Davis needed more than anything else. Now he could raise money. It was the discovery well for the Luling field, two miles by twelve miles in size. As the field opened up, it produced 57,000 barrels a day.

Four years later Davis sold his interests in the field to Magnolia for $12.1 million, leaving him much richer than he had ever been. Then he began doing what he was best at: giving away money. First, he threw a glorious entertainment, perhaps the biggest barbecue ever held in Texas, in a 100-acre cotton field, to which he invited everyone in three counties. Though it was bigger than anything Edna Ferber's fertile imagination ever produced, it was, to Davis, merely a gesture. He began handing out bonuses to his employees. Five managers each received a $200,000 check, and all the other employees received cash gifts in proportion to the amount of time they had worked for him. It was the biggest thing that had ever happened in Luling, and while most of the sudden money was spent in ways most citizens would approve, some went to drink, mistresses, and other high jinks that led to marital breakups. Davis then turned to community projects; he built the town two clubhouses, one for whites, one for blacks, at a cost of $100,000. He sent $1 million back to his native Brockton for welfare organizations. By now he had developed a genuine love for Texas, and he sponsored three annual scenery painting competitions, which cost him $65,000. Now, with a $1 million endowment, he established the Luling Foundation with a demonstration farm of 1,223 acres, designed to improve agriculture in the region. As it became self-supporting, its land, buildings, and livestock grew in value to $2 million. It was to be his most enduring legacy.

With these warm-up throwaways behind him, Davis was now ready for his main performance, for which he is remembered outside Texas—the financing and determined backing of a stage play on reincarnation, *The Ladder,* on Broadway and elsewhere. *The Ladder* cost him $1.5 million over a period of more than two years, an expenditure he apparently never regretted.

The genesis of *The Ladder* began when Davis ran into a boyhood friend, J. Frank Davis, a crippled newspaperman not related to him. The other Davis was broke, and as they talked, oilman Davis' mind turned to a subject he had often brooded over. Why didn't Frank Davis write a play about reincarnation, which Edgar Davis would finance and produce? The newspaperman accepted with alacrity and immediately went on the oilman's payroll at a very comfortable figure. Whatever Edgar Davis' deepest beliefs—and it appears that he believed in reincarnation not in the literal sense but in the meaning that "people's influence never really dies"—he soon had a finished script on his hands, named *The Ladder* from a stanza from nineteenth-century writer Josiah Gilbert Holland.

> Heaven is not reached at a single bound;
> But we build the ladder by which we rise
> From the lowly earth to the vaulted skies
> And we mount to its summit round by round.

The characters in the play went through four incarnations that began in 1300 in an English castle and from there developed through London in 1670, New York in 1844, and New York in 1926. Each progression in time was accompanied by an improvement in character, as well.

In the spring of 1926 Edgar Davis headed for New York and managed to induce Brock Pemberton, then beginning his Broadway career, to read the play. Pemberton expressed misgivings, but Davis finally gave him a share in the play, and it was cast and rehearsed. It tried out to unenthusiastic audiences in Stamford, Detroit, and Cleveland. After some doctoring by Edward Knoblock, author of *Kismet,* the production opened in New York at the Mansfield Theater on October 22, 1926, at a time when Mae West was starring in *Sex,* Marilyn Miller in *Sunny,* and with *An American Tragedy* and *Abie's Irish Rose* going strong on Broadway. Critically, *The Ladder* was a flop. Alexander Woollcott called it "a large, richly upholstered piece of nothing at all" in the *World,* and the most generous critique came from John Anderson in the *Evening Post:* "Mr. Pemberton presented quite a long play." Generally, it may be said, from that point it went downhill.

Displaying the same determination and cheerfulness with which he had drilled his discovery well after six dusters, Davis put more money behind *The Ladder*. "Here's the theater, and here's the play, and here's a million dollars," he told his producer. "How can it fail?" Somehow it did. *The Ladder* moved from one theater to another, about a half dozen in all, becoming the talk of the town and, to some degree, of the nation. Very few paid admission. Attendance at first was poor, then trailed off. But on several occasions, when free performances were given, thousands had to be turned away. As the play groaned on into 1927, producer Pemberton got out, but Davis bought his interest and continued the show. Davis pampered the cast, paid them well, usually whatever they asked, and dined and wined them, but despite various newspaper promotions, nothing improved attendance, except free tickets.

Obsessed, determined that it should succeed, Davis sought to hire Eugene O'Neill to doctor the play, but alas, O'Neill didn't as much as acknowledge the offer. Audiences grew smaller and smaller, often to thirty persons, once to ten, and the play's revenues hung at about $300 a week, a tenth of what it was costing. Actors changed as fast as those tired of it could be replaced by those out of work and eager for a job. Refusing to give up the idea, Davis brought in new people and had a new version written. Finally, eighteen versions of the play were written, five of them used. It became a lavish production, the finest that money could buy, but attendance remained slight. On November 10, 1928, New Yorkers saw *The Ladder* for the last time. It had run for 789 performances. Davis then took it for two weeks to Boston, where it did well with paid admissions. Then, before its record could catch up with it, Davis proclaimed that he had finally seen *The Ladder* succeed and called an end to it. Few parallels to his tenacity are likely to be found.

In the end Davis went broke. It was not *The Ladder* that broke him, but the same streak of independence that had made him his money in the first place. He stubbornly insisted on following his hunches and allocated his money according to whim, heedless of any warning. His business affairs grew tangled. Claiming him as a resident, the Commonwealth of Massachusetts sued him for back income taxes. Davis sternly protested that he legally lived in Texas at the time he sold his Luling field in 1926. The legal battle rocked along. Massachusetts secured a $700,000 judgment against him, but Davis sued Massachusetts for $1 million for harassment in a Texas court, and the jury awarded it. When the case got out of Texas, into the U.S. Circuit Court of Appeals in New Orleans, the decision was reversed. True to his nature, Davis refused to compromise on the back taxes case, although Massachusetts probably would have settled for less than $700,000. "When I said I was a citizen of Texas in 1926," he said, "I either lied or I didn't. If I lied, then I owe them the entire amount. But I didn't lie, and I don't owe them a cent." For twenty years he and his native state remained at an impasse, while interest on the $700,000 judgment mounted annually, and he, bankrupt after 1935, lived on in his beloved adopted Luling.

In the twilight of his life, when he was still trying for a comeback in the oil business, with the whole town pulling for him, he had $5,000 a month coming in from various oil properties but could not touch it because of the judgment back east. He did his own cooking (his weight had dropped to 200 pounds) and was the town's leading bridge player. Until his death in 1951 at the age of seventy-eight, still a local hero, he seemed not to have let any of his vicissitudes bother him, as he placidly lived one day at a time.

Years before, while he was in the process of giving away some of his great wealth, Davis had said, "I have no right to any of this money. I'm called a success, but there's as shadowy a line between success and failure as between sanity and insanity. When I share my money I'm just equalizing things a little." He had known sanity and perhaps insanity, success and failure in his time. If he had lived in a later era he might have ended up the subject of a movie, with his likeness on a T-shirt.[16]

4

Although H. L. Hunt noted that he didn't "specialize" in giving to charity, other oilmen have seemed preoccupied with one of the favorite pastimes of the rich—philanthropy. Giving away large sums of money may require the careful attention and calculation that was needed to make the money in the first place, since there are usually more applicants than recipients.

Philanthropy brings its own rewards, often greater than those brought by success in the oil business itself. While helping break down the barriers that wealth may have made between the giver and his fellowmen, philanthropy earns social recognition and respect, public honors, and prestigious publicity that, as Goronwy Rees said, "are not to be obtained from other ways of getting rid of his money." Gifts help erode some of the suspicion and distrust that face the wealthy man.[17]

Central to the philanthropic acts is the observation that social observer George G. Kirstein made: "In the case of the living gift a man is donating unneeded money; in the case of the bequest, he is donating an excess which obviously cannot follow him." [18] Many a man has gone broke looking for more oil, but few—perhaps none, if we exclude Edgar B. Davis' atypical case—have reduced themselves to penury through philanthropy.

The motivations behind it have presumably not been much different for Texas oilmen than for those in other states in other businesses. One is reminded of an old-time West Texas cattleman who made enough money from oil to become, along with other interests, vice-president of a bank even though, as one contemporary described him, "he didn't know any more about banking than a pig does about Sunday." In the early days of the income tax he was soon squabbling with a representative from the federal revenue service over the amount of his tax. Uncle George, as he was known, roared at the fellow as if he were going to devour him on the spot. He cursed him for everything he could think of in a voice that could be heard all over town. "I may die and go to hell," thundered Uncle George, "but I'm never paying that much income tax!" [19]

It is not recorded whether Uncle George finally established a foundation to achieve his ends, but the truth is that circumvention of the tax collector is not, by far, the only reason for philanthropy. Psychiatrist James A. Knight, examining the psychodynamics of giving, has divided motivations into four broad areas encompassing the human spirit (love of God, love of one's fellowman, social responsibility), self-interest (fear, guilt, evasion of taxes, social recognition and respect), religion (tithing, stewardship, fear of hell or purgatory, personal glorification), and power. Although giving to a certain extent may buy power in or over the recipient, the motivations behind the act will range as widely as the various individuals' emotions, which may involve family honor, sympathy, pity, snob appeal, altruism, patriotism, hope of immortality—from the simplest selfish, egoistic emotions to the highest forms of selfless love, in other words.[20]

Traditionally, the vehicle for giving, to whatever purpose, has been the foundation. On the basis of Texas' reputation as the oil giant, one would expect foundations established by Lone Star sheikhs to bubble close to the top of the list. However, this is not the case. Although H. L. Hunt, had he wished to, presumedly could have endowed a foundation that would have ranked in the top twenty, if not the top ten; at the last accounting not one Texas foundation ranked among the top ten. The Ford and Rockefeller foundations were first and second, respectively, with the Ford Foundations's $3.5 billion or so far and away outdistancing the Rockefeller's mere $890 million. (Of course, many fortunes have been divided into more than one foundation, so that a single foundation's assets do not accurately reflect the total worth of the fortune's residue.) In fact, only four Texas-based foundations of any description could be found in the top thirty-three of America's largest foundations. They were the Houston Endowment, sixteenth, with $214 million; Moody Foundation of Galveston, seventeenth, with $191 million; Brown Foundation, Inc., of Houston, twenty-fifth, with $108 million; and Sid W. Richardson Foundation of Fort Worth, twenty-eighth, with $106 million. Of these, only the Richardson foundation represents the residue of a fortune made primarily from oil, although oil has probably played a part in the endowment of other large foundations, especially, of course, the Rockefeller Foundation. The Pew Memorial Trust, established in Philadelphia in 1948 and with assets of $437 million ranking fifth, is one that owes an acknowledgment of some depth to Texas oil, tracing back to Sun Oil's operations at Spindletop.[21]

If their philanthropies are any indication, Texas oilmen—as individuals and through foundations—have been concerned with education, health (or staving off death), and, one presumes, the hereafter. The dominant areas in which gifts have been distributed have included schools and scholarships, hospitals and medical research, and religious institutions. The religious beneficiaries have been, almost invariably, Christian. After all, the industry, as Bill Rudman, a Jew, has remarked, is "a Christian business," whether run by Christian principles or not, and one gives to what is familiar to him.

J. G. "Uncle Gash" Hardin, who made millions during the Burkburnett boom, was one of the early oil millionaire philanthropists. Continuing to live in an unpretentious, modestly furnished home, frequently recalling the old days when he and his wife had lived in a dugout with only a wagon sheet to shut out the snow, Hardin gave away $4 million and left a huge trust fund behind him. He reputedly sent thirty young men and women through college, rescued half a dozen colleges from financial jeopardy during the Depression, and gave bountifully not only to Baptist organizations, but to other churches as well. "I believe that there are good people in every church," he said. Hardin-Simmons University was renamed in his honor; Mary Hardin-Baylor in his wife's honor. He also gave to Abilene Christian College, Baylor University, and Howard Payne College. "I never had an opportunity for educational advantages," he said, "and if doing this will build character and citizenship, then I am amply repaid."

An ironic footnote to Hardin's legacy came after the East Texas field came in. In 1932 trustees of the Hardin Trust were searching for safe, but well-paying, investments in which to put its funds. During the depth of the Depression this proved to be challenging. Those that were safe paid poorly, and others were risky. But as the East Texas field opened up, the trustees, familiar with the oil business, began making loans, first to a royalty company and then to other oilmen. As area bankers, until then distrustful of oilmen, saw the Hardin Trust loans being repaid, they began to loosen their credit strings. Thus, the Hardin Trust—endowed by oil—helped show the way. But ironically, the old Baptist's trust probably also financed the running of hot oil, for some loans were made, as Ruel McDaniel observed, to "men and corporations that ran hot oil." [22]

Oil wealth came too late for some to spend it in the usual ways. J. M. and Margaret Shannon, who came to the United States from Ireland, settled in Southwest Texas and lived out their lives alone on an isolated ranch. The town of Big Lake was forty miles away. When oil was found on their 50,000 acres, they were too old to travel or otherwise spend the new money. The white-bearded old gentleman and his wife preferred their large, quiet ranch. Their biggest expenditure while living was to endow the Shannon West Texas Memorial Hospital in San Angelo, memorializing their name through the wealth they did not live to enjoy.[23]

5

George Strake, Sr., a devout Catholic, so devoted himself to philanthropy that he became the most decorated Catholic layman in the United States. He reached the pinnacle in 1946, when Pope Pius XII personally decorated him with Knight, Grand Cross, of the Order of St. Sylvester, the oldest and most prized of papal orders.

"I have dedicated every venture to God," said Strake. "How foolish I would be to say that George Strake alone discovered the great Conroe oil field or any other, because I had God as my partner. I hope Divine Providence stays with me and never lets me commit the sin of pride in thinking I am a great man." [24]

Although Strake served on the boards of both St. Louis University and Notre Dame, one of his most interesting dispositions involved the famed Baptist minister Billy Graham. Strake owned what had been called "a fantastic paradise" in the Colorado mountains. One day Graham visited Strake for two hours in the oilman's Houston office. Neither ever reported what went on behind the closed doors, but when it was over, Strake had given the Graham organization the Colorado property as a sanctuary and Graham had asked the Catholic Strake to be the first speaker to the students there.[25]

His son, George Strake, Jr., remembered, "He used to say, 'It's hard to make money, it's hard to keep it, but it's even more difficult to give it away properly.'

"He knew the Bible better than any other layman I've ever known, and he tried to live that life that is taught in the Bible. A phrase in the Bible that used to worry him was the one which said it is as hard for a rich man to get to heaven as it is for a camel to go through the eye of a needle. He studied that, read books on it. The phrase came from the ancient days in Egypt when the people would ride their camels to the city. The camel, just like a dog, would develop affection for the owner, and when they would come into the marketplace, they would keep these camels in a corral. The camel would try to follow the owner into the marketplace. So what they did, they built a passageway there that was built big enough for a man to get through but very difficult for a camel to get through, because it'd hit his hump. And they called it 'the eye of the needle.' So that's what they were referring to, in the vernacular of the day, when the Bible was written. What he felt was, it wasn't impossible for a wealthy man to get into heaven, but the temptation to *not* get there was awfully great. And if he wasn't careful, it was as difficult for a rich man to get there as it was for the camel to get through the eye of this corral needle. Those kinds of things would disturb him to the point where he would research it and find an answer or change his way of living." [26]

Sid Richardson, the "billion-dollar bachelor" of Fort Worth, left his wealth to his relatives and to foundations. The true extent of his foundation's impact on Texas can be imagined only by carefully adding up the individual grants. The Richardson Foundation's primary impact has been in erecting buildings, such as gymnasiums for schools. In addition to private schools, it has benefited the state-supported University of Texas at Austin, to which the foundation gave $2 million in support of library collections on the history of science. In 1971 the oilman was memorialized on the Austin campus with the dedication of Sid Richardson Hall, a massive, splendid 942-foot long building behind the Lyndon B. Johnson Library.[27] But the full extent of the Richardson Foundation's contribution and influence is likely to be known only to its trustees.

The figures are not in yet, either, on Hugh Roy Cullen's gifts to society. Probably the champion Texas oilman-philanthropist, Cullen and his wife, Lillie, gave away huge portions of their money during their lifetimes. The estimates range from $200 million to more than 90 percent of their wealth.

"Giving away money is no particular credit to me," said Cullen. "Most of it came out of the ground—and while I found the oil in the ground, I didn't put it there. I've got a lot more than Lillie and I and our children and grandchildren can use. I don't think I deserve any great credit for using it to help people. It's easier for me to give a million dollars now than it was to give five dollars to the Salvation Army twenty-five years ago."

That earlier contribution to which he referred, a $5 check to the Salvation Army, had bounced because he had not realized his bank account was so low.

Cullen's entry into philanthropy came several months after his only son's death in an oil field accident. The former head of Houston's public school system and a founder of Houston Junior College, which grew into the University of Houston, went to Cullen to solicit his help in raising the money needed to enlarge the institution. At the moment Cullen was preoccupied with politics. Chewing on a cigar, he said, "I'm putting in most of my time trying to beat Roosevelt." Later he looked into the situation and, with the death of his son still fresh in his memory, wrote a check for $260,000 for the first University of Houston building, the Roy Gustave Cullen Memorial Building. With his eyes wet and his voice choked, he said, "There is only one condition to this contribution. The University of Houston must always be a college for working men and women and their sons and daughters. If it were to be another rich man's college, I wouldn't be interested."

Although Cullen attached no strings to his gifts, he appears to have checked his recipients for taints of liberalism in advance, if one anecdote is any indication. Approached with plans for a hospital for children with polio, operated by the Gonzales Warm Springs Foundation for Infantile Paralysis, a Texas institution, the old entrepreneur grew wary at the mention of "Warm Springs" even though it was at Gonzales, Texas. "Has this got anything to do with Mr. Roosevelt?" he asked. The man assured him that it had no connection with the Warm Springs, Georgia, institution made famous by FDR and that it might, in fact, be competitive and better. Cullen, put at ease, wrote a check for $35,000, with more to come.

The overwhelming bulk of Cullen's gifts went to education and medicine. He and his wife one night decided to donate money to some of Houston's hospitals and forty-eight hours later had given $4.5 million to four separate hospitals for new buildings and other purposes, with no strings attached. It came out of his oil payments. But all his beneficences were capped in March, 1947, during an address before the Texas Hospital Association, when from the stage of Houston's Music Hall he unexpectedly announced he and Mrs. Cullen were giving from 60 to 80 million barrels of oil to the University of Houston and the Texas Medical Center. With oil selling at $2.10 a barrel at the time, this would mean as much as $160 million from the production. He stated that he would form a foundation to distribute it. The largest single philanthropic act ever made in Texas, it was also the largest amount of money ever given by a single family during the lifetime of the donors. At that time the Cullen Foundation was said to have been exceeded only by the Ford and Rockefeller foundations.

Laurance S. Rockefeller, in Houston to attend a board meeting of Eastern Airlines, and a man who should have known what he was talking about, said it was "beyond anything I've ever run into."

But Cullen had a mundane explanation. "My wife and I are selfish," he said. "We want to see our money spent during our lifetime so we may derive great pleasure from it." [28]

Education has been a consistent concern of others as well. D. Harold Byrd recollected he had sent "twenty-six boys and two girls" to college on scholarships. His alma mater, the University of Texas at Austin, has been his favorite institution, and his interest has tended to focus on the UT band, to which he gave the "biggest drum in the world," standing seventy-eight inches high.[29]

Michel T. Halbouty has maintained scholarships at Texas A&M for about thirty years, "to help the underprivileged like I was helped," as he puts it. "I couldn't have finished school without borrowing money from Texas A&M, the development fund, and I vowed that if I ever reached the point where I could help anybody else, I was gonna do it. That was one of the first things I did. When I was able to, I established a scholarship just for underprivileged students who wanted to take geology and petroleum engineering." [30]

Giving land has frequently been used to help schools. W. B. Hamilton's company in Wichita Falls donated the forty acres on which that city's Midwestern University now has its main buildings. Also a two-term mayor of the city, Hamilton sold the university another forty acres at the low price of $200 an acre, even though he had already received a cash offer elsewhere of $750 an acre.[31]

One of the most original uses of oil money stemmed from a decision by Mrs. Walter B. Sharp, the widow of one of the Texas Company founders. She arranged for and paid for the tape recording of interviews with a large number of the surviving pioneers in Texas' oil history. This became the Pioneers in Texas Oil Oral History Project of the University of Texas at Austin, through which, under the supervision of Mody Boatright of the University and

William A. Owens of Columbia University, approximately 100 persons were interviewed during the 1950's. Many of the old-timers who were at Spindletop and the early Gulf Coast booms were still alive. Pattillo Higgins, for instance, left his memories of those nascent days on tape. Much of the material in the early chapters of this book came from the Pioneers in Texas Oil project.

When Mrs. Sharp died at ninety-two in the 1960's, she left about $25,000 with which to carry on the work. Her husband had died young, in 1912.

"She looked back on her life in the early days of the petroleum industry with my father as being a high point in her life," said Dudley C. Sharp, her son. "About 1951 we went to the fiftieth anniversary of Spindletop at Beaumont. We had a lot of old-timers there. I'm sure that's what stimulated her into doing this." [32]

If it had not been for her interest, all the old reminiscences would have been lost.

6

Some gifts, like Sid Richardson's funding struggling students, have gone unheralded. Claud Hamill remembered a time he and George Brown were out driving. "We came by some property out here where they have a retirement home for women—and Glenn McCarthy gave 'em that land. Twenty acres of it. And I mentioned that Glenn had given that, and George Brown's remark was that nobody knows anything about it. Glenn has done a lot for Houston." [33]

Most philanthropies, unlike that example of McCarthy's largess, are at least visible. Some of the most generous philanthropists have come from the ranks of the early oil families. Humble Oil-linked heirs have been especially active. Mrs. Harry C. Wiess, widow of a Humble Oil board chairman, gave Rice Institute $1,570,000 to establish a chair in geology, and two years later her three daughters added $1 million with which to erect a geology building. Before that John H. Blaffer, also Humble-related, built a wing of the Houston Museum of Fine Arts, an auditorium for Houston's Kinkaid School, and underwrote the publication of art portfolios for

the University of Texas Press. Nina Cullinan, of another family
tracing back to Corsicana before Spindletop, paid for another wing
of the museum.[34] Mrs. Walter Fondren, of another early Humble
Oil family, has made major contributions to institutions such as
Dallas' Southern Methodist University and Houston's Methodist
Hospital. "I don't think she has ever sold a share of Humble stock,"
said Claud Hamill, "but she sure has given a lot away." [35]

An oil fortune that without doubt was well spent was that
accruing to old Governor James S. Hogg's children. Their wealth
came after their father's death, from a plantation he had bought
years before. The three Hogg brothers, facing difficult times, had
been interested in selling the plantation, but their sister, Ima,
wouldn't let them sell "Papa's place." So they paid the taxes on it,
and it eventually produced a great fortune when the West Columbia field opened in 1919. Will Hogg, the governor's eldest son, died
in 1930 while vacationing with his sister in Europe. His will left a
major portion of his estate set aside for both Mike and Ima to
stipulate its use. With $2.5 million they established the Hogg
Foundation for Mental Hygiene, administered through the University of Texas; $600,000 more from his will went for student loan
funds at several universities. After Mike died in 1941 and Tom in
1949, only Ima was left.

She and her brothers looked on the oil money as theirs to hold in
trust, and she spent millions on philanthropy for the state, in
backing the Houston symphony, museums, and Memorial Park in
Houston. In 1958 she gave the state of Texas the Varner plantation,
on which the oil had been found, as a state park and museum. She
gave her Italian-style villa, Bayou Bend, and its fifteen acres of
gardens to the Houston Museum of Fine Arts, along with $750,000
in stocks to maintain it. In it was an Early American collection of
antiques and furniture, worth perhaps $10 million, that could be
rivaled only by that of the DuPont family. She not only used her
own money in her projects, but succeeded in bringing others in. In
her eighties she helped create the outdoor University of Texas
Winedale Museum at Round Top, personally supervising the
construction.[36]

7

Personal and family vicissitudes have provided the impetus for many acts of generosity. J. K. (for John Keener) Wadley, who operated from the Arkansas-Texas border, made philanthropy his major endeavor in his latter years. A deeply religious man who felt that the hand of God was in his business successes, Wadley had started out as a telegrapher and auditor whose attention to details won him rapid promotions. Then, proving that luck favors those who display pluck, he married into money. In the first decade of the century, before he was thirty, he made $100,000 and owned Texarkana's first automobile, an open-top one-cylinder Merry Oldsmobile. He was a rich man by the time he entered the oil business in 1919 in Louisiana, where within a few years he lost $400,000. But he bounded back handsomely when the East Texas field came in and was never to lack for money thereafter, as he added timber, hotels, and gold mining to his activities. Upon his death at ninety-three he left a sizable estate, of which about $1 million went to his Baptist church and $1 million to the Wadley Hospital, named after him, in his hometown—to which he had already provided huge contributions—as well as generous sums to about thirty individuals.

Much had been given away during his lifetime, of which the most noted recipient was probably Dallas' Wadley Research Institute of Molecular Medicine and Blood Bank. The inspiration for this came when a small grandson died of leukemia. During the last three months of the boy's life Grandpa Wadley stayed in Dallas to be near him. The end came for the six-year-old in Baylor Hospital.

"The night he passed away," said Wadley, "he kept calling for me, and when I walked into the room, he was suffering terribly with only a few hours to live. He cried, 'Papoo, I am not having a bit of fun!'"

The poignant memory of the little boy's plaintive wail never left Wadley's mind. The oilman vowed to work to eradicate the disease that had taken his grandson's life. The result became what then was one of the most complete blood research units in the world.[37]

When one possesses great wealth, there are subtle ways to make one's money count more and even to involve the rest of the community—sometimes without their knowing it. Texarkana journalist J. Q. Mahaffey played, to his surprise, a major role in such an event because of his friendship with millionaire Wadley.

"We were having a fund-raising project at the First Baptist Church, and I was making a speech in behalf of the fund and urging all of the other men of the church to give," said Mahaffey. "Almost right in the middle of the speech, I realized that although I was urging everyone else to give, I wasn't gonna give anything, because I was a lowly editor at the *Gazette* and I couldn't afford to give anything.

"Well, right in the middle of the thing J. K. Wadley walked up to me—he was sitting on the platform—and he said, 'You pledge five hundred dollars, and I'll pay it.' So I reared back, and I said, 'I feel so strongly about this fund that I will personally pledge *five hundred dollars!*' You could see the old-timers out there almost shocked. Oh, then I challenged them, and they began to give.

"So I went home that night, and Ruth was sitting up in bed. She said, 'Well, how did your speech go at the church?'

"I said, 'Oh, it was great! I got so enthusiastic that I personally pledged five hundred dollars.'

"She said, 'You did *what?*'

"I said, 'I pledged five hundred dollars to the building fund. But take it easy—J. K. Wadley's going to pay for it.'

"And then there was a long silence, and she said, 'How was he feeling when you saw him last?'

"And really, it was nearly two weeks that we worried. He hadn't come around with the money and we were scared to death that he would die and nobody would know the fact that he was going to pay that. Three or four weeks later, though, he paid it, and I got credit for pledging five hundred dollars to the church." [38]

8

Giving is never as simple as it seems and sometimes, as Dallas' Algur H. Meadows learned in the 1960's, it can become absolutely complicated—even heartbreaking. Meadows, a shrewd trader and controlling stockholder and chairman of the board of General American Oil Company of Texas, became what *Life* magazine called "the man who owns what may be the largest private collection of fake paintings in the world." A round-faced, balding, white-haired man in his sixties at the time, Meadows had begun his campaign of art acquisition in Europe, with many of his purchases subsequently going to Southern Methodist University.

"I had this compulsion," he said. "It's like self-hypnosis. Nothing satisfies except to continue to collect. All the time I thought I was creating something of immortal value. I kept thinking, what if I could have, in Dallas, Texas, a collection of art that might be considered a tiny Prado? I might be the only person in the country who could do this."

Meadows' wife, Virginia, had died in 1961, and he endowed SMU with $1 million to build a museum of Spanish art in her memory. After remarrying in 1962, he spent $500,000 on forty-one contemporary Italian sculptures, which went to a sculpture court and garden at SMU, dedicated to his second wife, Elizabeth.[39]

In April, 1964, Fernand Legros, a friend of Elmyr de Hory and supposedly a salesman of Hory's family art treasures, was introduced to Meadows in Dallas. Over the next two and a half years Legros and a partner, Réal Lessard, called on Meadows, eventually selling to him fifteen Dufys, seven Modiglianis, five Vlamincks, eight Derains, three Matisses, two Bonnards, one Chagall, one Degas, one Marquet, one Laurencin, one Gauguin, and a Picasso. The paintings were impressively documented, complete with certificates from a painter's family, sales records from auction houses, even statements of authenticity by experts in Paris. The French masters were valued at about $2 million, although Meadows, a trader always, bargained for much less. In the sale of one Modigliani, Legros and Lessard had asked $100,000 but were forced to drop to $75,000. When Meadows finally offered $45,000, they took it.

There was just one catch to the bargains Meadows had bought. They were fakes. They were painted by Elmyr de Hory.

When Meadows learned that his Spanish collection, given to SMU earlier, might not be authentic, he sought the advice of experts then in Dallas for a Picasso show. They assessed the work as forgeries.[40]

Meadows, by one account, had paid around $400,000 for what had been appraised at $1,362,750.[41] Aside from the paintings he had given to SMU, art dealers noted that his personal collection of French moderns might contain as many as forty-four fakes. Until the first suspicions had been aroused, however, not only Meadows but the entire art world had been taken in.

By now Meadows was busily replacing the forgeries with genuine works of art, costing millions more. Within a few months after disclosure of the racket, he had spent a couple of million dollars on paintings by Cézanne, Renoir, Bonnard, Murillo, Goya, and Pollock. "Oh, we've got our hands on some of the prettiest things you ever saw," he said.

Two years later, in 1969, SMU announced that Meadows had given the school a gift of $8 million for support of its school of the arts. It was the largest single gift SMU had received in its history and one of the largest gifts made by an individual to an American university. By that time it had run his total gifts to SMU to more than $15 million.[42]

9

The leading candidate for Texas oil money's most creative and, perhaps in the long run, most valuable contribution may be what second-generation oilman Tom Slick, Jr., did with his fortune. The basis for the wealth had been laid down by Tom, Sr., his Pennsylvania-born father who had drilled the discovery well in the Cushing, Oklahoma, field in 1912. Tom, Sr., had retired rich at thirty-one, but took poorly to idleness and went back into the oil business. He died of a cerebral hemorrhage in 1930 at age forty-six.

Young Tom, the eldest of three children, became known in later life for his expeditions to the mountains of Asia in search of yeti, the abominable snowman. But his more lasting expenditures stemmed out of his scientific interests developed as a youngster.

Educated at Yale, he established his home in San Antonio in 1939. As the Slicks and Urschels, his kinsmen, began finding more oil, in Mississippi and in Midland, Texas, he began to think of ways to achieve some of his boyhood dreams. As a youth he had conducted experiments and had frequently thought of becoming a laboratory scientist.

During World War II as he was serving as a naval officer in the South Pacific, Slick read a *Reader's Digest* article about the Armour Research Institute in Chicago, in which Harold Vagtborg of the institute was quoted as saying, "We can improve anything." After the war Slick, who felt strongly about the role of science in modern life, made contact with Vagtborg, telling him of the quotation that had impressed him so. Vagtborg explained, to Slick's dismay, that he had been misquoted. "Anything can be improved," it should have read. Vagtborg, by then president of Midwest Research Institute in Kansas City, soon became head of Slick's Southwest Research Institute, established in 1947.

"Tom was one of those rare individuals who seemed to have been born with the notion that scientific research could and would solve most of mankind's problems," said Vagtborg. "When he was of high school age, he was already doing complex experiments in biology; his inquisitiveness was unbounded. While other boys were reading the popular novels of the day, Tom was reading *Scientific American, Popular Mechanics,* and many books on science."

Slick earlier had founded the Southwest Foundation for Research and Education in 1941, when he was twenty-five, but the war had interrupted his plans.

Despite his pursuit of the abominable snowman that became linked with his name, Slick was nearly the opposite of the flamboyant oilman. In his western hat and gray business suit, he might have passed on a San Antonio street as just another South Texas businessman or rancher. Since his graduation from Yale his interests had spread from general science to medicine, biology, engineering, physics, and chemistry. From his original philanthropy four research institutions evolved, two of them surviving him. He also established the Mind Science Foundation and the Human Progress Foundation, while providing substantial financial support to education, the cause of peace, and other institutions.

He was a restless person, often taking chances while flying on his global journeys. He had one narrow escape in the Brazilian jungles in the 1950's while on a geological exploration, and he had taken many risks on trips to Tibet and other places in search of the abominable snowman.

One day he told Vagtborg, "Harold, don't be so concerned about the hopping around I do in small planes in foreign countries and in the mountains looking for the snowman or mines or even going hunting. I have a million-dollar insurance policy with the institutions as beneficiary that you can rely on."

In 1962, at the age of forty-six, the same point in life his father had reached, Tom Slick, Jr., and his pilot were killed when their plane crashed near Dillon, Montana, while flying into a storm area without the aid of navigation instruments.

His will took care of the institutions he had fathered, with one-sixteenth of the funds directed toward "furthering peace efforts, particularly in the direction of long-range and comprehensive planning." Among those whose opinions he wanted "solicited, carefully considered, and followed as far as seems advisable" were Norman Cousins, editor of *Saturday Review*.

At the time of Slick's death the staffs of the research organizations totaled 700 persons, with facilities and equipment valued at more than $6 million. The existing three organizations had total budgets of more than $7 million with cumulative budgets having reached $60 million.

In all, his estate has given $12 million to three research institutions and three universities. Endowments went to Texas A&M and Texas Christian University for range management programs and fellowship programs and for "peace studies" at the LBJ School of Public Affairs at the University of Texas at Austin. An extensive art collection was given by his executors to the Witte Memorial Museum and the Marion Koogler McNay Art Institute in San Antonio.

Although many tried to dissuade him from locating his research institutions in San Antonio, which was supposed to be the "wrong place," they have flourished. The Southwest Foundation for Research and Education works on basic medical research. The Southwest Research Institute concentrates on applied research and development. Together they employ more than 1,400 people and have combined assets of more than $20 million with annual budgets in excess of $25 million. Samples of their ongoing research in 1975 included cholesterol metabolism related to heart disease; nutrition and vitamins; quality in meat research; cellular physiology and microbiology; horticulture; hormone biochemistry; pathology cancer research; water conservation; lubrication technology in nuclear-powered aircraft; study of air contamination in Houston; land utilization in New Mexico and East Texas, and environmental control.

After the spacecraft fire at the Kennedy Space Center in 1967, Southwest Research Institute was called on by NASA to study the combustion characteristics in pure oxygen of all nometallic materials used in the Apollo command module and to investigate measures to prevent, retard, or extinguish spacecraft fires. Its recommendation was accepted by NASA, and the institute was awarded a contract to develop a prototype portable extinguisher capable of putting out fires in a pure oxygen atmosphere. Once it had been worked out, the extinguishers were used in all subsequent Apollo flights.

The legacy promises to be a permanent display of Slick's faith in his favorite subject, for as Vagtborg said, "The depth of his convictions of what scientific research could do cannot be measured." [43]

10

One of the most intriguing cases of "what they did with it" involved a couple who were not oil people to begin with or inheritors of oil money—but they thought they were. Ernest and Margaret Medders enjoyed a six-year spending spree with $3 million worth of Texas high life that was an Aladdin's lamp full of wishes come true. They bought a Texas-rich home and ranch, dined at Lyndon Johnson's White House, and flew home on Air Force One. It was a grand, sheikhlike life-style—all on credit.

Everyone seemed eager to extend the Medderses credit because the word spread like a gas blowout that they were heirs to the estate of William Pelham Humphries, who had owned Spindletop land before oil came. The contention was that Humphries had not sold the land legally, and therefore, the Humphries heirs rightfully owned fortunes that others had collected. Responding to a newspaper ad from Tuscaloosa, Alabama, Memphis resident Ernest Medders attended a meeting of people with his name or a similar variation who might be heirs of Humphries on the Ruben Medders side of the family. The story circulated that the "true heirs" might have $6 billion coming, mainly from oil companies. Ernest Medders was a grandnephew of Ruben Medders. W. T. Weir, a Mississippi attorney, handled the case. Until his death at ninety-three in 1972 Weir's principal efforts were directed toward the Spindletop case.

In 1961 Weir filed suit in behalf of the Medderses, who were striving to make ends meet. Margaret Medders had been so destitute at one time that she had placed her children in an orphanage and had worked sixteen-hour shifts as a nurse in Memphis, while her husband, who left school after the third grade, had earned $65 a week as a mechanic's helper. The lawsuit changed all this. Faster than a bad rumor, the news spread of their impending wealth, bringing them offers of credit that eventually extended into the millions.

Borrowing $20,000 from Subiaco Academy, a Roman Catholic school in Arkansas where two of Mrs. Medders' sons were sent, the couple moved from Memphis to Muenster, Texas, in search of a better climate for the husband's health. Both were middle-aged. When they decided to buy 185 acres of land, costing $60,000 over four years, they found the Poor Sisters of St. Francis Seraph, Inc., of Mishawaka, Indiana, willing to put up the money. The couple built a twenty-room house that they called Colonial Acres. The nuns paid for it because Medders had made out his will stipulating that in his lifetime he intended to give $10 million to the order and that if he failed to do so, the sum was to be given the order from his estate at his death.

In all, the Medderses acquired about 1,400 acres, including eighteen oil wells and prime Angus cattle, prize-winning Appaloosa horses, an irrigation system, and a huge show barn with a kitchen, office, and a movable floor. Their house was up to the Texas-rich standards, with three dens, a swimming pool, all furnished with the finest that borrowed money could buy.

The nuns lent them a total of $1.94 million.

Then the Beaumont court denied the claim by the Humphries descendants. On appeal, the Texas Court of Civil Appeals also ruled against them. The case went to the U.S. Supreme Court, which in October, 1965, dismissed it. But Weir, undaunted, began seeking other ways of recovering the fortune, while the Medderses continued spending.

Margaret Medders had a $60,000 ring, a spectacular necklace, and had ordered an $80,000 mink coat. Since their relatives had gained nothing from the lawsuit, suspicions were aroused. One of them filled suit to seek a declaration on the source of the Medders money. In court, Ernest Medders explained that it was all based on credit. His only income, Social Security checks, couldn't even pay the utility bills at Colonial Acres. This precipitated the deluge, as 200 creditors filed suit, crushing the couple into bankruptcy. Cars, trucks, farm equipment, livestock, land, houses, and oil wells went up for auction. But under Texas bankruptcy law, they retained a Cadillac (their "carriage") and the twenty-room home and 185 acres (their "homestead"). They were forced to sell the farm when they couldn't afford to keep it up.

The six-year merry-go-round ended in 1967. But several years later, in the 1970's, they were better off than when it had started, with a four-bedroom brick and frame two-story home in Memphis, a new Cadillac, and a cook. Mrs. Medders had written a book about it and was talking about there being a movie of their experience. "We're not destitute," she said. Most creditors had settled for 12½ cents on the dollar, and Subiaco was repaid its $20,000. But the Poor Sisters remained nearly $2 million the poorer.

"We was just ignorant," said Mrs. Medders. "We just didn't know how to live rich." [44]

11

While oil wealth has improved many a person's life, a few have spent their time and money in defending their claims to it. A landowner who became rich from oil, Mrs. W. A. Monroe Smith died unhappy at seventy-five in 1929 in San Angelo in West Texas after years of litigation over the money, with her children aligned against her. The frail little woman was almost blind in her declining years as she occupied witness chairs and matched wits with her children's attorneys, who tried to have her declared mentally incompetent.

She and her first husband, John Monroe, had gone to West Texas as a young couple, fighting droughts and other frontier hardships in the rough Pecos country. Monroe died, and she married W. A. Smith, a cowboy. When oil was found on her ranch lands, it brought in millions of dollars. Then began the litigation. She sued a son on a grass lease. Her children then sued to have a receiver appointed, claiming she was not competent to manage her affairs. A receiver was named and filed suit against the oil companies, seeking to break Mrs. Smith's leases. Nearly blind and almost inarticulate, the old woman fought the suit. But shortly before her death she viewed it all with sorrow.

"Oil has been a curse to me," she said. "I wish I had never seen an oil well. I wish they had never found a drop of oil on my ranch. It has brought me nothing but trouble and sorrow and definitely set my children against me and made me poor again." [45]

XV

A DECLINING GIANT

1

Seventy-five years after its first bonanza at Spindletop, Texas is a declining oil giant, faced with the prospect of becoming substantially drained in one long lifetime.

A very brief era, the years since 1901 lie within the lifetime of a large segment of our population. Many of the persons interviewed for this book were born before Spindletop. Yet within that time more has happened to more people in the world at large than occurred in all previous time. Our technology has expanded with dizzying speed. Our population has proliferated. Most of all, we have flagrantly, insatiably consumed nonrenewable resources, especially petroleum, as recklessly as those old Spindletop operators who opened up their gushers on a Sunday afternoon just to impress the visitors. They thought it would last forever. So, it appears, did we.

As an oil producer Texas—barring a totally unexpected huge discovery—is over the hill. Estimates of the giant, East Texas, give it another fifteen to twenty years of production, maybe more. It could be less, for with wells producing 100 percent of allowable, there are the risks of lowered field pressure and water encroachment.

As long ago as the 1960's the domestic oil situation was far from bright. During the crisis in the Middle East that resulted from the closing of the Suez Canal, Texas production was raised to take up the slack. Increasing allowables would push the good fields to their limits, but, said one oilman, "The old fields physically can't do it. They are worn out." Some Texas districts in 1967 fell 30 percent short of their legal allowables.[1] Seven years later Sherman Hunt, while president of the Texas Mid-Continent Oil and Gas Association, said, "We don't have an oil field that I know of that could stand to produce more than it is producing right now, over a period of time. And if you produce it over what we call the maximum efficient rate (MER), you would leave so much oil behind that you would never recover. You know," he added, "we find a major discovery in the United States about every ten years. Just go back through history. And, of course, every time one of them is found there's just that one less to find again. I would be surprised if, domestically, it could ever be where we could be totally self-sufficient." [2]

Texas remains the number one oil state, but by the 1970's it was undergoing a "traumatic transition from being an oil exporter to being an oil importer," as the *Texas Observer* phrased it. In 1975, after three consecutive years with allowables set at 100 percent, Texas was importing 4,432,000 barrels a day, while major buyers were purchasing 3,774,509 barrels a day of Texas oil. With about 28 percent of the nation's refinery capacity in Texas, the industry's base will remain there for a long time, but more and more it will be processing foreign crude.[3] It is a time of flux not only for Texas, but for the nation; if the number one oil state faces these prospects, the nation obviously is in a similar situation.

Back before Ranger's boom, when Jay Hall, for many years the oil editor of the Dallas *Morning News,* was born, Pennsylvania and West Virginia were the leading oil states. Now Texas is in their position. "In my planning for my own personal life," said Hall as he sat sipping a late-afternoon drink in his retirement home near Tyler within walking distance of the golf course, "I always said that the oil business in Texas and Jay Hall would go out about the same time. I set 1975, which would make me sixty-five. But actually Texas reached its peak in 1962. I'm not saying somebody won't come along and find another East Texas field, but I guarantee you it's like me shooting par golf—I don't think it's gonna be done!

"There have been too many wells drilled in Texas, too many

areas explored, too much geophysical work done. There shouldn't be an inch of ground in the state of Texas that isn't pretty well known by the explorer. Now that doesn't say we're just going to fade out of the oil business, because we still have quite a bit of reserves and we could still find, you know, small stuff to keep the thing from falling altogether apart. It's going to take a long time to exhaust this state. But Texas is becoming an old oil province. That's the only way I can say it. We're not virgin anymore. We've been had!" [4]

2

During that three-quarters of a century Texas has come a great distance. "In the roster of the great and dynamic states Texas has now won a place," wrote Theodore H. White more than twenty years ago. "The struggle for control of its bursting energy and industrial power cannot leave American life unchanged; whichever way it goes, the rest of the nation will be tugged to follow—or to resist." [5] Events have proved White accurate. Texas today is the industrial power that he foresaw in 1954. By the mid-1970's Texas had moved into the number three spot of the most populous states with more than 12 million people, behind California and New York, brusquely shoving ahead of Pennsylvania. Texas' population was increasing at the rate of 8 percent, ahead of California's 5.4 percent, while New York actually lost population. Texas led all other states in the use of fuel and electric energy in manufacturing.[6] Petroleum has made it possible, by providing an abundant supply of cheap energy to fuel the industries that have transformed the state.

Energy-intensive industries have tended to follow major discoveries. This has made the difference, for better or for worse, in creating a booming Texas. "I'd say you wouldn't have a rustling type of economy without oil," said historian-oilman Ed Owen. "All you have to do is to look at the counties that have had no oil and contrast them with the counties that have had the oil. A lot of Texas would be just like Mexico. A lot of it was, the first time I saw it." [7] Without oil and gas, others agree, Texas "wouldn't be worth a damn," "wouldn't be anything but an old cow country," and its smaller population would have to depend largely on cattle, timber, farming, and fishing.[8]

Today Texas has more oil and gas wells than Jim Hogg and

"Buckskin Joe" Cullinan could ever have envisioned. Wells are in every region of the state: prairies, piney woods, sand dunes, swamps, high plains, coastal waters, out into the Gulf of Mexico—quietly, steadily flowing the lifeblood that moves Texas and a good part of the nation. An obvious reason for Texas' prolific record is its size. Enlarge the boundaries of any state in a region where there is a lot of petroleum and that state will become a leader.

Statistics may be dry, but they tell an amazing story. From the beginning of recorded production in 1889 until January, 1975, the total value of Texas crude oil was a staggering $99,409,358,005— nearly $100 billion. Since this represents the wellhead price, which went as low as 5 cents per barrel and often hovered around $1, it is a colossus. This amounted to 39.4 percent of the United States' production during that time—and 6.14 percent of the world's total.[9] Texas had seen 17,964 separate oil *fields* developed within its boundaries, with 8,075 of them still active. A total of 219 of its 254 counties have produced oil; 212 of them still do.[10] And the Texas Mid-Continent Oil and Gas Association reported that the state has had 35 of the nation's largest 100 oil fields, which hold an estimated 7.5 billion barrels yet of Texas' 11-billion-barrel reserve. Seven of the ten biggest fields are in Texas, the Yates field in West Texas with 1.3 billion barrels left, the East Texas field with 1.2 billion to go. (The United States' largest field was Prudhoe Bay on Alaska's North Slope, awaiting the completion of the Trans-Alaska Pipeline to produce its estimated 9.6 billion barrels.)[11] The data overwhelmingly pronounce Texas to have been the richest, in natural wealth, of all the fifty states. "Even if you take California's oil production, add the gold and everything else," said Ed Owen, "Texas would still win."[12]

Enriched though Texas has been, it is still debated whether eastern and other out-of-state capital has dominated the profits that have come from under the soil. Undeniably much of its wealth has gone out of state. John Gunther thought of Texas as a "colony," the state has been labeled New York's most valuable possession by others, and there are even some who insist that the official state song, "Texas, Our Texas," should be retitled to reflect more accurately the economic realities—"Texas, Their Texas." When Standard Oil scion Winthrop Rockefeller dropped out of Yale in the 1930's and went to work as a 78-cents-an-hour roustabout in the

Texas oil fields, becoming the only Rockefeller brother to be a paid employee of the family's oil companies, it was as in a Kiplingesque legend of the black sheep sailing for the colonies.

Yet as seductive as it is, the colonial analogy has its flaws. How is one to equate Texas, with its private ownership of land and an environment that gave rise to thousands of independent oilmen, to Mexico during the heyday of the British and American interests there? And whereas in the early Hogg era corporations exploited Texas from headquarters in the North and the East, many of the large oil companies' domestic headquarters are now in Texas, especially in Houston. Undoubtedly "outsiders" have profited from Texas' wealth, perhaps more than the Texans themselves, but their outside capital also has helped make the state the oil leader.

How much of the oil business in the state is owned by Texans? Two decades ago Fain Gillock, an old-timer, estimated that 92 percent was owned by nonresidents.[13] That figure may or may not be accurate; the majors, controlled elsewhere, do have major shares. But this is not the same question as a companion one: How much of Texas' oil money has remained in the state? The percentage undoubtedly is higher than a mere 8, although supplying the full answer involves ramifications. To start with, landowners—most of whom have been Texas residents—have received one-eighth, or 12½ percent, royalties on their oil and gas. A certain amount of wealth was "created" locally by leasing, jobs, purchases, and the mechanics of exploring and producing. Texas' tax bill is the fifth lowest in the nation, and oil and gas revenues have been lauded as responsible for this; without them, it is argued, there would be "a tremendous increase" in sales and property taxes or even an income tax.[14] The majors also reinvested much of their earnings back into the state until recent years, and Texans have held large blocks of stock in many of the major companies.

Men like Ed Owen, who doubts that the state was ever a "province" of eastern lords of finance, point out that not all native operators lost control when their corporations were financed by eastern capital. The point is well taken. Most of the majors that were controlled in the East, such as Gulf, Sun, Marathon, and Magnolia, actually originated there but hit the jackpot in Texas.[15] On the other side of the ledger, Texaco long ago passed into the hands of easterners, and the example of Humble can be used to prove either side of the point. The founders of Humble retained 50 percent of the stock when they sold to Jersey Standard and continued to run the business without interference from New York, even becoming the top management of Jersey decades later. But today Humble has been digested by the giant Exxon.

The jury is still out. Benefits have flowed both ways. Ultimate control of the industry largely resides outside Texas and has shaped the state's growth over the years; at the same time outside capital has been a godsend, making possible growth and development that otherwise would have lagged. Most of the time in the past, capital-hungry Texas operators and landowners were pleased to accept the terms. Only in hindsight is vision perfected.

Despite the blessings that have flowed from Texas' earth, the status of the state's wealthiest on the whole does not yet match those in the more established centers of the nation. Contrary to its reputation, Texas does not have the richest people, although it boasts *some* of the richest. This kind of information is difficult to pin down precisely, because the U.S. Department of Commerce's Bureau of Economic Analysis does not measure wealth of individuals by state. However, in a listing of 25 counties with the greatest per capita income for the calendar year 1974, only one Texas county was listed; it was Sherman County, fifth in the nation, with $11,040, obviously no clue to the ranking of the Big Rich in Dallas and Houston. But from talking with oilmen and other wealthy persons, one gains the impression that the fortunes extant in older population centers far exceed those acquired more recently. The wealth of the East, for instance, remains greater than the wealth of Texas, H. L. Hunt and a few others to the contrary. It is like comparing the Hunt family, wealthy though it is, to the Rockefellers and the Fords. A head start makes a significant difference. The older money is, the more time it has to grow. In fact, one popular attempt at ranking states with the richest people places Texas sixth, after New York, California, Illinois, Pennsylvania, and Ohio, which would seem to be a reasonable conclusion. Sixth place may not be bad, considering Texas did not take over the lead in oil and gas production for good until 1928. Yet no other has *produced* so much wealth.

Then there is a disturbing companion fact. The 1974 Bureau of Economic Analysis report that listed only one Texas county in the top 25, according to per capita income, also listed three Texas counties among the 25 with the lowest per capita income. At the same time, a Southern Regional Council study demonstrated that of the eleven states which once formed the Confederacy, Texas has the most poor people—more than 2 million whites, blacks, and Chicanos living under the four-member family poverty level of $3,745 per year.[16]

Texas has become, as well as a home for millions of people in between, the land of the filthy rich and the dirt poor.

3

Although oil money oozes through Texas, its influence seems to be slight upon the state's financial institutions. In Dallas, only four of nineteen directors of First International Bancshares are related directly to oil, and three of twenty-eight at Republic of Texas. In size, Texas also lags. In 1976 Dallas' First International ranked twenty-sixth in the nation in deposits, Republic twenty-eighth, and First City in Houston forty-third. "No Texas bank has even one-tenth the assets of the nation's largest banks," concluded journalists William Broyles and Alex Sheshunoff.[17]

Other signs indicate that Texas' oil has attracted and helped build great business empires that are controlled elsewhere. While their presence has meant a boon to the local economies, the role of the major corporations in Texas economic life remains ambiguous. Antitrust legislation rooted in the Hogg era has become relatively ineffectual over the decades. Corporation lawyers have designed ways to pacify the courts while achieving corporate goals inimical to some of the early laws. The *Texas Observer* once commented, "With the ebbing of public indignation that marked the era of the robber barons, greater and greater industrial combinations have been formed and put into operation while the long test cases have droned through the courts unnoticed by public and press alike." [18]

In Texas today, six of the top ten—and eleven of the top twenty—largest corporations, which include the first and second biggest, deal primarily in oil and gas or related industries. Eight of these big oil corporations have offices in Houston, where their buildings, such as the Exxon, Tenneco, and Shell edifices, have become major down-town landmarks. (Shell, reputed to be the largest Texas-based corporation, moved its headquarters to Texas in 1970; it is controlled by the Royal Dutch/Shell in The Netherlands.) Writing in the *Texas Monthly*, Harry Hurt III has noted that the largest stockholders in most of Texas' biggest corporations are eastern financial institutions, such as the Chase Manhattan, First National City, and Morgan Guaranty banks. "From this perspective," wrote Hurt, "the Rockefeller family, who dominate Chase Manhattan and much else, should receive due consideration as being among the most powerful people in Texas, especially since the Vice President [Nelson Rockefeller] has established a partial claim to residency by virtue of purchasing a South Texas ranch." [19]

The multinational oil companies, which would include some of these, are being watched closer than ever before. The liberal Houston oilman J. R. Parten thinks the scrutiny is justified but perceives the conglomerate corporation as being the more severe threat to the economic system, not only in Texas, but also in the rest of the nation. "I think that if the free enterprise system is lost in this country," he said, "it will be primarily due to the development of the conglomerate corporation. I think a multinational oil company is all right, but it should be strictly regulated. I don't think that one multinational business confined to one line of business is nearly as bad as a conglomerate that is in twenty lines of business because when a company goes into a multitude of businesses, it tends to eliminate competition. And when you eliminate competition beyond a certain margin, you destroy the free enterprise system. I think we ought to come back to the method of specifically defining the purpose for which a corporation is allowed to do business. I believe in it very strongly, and I think that free enterprise is really on trial. And the multinational oil company is as much responsible for that as is the conglomerate." [20]

4

Conglomerates, multinational oil companies, a long-closed oil frontier—the old days are gone forever. A man can no longer start out with a notebook and a few leases and make a fortune, as many did in the early years. Everything about the oil business has grown exceedingly complex. Crews now drill to depths that, several decades ago, would have been unheard of. A crewman may take his break in an air-conditioned trailer with a flushing toilet. He may live twenty, thirty, even fifty miles from the drill site and drive to work every day. Brute strength and size no longer count. Tools are different. Machines put drill pipe together. Engineers and geologists, college graduates, are on hand to advise. A technological revolution has transformed the industry.

It was never made clearer than by an old driller, retired after forty years in the business, whom folklorist Mody Boatright interviewed. The old man pointed toward a residence in the next block.

"A driller lives in that house," he said. "He is thirty years old, and he has already drilled more wells than I did in my forty years."

The old man confessed that he would not know how to use the new equipment the young driller was using.[21]

Business has grown more complicated, with deals concluded not by a handshake but by lengthy contracts spelled out in excruciating detail by methodical lawyers. "It's a regular lawyer's paradise now," said Carrol M. Bennett. "You can't turn around without a lawyer at your side." Claud B. Hamill remembered that he used to visit at the Humble offices when Walter Fondren, then its president, answered his own telephone. The colorful old wildcatter, O. W. Killam, could see the changes back in the 1950's. "Thirty or forty years ago," he said then, "the oil business was carried on by individuals. Now it's carried on by an organization. And you've got to go through that organization, and it takes a lot of time before you get any results. I remember going to Dallas and Houston at various times and making deals involving a hundred thousand to a million dollars. Get there in the morning, make the trade, and leave in the evening with the check in your pocket for several hundred thousand dollars. You couldn't do that now in weeks and weeks of time, you would have to go through so many hands." [22]

Without exception, oilmen complain of the skyrocketing costs of finding and producing oil in an inflationary economy. The *Oil and Gas Journal* in 1976, reporting a decline in oil companies' profits, noted that the rate of return on stockholders' equity was equal to that of manufacturing firms, with the top company, Exxon, lagging behind returns of industries such as soft drinks, drugs, tobacco, office equipment, and computers.[23] The small independents are hit hardest. The cost of drilling has tripled. With rises in steel prices, all tubular supplies have gone up accordingly—when they are available. Labor, taxes, and insurance have joined the soaring trend. R. J. McMurrey, a small independent, contends that his father made more money during the Hot Oil War selling crude at six cents a barrel than he makes today. "Now that's a proven fact, because we ran through the records." 24

Oilmen often complain, along with other businessmen, of the increasing burden of governmental regulations that clutter their days and complicate the task of producing oil. Government reporting procedures, Carrol Bennett said, consume a large portion of his company's time. "I'll bet you we've got thirty people that do nothing but work on reports. That would have been impossible prior to computers because we have to break those down by wells monthly. You couldn't hire enough people to file this information." 25

Everything has changed drastically and irrevocably. Eddie Chiles of Fort Worth, musing over the new picture, characterized the past, since Spindletop, as a time of "giants"—outstanding individuals who by their personal efforts guided the industry forward. "I don't think that will be true in the future," said Chiles. "It will be faceless figures, management people and computers and things like that." 26

The oil business, in other words, is rushing inexorably toward that same rendezvous—or vortex—the rest of us are drawn toward at an accelerating pace.

5

Everyone had a scapegoat for the energy crisis. Oilmen—and coalmen—accused the environmentalists and the government; consumers and politicians blamed the oilmen, especially the major companies, and the Arabs. Embattled oilmen bewailed the loss of the depletion allowance and the injustice of price ceilings that, they claimed, discouraged the discovery and development of new petroleum reserves; congressmen argued about the process of divestiture, or breaking up, of the major companies. Consumers complained bitterly about the high costs of gasoline and other energy, while still driving two, even three, cars per family.

It was as confusing an era as one was likely to find in the history of petroleum. Unlike earlier periods when the issues were simpler and the world less complex, the national policies likely to result from today's political solutions would profoundly affect every other facet of our society, along with the economies—for better or for worse—of the other nations in this finite, interdependent world system.

Although conditions had been building up for years, to many people it was as if the petroleum crisis of the middle 1970's had occurred overnight. There was, suddenly, such a sharp break with the abundance of the easygoing past that many refused to accept what was before them. Some even doubted that there was an energy crisis.

In Texas controversy flared perhaps more fiercely than elsewhere. There seemed to be few areas of agreement. A case in point was the Wise County field, where in 1976 Mitchell Energy was piping natural gas to Chicago at the Federal Power Commission-fixed price of 30 cents per thousand cubic feet. However, while the FPC was forcing interstate producers to hold the line, sharp price increases on natural gas were being permitted inside Texas by state regulators. This meant that some gas produced near the Chicago-bound gas in Wise County was selling at prices four times as high as the northern gas. While oilmen complained bitterly of the uneven price structures, Texas consumers were incensed to learn that people in other states were enjoying the benefits of Texas gas for a fraction of what they were paying in their own state. Others charged that Texas was being drained of its natural gas for northerners and easterners—and at cheaper prices.

The petroleum business is one of the most complicated industries going today. This is one reason many people shy away from a thorough, searching study of it. Answers to its problems are likely to be equally complex. A glance at the natural gas shortage, which also generally parallels the oil crisis, will illustrate some of the historical factors involved. To simplify the matter as much as possible, it is useful to examine four factors that have played large roles in the growing shortage: federal price ceilings on gas at the wellhead, the industry's campaigns in the past to sell its products cheaply, the shift of drilling emphasis from domestic to foreign sites (especially in the Middle East), and a scaled-down reassessment of reserves.[27]

1. *Federal price ceilings on gas at the wellhead.* This, stemming from the 1954 Supreme Court decision, has become a classic liberal-conservative battle. More realistically, it should be viewed as a struggle of the gas-producing states versus the nonproducing states. A petroleum-producing state tends to be concerned with the economic health of the industry; the consumer-oriented state concentrates on low prices and an adequate supply. Although producing states must also be concerned with consumers' happiness, in the past Texans have had no reason to complain: They had a plentiful supply, and because of the lower transportation expense, they paid less for their gas than did the more numerous interstate customers hundreds and thousands of miles away.

At first, because of abundant supplies, this decision had no apparent effect on the natural gas industry. But federal regulation of wellhead prices had a delayed impact. It eventually led to a gross underpricing of gas, as the FPC consistently kept interstate gas cheap. "That was such a cheap price, and it was such a great fuel that this created a terrible waste," said oil writer Nancy Heard Toudouze, herself a liberal Democrat. "It caused the coal to be abandoned in the Appalachian area, because they couldn't mine the coal and compete with this gas from Texas and Louisiana. And it was just awful, the waste." [28] Eventually the federal price regulation became a damper on exploration; in an era of rising costs the stakes became too low for the economic risks involved.

The waste—or, at least, unwise use—continued into the 1970's, inspiring one observer to note that "intelligent legislation on the natural gas problem will be undertaken only after front yard gaslights in the suburbs of Washington, D.C., begin to dim." [29]

2. *The industry's campaigns to sell its products cheaply.* Gas in the early years was considered largely a nuisance; much of it was "flared off," or burned in flares to get rid of it, on a grand scale as recently as the East Texas field in the 1930's. Over the past few decades, in their enthusiasm to profit from gas discoveries, oilmen and gas companies did all they could to make gas popular, urging it upon consumers with special discounts, advertising its advanges over other fuels, anything to make it more appealing than coal. Consumers—both individual and corporative—responded with alacrity. This cooperative venture in which the principals were largely ignorant of much that we know today led to waste, or at best overuse, of gas on a large scale.

3. *The shift of drilling emphasis from domestic to foreign sites, especially the Middle East.* Oilmen (especially the majors and the large independents), government, and consumers—all had interests in the Middle East's development. It brought in cheap oil, which satisfied the consumers, and there was enough of it to meet the companies' market demands. As independents sought import limits through one process or the other, usually to a deaf political ear, the flood of Middle Eastern oil continued. As a consequence, Americans became "hooked" more and more on cheap petroleum, while the economics of the situation forced thousands of independents out of business. A net result was that there was less drilling in this country. This meant less exploration for gas, and the Middle East would not be bringing gas supplies to this country since, unlike oil, gas is not transported by tanker but must be carried by pipelines. Gas-producing potential steadily declined.

There is an ironic twist. If Middle Eastern imports had been restricted in earlier years, there would have been more drilling in this country, with more proved gas reserves. This would mean, perhaps, that our domestic gas reserves would have been more depleted, but the industry would have been better able to discover more reserves. In one sense, then, reliance on Middle Eastern imports "saved" some domestic reserves—because they were not found—but at the same time Americans lost much of the capacity to find and produce the gas reserves in time of critical need.

4. *A scaled-down reassessment of reserves.* Another reason that the natural gas shortage has descended on the country almost unexpectedly, to the surprise of consumers and politicians, is that the statistics of reserves have changed. Figures on reserves have been reduced, simply because reserves were not as high as originally estimated. Knowledgeable insider Ed Owen explained, "One of the big problems right now with our gas supply is that the gas reserves estimates are made by licensed engineers, and they are made to fit the bankers' formula that promotes the bond issues and so forth to the transmission companies, and they are just desk exercises. Most of them are made before you have any drawdown so that you know how much pressure declined per billion cubic feet that was withdrawn, and I don't know of a damned one of them that wasn't grossly overestimated. So here we are with these cities and industries relying on contracts that were made on the basis of these estimates— and the gas ain't there to satisfy those contracts. It's the same

everywhere, to some degree. So it's going to be a toughie." [30]

The energy crisis was a long time building. Many oilmen had predicted it years before. Everette L. DeGolyer warned a House subcommittee in 1948 of future consequences flowing from the hard companion facts that the United States was the greatest consuming area of the world, while the Middle East held the largest proved reserves on earth.[31] In 1951 the Paley Commission, on which Texan George R. Brown served, forecast shortages and cautioned against increasing dependence on foreign, especially Middle Eastern, oil.[32] Michel T. Halbouty, one of the more energetic forecasters, not only heralded the shortage, but expressed optimism over solving it—if the economic incentives are adequate. "There is no evidence that gas cannot be found to supply any market as long as the explorer can be compensated for his efforts," he wrote in 1964. "He will have to drill more wells, suffer a greater ratio of dry holes, and drill them deeper; and millions will have to be spent on new tools, techniques, and technology. But who knows how many and where great gas fields are to be found?" [33]

Convincing the public of what was to come became a major source of frustration to many who understood the inner workings of the industry. And as the energy controversy raged from the living-room dens to the halls of Congress, the depletion allowance became a center of contention. Once a glorious 27½ percent, it had been slashed first to 22 percent and then eliminated completely for all but certain small independents, following a strict formula. Embattled oilmen, large and small, replied with indignation and frustration. The small independents, who often depend on dry hole money from the majors, expected a decrease in cooperative funding from this source because of the depletion cut. Others believed it would precipitate a sharp decline in outside investors, on whom independents have depended for much of their exploration support. Citing as his example a person looking for a way to invest $20,000, George Strake, Jr., said, "If you want to try something really exotic, the only way you can take your twenty thousand dollars and maybe make a half million dollars—the one business that you can do that in is the oil business. But to be realistic, ninety-five percent of the time you are going to lose that twenty thousand dollars. For every one person like my dad who is successful, man, there are a hundred bones in the cemetery who tried it and missed it. Unless we keep that incentive there, we've had it." [34]

Most oilmen seemed either amazed or chagrined that other people did not see what to them were obvious, logical needs for a depletion allowance and similar incentives; to a man they argued against price controls and the breaking up of the major companies. After all, said independent Glenn McCarthy, a gallon of gasoline was as cheap as a bottle of beer; nobody complained about the price of beer, he said, while in other countries the same gasoline would sell for $1.75 per gallon. Oilmen, he contended, had kept the price down in this country.[35]

The only valid argument against the depletion allowance, added the liberal J. R. Parten, is that it has made the price of gasoline, before the tax is added, so cheap that it has resulted in waste. Eric Schroeder tried to explain the depletion allowance in ordinary business terms: A building, depreciated 10 percent a year, can be depreciated in ten years while the owner still has it and it may be worth even more than in the beginning, but an oil well produces one's capital and is likely to be gone in ten years. In the same vein, W. A. Moncrief, Sr., chided politicians for talking of Operation Independence and then proposing "heavy taxes on the only people who can deliver that 'independence.' " [36]

Price controls and tightening governmental regulations rankled oilmen, whether they were top executives with major companies or small independents. Parten, the old Democrat, views such stringent economic reins as antithetical to the democratic process and a free society. Nationalization, he believes, would usher in "the beginning of the end of our democracy" because the next step would be the nationalization of other raw materials. "You'd wind up with a police state," he said. "Without competition in business there's essentially no way for a free society to function." [37]

Furthermore, added Carrol M. Bennett of Texas Pacific Oil, the ambivalent signals from Washington have been so negative economically that it is impossible to make long-term plans for the next five or ten years, including expansion programs. "Hell," he said, "we can't even plan for next week now. We don't know what's going to happen. And all the other companies are in the same boat." [38]

They just as solidly deplored the moves to divest the huge major companies of segments of their operations. Divestiture would divide a company into four parts—production, transportation (pipelines), refining, and marketing—and force it to choose which one to keep, which three to turn loose. It would be similar to the restrictions upon oil corporations in Texas at the time Spindletop roared in. While some political leaders contended that divestiture would engender more competition and greater efficiency, oilmen argued the business was already highly competitive and more efficient than it would be under conditions of divestiture. Parten predicted that divestiture would create "enormous confusion and added overhead expenses that would cost the consumer of oil products greatly," while producing no additional oil and gas.[39]

Historically, efficiency and competition have not always gone together. Old Standard Oil, because it *was* a monopoly, handled the development of a field more efficiently than did the flood of variegated independents in the East Texas field, which probably created a more competitive atmosphere than has any other field except perhaps Spindletop. However, that sort of efficiency is not much of a question today; proration and other governmental regulations work toward preventing the old-time production inefficiency that led to waste. But a point not to be lost is that Standard also was able to nose out competition because it operated in all four phases of the petroleum industry. One—though not the only—reason it could undercut competitors was that it could save on one phase— such as pipelines or transportation—and thus reduce its market price to the consumer; of course, once the enemy was eliminated, Standard then could hike the price up higher than ever. But behind the greed was a certain efficiency that smaller competitors could not afford, though one should not overlook the obvious fact that Standard's size itself enabled it to deal more harshly with competitors than did anything else. There looms the possibility, then, that competition is not essential to efficiency of operation: A few huge companies may produce more and better petroleum products at a more reasonable cost to the consumer than might scores or hundreds or thousands of smaller companies. The thrust of this argument, though, is that if a few can do so well, then one might do best of all. In turn, critics favoring nationalization might just as logically insist that the federal government should be that one.

Since there is no way to prove conclusively whether divestiture would result in more, or less, efficiency, the focus of the controversy has hinged on competition. Is there now competition, or is there a monopoly? Contending that the oil industry is one of the most competitive, Dallas *Morning News* columnist William Murchison cited that Exxon, the biggest of all, in 1974 controlled only 7.8 percent of total refinery capacity, with other large companies trailing behind; Texaco held the greatest share of the market, with a mere 8.1 percent. Examining congressional critics' argument that the twenty largest oil companies bought and sold 76.3 percent of the nation's crude oil in 1973, Murchison responded that four automobile companies produced 100 percent of American cars and trucks the same year, yet no one had demanded their breakup.[40] It was a telling point, although Murchison's argument was flawed in comparing the petroleum business, in which a major company takes part in the entire process from drilling a new well to selling of the refined product, to the automobile business, in which the Detroit manufacturers do not mine the iron ore or operate the steel mills which produce the materials used to make automobiles. Without a doubt, though, there were more oil companies than there were automobile-manufacturers-plus-steel-companies.

Aside from wistful thinking, most people seemed to accept that the days of cheap energy—whatever the form might be—were over. As inflation raised the cost of everything else, it appeared only logical that oil, gasoline, and natural gas would follow suit. But there were other factors in the petroleum industry not readily accepted by outsiders, and the most important one was that each year there will be less of a nonrenewable resource to find and use. This is as true of metals as it is of oil and gas. And, as the oilmen keep emphasizing, all the "easy" oil is found first. "It was off the good roads, accessible places, and in areas where weather was not too great a factor," said Eric Schroeder. "Obviously, as time went on and those areas became exhausted, they had to go further and further into the wilds and inaccessible places to look for it. If you follow what has been done on the North Slope in Alaska, you get some conception of what oilmen are doing in order to produce oil. And that meant that the wells went deeper and deeper and deeper. The shallow stuff was gone. I don't know where there is any shallow stuff today." [41]

By the middle 1970's oilmen generally were at a loss to understand why what seemed so clear to them was not readily grasped by the public. "The oil industry has been one of the finest industrial citizens there has been," said retired Humble chief Carl Reistle.

"There's no doubt about it. We've been paying our people better. We've had good retirement practices. We supplied our customers conscientiously with a better quality. We've worked hard. You know, it's just heartbreaking to end a career in the oil industry and see the industry blamed. You can't help but be kinda heartsick to see the public and their misunderstanding of what's happened." [42]

There is truth in the oilmen's arguments, though how far one is willing to go along with them will depend on conflicting interpretations and one's own position as a consumer or businessman. Incentives are clearly necessary in such a high-cost, high-risk enterprise. An oilman can't be forced to drill for oil and gas; he must be lured. But answers to such a complex problem can be expected to be correspondingly complex. Whether these incentives should take the form of a depletion allowance or other tax benefits is a point that can be settled satisfactorily only after a searching examination of the intimate economics of the industry and of the nation's needs. Although economic incentive is needed, so is some responsible form of social control over such a crucially important industry. It may be, for instance, that the only fair way to restrict oil profits would be to limit them through an excess profits tax. But if oil profits were limited to, say, 8 percent, then to be fair the government would also have to limit all other businesses to an 8 percent profit ceiling. Such a maneuver, no doubt, would be resisted by all businessmen, if not most citizens; this provides some small insight into the complexity of the matter.

Oilmen seem to be correct in contending that most, if not all, of the "easy" oil has been found and that from now on finding oil and gas will cost very much more. At the same time, with the nation intertwined economically as never before, it should be possible for consumers to expect uniform prices, after allowing for transportation costs and other differentials, throughout the country. These are knotty problems, affecting everyone but in varying ways, and they remind us that more than government regulation is responsible for the uncertainties that we all face. If the oilman is frustrated over his inability to make long-range plans, so are many average citizens, for it is an era of unheralded flux that has no simple solution.

To be sure, Carl Reistle is probably correct when he states that the public misunderstands the petroleum industry and its motives. Such a highly technical, complicated industry is frequently poorly grasped even by persevering journalists, and many times a thorough understanding of an industry's operations is needed in order to interpret correctly its leaders' motives. But the fault of poor communication, in this instance, is not particularly the public's. As energy writer Clyde La Motta has noted, the petroleum industry, while achieving unexcelled technological goals, "still is in the kindergarten when it comes to swaying public opinion." [43] This was the problem that outspoken Michel T. Halbouty had in mind when he accused oilmen of creating their own crisis in public opinion through "self-serving communications." The industry itself, he said, not the news media, was to blame for its ineffective communication with the public.

"We have been concentrating on propaganda and promotion when we should have been concentrating on facts and the industry story," Halbouty said in 1970 to a petroleum landmen's convention. "We must give the people honest light so they can find their own way. Through our system of controlled public relations and public affairs ... we have been mouthing a set of clichés about high risks, low profits, excessive imports, tax matters, and price controls. These are *our* problems. Now we must concern ourselves with *public* problems."

The public, he said, isn't interested in the oilmen's woes; therefore, the oilmen must become interested in the public's concerns— among which is the threat presented by the Soviet Union's closeness with Middle Eastern, African, and South American nations with large reserves—and open lines of communications on that basis.

"If the people in industry, business, the professions, and labor do not begin to speak up, educate, inform, and create a dialogue with the man in the street, if we don't end our monologue with ourselves and our talking to instead of with the people, or answer some simple questions and give some straight answers, nationalization is what we are going to get!" [44]

Whatever its intentions, the industry was not convincing the public of its virtues. The public image of the oilman, especially of the mythical Texan variety, has hampered the industry to some extent in getting its message across to the public, but this was not the only, or main, problem. Other reasons were endemic to the business itself. Like medicine, the oil business has a formidable technical language barrier that most nonoilmen find impenetrable;

without explaining some of the basic facts and documenting them, oilmen usually lose their listeners before they have started. Laying the predicate for one's case is never more essential than in their industry.

Add to this the fact that oilmen are traditionally and habitually tight-lipped regarding details of their business, a deeply ingrained way of life in an industry where information is so valuable. In oil field terms, this is the "tight well" mentality. A tight well is one on which no information at all is given out as it is being drilled, for fear competitors will benefit more than they. This has carried over into other aspects of their lives, into a period when they have a great need to talk with the public about their industry.

"I can remember the time when Getty Oil wouldn't permit a newspaperman anywhere on the premises, in the field or anywhere," said writer-historian James A. Clark. "Not that they were afraid of the newspaperman. They were just afraid of the fact that the reporter might put something in the paper that they didn't want Texaco to know about. That information would be very valuable, to Texaco or anybody else. Now it's multiplied—you've got radio people and television people on top of that. That's a basic reason why the oil business has a bad image, because nobody has ever been able to tell its story.

"I've never seen a sincere man—member of the legislature, writer, anybody—who, when he found out the truth about this business, wasn't fascinated by it and who didn't become a friend. That's why I have always advocated to the industry that all it has to do is to just tell the truth and let people look into it, as far and as deep as they want to, because the farther and deeper they go, the more admiration they'll have for what has been accomplished and how much it has meant for the public."

Clark, author of a number of books about oilmen and oil fields, has been critical of the industry for just making statements without giving the public an opportunity to ask questions—a cavalier treatment that is now boomeranging.

"They have a great story and just don't know how to tell it," lamented Clark. "They think you tell it by Madison Avenue. My God, Nixon should have known you can't do that. He tried that, and it didn't work. Everybody else has tried it and it didn't work. Now, they can sell their gasoline that way, but not . . . ." [45]

Halbouty and Clark are insiders offering pointed, practical advice to an industry they love. Geologist Halbouty has become one of the richest independents in the country; Clark has spent most of his life writing about the petroleum business and its personalities. Whether the honest dialogue between oilmen and the average American, as envisioned and advocated by Halbouty, would solve the industry's pressing problems remains to be seen, but it would inaugurate a momentous departure from the past, which of itself would improve communications. And whether people generally would admire the industry as much as Clark believes, after having examined it "as far and as deep as they want to," in this day of full disclosure any step in that direction would earn a sparkling round of applause. Although genuine frankness might at times provide ammunition to the industry's longtime critics, in an open society Clark's formula for reaching rapport with the public is an impeccable model that would ensure a deep impression on the citizenry and set a lasting precedent for other industries. Its adoption might not precipitate an unbridled orgy of adoration on the part of all Americans for the industry, but it would deliver an unanswerable reply to some of its fiercest critics. As for doubters who scorn the advice as utopian and out of touch with the reality of a harsh, competitive world, they might be reminded that such openness, initiated voluntarily, registers on a far higher scale than revelations forced out under oath in the midst of a crisis.

Such a process would enable the public to judge whether or not Carl Reistle's contention is correct: that the industry has been "one of the finest industrial citizens." As the facts appear now, the statement leaves openings for criticism. Oil company employees *have* been paid well and have generally had good retirement practices. But today this is a virtual necessity if a company is to retain skilled technicians, and labor unions have also been responsible for the adoption of some of these practices. Furthermore, if one traces back to the early decades of the century, one finds that rules of industrial safety and conservation, all too often, were imposed on the industry by legislation. And while petroleum has enriched the areas in which it has been produced—through royalties, jobs, and other outlays—the industry has also frequently helped shape political conditions to its own liking. Reistle himself, for instance, took a leading role in passing a sales tax in Texas—a revenue that many people consider a tax on poverty and that is certainly favorable to large oil companies. Other oil company executives and independents have been just as energetic at deflecting the potshots of tax reformers from their industry. The political smoke screen raised in 1952 over the tidelands is a memorable documentation of how oil money has been spent to disguise the industry's underlying motives.

The impact of the industry on Texas, and on the nation, is as great as that of any other event in history. In the final analysis, an elaborate collection of pluses and minuses involving economic, social, and political factors will likely emerge. Is the large refinery that comes to a city more an economic boon or a long-term hazard? Computing the final balance sheet of economic and social debts and credits will probably keep historians occupied for many years into the future.

6

The petroleum industry has never been an island to itself. The consuming public that has fed the industry has also played an integral role in bringing about today's crisis, through high levels of consumption of the seemingly endless products made from petroleum. Amazingly, though, relatively little serious attention has been steadily focused on consumer conservation, admittedly not a popular political position to advocate. Although the fifty-five-mile-per-hour speed limit was instituted with wide success at first, its effectiveness began to erode as some states practically ignored strict enforcement. Drivers of both trucks and automobiles flagrantly disobeyed the speed laws, often with the aid of Citizens Band radios. Nor had homeowners in the mid-1970's cut back enough on energy use to indicate that they seriously considered the shortages real or persistent. Much of this was due to the failure of government, on both national and state levels, to make clear the critical nature of the crisis.

In the past many segments of the economy played their parts in making this a nation of energy gluttons. Lobbyists for highways pushed good, speedy highways, which, in turn, expanded the market for gasoline by encouraging road use. The freeway system allowed people to live thirty, forty, even fifty miles from their jobs and

encouraged weekenders and vacationers to drive distances far
beyond what they once did. The automobile industry, for its part,
manufactured powerful gasoline drinkers.

"We must face the proposition that we *must* arrest the annual rise
in consumption of petroleum and gas," said J. R. Parten.[46] The
means by which this could be done were near at hand but relatively
ignored: car pooling, the avoiding of unnecessary trips (such as a
two- or three- or ten-mile drive for a loaf of bread), and similar
changes in life-styles as occurred during World War II, when
gasoline was rationed. But Americans chose to use their cars instead
of their legs and generally to continue their affluent way of life. It
was this social environment that inspired Buckminster Fuller to
have a geologist compute the amount of energy spent by nature in
making petroleum. "We found it cost nature, over the eons, a
million dollars to produce a gallon of petroleum, at the rate at
which you and I pay for electricity," reported Fuller. "All those
people driving in to work every day—they're each spending two or
three million dollars a day, at least by nature's accounting." [47]

For once in the nation's history the answer to overconsumption
was not to be found in stepped-up production, except possibly on a
temporary basis, for the "new frontiers" of petroleum remain largely
illusory. The only two frontiers, if they can be called that, are
offshore and Alaska; both are essentially technological frontiers.
Additionally, there is always an economic basement in each locale,
related to drilling depth, beyond which it is not economically
feasible to recover oil and gas. "There are some fields where more
units of energy were spent looking for energy than were produced,"
Ed Owen said. "This is what we have to look out for now. This
frantic search for energy may expend more energy than we end up
capturing."

Scholarly, hoarse-voiced Owen, a tall, white-haired, straight-
spoken man approaching eighty, a former president of the American
Association of Petroleum Geologists and author of the encyclopedic
Trek of the Oil Finders (which he spent twelve years writing), was not
encouraged by what he saw ahead.

"I can just see it, coming in on all sides. Some of these energy
projects we are committing ourselves to are going to be self-
defeating. Oil shales—about thirty gallons of recoverable oil in a ton
of the best oil shale. Now they talk about a billion barrels of oil in

shale. There are ~~thirty-two~~ 42 gallons of oil in a barrel. So put a computer to work to tell you how much tailings you'll have out there in the Rocky Mountain country to extract that oil—plus the fact that there is no water out there to perform that operation. It comes about as near being a crisis as I think we'll ever be able to get."

He gave a wry chuckle and added, "I feel like I've lived in the golden age." [48]

7

As Texas has declined in the production of petroleum, so has the United States. Other world leaders are edging up. In 1974, for the first time, the Soviet Union became the world's leading oil producer, with 3.4 billion barrels that year as U.S. production slipped to 3.2 billion barrels. Meanwhile, for the same period the Organization of Petroleum Exporting Countries—OPEC, which included the Arab nations—produced 11.2 billion barrels.[49] Nor do the changing trends end there. China has come upon the horizon as a major producer. By 1988, a short time, it is expected to reach the current oil production of Saudi Arabia. For the past several years China has acquired sophisticated French, American, and Japanese petroleum survey equipment, while keeping American companies out.[50] Elsewhere, large discoveries have been reported in southern Mexico and in the North Sea, which will enrich both Great Britain and Norway. Pipelines from deep in Mexico will deliver natural gas to Texas for U.S. needs. Everywhere the oil picture is changing. In 1976 Venezuela took over its multibillion-dollar industry. One of the world's biggest negotiated nationalizations of foreign industry, it ended sixty years of direct foreign involvement in the country by Exxon, Shell, Gulf, Mobil, and Texaco. The $1 billion they accepted for their assets was reported to be one-fifth of the $5 billion book value.[51]

Meanwhile, the parade of oil moved away from Texas. In 1974 oil companies put up $1.5 billion for 123 tracts of sea bottom in the Gulf, off Texas' shore. But it was outside the state's jurisdiction, onto offshore tracts handled by the Department of the Interior. Mobile bid a whopping $650 million.[52] The good luck had just missed Texas, and it was perhaps a portent of things to come.

Then there is Texas' challenger among its sister states—Alaska.

The state that usurped Texas' distinction as the nation's largest state now may take over the number one oil producer's role, in time. The Dallas *Morning News,* a staunch champion of all things conservatively Texan, has already drafted an official concession in an editorial entitled, "Alaska—The New Oil King." [53] However, to outdo Texas' record over the past three-quarters of a century will take some doing. There are problems in Alaska that never existed in Texas. On the North Slope with the weather sixty degrees below zero, a tractor driver may go seventy-five miles at night to build a pad for a drilling rig. The driver wears insulated underwear; it's a comfortable zero degrees inside the cab. When Atlantic-Richfield brought in the first commercial producer on the North Slope, workers hauled equipment 350 miles over the ice with a bulldozer.

It takes big money, more than for any of Texas' toughest fields, to explore and develop the North Slope, and it comes as no surprise that the entrants are big companies—Atlantic-Richfield, British Petroleum, Exxon, Mobil, Sinclair, and Hamilton Oil Company. If it lives up to expectation, the stakes will have been sufficiently high to justify the risk.

Alaska is so huge that it continually challenges Texans to design formulas by which their homeland will emerge the larger. The earliest one uttered was: "Take away Alaska's snow and ice, and Texas would be bigger." But a more interesting one, and of considerable significance in comparing the two states as petroleum producers, is one advanced by the late Texas Congressman Wright Patman: If federally owned land were excluded from Alaska's area, Texas would be more than 13.6 times larger; almost 97 percent of Alaska's land is owned by the federal government.[54] In the long run this may benefit more people, for with the passage of the native claims bill the Indians and Eskimos were assured of a significant share of the proceeds. Whatever the end results, however, the dominant pattern of Alaskan landownership, being radically different from that in Texas, will represent a significant departure from, and perhaps contrast with, what has occurred in Texas.

There are other reasons, of course, why Alaska will never be another Texas, whether or not it produces 100 billion barrels, as some high estimates indicate. No matter how much oil is found, no Alaskan city is going to supplant Houston as the oil capital of the world. Aside from matters of climate and geography, it is no longer necessary to move the center of the oil business to the oil fields. With airplanes, radio and telephone communication, people can continue to live in Houston and Dallas and other such cities while operating in the frozen north.

8

Billie Edgington, a Texas native who has accompanied her husband on foreign assignments with Standard of California, told of a Canadian woman who "finally made it"—she was mistaken for a Texan.[55] Abroad all Americans in the oil business are known as Texans. Wherever there is oil, in non-Communist countries, one is likely to find Texans. The pattern will probably continue as long as Texas is an oil center, and that, despite the state's declining trends, is likely to be for a long time yet.

Men like independent Mike Halbouty of Houston think a lot of oil and gas will still be found in Texas, and even as he said it, a new huge gas-producing area was opening up near Laredo in South Texas, one that *World Oil* estimated may produce as much as 10 trillion cubic feet. But even without such production, Texas will remain a focal point for the oil business for some time because of the bank of people, equipment, organization, and technical know-how that is headquartered in Texas—particularly in Houston. Even when Texas is drained, Houston will continue to be an important place for the energy industry.

Houston is basking in the blessings of decades of oil's benefits. The ship channel and the prolific Gulf Coast fields made Houston the oil capital of the world, but today it is much more than an oil center. It has become the fastest-growing big city in America and now the sixth largest in the country. Some predict it will pass Detroit and Philadelphia within the coming few years, Los Angeles and Chicago within the next twenty-five. Other exuberant boosters believe that within the century ahead Houston will become the world's most populous city.

That remains to be seen, but the symbols of Houston's ascendancy are large and clear. Much of the nation's chemical manufacturing is done in Texas because of Houston and its ship channel, making the state a runner-up to New Jersey in that category. Du

Pont, Monsanto, Union Carbide, Dow, Celanese, and Ethyl are some of the companies now located there. Tenneco, Pennzoil, Gulf, Exxon, and Shell have domestic or main headquarters there, plus a myriad of independents of all sizes. The Bank of Rome has opened a branch office in Houston, joining those from the Middle East, Scotland, and other countries.[56]

While, for some of the companies, major economic decisions may be made in the East or by eastern board members, where control may ultimately reside, production and technological decisions are made predominantly in Houston. "When I first moved to Houston from Los Angeles," said Howard Marshall, "somebody said, 'You can get more done from a street corner in Houston in a day than you can get done in the oil business in Los Angeles in a year.'" [57] Houston is *the* place to find an oil deal, whether with a major company or with a small or large independent.

Oilmen tend to cluster. "Most of the companies left New York City because of the tax rates and because it's hard to retain the employees," said LeRoy Menzing. "So they moved to Houston—and Houston is a better place to operate, strictly because that's where oil people are. You have to operate where oil people are, and they're all down there." [58]

None of the other oil-center cities of the world—London, Amsterdam—can compare with Houston, said historian-geologist Ed Owen. "The rest of them are parochial. Texas is such a technological center for petroleum that I have a feeling it will maintain the top position for quite a long time. You do have this fantastically complicated technological setup in Texas, and it interlocks with research facilities elsewhere. You have to have industry-coupled research to get technological advances.

"The United States," he continued, "predominates in the world oil industry because this was the only place where ownership of the minerals was disseminated among millions of people. And that disseminating ownership gave rise to hundreds of thousands of operating oilmen, while in any other country there were only tens or a few hundred. And there were more of 'em in Texas than in any other place. So there were more oilmen of experience in Houston, probably, than in all of Europe or all of the Middle and Far East. And that is something that outweighs damned near everything else, except having the stuff in the ground." [59]

Houston's oilmen are their city's most exuberant boosters. Armed
with population trends and economic indexes, most of them are
likely to agree with Michel T. Halbouty: "I think Houston is going
to be one of the largest cities of the world, twenty-five years from
now." [60] George P. Mitchell echoes the assessment. "I think that
Houston is probably, of all the cities, the most dynamic in the
country, and everybody else is beginning to think so, too. It's the
most open of the cities. Socially open, too. I'm not that close to
Dallas, but I think Dallas has a little bit more of that blue-blood
instinct, of being a little more conservative, just a little more
Republican, than Houston." Houston's serious problems related to
its growth can injure the city if they are covered up and not faced
squarely, admitted Mitchell, "but we have the dynamics to solve
them here and I think we can help show others how we can solve
them over the next fifteen years."

Meanwhile, Mitchell insisted, Houston will continue to be the
energy capital of the world.

"Why should somebody be in Paducah when they can have their
top talent brainstorming with other top talent in this region?" [61]

9

Even while Texas adjusts to its unaccustomed role as a declining
petroleum producer, it remains a growing, bustling giant in almost
all other ways. The wealth from petroleum will remain and
multiply long after the last drop of oil is finally pumped out. But
the transformation is accompanied by its own peculiar pains. As the
conditions that created the wealth gradually fade from human
memory, they leave in their wake a cluster of inescapably evocative
symbols that bind us even more forcibly to the past.

Symbols are an intimate, inevitable part of our lives, reminding
us, sometimes unconsciously, of more than is on the surface. They
plug our memories infrangibly into history. In the middle 1970's as
the oil industry, and particularly Texas, wound up an era and
headed toward largely uncharted tomorrows, the symbols of the
passing of the old were so plentiful that one could hardly miss the
point.

Pegasus, the flying red horse perched atop the Magnolia (now

Mobil) Building in downtown Dallas since 1934, once synonymous with Dallas, is no longer the highest point in town as the towering skyscrapers stretch up to obscure it, and in 1974 it faced the ax of a new city ordinance prohibiting signs to extend more than three feet from the top of a building. To save Pegasus from the consequences of the growth it has symbolized, the city declared the sign a historical landmark, exempt from the rule.[62]

In the oil patch there were other changes, both real and symbolic. "Let me tell you," said Dallas oilman Sherman Hunt. "You wouldn't believe, twenty years ago, that they would ever reverse a pipeline—when oil was going from the Midland-Odessa area to Port Arthur and Beaumont for refineries and for export on tankers, that they would ever turn those pipelines around and be shipping oil back out to the refineries in West Texas."

In the early 1970's, he said, one large refinery at Big Spring in West Texas started using imported foreign oil mostly from Venezuela and Nigeria, pumping it in the opposite direction from the coast through pipes that had once flowed native crude.

"Josh Cosden built that refinery, I guess, back in the twenties," said Hunt. "He had a refinery there, and he had one in Colorado City. They have been there a long, long time, back in the days when there were regional refineries that got their crude in the local area.

"I will guarantee you that twenty years ago, if you had told me this was going to happen, I would have laughed at you. I'd have said you were a candidate for Terrell! * And right here it is." [63]

There were other changes, unrelated to petroleum. The Alien Land Act, enacted in the Hogg era to protect the state from the encroachments of absentee English and Scottish landowners, was repealed in 1965 by the state legislature. Its original purpose was long forgotten, as its amendment brought the rights of aliens, such as many Mexicans who had been longtime residents of the state, into line with those of other American citizens.[64] But ironically, a decade later in a drastically changed economic situation some wondered if it legally opened the door to Arab and Japanese economic intrusion.

Fears acquired substance in the 1970's when Arabs, seeming richer than Texans ever were, began scouring the United States for

* Terrell is the town in which a Texas state hospital for the mentally ill is situated.

investments. The old rich Texan jokes began to lose their power to amuse. Remember the one about the Texan who wanted a Cadillac for his nine-year-old, so he could drive around the living room, or who wanted to buy the Empire State Building? They had grown hollow. The rich Arab had supplanted them, but it was no joke when Sheikh Al-Aharif Al-Hamdan of Saudi Arabia attempted to buy the Alamo, the shrine of Texas freedom in San Antonio. While Texans passed it off lightly, if nervously, the sheikh was serious.[65]

But the symbols most forcibly reminding us of the relative briefness of time in which Texas has risen and then commenced its decline as an oil producer, though not as a center of wealth have been a series of deaths, of people whose lives have spanned the years encompassed in this book. Within a two-year period, the world's three billionaires with oil links have died. H. L. Hunt was the first to go, in late 1974; J. Paul Getty, a non-Texan but an oilman, the last, in 1976. Howard R. Hughes, marking the end to an era he may have scarcely been aware of, died in April, 1976. He was seventy, having been born in late 1905. Hughes' life had been a symbol of what Texas oil wealth had branched out into, and his death, on an airplane rushing desperately to Houston, which is now a medical center as well as the petroleum capital and his burial place, had its own ironic touches and symbolism.

By then Curt G. Hamill, who was up in the derrick when the Spindletop discovery well roared in to inaugurate the age of liquid fuel, was already dead. He had died in 1974, three days before his hundred and first birthday. Curt Hamill had lived through it all, had remembered it all, had drilled a well when he was ninety-five, and was still raring to go when he died. He'd always said the mother pool had not yet been found. His son, Claud Hamill, twenty-one months old when the Lucas well came in, was still active in Houston in 1976, looking for the mother pool.

Perhaps the most remarkable symbol of all was the death of Ima Hogg, the only daughter of Governor Jim Hogg, who went into the oil business at Spindletop. Miss Ima, as she was known to generations of Texans, died at ninety-three while on a trip to London where she had gone for the 1975 music season. ("When you're over ninety," she once said in her clear-eyed way, "it doesn't matter much where you die.") She had survived her brothers, Will, Mike, and Tom, by decades. As the last member of that stouthearted

Texas pioneer family, she had seen that its oil wealth went for worthy causes in her beloved Texas. She loved music (especially Bach), wild Texas flowers, art (particularly Picasso and Rivera), and politics. She reigned like the grand duchess of Texas from her stately home in Houston, a Democrat to the end.[66] She had been a young lady when Spindletop blew in, and she was a very old lady when she died, with everything about the oil industry changed forever. Like Curt Hamill, she had seen it all.

The Texas oil experience has been compressed within the span of a moment in the life of the earth, during which the age of liquid fuel has merged into the age of energy—in the process helping to make the world smaller, tying it together in to one interdependent system and, most of all, changing us, the world, and the industry itself, forever. The days that the Hamills, the Hoggs, and the older Hunts represented are gone now, a folded era never to come again, like adolescence, like a simpler America itself. Like a flickering flame, soon gone, the close of the era marks for all time the end of cheap, plentiful energy, as the example of an earlier Texas, not so long ago, becomes a lesson for all humanity.

It is a way of life that has vanished while we were looking at it.

NOTES

I. OUTSIDERS, KEEP OUT!

1. Robert C. Cotner, *James Stephen Hogg: A Biography* (Austin: University of Texas Press, 1959), p. 475.

2. *Ibid.,* pp. 538–39; Claude Vaden Hall, "The Life and Public Services of James Stephen Hogg," typescript, East Texas State University Library, n.d., pp. 16–17.

3. Cotner, *Hogg,* pp. 5, 44–48, 93.

4. *Ibid.,* p. 74.

5. *Ibid.,* pp. 52–96.

6. Herbert Gambrell, "James Stephen Hogg: Statesman or Demagogue?," *Southwest Review,* Vol. XIII, No. 3 (April, 1928), p. 348.

7. Cotner, *Hogg,* pp. 134–36.

8. Gambrell, "Hogg," p. 348.

9. Cotner, *Hogg,* pp. 147–66; Sam H. Acheson, "Big Governor," in Edwin Diller Starbuck, ed., *Lives That Guide* (New York: World Book Co., 1939), pp. 152–89.

10. Tom Finty, Jr., *Anti-Trust Legislation in Texas* (Dallas: A. H. Belo Co., 1916), p. 48.

11. Cotner, *Hogg,* pp. 184–85.

12. *Ibid.,* p. 195.

13. *Ibid.,* p. 172.

14. *Ibid.,* pp. 193–95.

15. Robert C. Cotner, ed., *Addresses and State Papers of James Stephen Hogg* (Austin: University of Texas Press, 1951), pp. 100–1.

16. Cotner, *Hogg,* pp. 236–38.

17. *Ibid.,* pp. 244–47.

18. Gambrell, "Hogg," pp. 339–40.

19. Cotner, *Hogg,* p. 443.

20. *Ibid.,* pp. 336–42.

21. Claude L. Witherspoon Interview, Pioneers in Texas Oil Oral History Project, University of Texas at Austin, hereafter cited as PTO-UTA.

22. Barret's story is told in Frank X. Tolbert, *The Story of Lyne Taliaferro (Tol) Barret Who Drilled Texas' First Oil Well* ([Dallas]: Texas Mid-Continent Oil & Gas Assn., 1966).

23. Dallas *Morning News,* March 24, 1889.

24. Max W. Ball, *This Fascinating Oil Business* (Indianapolis: Bobbs-Merrill Co., 1940), pp. 353–54; John S. Spratt, *The Road to Spindletop: Economic Change in Texas, 1875–1901* (Dallas: Southern Methodist University Press, 1955), pp. 293, 302.

25. John O. King, *Joseph Stephen Cullinan: A Study of Leadership in the Texas Petroleum Industry, 1897–1937* (Nashville: Vanderbilt University Press and Texas Gulf Coast Historical Association., 1970), p. 13.

26. *Ibid.,* pp. 7–8.

27. Arthur Elliot Interview, PTO-UTA.

28. Ralph W. Hidy and Muriel E. Hidy, *Pioneering in Big Business, 1882–1911; History of Standard Oil Co. (New Jersey)* (New York: Harper & Bros., 1955), pp. 276–77.

29. King, *Cullinan,* pp. 32 ff.

30. *Ibid.,* photograph opposite p. 86.

31. C. A. Warner, "Texas and the Oil Industry," *Southwestern Historical Quarterly,* Vol. L, No. 1 (July, 1946), p. 7.

II. SPINDLETOP—WHERE IT ALL BEGAN

1. Pattillo Higgins Interview, PTO-UTA.

2. Presto Mowbray, W.C. Gilbert interviews, PTO-UTA., tell of

the shooting incident with Patterson. Higgins' widow (Mrs. Pattillo Higgins Interview with J. P.) asserted it was a boyhood accident.

3. Higgins Interview, PTO-UTA; Robert C. Cotner interview of Pattillo Higgins, 1952, cited in Cotner, *James Stephen Hogg: A Biography* (Austin: University of Texas Press, 1959), p. 519.

4. Higgins Interview, PTO-UTA; James A. Clark and Michel T. Halbouty, *Spindletop* (New York: Random House, 1952), pp. 5–6.

5. Higgins Interview, PTO-UTA.

6. Personal communication, James A. Clark. Clark's information came from an interview with Higgins.

7. Higgins Interview, PTO-UTA.

8. Clark and Halbouty, *Spindletop*, pp. 10–14; Higgins Interview, PTO-UTA.

9. Higgins Interview; Cotner Interview of Mrs. Walter B. Sharp cited in Cotner, *Hogg*, pp. 519–20. Returning to water well work, Sharp roamed from Texas to North Carolina. By 1897 in the Corsicana boom he and his brothers, John and James, were working with much improved rotary rigs. In 1901 he returned to Beaumont.

10. W. C. Gilbert Interview, PTO-UTA.

11. Max Theodore Schlicher Interview, PTO-UTA.

12. Higgins Interview, PTO-UTA.

13. Reid Sayers McBeth, *Pioneering the Gulf Coast: A Story of the Life and Accomplishments of Capt. Anthony F. Lucas* (New York: n. pub., 1918), pp. 6–9.

14. Clark and Halbouty, *Spindletop*, pp. 30–41; E. DeGolyer, "Anthony F. Lucas and Spindletop," *Southwest Review*, Vol. XXXI (Fall, 1945), p. 85.

15. Curtis G. Hamill, *We Drilled Spindletop!* (Houston: n. pub., 1957), pp. 10–12.

16. Descriptions of the Hamill brothers are in the Claud Deer Interview, PTO-UTA, and Claud B. Hamill Interview (J. P.).

17. Hamill, *Spindletop*, p. 16.

18. *Ibid.*, pp. 22–27.

19. *Ibid.*, p. 27–29; Al Hamill Interview, PTO-UTA.

20. Clark and Halbouty, *Spindletop*, p. 62.

21. Al Hamill's account is also in Mody C. Boatright and William A. Owens, *Tales from the Derrick Floor: A People's History of the Oil Industry* (Garden City, N.Y.: Doubleday, 1970), p. 41.

22. Curt Hamill, Al Hamill Interviews, PTO-UTA.

23. "Texas Oil Scrapbook," PTO-UTA, Archives.

24. Pattilo Higgins Interview, PTO-UTA.

25. John S. Wynn, Al Hamill Interviews, PTO-UTA.

26. Hamill, *We Drilled,* pp. 30–31; Al Hamill Interview, PTO-UTA.

27. Al Hamill Interview, PTO-UTA.

28. Carlton D. Speed Interview, PTO-UTA.

29. E. W. Mayo, "The Oil Boom in Texas," *Harper's Weekly* (June 22, 1901), pp. 624–25.

30. Ashley Weaver, Claude L. Witherspoon Interviews, PTO-UTA; George Parker, *Oil Field Medico* (Dallas: Banks-Upshaw & Co., 1948), pp. 2–3; Ray Sittig, Clint Wood Interviews, PTO-UTA; Clark and Halbouty, *Spindletop,* pp. 77–78.

31. *Memoirs of George W. Armstrong* (Austin: n.pub., 1958), pp. 67–68.

32. Claude L. Witherspoon Interview, PTO-UTA.

33. Isaac F. Marcosson, "The Black Golconda," *Saturday Evening Post* (April 19, 1924), p. 198; Mayo, "Oil Boom," pp. 624–25.

34. Claud Deer, H. P. Nichols, Harry R. Paramore, Benjamin "Bud" Coyle interviews, PTO-UTA; Boatright and Owens, *Tales,* pp. 64–67.

35. George Sessions Perry, *Texas, A World in Itself* (New York: Whittlesey House, 1942), p. 168.

36. R. R. Hobson Interview, PTO-UTA.

37. Frank Redman, Frank Dunn Interviews, PTO-UTA; Boatright and Owens, *Tales,* pp. 68–69.

38. Harry R. Paramore Interview, PTO-UTA.

39. John Little, Claud Deer, Frank Redman Interviews, PTO-UTA. The boom's aftermath, or taming-down period, is examined in Paul E. Isaac, "Municipal Reform in Beaumont, Texas, 1902–1909," *Southwestern Historical Quarterly,* Vol. LXXVIII, No. 4 (April, 1975), pp. 409–30.

40. Burt E. Hull Interview, PTO-UTA.

41. Carl F. Mirus Interview, PTO-UTA.

42. Cotner, *Hogg,* pp. 523–24.

43. *Ibid.,* pp. 526–27; Benjamin "Bud" Coyle Interview, PTO-UTA.

44. Frank Redman, Claud Deer, John S. Wynn Interviews, PTO-UTA.

45. Burt E. Hull Interview, PTO-UTA.

46. Early C. Deane Interview, PTO-UTA.

47. Clark and Halbouty, *Spindletop,* pp. 128–42; Craig Thompson, *Since Spindletop: A Human Story of Gulf's First Half-Century* (Pittsburgh: Gulf Oil Corp., 1951), pp. 9–14, 17–18, 23.

48. John O. King, *Joseph Stephen Cullinan* (Nashville: Vanderbilt University Press & Texas Gulf Coast Historical Association, 1970), pp. 94–101.

49. Lloyd Wendt and Herman Kogan, *Bet A Million! The Story of John W. Gates* (Indianapolis: Bobbs-Merrill Co., 1948), pp. 158, 202–3, 243, 130, 134, 150, 231.

50. *Ibid.,* p. 243.

51. Ima Hogg Interview, PTO-UTA.

52. King, *Cullinan,* pp. 106, 128; Cotner, *Hogg,* pp. 540–47.

53. H. P. Nichols Interview, PTO-UTA.

54. Marquis James, *The Texaco Story: The First Fifty Years, 1902–1952* (N.p.: The Texas Co., 1953), pp. 35–36; King, *Cullinan,* pp. 6–7, 194.

55. Robert Henriques, *Bearsted: A Biography of Marcus Samuel, First Viscount Bearsted and Founder of "Shell" Transport and Trading Company* (New York: Viking Press, 1960), pp. 340–45, 350, 353. Henriques states that these figures come from the original documents and that other accounts giving 4.5 million barrels are inaccurate.

56. *Ibid.,* pp. 348–49, 357–58, 445, 462–67.

57. King, *Cullinan,* p. 149; Clark and Halbouty, *Spindletop,* pp. 169–82.

58. Clark and Halbouty, *Spindletop,* pp. 157–68; John G. "Jack" Pew Interview (J. P.)

59. The genesis of Humble is in Henrietta M. Larson and Kenneth Wiggins Porter, *History of Humble Oil & Refining Company: A Study in Industrial Growth* (New York: Harper & Bros., 1959), pp. 22–56, 73–76; Clark and Halbouty, *Spindletop,* pp. 183–202; Edgar Welsey Owen, *Trek of the Oil Finders: A History of Exploration for Petroleum* (Tulsa: American Association of Petroleum Geologists, 1975), p. 313.

60. David Rockefeller, "The Cost of All Out Mobilization," in *Spindletop: Symbol of Free Enterprise: Preprint of a Series of Speeches Commemorating the 50th Anniversary of the Discovery of the Spindletop Oil Field, Beaumont, Texas* (Beaumont: Spindletop 50th Anniversary Committee, 1951), p. 37.

61. H. A. Rathke Interview, PTO-UTA.

62. DeGolyer, "Lucas and Spindletop," p. 86.

63. Cotner, *Hogg*, pp. 530–31.

64. Owen, *Trek of Oil Finders*, p. 199; Thelma Johnson et al., *The Spindle Top Oil Field: A History of Its Discovery and Development* (Beaumont: George Norvell, 1927).

65. Mrs. Pattillo Higgins Interview (J. P.); Mrs. Higgins, a number of years younger than her husband, was still alive in 1978.

III. THE SCANDAL OF THE SENATOR AND STANDARD OIL

1. "Men We Are Watching: The Lion in a Snare," *The Independent* (January 24, 1907), pp. 208–9.

2. Jesse Guy Smith, "The Bailey Controversy in Texas Politics" (Unpublished M.A. Thesis, University of Chicago, 1924), p. 7.

3. Sam Hanna Acheson, *Joe Bailey, The Last Democrat* (New York: Macmillan Co., 1932), pp. 1–25, 30–31, 37, 48.

4. Smith, "Bailey Controversy," p. 13.

5. Lonn Taylor, "Miss Ima," *Texas Observer* (September 5, 1975), p. 10.

6. Smith, "Bailey Controversy," p. 15.

7. Acheson, *Bailey*, pp. 137–39, 38, 160.

8. Tom Finty, Jr., *Anti-Trust Legislation in Texas* (Galveston: A. H. Belo & Co., 1916), p. 21.

9. Smith, "Bailey Controversy," p. 22; Bailey speech at Greenville, Texas, as reported in Galveston *News*, October 2, 1906; Frederick Upham Adams, *The Waters Pierce Case in Texas* (St. Louis: Skinner & Kennedy, 1908), pp. 1 ff.

10. Galveston *News*, October 2, 1906.

11. Acheson, *Bailey*, pp. 229 ff.

12. *Ibid.*, pp. 176–77.

13. Smith, "Bailey Controversy," pp. 20–21.

14. Texas Legislature, House. *Proceedings and Reports of Bailey Investigation Committee* (Austin: Von Boeckmann-Jones Co., 1907), p. 841.

15. Smith, "Bailey Controversy," pp. 22–23.

16. Robert C. Cotner, ed., *Addresses and State Papers of James Stephen Hogg* (Austin: University of Texas Press, 1951), pp. 478–82.

17. Cotner, *Hogg*, pp. 505-11.

18. Joseph W. Bailey, *In Reply to "Muckrakers"; Personal Explanation Speech in U.S. Senate, June 27, 1906* (Washington: n.pub., 1906), p. 9; Smith, "Bailey Controversy," p. 27; Cotner, *Hogg*, pp. 511-13; Acheson, *Bailey*, p. 151.

19. Smith, "Bailey Controversy," pp. 29-30; David Graham Phillips, "The Treason of the Senate," *Cosmopolitan Magazine* (July, 1906), pp. 270-71.

20. Bailey, *In Reply to "Muckrakers,"* pp. 10, 13-15.

21. Adams, *Waters Pierce Case*, a pro-Waters Pierce view, seeks to show that Pierce was an innocent victim of the controversy, not a conspirator and cat's paw of Standard Oil. See especially pp. 20-22, 36-39, 47, 54, 60.

22. Galveston *Daily News*, September 16, 1906.

23. Finty, *Anti-Trust Legislation*, p. 22; Smith, "Bailey Controversy," pp. 29-30.

24. Galveston *News*, October 2, 1906.

25. *Ibid.*, October 7, 1906.

26. Acheson, *Bailey*, pp. 176-77; Smith, "Bailey Controversy," p. 31.

27. A copy of Bailey's letter is in Texas House, *Bailey Investigation Committee*, pp. 813-19.

28. Alfred Henry Lewis, "The Hon. (?) J. W. Bailey," *Cosmopolitan Magazine* (April, 1913), p. 602; Smith, "Bailey Controversy," p. 35.

29. Texas House, *Bailey Investigation Committee*, p. 202-3.

30. *Ibid.*, pp. 208-9.

31. *Ibid.*, pp. 668-69, 678-79.

32. *Ibid.*, pp. 817, 847-50.

33. *Ibid.*, p. 899, 944.

34. *Ibid.*, pp. 984-85.

35. *Ibid.*, pp. 1056-58, 1084-85, 1090-91.

36. A brief account of the whole controversy is in Acheson, *Bailey*, pp. 229-40. For an anti-Bailey view see E. G. Senter, *The Bailey Case Boiled Down* (Dallas; Flag Publishing Co., 1908), or the prosecutor's account, William A. Cocke, *The Bailey Controversy in Texas, with Lessons from the Political Life-Story of a Fallen Idol* (San Antonio: The Cocke Co., 1908), 2 vols.

37. Finty, *Anti-Trust Legislation, p. 22;* Rupert Norval Richardson, *Texas, The Lone Star State* (Englewood Cliffs, N.J.: Prentice-Hall,

1942), pp. 375–76; Allan Nevins, *John D. Rockefeller* (New York: Charles Scribner's Sons, 1959), p. 324.

38. Ralph W. Hidy and Muriel E. Hidy, *Pioneering in Big Business, 1882–1911. History of Standard Oil Company (New Jersey)* (New York: Harper & Bros., 1955), pp. 276, 393–94, 696; "A History of Texas Anti-Trust in Oil," *Texas Observer* (September 18, 1959), p. 2.

39. "The Laborer and His Hire—Another Standard Oil Lesson," *Hearst's Magazine* (February, 1913), pp. 174–88; Alfred Henry Lewis, "The Hon (?) J. W. Bailey," *Cosmopolitan Magazine* (April, 1913), pp. 601–5. In 1908 Hearst had published copies of documents linking prominent politicians to Standard Oil. A few had been forgeries, but not those concerning Bailey. See Oliver Carlson and Ernest Sutherland Bates, *Hearst, Lord of San Simeon* (New York: Viking Press,1936), pp. 166–68, 171–74.

IV. MUD 'N' BLOOD IN ROARING RANGER

1. Edgar Wesley Owen, *Trek of the Oil Finders: A History of Exploration for Petroleum* (Tulsa: American Association of Petroleum Geologists, 1975), pp. 284ff., 318, 363–65.

2. Boyce House, *Oil Field Fury* (San Antonio: Naylor Co., 1954), pp. 98–99.

3. Boyce House, *Were You in Ranger?* (Dallas: Tardy Publishing Co., 1935), pp. 1–12; House, *Oil Field Fury*, p. 32; Boyce House, *Roaring Ranger: The World's Biggest Boom* (San Antonio: Naylor Co., 1951), p. 4; Owen, *Trek of Oil Finders*, pp. 318–19; Samuel W. Tait, Jr., *The Wildcatters: An Informal History of Oil-Hunting in America* (Princeton: Princeton University Press, 1946), p. 131.

4. John F. Rust Interview, PTO-UTA.

5. E. P. "Matt" Matteson Interview, PTO-UTA.

6. R. S. Kennedy, O. G. Lawson, Clair McCormick, Carl Angstadt Interviews, PTO-UTA; Jake L. Hamon Interview (J.P).

7. McCormick Interview, PTO-UTA.

8. Lucille Glasscock, *A Texas Wildcatter: A Fascinating Saga of Oil* (San Antonio: Naylor Co., 1952), p. 21.

9. Rust Interview, PTO-UTA.

10. Matteson Interview, PTO-UTA.

11. House. *Were You in Ranger?*, pp. 160–91.

12. James Donohoe Interview, PTO-UTA.

13. Boyce House, "It Was Fun While It Lasted," *Saturday Evening Post* (October 16, 1937), p. 14.

14. House, *Roaring Ranger*, p. 1. These estimates may be inflated.

15. Rust Interview, PTO-UTA.

16. Richard R. Moore, *West Texas After the Discovery of Oil: A Modern Frontier* (Austin: Jenkins Publishing Co./Pemberton Press, 1971), pp. 93–94.

17. House, *Roaring Ranger*, pp. 13–15; House, *Were You in Ranger?*, pp. 35–38; House, *Oil Field Fury*, p. 37.

18. Landon H. Cullum Interview, PTO-UTA.

19. Lesley Hill True Interview (J.P.)

20. House, *Roaring Ranger*, p. 14.; Gerald Forbes, *Flush Production: The Epic of Oil in the Gulf-Southwest* (Norman: University of Oklahoma Press, 1942), p. 165.

21. House, *Oil Field Fury*, pp. 41–42.

22. Cullum Interview.

23. House, *Were You in Ranger?*, pp. 132–33.

24. Rust, McCormic interviews; House, *Oil Field Fury*, p. 33; H. P. Hodge Interview, PTO-UTA.

25. Matteson Interview.

26. McCormick Interview.

27. James A. Clark, *The Chronological History of the Petroleum and Natural Gas Industries* (Houston: Clark Book Co., 1963), p. 119.

28. Owen, *Trek of Oil Finders*, p. 323.

29. House, "Fun While It Lasted," p. 89.

30. Rex Beach, *Flowing Gold* (New York: Harper & Bros., 1922), p. 101.

31. Walter Cline, H. P. Hodge, Jack Knight, Frank Hamilton Interviews, PTO-UTA; Beach, *Flowing Gold*, p. 102; Pauline Naylor Interview (J.P.); House, *Oil Boom*, pp. 64–69. See also Mody C. Boatright, *Folklore of the Oil Industry* (Dallas: SMU Press, 1963), p. 67.

32. E. M. Friend Interview, PTO-UTA.

33. Electra *News*, Anniversary Edition, March 29, 1923.

34. "History of the Texas Railroad Commission," mimeo. ms., pp. 4–5; "A Chronological Listing of Important Historical Events, Legislative Acts, Judicial Decisions, Orders, and Other Relevant

Data Regarding The Railroad Commission of Texas," mimeo. ms., [Austin], Railroad Commission of Texas, n.d., p. 2.

35. Jay Hall Interview (J.P.).

36. W. B. Hamilton Interview, PTO-UTA.

37. Charles N. Gould, *Covered Wagon Geologist* (Norman: University of Oklahoma Press, 1959), p. viii; Edward B. Garnett, "Oil Is King in the Texas Panhandle," *World's Work* (December, 1927), pp. 170-174; Carl Coke Rister, *Oil! Titan of the Southwest* (Norman: University of Oklahoma Press, 1949), pp. 276-280; James Levi Horlacher, *A Year in the Oil Fields* (Lexington: The Kentucky Kernel, 1929), pp. 38-39; George W. Gray, "The Roaring Tides of the Oil Fields," *New York Times Magazine,* Sept. 30, 1931, V, p. 4. Also see C. C. McClelland, Landon W. Cullum Interviews, PTO-UTA, and Interview with officials of International Union of Operating Engineers, Local 351: James E. Garrett, Earl Snider, Burl Cartright, L.V. McCarthy, T.W. Ozmer, PTO-UTA.

38. Owen, *Trek of Oil Finders,* pp. 943-944.

39. Edgar W. Owen Interview (J.P.); Owen, *Trek of Oil Finders,* p. 284; Moore, *West Texas After Discovery of Oil,* pp. xi–xii.

40. Rupert Norval Richardson, *Texas, The Lone Star State* (Englewood Cliffs, N.J.: Prentice-Hall, 1943), pp. 441, 509; Max W. Ball, *This Fascinating Oil Business* (Indianapolis: Bobbs-Merrill Co., 1940), p. 339.

V. OIL FOR THE LAMPS OF LEARNING

1. Ronnie Dugger, *Our Invaded Universities: Form, Reform and New Starts, A Nonfiction Play for Five Stages* (New York: W. W. Norton & Co., 1974), p. 252.

2. Edith Helene Parker, "History of Land Grants for Education in Texas" (Unpublished Ph.D. Thesis, University of Texas at Austin, 1952), pp. 223–24, 254–56; Rupert Norval Richardson, *Texas, The Lone Star State* (Englewood Cliffs, N.J.: Prentice-Hall, 1943), pp. 331, 339–41; Mody C. Boatright, *Folklore of the Oil Industry* (Dallas: SMU Press, 1963), pp. 54–56.

3. H. Y. Benedict, *A Source Book Relating to the History of the University of Texas: Legislative, Legal, Bibliographical, and Statistical*

(Austin: University of Texas Bulletin No. 1757, October 10, 1917), p. 831.

4. Parker, "History of Land Grants," pp. 271–72, 281–82.

5. Martin W. Schwettmann, *Santa Rita: The University of Texas Oil Discovery* (Austin: Texas State Historical Association, 1943), pp. 24–35; Jean Sladek, "Our Saint Came Marching In," *Alcade: The University of Texas at Austin Alumni Magazine* (January, 1974), pp. 9–11; Richard R. Moore, *West Texas After the Discovery of Oil: A Modern Frontier* (Austin: Jenkins Publishing Co., 1971), pp. 10–11, 91; Samuel D. Myres, *The Permian Basin, Petroleum Empire of the Southwest: Era of Discovery, from the Beginning to the Depression* (El Paso: Permian Press, 1973), pp. 223–24; Clarence C. Pope, *An Oil Scout in the Permian Basin, 1924–1960* (El Paso: Permian Press, 1972), p. 70. The full story of the Reagan County bonanza is given in Myres, pp. 194–273.

6. Letter, W. L. Lobb, associate deputy chancellor for investment, trusts, and lands of the University of Texas System, to J. P., November 6, 1975, with inclosure, Permanent University Fund Receipts From the Beginning Through August 31, 1975; letter, Berte R. Haigh, consultant on University of Texas lands, to J. P., November 14, 1975; letter, W. C. Freeman, executive vice-president for administration of the Texas A&M System, to J. P., November 10, 1975, with Special Mineral Fund ledger page inclosed.

7. Edgar W. Owen Interview (J. P.).

8. Dugger, *Invaded Universities*, pp. 107–8, 253, 266–67.

9. Willie Morris, *North Toward Home* (Boston: Houghton Mifflin Co., 1967), pp. 186, 189, 191–92.

10. San Angelo *Morning Times,* October 28, 1936. The story of the Yates pool is told in this issue.

11. Pope, *Oil Scout,* pp. 67–68.

12. Thomas Lloyd Miller, *The Public Lands of Texas, 1519–1970* (Norman: University of Oklahoma Press, 1971), pp. 271–80; statement, Texas Land Commissioner Bob Armstrong, December 4, 1975; letter, Mary Beth Rogers to J. P., December 11, 1975, with statement of mineral leases revenue, June 9, 1922, to August 31, 1975. (Mrs. Rogers was administrative assistant to Commissioner Armstrong).

13. Letter, Patrick J. Nicholson, vice-president, university devel-

opment, at the University of Houston, to J. P., November 13, 1975.

14. W. Vance Grant and C. George Lind, *Digest of Education Statistics* (Washington: U.S. Government Printing Office, 1976; 1975 edition), pp. 63–64, 78, 123, 126, 180.

VI. EAST TEXAS–THE GRANDDADDY OF THEM ALL

1. James A. Clark and Michel T. Halbouty, *The Last Boom* (New York: Random House, 1972), pp. 6–9, 18–19; Dallas *Morning News,* March 29, 1947, Sect. II, pp. 1, 3; Ralph Farmer Interview (J.P.).

2. Harry Harter, *East Texas Oil Parade* (San Antonio: Naylor Co., 1934), pp. 59–60; Clark and Halbouty, *Last Boom,* pp. 15–17.

3. W. Dow Hamm Interview (J.P.). Hamm also recalled this experience in Edgar Wesley Owen, *Trek of the Oil Finders* (Tulsa: American Association of Petroleum Geologists, 1975), pp. 857–58. A copy of Lloyd's report, possibly of a later date and apparently not the one that Hamm saw, is in Clark and Halbouty, *Last Boom,* pp. 295–300.

4. E. G. Laster, Mrs. H. C. Miller et al. interviews, PTO-UTA; Clark and Halbouty, *Last Boom,* pp. 34–39; Harter, *East Texas Oil Parade,* p. 59.

5. A good survey of the Van field is in Owen, *Trek of the Oil Finders,* pp. 856–57.

6. Laster Interview; Clark and Halbouty, *Last Boom,* pp. 56–61.

7. Laster Interview.

8. Henderson *Times,* September 9, 1930.

9. *Ibid.,* September 23, 1930.

10. *Ibid.,* September 16, 1930.

11. Clark and Halbouty, *Last Boom,* pp. 79–81; Harter, *East Texas Oil Parade,* pp. 69–74; Laster Interview; D. Harold Byrd Interview (J. P.). Other sources for the Laster account include Dorman H. Winfrey, "A History of Rusk County, Texas" (Unpublished M.A. Thesis, University of Texas at Austin, 1951), p. 151, and Dallas *Morning News,* September 14, 1930.

12. Henderson *Times,* October 21, 1930.

13. L. L. James Interview, PTO-UTA; H. L. Hunt, *Hunt Heritage: The Republic and Our Families* (Dallas: Parade Press, 1973), pp. 81–84.

14. Sherman Hunt Interview, (J.P.); H. L. Hunt, *Hunt Heritage,*

pp. 6–11; H. L. Hunt, *H. L. Hunt Early Days* (Dallas: Parade Press, 1973), pp. 1–2.

15. Hunt, *Hunt Heritage,* pp. 15–22.

16. Tom Buckley, "Just Plain H. L. Hunt," *Esquire* (January, 1967), p. 66; Hunt, *Hunt Heritage,* pp. 23–42.

17. Hunt, *Hunt Heritage,* pp. 42–48, 69–71; Buckley, "Just Plain H. L. Hunt," p. 66.

18. Buckley, "Just Plain H. L. Hunt," pp. 66–67.

19. *Ibid.,* pp. 67–68; Hunt, *Hunt Heritage,* pp. 71–74.

20. Hunt, *Hunt Heritage,* pp. 84–90; Clark and Halbouty, *Last Boom,* pp. 90–96. Both sources give the crucial terms of the agreement.

21. Clark and Halbouty, *Last Boom,* pp. 10–12, 84–87, 97–100, 101–3.

22. NEA story, March 20, 1931, University of Texas at Austin Pioneers in Texas Oil Scrapbook.

23. W. A. Moncrief, Sr., Interview (J. P.); "Moncrief Recalls Core Looking Like Oil-Dipped Brown Sugar," Longview *Daily News,* January 26, 1966; letter, W. A. Moncrief to J. P., September 4, 1975.

24. Moncrief Interview.

25. Lesley H. True Interview (J. P.).

26. George W. Pirtle Interview (J. P.).

27. Owen, *Trek of Oil Finders,* pp. 859–60; Ruel McDaniel, *Some Ran Hot* (Dallas: Regional Press, 1939), p. 71; Harter, *East Texas Oil Parade,* pp. 86–88; Clark and Halbouty, *Last Boom,* pp. 108–9.

28. L. L. James Interview, PTO-UTA.

29. "East Texas, Oil Terror," *Business Week* (January 19, 1935), p. 21.

30. James Interview.

31. Sherman M. Hunt Interview.

32. A roundup of the suit is in Clark and Halbouty, *Last Boom,* pp. 197–208.

33. James Interview; Harter, *East Texas Oil Parade,* pp. 208–9, 219.

34. George W. Gray, "The Roaring Tides of the Oil Fields," *New York Times Magazine,* September 20, 1931, V, p. 5; Harter, *East Texas Oil Parade,* pp. 96–97.

35. Laster Interview.

36. Joe Zeppa Interview (J. P.).

37. Pirtle Interview.

38. Laster Interview.

39. Clark and Halbouty, Last Boom, pp. 110, 118; Robert W. Eaton Interview (J. P.).

40. John G. "Jack" Pew Interview (J. P.).

41. Clark and Halbouty, *Last Boom,* pp. 111, 289.

42. Dallas *Morning News,* March 29, 1947, Sect. II, pp. 1, 3; *ibid.,* March 31, 1947, editorial.

43. John T. Scopes Interview, May, 1970 (J. P.).

44. Dallas *Morning News,* November 10, 1975; John William Rogers, *The Lusty Texans of Dallas* (New York: E. P. Dutton, 1960), pp. 275, 360.

45. H. L. Hunt, *Hunt Heritage,* p. 101.

46. James S. Hudnall Interview, PTO-UTA.

47. Max W. Ball, *This Fascinating Oil Business* (Indianapolis: Bobbs-Merrill Co., 1940), p. 315; H. L. Hunt, *Hunt Heritage,* pp. 86–88, 102.

48. Owen, *Trek of Oil Finders,* p. 860.

49. J. Howard Marshall Interview (J. P.).

VII. THE HOT OIL WAR

1. Kilgore *News Herald,* August 24, 1941.

2. James A. Clark and Michel T. Halbouty, *The Last Boom* (New York: Random House, 1972), pp. 144–45.

3. Carl E. Reistle, Jr., Interview (J. P.).

4. Clark and Halbouty, *Last Boom,* p. 162–63; J. Howard Marshall Interview; Edgar Wesley Owen, *Trek of the Oil Finders* (Tulsa: AAPG, 1975), p. 454.

5. William Atherton Dupuy, "Once More 'Hot Oil' Gushes Ruinously," *New York Times Magazine,* January 27, 1935, Sect. VI, p. 2.

6. Clark and Halbouty, *Last Boom,* pp. 162–65.

7. *Ibid.,* pp. 166–70; James A Clark, *Three Stars for the Colonel* (New York: Random House, 1954), pp. 65–66, 73; Harry Harter, *East Texas Oil Parade* (San Antonio: Naylor Co., 1934), p. 106.

8. Clark and Halbouty, *Last Boom,* p. 171.

9. Richard O'Connor, *The Oil Barons: Men of Greed and Grandeur* (Boston: Little, Brown, 1971), p. 309.

10. Gladewater *Gusher,* August 19, 1931.

11. Clark and Halbouty, *Last Boom,* pp. 172–73; Luther A. Reed, J. R. Lyne Interviews (J. P.).

12. Clark and Halbouty, *Last Boom,* pp. 173–79, 182–83; Harter, *East Texas Oil Parade,* pp. 110–14.

13. Ruel McDaniel, *Some Ran Hot* (Dallas: Regional Press, 1939), pp. 198, 209–10; Clark and Halbouty, *Last Boom,* p. 185.

14. Clark, *Three Stars,* pp. 63–64, 66–68.

15. *Ibid.,* pp. 19–62.

16. LeRoy Menzing Interview (J. P.).

17. Clark, *Three Stars,* pp. 88–90.

18. Harold L. Ickes, *The Secret Diary of Harold L. Ickes: The First Thousand Days, 1933–1936* (New York: Simon & Schuster, 1953), pp. 29, 31–32.

19. J. R. Parten Interview (J. P.).See also *New York Times,* May 7, 1933, Sect. II, 7:3, and May 12, 1933, 28:1.

20. Ickes, *Secret Diary,* pp. 158–59.

21. *New York Times,* May 6, 1934, II, 9:7; May 30, 1934, 31:1; June 15, 1934, 41:1; June 16, 1934, 7:1.

22. U.S. Congress, House. 73rd Congress (Recess). *Hearings Before a Subcommittee of the Committee on Interstate and Foreign Commerce. Sept. 17–22, 1934* (Washington: U.S. Government Printing Office, 1934), Part 1, pp. 6–7, 196.

23. *Ibid.,* Part 3, pp. 1607–11.

24. *Ibid.,* Part 4, pp. 2289, 2293–94.

25. *Ibid.,* Part 3, pp. 1521–27.

26. *Ibid.,* pp. 1772; see also 1776, 1782–83, 1810–11.

27. Parten Interview.

28. Parten Interview; letter, J. R. Parten to J. P., January 21, 1976; Sherman Hunt Interview (J. P.); Austin *American,* April 25, 26, 29, May 2, 3, 1933. Also see Clark and Halbouty, *Last Boom,* pp. 195–96, 209–10.

29. House, *Hearings, 1934,* Part 4, pp. 2000–1.

30. Ickes, *Secret Diary,* p. 142.

31. Clark, *Three Stars,* pp. 107–8.

32. J. Howard Marshall Interview (J. P.).

33. R. J. McMurrey, Jr., Interview (J. P.).

34. F. W. Fischer Interview, PTO-UTA.

35. George W. Pirtle Interview (J. P.).

36. Fischer Interview, PTO-UTA.

37. Marshall Interview.

38. *Ibid.; New York Times,* August 24, 1934, (2:5), August 27, 1934 (33:2), August 28, 1934.

39. "Hot Oil Cooler," *Business Week* (December 22, 1934), p. 11.

40. Marshall Interview.

41. Thomas G. Kelliher Interview (J. P.).

42. Luther Reed Interview (J. P.).

43. Fischer Interview.

44. Jay Hall Interview (J. P.).

45. John D. Murchison Interview (J. P.).

46. Pirtle Interview. Pirtle was told this account by Marvin McMurrey, who is now dead.

47. R. J. McMurrey, Jr., Interview (J. P.).

48. Marshall Interview. Story verified by McMurrey's son, R. J., Jr.

49. Marshall Interview; Ickes, *Secret Diary,* pp. 306 – 7; letter, J. Howard Marshall to J. P., November 4, 1975; Fischer Interview; Clark and Halbouty, *Last Boom,* pp. 224–31; Kelliher Interview; McDaniel, *Some Ran Hot,* pp. 227–29; Harter, *East Texas Oil Parade,* pp. 126–34.

50. Marshall Interview; Clark and Halbouty, *Last Boom,* pp. 231– 32; Samuel B. Pettengill, *Hot Oil: The Problem of Petroleum* (New York: Economic Forum Co., 1936), p. 207. Pettengill provides the text of the Connally Act in pp. 296–300.

51. Marshall Interview.

VIII. LONE STAR SHEIKHS

1. Tom Buckley, "Just Plain H. L. Hunt," *Esquire,* January, 1967, pp. 68-69.

2. George G. Kirstein, *The Rich: Are They Different?* (Boston: Houghton Mifflin, 1968), p. 244.

3. Goronwy Rees, *The Multimillionaires: Six Studies in Wealth* (New York: Macmillan Co., 1961), pp. 107–9.

4. Robert W. Eaton Interview (J. P.).

5. *Ibid.*

6. LeRoy A. Menzing, D. H. Byrd, Bess Bond Interviews (J. P.).

7. Ralph Spence, Robert Eaton interviews (J. P.).

8. Stanley Marcus, *Minding the Store: A Memoir* (Boston: Little, Brown, 1974), pp. 194–95; George Fuermann, *Houston, Land of the Big Rich* (Garden City, N.Y.: Doubleday, 1951), pp. 17–21; George Fuermann, *Reluctant Empire* (Garden City, New York: Doubleday, 1957), p. 33.

9. Spence Interview.

10. Nancy Heard Toudouze Interview (J. P.).

11. Jay Hall Interview (J. P.).

12. Edna Ferber, *Giant* (New York: Pocket Books, 1954), pp. 342–43.

13. Glenn H. McCarthy Interview (J. P.).

14. "King of the Wildcatters," *Time* (February 13, 1950), p. 18.

15. McCarthy Interview.

16. Lynn Ashby, "The Wildcatter's Wildcatter," *Texas Monthly* (November, 1974), pp. 67, 162; George Fuermann, *Houston, City of Big Rich,* pp. 96–98; McCarthy Interview.

17. McCarthy Interview.

18. James Clark Interview (J. P.).

19. H. L. Hunt, *Hunt Heritage: The Republic and Our Families* (Dallas: Parade Press, 1973), p. 2.

20. Buckley, "Just Plain H. L. Hunt," p. 69.

21. Frank X. Tolbert, " 'Richest Man'–? Dallasite Doubts It," Dallas *Morning News,* April 4, 1948, Sect. 4, p. 1.

22. H. L. Hunt, *H. L. Hunt Early Days* (Dallas: Parade Press, 1973), p. 71.

23. Welch Wright Interview (J. P.).

24. Art Brenton Interview; Buckley, "Just Plain H. L. Hunt," p. 152.

25. Buckley, "Plain H. L. Hunt," p. 148.

26. Rena Pederson, "A Day in the Lives of the Hunts," Dallas *Morning News,* September 14, 1975, p. 30-A.

27. Hunt, *Hunt Heritage,* p. 135, reproducing letter from H. G. Green, November 17, 1972.

28. Devin Garrity Interview (J. P.).

29. Karl Hess Interview (J. P.); Letter, Karl Hess to J. P., July 27, 1977.

30. Les H. True Interview (J. P.).

31. McCarthy Interview.

32. J. Clarence Karcher Interview (J. P.).

33. Jake L. Hamon Interview (J. P.).

34. Buckley, "Just Plain H. L. Hunt," p. 154; Hunt, *Hunt Early Days,* p. 188; Bill Porterfield, "H. L. Hunt's Long Goodbye," *Texas Monthly* (March, 1975), pp. 64–67; Dallas *Morning News,* November 30, 1974; Frank X. Tolbert, "Tolbert's Texas: Hunt's 'Floating' Checkers Contest," Dallas *Morning News,* December 3, 1974; James R. Gaines et al. "A Scandal for the Hunt Clan," *Newsweek* (March 24, 1975), p. 26.

35. Pederson, "Day in Lives of Hunts." An interview with Ray Hunt by Cheryl Hall is in Dallas *Morning News,* October 9, 1977, p. 1-H.

36. "Richest of All," *Fortune* (May, 1968), p. 157.

37. Dallas *Morning News,* July 11, 1973.

38. "Now, a Silver Rush," *Newsweek* (February 25, 1974), p. 83.

39. Dallas *Morning News,* December 10, 12, 19, 20, 1974.

40. Gaines et al., "Scandal," pp. 26–27; Dallas *Morning News,* March 21, September 17, 18, 26, 1975 *et seq.*

41. Will Grimsley, "Hunt Fortune Uncovers Riches in Chiefs' World Football Title," AP story in Memphis *Commercial Appeal,* June 7, 1970, p. 3.

IX. LONE STAR SHEIKHS (CONT'D)

1. Tony Castro, "Mr. Brown of Brown & Root: Power and Money in Houston," *Texas Observer* (July 25, 1975), pp. 15–16.

2. Francis Russell, *The Shadow of Blooming Grove: Warren G. Harding in His Times* (New York: McGraw-Hill Book Co., 1968), pp. 348–49 ff. Russell noted that a lawyer had indicated that the elder Hamon had been promised a third interest in the Teapot Dome lease. The junior Hamon, in a personal communication to me, said that this was inaccurate and that he had never heard of it.

3. Jake L. Hamon, Jay Hall, Lesley Hill, True, LeRoy Menzing interviews (J.P.); *Who's Who in America,* 38th ed., 1974–75; letter, Jake L. Hamon, April 3, 1975, to J.P.

4. "Surprise Package," *Time* (December 17, 1965), p. 80.

5. Freeman Lincoln, "John Mecom's Delightful Dilemma," *Fortune* (June, 1957), pp. 169–72 ff.; "The Midas Touch of John Mecom," *Business Week* (October 10, 1964), pp. 90–92 ff. in the Houston *Chronicle* deal see Stanley H. Brown, "The Big Deal That Got Away," *Fortune* (October, 1966), pp. 164–66 ff., and Ben H. Bagdikian, "Houston's Shackled Press," *Atlantic* (August 1966), pp. 87–93.

6. Louis Alexander, "Louis Alexander Calls on Bob Smith," *Oil*, Vol. XX, No. 4 (April, 1960), pp. 13–17; "Keeping a City in Good Shape," *Business Week* (June 6, 1964), pp. 110–14; "Biographical Data and List of Club and Committee Memberships of R. E. Smith," mimeo., n.d.; Texarkana *Gazette*, November 12, 1971; Sherman Hunt, Jake L. Hamon, Claud B. Hamill, M. B. Rudman, William N. Finnegan, Dooley Dawson, D. H. Byrd interviews (J.P.)

7. Ed Kilman and Theon Wright, *Hugh Roy Cullen: A Story of American Opportunity* (New York: Prentice-Hall, 1954), pp. 5–7.

8. Thomas G. Kelliher Interview (J.P.).

9. Kilman and Wright, *Cullen,* pp. 20–115.

10. "The Billionaire," *Newsweek* (July 15, 1957), p. 169.

11. Kilman and Wright, *Cullen,* pp. 121–85.

12. George Fuermann, *Reluctant Empire* (Garden City, N.Y.: Doubleday, 1957), p. 34.

13. "Texans on Wall Street," *Time* (June 16, 1961), p. 80.

14. John D. Murchison Interview (J.P.).

15. Robert Lubar, "Henry Holt and the Man from Koon Kreek," *Fortune* (December, 1959), pp. 104–9 ff.

16. Murchison Interview.

17. Frank X. Tolbert, "Tolbert's Texas: Billionaire's First Financial Triumph," Dallas *Morning News,* February 2, 1976.

18. H. H. Anderson Interview (J.P.).

19. Edgar W. Owen Interview (J.P.).

20. Anderson Interview.

21. Dudley C. Sharp, Sr., Interview (J.P.).

22. Sherman Hunt Interview.

23. Pauline Naylor Interview (J.P.).

24. Ralph Spence Interview (J.P.).

25. Murchison Interview; "Texans on Wall Street," pp. 80–81.

26. George W. Strake, Jr., Interview (J.P.).

27. Johnny Mitchell Interview (J.P.).

28. Stanley Marcus, *Minding the Store: A Memoir* (Boston: Little, Brown, 1974), p. 246.

29. John William Rogers, *The Lusty Texans of Dallas* (New York: E. P. Dutton, 1960), pp. 275–76; George Fuermann, *Houston, Land of the Big Rich* (Garden City, N.Y.: Doubleday, 1951), pp. 58–59.

30. Dooley Dawson, Glenn McCarthy Interviews (J. P.).

31. Brown, "Big Deal That Got Away," p. 192.

32. Fuermann, *Houston*, pp. 174–75; Kilman and Wright, *Cullen*, pp. 208–9.

33. Walter Cline Interview, PTO-UTA.

34. Byrd Interview.

35. Hamon Interview; Ralph Hewins, *Mr. Five Per Cent: The Story of Calouste Gulbenkian* (New York: Rinehart & Co., 1958), pp. 5–6, 181–85, 220–22.

36. John Grover, "Texas-Born He-Men Pile Jillions Upon Jillions," Los Angeles *Mirror*, September 1, 1954, and "Texans Like Fast Horses and Fistfuls of Dough," *ibid.*, September 2, 1954.

37. Ann Miller with Norma Lee Browning, *Miller's High Life* (Garden City, N.Y.: Doubleday, 1972), pp. 168–202.

38. Byrd Interview.

39. W. A. Moncrief Interview (J. P.); " 'You Have Made Yourself a Deal,' Said Monty Moncrief," *Petroleum Independent* (November–December, 1972), p. 8.

X. OF ETHNICS AND WOMEN

1. James A. Clark Interview (J. P.). On blacks, see also Carl B. King and Howard W. Risher, Jr., *The Negro in the Petroleum Industry* (Philadephia: University of Pennsylvania Press, 1969).

2. Joe Zeppa Interview (J.P.).

3. Michel T. Halbouty Interview (J. P.); James A. Clark, "Outline of Personal History of Michel T. Halbouty," "Brief Biography of Michel T. Halbouty," "Bibliography of Publications of Michel T. Halbouty," mimeo. A collection his speeches in James A. Clark, editor, *Ahead of His Time: Michel T. Halbouty Speaks to the People* (Houston: Gulf Publishing Co., 1971).

4. Johnny Mitchell Interview; "He's Half Wildcatter, Half Big Businessman," *Business Week* (November 14, 1964), pp. 103–4;

George P. Mitchell Interview. Additional material on Sam Maceo came from William Kugle. For another view, of George Mitchell's new town, the Woodlands, including criticism, see Sandy Sheehy, "Problems in Paradise," *Houston City Magazine* (April, 1978), pp. 57–61. A financial report on Mitchell Energy can be seen in the *Wall Street Journal*, June 30, 1977.

5. M. B. Rudman Interview (J.P.); Ruth Goddard, "The Wildcatter of Running Duke," *Texas Star* (January 16, 1972), pp. 10–11; Patrick Bailey, "Flashy Rudman Likes to Win Often," Dallas *Times Herald*, June 27, 1971, p. D-9; Larry Grove, "Dapper Oilman Feels Spats Would Be Sensible in Cold," Dallas *Morning News*, February 4, 1963. Sect. 1, p. 6; *ibid.*, November 25, 1966; Alex L. Acheson, "Wildcatter Has 9 Lives," Dallas *Times Herald*, December 24, 1967, p. C-5.

6. Elizabeth Kathryn Martin, "Lexicon of the Texas Oil Fields" (Unpublished Ph. D. Thesis, East Texas State University, 1969) pp. 62–63. Her chapter, "Primal Sexuality and Obscenity," pp. 62–84, is especially relevant.

7. Nancy Heard Toudouze Interview (J. P.).

8. Catherine Terrell Smith Interview (J. P.).

XI. ON THE TRAIL OF A DREAM

1. John G. "Jack" Pew, Claud B. Hamill, Edgar W. Owen, D. H. Byrd, Lesley Hill True, George W. Pirtle Interviews; George W. Pirtle manuscript, 1975; Carl E. Reistle, Jr., Interview (J.P.); "Carl Ernest Reistle Jr." (biographical sketch), mimeo.; Carrol M. Bennett Interview; Lewis Nordyke, "Heap Big Uncle Frank," *Saturday Evening Post* (July 29, 1944), pp. 20–21, 34; Eric Schroeder Interview (J.P.)' [American Petroleum Institute], *History of Petroleum Engineering* (New York and Dallas: American Petroleum Institute, 1961), pp. 331–34; J. R. Parten, George W. Strake, Jr. Interviews (J.P.); Osborn Elliott, *Men at the Top* (New York: Harper & Brothers, 1959), pp. 55–56; John William Rogers, *The Story of General American Oil Company of Texas* ([Dallas: General American Oil Co. of Texas], 1955), pp. 1–19; David Nevin, *The Texans:What They Are—And Why* (New York: William Morrow & Co., 1968), pp. 34–42.

2. Frank Luther Mott, *American Journalism: A History, 1690–1960,* 3rd ed. (New York: Macmillan Co., 1962), p. 564.

3. A. J. Thomon and J. H. Anderson Interviews, PTO-UTA.

4. Larry Secrest (interviewer), "Entrepreneurship in Oil: Transcribed Interviews with Mr. Paul R. Haas, Mr. John W. Crutchfield, Mr. Larry A. McNeil, Mr. Emmet C. Wilson" (Oral Business History Project, Graduate School of Business, University of Texas at Austin, 1971), pp. 78–79; H.E. "Eddie" Chiles Interview (J.P.).

5. Morgan J. Davis Interview (J.P.).

6. Byrd Interview.

7. Jake L. Hamon Interview (J.P.).

8. True Interview.

9. Letter, Edgar W. Owen to J.P., April 30, 1976.

10. Ralph Spence Interview (J.P.).

11. William Broyles and Alex Sheshunoff, "How First National Passed Republic and Other Stories of the Banking Game," *Texas Monthly* (May, 1974), pp. 48, 50, 96; Stanley Marcus, *Minding the Store: A Memoir* (Boston: Little, Brown, 1974), pp. 246–47; D. H. Byrd Interview; M. B. Rudman Interview.

12. H. L. Hunt, *Hunt Heritage: The Republic and Our Families* (Dallas: Parade Press, 1973), pp. 90–92.

13. Eric G. Schroeder Interview (J.P.).

14. John H. Wynne Interview, PTO-UTA.

15. Sherman M. Hunt Interview (J.P.).

16. Boyce House, "The Colonel Left Tracks," *Saturday Evening Post* (June 5, 1937), p. 69.

17. Ruth Sheldon Knowles, *The Greatest Gamblers: The Epic of American Oil Exploration* (New York: McGraw-Hill Book Co., 1959), pp. 122–23.

18. Hamill Interview.

19. Byrd Interview.

20. Sara H. Stone Interview (J.P.).

21. George G. Kirstein, *The Rich: Are They Different?* (Boston: Houghton Mifflin, 1968), pp. 111–12.

22. Hunt Interview.

23. J. Howard Marshall Interview (J.P.).

24. Owen Interview.

25. Spence Interview.

26. Otis T. Dunagan Interview (J.P.).

27. Spence Interview.

28. John A. Jackson Interview (J.P.).

29. Luther A. Reed Interview (J.P.).

30. Hunt Interview.

31. Edgar Wesley Owen, *Trek of the Oil Finders* (Tulsa: American Association of Petroleum Geologists, 1975), p. 1576.

32. Hamill, M. B. Rudman interviews (J.P.)

33. Hunt Interview.

34. Charlie Lane Interview, PTO-UTA.

35. Clarence C. Pope, *An Oil Scout in the Permian Basin* (El Paso: Permian Press, 1972), p. 118.

36. George Fuermann, *Reluctant Empire* (Garden City, N.Y.: Doubleday, 1957), p. 32; John D. Murchison Interview.

37. Glenn H. McCarthy Interview (J.P.).

38. J. A. Presley Interview (J.P.).

39. Marshall Interview; Owen, *Trek of Oil Finders,* p. 254; Lon Tinkle, *Mr. De: A Biography of Everette Lee DeGolyer* (Boston: Little, Brown, 1970), pp. 186–87, 202.

40. See Stewart Alsop, "America's New Big Rich," *Saturday Evening Post* (July 17, 1965), pp. 23–27 ff.

41. H. E. Chiles Interview. (J.P.).

42. Spence Interview.

43. Michel T. Halbouty Interview (J.P.).

44. Sue Buffington Interview (J.P.).

45. Dooley Dawson Interview (J.P.).

46. Hunt Interview.

47. W. A. Moncrief Interview (J.P.).

48. Carrol M. Bennett Interview (J.P.).

49. Owen Interview.

50. J. Q. Mahaffey Interview (J.P.).

51. "George Strake Featured Speaker at Houston's Executive Night Program," *The Landman* (February, 1965), pp. 76–77. This is the text of Strake's speech.

52. George W. Strake, Jr., Interview (J.P.).

53. Owen, *Trek of Oil Finders,* p. 622.

54. True Interview.

55. O. W. Killam Interview, PTO-UTA.

56. True Interview.

57. Hamon Interview.
58. Pew Interview.
59. Rudman Interview.
60. Hamon Interview.
61. Hunt Interview.
62. Hamon Interview.
63. Kirstein, *The Rich,* pp. 113–14.
64. Spence Interview.
65. U.S. Congress, Senate, *Hearings Before a Special Committee Investigating Petroleum Resources—The Independent Petroleum Company, 79th Congress, 2nd Session, March 19–22, 27 and 28, 1946* (Washington: Government Printing Office, 1946), p. 345.

XII. MILLION-DOLLAR IDEAS

1. John A. Jackson Interview (J.P.).
2. *Ibid.*; John T. Scopes, George P. Mitchell, Johnny Mitchell interviews (J.P.); John A. Jackson, *Wise County: 25 Years of Progress* (Dallas: priv. pub., 1972), *passim;* Dudley Lynch, "Excitement in Frustration," *Midwest: Magazine of the Chicago Sun-Times,* January 14, 1973, pp. 32, 34, and "The Frustration Fields Gang Rides Again," *Southwest Scene, Dallas Morning News Sunday Magazine,* December 10, 1972, pp. 14–19.
3. Carroll Deely Interview (J.P.); letter, Carroll Deely, January 11, 1978.
4. J. Clarence Karcher Interview (J.P.); J. Clarence Karcher, "The Reflection Seismograph: Its Invention and Use in the Discovery of Oil and Gas Fields" (Unpublished Monograph, Center for History of Physics at the American Institute of Physics, February 15, 1974), pp. 1–46.
5. John S. Wynn Interview, PTO-UTA. Although I have followed Wynn's account, his version probably is telescoped in time. Hughes filed application for patents on November 20, 1908, and on August 10, 1909, he was granted two basic patents for the Hughes rock bit. Most accounts of the rock bit do not mention Wynn's role. See Walter Prescott Webb and H. Bailey Carroll, eds., *The Handbook of Texas* (Austin: Texas State Historical Association, 1952), Vol. I, p. 860.
6. Wynn Interview.

7. Benjamin Coyle, James Donahoe, J. A. Rush interviews, PTO-UTA: Dudley C. Sharp, Sr., Interview (J.P.). She sold her stock to Ed Prather, who sold out to Hughes in 1918. See Webb and Carroll, *Handbook of Texas*, I, p. 860.

XIII. POLITICS AMONG THE PETRO-RICH

1. Earl Golz, "Bunker Hunt Emerging as Hot News Item," Dallas *Morning News*, July 11, 1973.
2. Ronnie Dugger, "John Connally: Nixon's New Quarterback," *Atlantic Monthly* (July, 1971), p. 85.
3. Robert L. Heilbroner, *The Quest for Wealth: A Study of Acquisitive Man* (New York: Simon & Schuster, 1956), pp. 106–7, 114–15.
4. Al Reinert, "Bob and George Go to Washington or the Post-Watergate Scramble," *Texas Monthly* (April, 1974), pp. 53 ff.
5. Carl E. Reistle, Jr., Interview (J.P.).
6. John D. Murchison Interview (J.P.).
7. Carrol M. Bennett Interview (J.P.).
8. Lloyd Wendt and Herman Kogan, *Bet A Million! The Story of John W. Gates* (Indianapolis: Bobbs-Merrill Co., 1948), p. 302.
9. Jay Hall Interview (J.P.).
10. *Ibid.*
11. Edgar W. Owen Interview (J.P.).
12. Otherwise undated clipping, Austin *American*, 1925, in Oil Scrapbook, University of Texas at Austin, Barker Texas History Center Archives.
13. "Exploiting Texas: An Editorial," *Texas Observer* (April 18, 1959), p. 1.
14. Reistle, Jr., Interview; letter, Carl E. Reistle, Jr., to J. P., June 13, 1975.
15. Ronnie Dugger Interview (J.P.).
16. Molly Ivins, "The Texas Research League," *Texas Observer* (February 1, 1974), p. 3.
17. Texarkana *Gazette*, May 2, 1976.
18. John O. King, *Joseph Stephen Cullinan: A Study of Leadership in the Texas Petroleum Industry, 1897–1937* (Nashville: Vanderbilt University Press & Texas Gulf Coast Historical Association, 1970), pp. 210–12.
19. Nancy Heard Toudouze Interview (J.P.). In 1961, when John

Connally, during confirmation hearings on his appointment as secretary of the navy, was questioned about any part he may have had in the scandal, he replied: "I had no part in the incident any more than anybody else who was interested in the oil and gas business." See Dugger, "John Connally," pp. 85–86.

20. James A. Clark, ed., *Ahead of His Time: Michel T. Halbouty Speaks to the People* (Houston: Gulf Publishing Co., Book Division, 1971), p. 51.

21. Glenn H. McCarthy Interview (J.P.).

22. Ernest R. Bartley, *The Tidelands Oil Controversy: A Legal and Historical Analysis* (Austin: University of Texas Press, 1953), pp. 79–94.

23. A detailed account of *U.S. v. Texas* is in *ibid.*, pp. 195–212.

24. Theodore H. White, "Texas: Land of Wealth and Fear," *The Reporter* (June 8, 1954), pp. 35–36.

25. Dugger Interview.

26. For a survey of the events in the controversy see *Texas Almanac, 1972–1973* (Dallas: A. H. Belo Co., 1974), pp. 389–91.

27. Hall Interview.

28. T. R. B., "Most Valuable Senator," *New Republic* (April 8, 1957), p. 2.

29. Ronnie Dugger, "Oil and Politics," *The Atlantic* (September, 1969), p. 71; Carl Solberg, *Oil Power* (New York: Mason/Charter, 1976), pp. 73–78.

30. James A. Clark Interview (J.P.).

31. McCarthy Interview.

32. Johnny Mitchell Interview (J.P.).

33. M. B. Rudman Interview (J.P.).

34. Harry Hurt III, "The Most Powerful Texans," *Texas Monthly* (April, 1976), pp. 76, 107.

35. Dugger Interview.

36. Clark Interview.

37. Dugger, "Oil and Politics," p. 72.

38. Stanley Marcus, *Minding the Store: A Memoir* (Boston: Little, Brown, 1974), p. 250.

39. Personal conversation with Ronnie Dugger and Creekmore Fath, 1960.

40. Ed Kilman and Theon Wright, *Hugh Roy Cullen: A Story of American Opportunity* (New York: Prentice-Hall, 1954), pp. 69–72.

41. *Ibid.*, pp. 168–70, 211–20, 258–60, 281–83, 285, 295, 327; Devin Garrity Interview (J.P.).

42. Dugger Interview.

43. *Ibid.*, George Fuermann, *Reluctant Empire* (Garden City, N.Y.: Doubleday, 1957), pp. 92–93.

44. Jake L. Hamon Interview (J.P.).

45. H. L. Hunt, *H. L. Hunt Early Days* (Dallas: Parade Press, 1973), p. 78.

46. Hunt, *Early Days*, p. 183.

47. White, "Texas: Land of Wealth and Fear," p. 31; Robert G. Sherrill, "H. L. Hunt: Portrait of a Super-Patriot," *The Nation* (February 24, 1964), pp. 188, 190; Bill Porterfield, "H. L. Hunt's Long Goodbye," *Texas Monthly* (March, 1975), p. 94.

48. Karl Hess Interview (J.P.).

49. *Ibid.*, p. 60; Tom Buckley, "Just Plain H. L. Hunt," *Esquire* (January, 1967), pp. 142, 144.

50. Hunt, *Early Days*, pp. 74–76.

51. Sherrill, "H.L. Hunt," pp. 186–87.

52. Texarkana *Gazette*, July 16, 1964.

53. *Ibid.*, November 30, 1974.

54. Earl Golz Interview.

55. Letter, Charles Dickey to J.P, Aug. 26, 1976.

56. H. L. Hunt, *Alpaca Revisited* (Dallas: H. L. Hunt Products, 1967), pp. 83–85.

57. *Ibid.*, pp. 191–92.

58. *Ibid.*, pp. 184–86.

59. *Ibid.*, pp. 164, 78.

60. William F. Buckley, Jr., "Speaking Out: God Bless the Rich," *Saturday Evening Post* (December 30, 1967), pp. 4 ff.

61. William F. Buckley, Jr., "The Trials of the Very Rich," Shreveport *Times*, December 8, 1974.

62. Johnny Mitchell Interview.

63. Hamon Interview.

64. King, *Cullinan*, p. 212.

65. Lonn Taylor, "Miss Ima Hogg," *Texas Observer* (September 5, 1975), p. 10.

66. Texarkana *Gazette*, September 18, 1975.

67. J. R. Parten Interview (J.P.).

XIV. WHAT DID THEY DO WITH IT?

1. Reproduced in Stanley Marcus, *Minding the Store: A Memoir* (Boston: Little, Brown, 1974), from *The New Yorker* in 1956.

2. Dickson Terry, "West Gets a Bang Playing Policeman," *Texas Observer* (March 14, 1955), p. 6.

3. M. B. Rudman Interview (J.P.)

4. Lesley Hill True, J. Clarence Karcher, John D. Murchison, LeRoy A. Menzing interviews (J.P.).

5. Dooley Dawson Interview (J.P.).

6. Jake L. Hamon Interview (J.P.).

7. Del Deterling, "Hay System for Fewer Backaches and Head-aches," *Progressive Farmer* (June, 1975), pp. 16–17.

8. Tom Lea, *The King Ranch* (Boston: Little, Brown, 1957), Vol. 2, pp. 612, 679–83, 713–20; Edgar Wesley Owen, *Trek of the Oil Finders* (Tulsa: American Association of Petroleum Geologists, 1975), pp. 777–79; "King Ranch Riches Multiply," *Business Week* (December 7, 1946), p. 22; Dudley C. Sharp, Sr., Interview (J.P.); Richard West, *"Texas Monthly Reporter:* Succession at the King Ranch," *Texas Monthly* (December, 1974), pp. 11–12.

9. Jack Olsen, "The Big Itch They Call Little John," *Sports Illustrated* (January 11, 1965), pp. 52, 61.

10. D. H. Byrd Interview (J.P.).

11. Hamon Interview.

12. Olsen, "Big Itch," pp. 53–54 ff.

13. Boyce House, *Oil Boom: The Story of Spindletop, Burkburnett, Mexia, Smackover, Desdemona, and Ranger* (Caldwell, Idaho: Caxton Printers, 1941), p. 85.

14. Lon Tinkle, *Mr. De: A Biography of Everette Lee DeGolyer* (Boston: Little, Brown, 1970), pp. 221 ff.

15. Byrd Interview.

16. Stanley Walker, "Where Are They Now? Mr. Davis and His Millions," *New Yorker* (November 26, 1949), pp. 35–49; Austin *American,* November 23, 1938; San Antonio *Express-News,* July 6, 1974.

17. Goronwy Rees, *The Multimillionaires: Six Studies in Wealth* (New York: Macmillan Co., 1961), pp. 119–20.

18. George G. Kirstein, *The Rich—Are They Different?* (Boston: Houghton Mifflin, 1968), p. 121.

19. E. M. Friend Interview, PTO-UTA.

20. James A. Knight, *For the Love of Money: Human Behavior and Money* (Philadelphia: J. B. Lippincott Co., 1968), pp. 130–54, provides an excellent analysis of motivations in philanthropy. Also see Kirstein, *The Rich*, pp. 115–42.

21. Maxwell S. Stewart, *The Big Foundations* (New York: Public Affairs Pamphlets, 1975), Public Affairs Pamphlet No. 500, based on the Twentieth Century Fund Study by Waldemar A. Nielsen.

22. House, *Oil Boom*, pp. 83–85; Ruel McDaniel, *Some Ran Hot* (Dallas: Regional Press, 1939), pp. 242–44.

23. Clarence C. Pope, *An Oil Scout in the Permian Basin, 1924–1960* (El Paso: Permian Press, 1972), pp. 114–15.

24. Patrick O'Bryan, *The Great Conroe Oil Field* (Houston: n. pub., n.d.), p. 40.

25. Patrick O'Bryan, "Men of Houston: George W. Strake," *Houston Town*, (October, 1958), p. 44.

26. George W. Strake, Jr., Interview (J.P.).

27. Ronnie Dugger, *Our Invaded Universities* (New York: W. W. Norton, 1974), pp. 79, 293–94.

28. Ed Kilman and Theon Wright, *Hugh Roy Cullen: A Story of American Opportunity* (New York: Prentice-Hall, 1954), pp. 190–95, 221–32, 248–50; Dickson Terry, "Hugh Roy Says He's Selfish," *Texas Observer* (March 7, 1955), p. 6; Dallas *Morning News*, March 30, 1947.

29. Byrd Interview.

30. Michel T. Halbouty Interview (J.P.).

31. W. B. Hamilton Interview, PTO-UTA.

32. Dudley C. Sharp, Sr., Interview (J.P.).

33. Claud B. Hamill Interview (J.P.).

34. George Fuermann, *Reluctant Empire* (Garden City, N.Y.: Doubleday, 1957), pp. 102–3.

35. Hamill Interview.

36. Robert C. Cotner, *James Stephen Hogg: A Biography* (Austin: University of Texas Press, 1959), pp. 584–85; Lonn Taylor, "Miss Ima Hogg," *Texas Observer* (September 5, 1975) pp. 10–11; Dudley C. Sharp, Sr., Interview; Frank Tolbert, "Texas Philanthropist Dies," Dallas *Morning News*, August 21, 1975, p. 35A.

37. James E. Coggin, *J. K. Wadley: A Tree God Planted* (Texarkana, Ark.: Southwest Printers & Publishers, n.d.), pp. 8, 52, 133; J. Q. Mahaffey Interview.
38. J. Q. Mahaffey Interview (J.P.).
39. William A. McWhirter, "How Art Swindlers Duped a Virtuous Millionaire," *Life* (July 7, 1967), pp. 52–61.
40. Clifford Irving, *Fake: The Story of Elmyr de Hory, the Greatest Art Forger of Our Time* (New York: McGraw-Hill Book Co., 1969), pp. 8–9, 170, 195.
41. "Meadows' Luck," *Time* (May 19, 1967), p. 94.
42. McWhirter, "Art Swindlers," p. 61; "Back to Market," *Time* (June 9, 1967) p. 84; San Antonio *Light,* April 16, 1969; Marcus, *Minding the Store,* pp. 291–93.
43. Harold Vagtborg, *The Story of Southwest Research Center: A Private, Nonprofit, Scientific Research Adventure* (San Antonio: Southwest Research Institute, 1973), pp. 8–17, 31–32, 398, 538, 567–72.
44. Bill Simmons, "Camelot on Credit Almost Real for Margaret, Ernest Medders," Fort Worth *Star-Telegram,* November 17, 1974. See also Memphis *Commerical Appeal,* September 7, 1973. Mrs. Medders' account is her book, *The Medders Story* (Memphis: Marest Publishing Co., 1973).
45. Austin *American,* April 19, 1929.

XV. A DECLINING GIANT

1. "Where Texas Falls Short," *Business Week* (July 29, 1967), p. 32.
2. Sherman M. Hunt Interview (J.P.).
3. "Maxima," *Texas Observer* (February 1, 1974), p. 6; Texarkana *Gazette,* September 19, 1975.
4. Jay Hall Interview (J.P.)
5. Theodore H. White, "Texas: Land of Wealth and Fear," *The Reporter* (June 8, 1954), p. 37.
6. "Wright Patman's 1924th Weekly Letter," November 21, 1974; Dallas *Morning News,* December 19, 1974.
7. Edgar W. Owen Interview (J.P.).
8. D. H. Byrd, Nancy Heard Toudouze, Glenn H. McCarthy interviews (J.P.).
9. Texarkana *Gazette,* August 31, 1975; letter, Virginia M. Smyth,

librarian, American Petroleum Institute, to J. P., November 7, 1975; "Wright Patman's 1970th Weekly Letter," October 16, 1975.

10. Personal communication, Elizabeth Mavropoulis, secretary, Railroad Commission of Texas, citing Texas Mid-Continent Oil and Gas Association statistics, November 6, 1975.

11. Dallas *Morning News*, April 26, 1975.

12. Owen Interview.

13. Fain Gillock Interview, PTO-UTA.

14. Texarkana *Gazette*, July 31, 1975.

15. Letter, Edgar W. Owen to J. P., April 30, 1976.

16. Letter, Lowell D. Ashby (assistant chief, Regional Economic Measurement Division, Bureau of Economic Analysis) to J.P., August 5, 1976, with enclosures on personal income data. See, for example, "What in the World: Marrying for Money?", *Family Weekly* (October 20, 1974), p. 17, based on Department of Commerce and various almanac data; Dallas *Morning News*, January 31, 1975.

17. William Broyles and Alex Sheshunoff, "How First National Passed Republic and Other Stories of the Banking Game," *Texas Monthly* (May, 1974), pp. 51, 94.

18. "A History of Texas Anti-Trust in Oil," *Texas Observer* (September 18, 1959), p. 1.

19. Harry Hurt III, "The Most Powerful Texans," *Texas Monthly* (April, 1976), pp. 110–11, 121.

20. J. R. Parten Interview (J.P.).

21. Mody C. Boatright, *Folklore of the Oil Industry* (Dallas: SMU Press, 1963), pp. 130–31.

22. Carrol M. Bennett, Claud B. Hamill interviews (J.P.); O. W. Killam Interview, PTO-UTA.

23. Texarkana *Gazette*, May 2, 1976.

24. R. J. McMurrey, Jr., Interview (J.P.).

25. Bennett Interview.

26. H. E. Chiles Interview (J.P.).

27. Associated Press writer Stan Benjamin presented these in an analysis published, among other places, in Texarkana *Gazette*, November 24, 1975.

28. Toudouze Interview.

29. "Gassing Game," *Texas Monthly* (April, 1976), p. 56.

30. Edgar W. Owen Interview (J.P.).

31. Lon Tinkle, *Mr. De: A Biography of Everette Lee DeGolyer* (Boston: Little, Brown, 1970), p. 285.

32. Texarkana *Gazette,* October 26, 1975.

33. James A. Clark, ed. *Ahead of His Time: Michel T. Halbouty Speaks to the People* (Houston: Gulf Publishing Co., Book Division, 1971), p. 72.

34. George W. Strake, Jr., Interview (J.P.).

35. Lynn Ashby, "Wildcat Wisdom," Houston *Post,* March 28, 1975.

36. "Parten Proves Movie Industry Saying: The Bigger They Are, The Nicer They Are," *Business & Energy International* (2nd Quarter; June 1, 1976), p. 25; Eric Schroeder Interview; W. A. Moncrief and R.C. Cowan, "A Different Kind of Pollution," *Atlantic* (May, 1975).

37. "Parten Proves," *Business & Energy International,*

38. Bennett Interview.

39. "Parten Proves," *Business & Energy International*

40. Dallas *Morning News,* June 22, 1976.

41. Eric Schroeder Interview (J.P.).

42. Carl E. Reistle, Jr. Interview (J.P.).

43. Dallas *Morning News,* May 30, 1976.

44. Clark, ed., *Ahead of His Time,* pp. 277–78.

45. James A. Clark Interview (J.P.).

46. "Parten Proves," *Business & Energy International*

47. "Five Noted Thinkers Explore the Future," *National Geographic* Vol. 150, No. 1 (July, 1976), pp. 72–73.

48. Owen Interview.

49. Dallas *Morning News,* September 5, 1975.

50. Texarkana *Gazette,* September 5, 1975.

51. *Ibid.,* December 28, 1975.

52. *Ibid.,* May 30, 1974.

53. Dallas *Morning News,* April 27, 1976.

54. "Wright Patman's 1975th Weekly Letter," November 20, 1975.

55. Billie Edgington Interview (J.P.).

56. Noel F. Busch, "Dizzying, Dazzling Houston," *Reader's Digest* (April, 1975), pp. 114–18.

57. J. Howard Marshall Interview (J.P.).

58. LeRoy A. Menzing Interview (J.P.).

59. Owen Interview.

60. Michel T. Halbouty Interview (J.P.).

61. George P. Mitchell Interview (J.P.).

62. Texarkana *Gazette,* March 15, 1974; Dallas *Morning News,* November 10, 1975.

63. Sherman M. Hunt Interview (J.P.).

64. Letter, J. Milton Richardson, assistant attorney general of Texas, to J. P., May 30, 1975; *Vernon's Annotated Texas Civil Statutes* (1965), Title 5, pp. 1–4.

65. "Sold Arabian," *Texas Monthly* (April, 1975), p. 46.

66. Lonn Taylor, "Miss Ima Hogg," *Texas Observer* (September 5, 1975), pp. 10–11.

BIBLIOGRAPHY

ORAL HISTORY

Pioneers in Texas Oil Oral History Project of the University of Texas at Austin (PTO-UTA)

This extremely valuable collection, consisting of more than 100 interviews and more than 200 transcripts, was created in the 1950's under the direction, primarily, of Professors Mody C. Boatright of the University of Texas and William A. Owens of Columbia University. Boatright and Owens conducted most, but not all, of the interviews, which covered the period from Spindletop to East Texas. Many of the veterans of Corsicana and Spindletop, such as Pattillo Higgins, were still alive then. The PTO-UTA transcripts, as I have abbreviated it in the notes, are housed in the Archives of the Barker Texas History Center at the University of Texas at Austin. All such transcripts of interviews used in this text have been cited with the PTO-UTA identification to distinguish them from interviews that I conducted.

Oral Business History Project, Graduate School of Business, The University of Texas at Austin

Secrest, Larry, interviewer, "Entrepreneurship in Oil: Mr. Paul R. Haas and the Prado Oil and Gas Company: Transcribed Interviews with Mr. Paul R. Haas, Mr. John W. Crutchfield, Mr. Larry A. McNeil, Mr. Emmet C. Wilson." (Oral Business History Project, The University of Texas at Austin, 1971), transcript, bound.

Interviews by the Author
These interviews ranged, for the most part, from two hours to all day. All but a few were tape-recorded; most of them will eventually become a part of the Oral Business History Project at the University of Texas at Austin.

Ames, Bill, Texarkana, Texas, July 6, 1974.
Anderson, H. H. "Andy," Dallas, June 23, 1975.
Bennett, Carrol M., Dallas, March 7, 1975.
Bond, Bess, Dallas, August 27, 1974.
Brenton, Art, Dallas, June 23, 1975.
Buffington, Sue, Houston, June 5, 1975.
Byrd, D. Harold, Dallas, August 27, 1974.
Cape, R. Randall, Tyler, March 25, 1975.
Chiles, H. E., Fort Worth, February 8, 1975.
Clark, James A., Houston, June 5, 1975.
Clark, W. Ray, Texarkana, Texas, March 15, 1971.
Davis, Morgan J., Houston, June 2, 1975.
Dawson, Dooley, Crockett, April 12, 1975.
Deely, Carroll, Dallas, November 6, 1974.
Diehl, Kemper, San Antonio, November 18, 1968; August 5, 1974.
Dugger, Ronnie, Austin, March 31, 1975.
Dunagan, Otis T., Tyler, March 25, 1975.
Eaton, Robert W., Tyler, March 25, 1975.
Edgington, Billie, Texarkana, Texas, November 15, 1975.
Elliott, Travis, Texarkana, Texas, May 17, 1974.
Farmer, Ralph, Texarkana, Texas, February 22, 1976.
Finnegan, William N., Houston, June 5, 1975.
Garrity, Devin, Atlanta, Texas, July 31, 1976.
Golz, Earl, Dallas, January 25, 1975.
Halbouty, Michel T., Houston, June 4, 1975.
Hall, Jay, Lindale, Texas, March 25, 1975.
Hamill, Claud B., Houston, June 3, 1975.

Hamon, Jake L., Dallas, March 15, 1975.

Hamm, W. Dow, Dallas, November 2, 1974.

Hess, Karl (telephone, Kearneysville, West Virginia), October 17, 1977.

Higgins, Mrs. Pattillo (telephone, San Antonio), January 20, 1978.

Hunt, Sherman M., Dallas, November 20, 1974.

Jackson, John A., Dallas, June 17, August 29, 1974.

Karcher, J. Clarence, Dallas, June 24, 1975.

Kelliher, Thomas G., Willis, Texas, April 5, 1975.

King, Frank L., Texarkana, Texas, October 1, 1974.

Kugle, William (telephone, Athens, Texas), October 17, 1977.

Ledbetter, Cam, Wimberly, Texas, April 2, 1975.

Lyne, J. R., Houston, June 4, 1975.

Mahaffey, J. Q., Texarkana, Texas, December 5, 1974.

Marshall, J. Howard, Houston, April 5, 1975.

McCarthy, Glenn H., Houston, April 4, 1975.

McLeckie, H. W., Naples, Texas, July 5, 1974.

McMurrey, R. J., Tyler, February 17, 1976.

Menzing, LeRoy A., Fort Worth, May 13, 1975.

Mitchell, George P., Houston, June 4, 1975.

Mitchell, Johnny, Houston, June 3, 1975.

Moncrief, W. A., Fort Worth, February 8, 1975.

Murchison, John D., Dallas, June 24, 1975.

Naylor, Pauline, Fort Worth, August 28, 1974.

Owen, Edgar W., San Antonio, April 1, 1975.

Parten, J. R., Madisonville, Texas, April 12, 1975.

Pew, John G. "Jack," Dallas, March 14, 1975.

Pirtle, George W., Tyler, March 8, 1975.

Presley, J. A., Texarkana, Texas, September 27, 1975.

Ray, C. L., Texarkana, Texas, January 9, 1975.

Reed, Luther A., Texarkana, Texas, October 1, 1975.

Reistle, Carl E., Jr., Houston, June 2, 1975.

Rudman, M. B. "Bill," Dallas, May 23, 1975.

Schroeder, Eric G., Dallas, May 23, 1975.

Scoggins, Monroe, Texarkana, Arkansas, November 10, 1975.

Scopes, John T., Shreveport, Louisiana, May, 1970.

Sharp, Dudley C., Sr., Houston, June 3, 1975.

Smith, Catherine Terrell, Fort Worth, May 13, 1975.

Spence, Ralph, Tyler, March 25, 1975.
Stone, Sara H., Texarkana, Arkansas. September 30, 1975.
Strake, George W., Jr., Houston, April 3, 1975.
Toudouze, Nancy Heard, San Antonio, April 2, 1975.
True, Les H., Wimberly, Texas, April 2, 1975.
Wright, Welch, Dallas, June 24, 1975.
Zeppa, Joe, Tyler, March 25, 1975.

LETTERS (All to J. P. unless otherwise noted)

Ashby, Lowell D. (Bureau of Economic Analysis, U.S. Department of Commerce), August 5, 1976.
Byrd, D. Harold, to Henry R. Luce, April 23, 1946.
Chiles, H. E., February 26, 1975.
Deely, Carroll, January 11, 1978.
Dickey, Charles, August 26, 1976.
Ernst, Joseph W. (archivist, Rockefeller Family & Associates), February 18, 1976.
Freeman, W. C., November 10, 1975.
Haigh, Berte R., November 14, 1975.
Hamon, Jake L., April 3, 1975
Hess, Karl, July 27, 1977.
Hunt, Sherman M., November 3, 1975.
Lobb, W. L., November 6, 1975.
Marshall, J. Howard, November 4, 1975, May 17, 1976.
Menzing, LeRoy A., May 22, 1975.
Mitchell, George P., May 13, 1976.
Moncrief, W. A., September 4, 1975.
Nicholson, Patrick J., November 13, 1975.
Owen, Edgar W., January 5, April 30, 1976.
Parten, J. R., January 21, August 11, 1976.
Reistle, Carl E., Jr., June 13, 1975.
Rogers, Mary Beth, December 11, 1975.
Smyth, Virginia M. (librarian, American Petroleum Institute), November 7, 1975.
Sutton, Calvin, November 3, 1975.
Toudouze, Nancy Heard, September 20, 1975, May 25, 1976.

MANUSCRIPTS AND OTHER UNPUBLISHED MATERIAL

Hall, Claude. "The Life and Public Service of James Stephen Hogg." Typescript, East Texas State University Library, n.d.

Karcher, J. Clarence. "The Reflection Seismograph: Its Invention and Use in the Discovery of Oil and Gas Fields." Monograph written for the Center for History of Physics at the American Institute of Physics, 1974.

Mitchell, Johnny. "The Private War of Captain Johnny Mitchell." Manuscript.

Pirtle, George W. "Introduction: About the Author." Manuscript, 1975.

"Southern Methodist University Presents the SACROC Transaction." Volume of instruments pertaining to SMU et al. acquiring interest in Scurry County, Texas, oil and gas properties. SMU, Dallas, 1956.

BOOKS

Abels, Jules. *The Rockefeller Millions: The Story of the World's Most Stupendous Fortune.* London: Frederick Muller, 1967.

Acheson, Sam Hanna. *Joe Bailey, The Last Democrat.* New York: Macmillan Co., 1932.

Adams Frederick Upham. *The Waters Pierce Case in Texas.* St. Louis: Skinner and Kennedy, 1908.

Armstrong, George W. *Memoirs.* Austin: n. pub., 1958.

Bainbridge, John. *The Super-Americans: A Picture of Life in the United States, As Brought into Focus, Bigger Than Life, In the Land of the Millionaires—Texas.* New York: Doubleday, 1961.

Bailey, Joseph W. *In Reply to "Muckrakers": Personal Explanation Speech in U.S. Senate, June 27, 1906.* Washington: n. pub., 1906.

Ball, Max W. *This Fascinating Oil Business.* Indianapolis: Bobbs-Merrill Co., 1940.

Bartley, Ernest R. *The Tidelands Oil Controversy: A Legal and Historical Analysis.* Austin: University of Texas Press, 1953.

Beach, Rex. *Flowing Gold.* New York: Harper & Bros., 1922.

Beaton, Kendall. *Enterprise in Oil: A History of Shell in the United States.* New York: Appleton-Century-Crofts, 1957.

Benedict, H. Y. *A Source Book Relating to the History of the University of Texas: Legislative, Legal, Bibliographical, and Statistical.* Austin: University of Texas Bulletin No. 1757, October 10, 1917.

Blair, John M. *The Control of Oil.* New York: Pantheon Books, 1977.

Boatright, Mody C. *Folklore of the Oil Industry.* Dallas: Southern Methodist University Press, 1963.

Boatright, Mody C., and William A. Owens. *Tales from the Derrick Floor: A People's History of the Oil Industry.* Garden City, N.Y.: Doubleday, 1970.

Brantly, J. E. *History of Oil Well Drilling.* Houston: Gulf Publishing Co., 1971.

Brown, Stanley *H. L. Hunt.* Chicago: Playboy Press, 1976.

Bryan, Cooper. *Alaska, The Last Frontier.* New York: Morrow, 1973.

Carlson, Oliver, and Ernest Sutherland Bates. *Hearst, Lord of San Simeon.* New York: Viking Press, 1936.

Chasan, Daniel Jack. *Klondike '70: The Alaskan Oil Boom.* New York: Praeger Publishers, 1971.

Clark, J. Stanley. *The Oil Century: From the Drake Well to the Conservation Era.* Norman: University of Oklahoma Press, 1958.

Clark, James A., ed. *Ahead of His Time: Michel T. Halbouty Speaks to the People.* Houston: Gulf Publishing Co., Book Division, 1971.

———. *The Chronological History of the Petroleum and Natural Gas Industries.* Houston: Clark Book Co., 1963.

———. and Michel T. Halbouty. *The Last Boom.* New York: Random House, 1972.

———and———. *Spindletop.* New York: Random House, 1952.

———. *Three Stars for the Colonel.* New York: Random House, 1954.

Cocke, William A. *The Bailey Controversy in Texas, with*

Lessons from the Political Life-Story of a Fallen Idol. San Antonio: The Cocke Co., 1908. 2 vols.

Coggin, James. E. *J. K. Wadley: A Tree God Planted.* Texarkana, Ark.: Southwest Printers & Publishers, n.d.

Collier, Peter, and David Horowitz. *The Rockefellers: An American Dynasty.* New York: Holt, Rinehart & Winston, 1976.

[Continental Oil Company]. *CONOCO: The First One Hundred Years.* New York: Special Marketing Division, Dell Publishing Co., 1975.

Cotner, Robert C., ed. *Addresses and State Papers of James Stephen Hogg.* Austin: University of Texas Press, 1951.

———. *James Stephen Hogg: A Biography.* Austin: University of Texas Press, 1959.

———, ed. *Texas Cities and the Great Depression.* Austin: University of Texas Memorial Museum, 1974.

Cotton, Catherine. *The Saga of Scurry.* San Antonio: Naylor Co., 1957.

Crawford, W. L. *Crawford on Baileyism: The Greatest Exposé of Political Degeneracy Since the Crédit Mobilier Scandal.* Dallas: Electer News Bureau, 1907.

Davis, Wallace. *Corduroy Road: The Story of Glenn H. McCarthy.* Houston: Anson Jones Press, 1951.

Dugger, Ronnie. *Our Invaded Universities: Form, Reform and New Starts, A Nonfiction Play for Five Stages.* New York: W. W. Norton Co., 1974.

East Texas Chamber of Commerce. *A Book of Facts: Martial Law in East Texas, What It Has Meant to the State and the Nation.* Fort Worth: Texas Oil and Gas Conservation Association, 1932.

Elliott, Osborn. *Men at the Top.* New York: Harper & Brothers, 1959.

Engler, Robert. *The Politics of Oil: A Study of Private Power and Democratic Directions.* Chicago: University of Chicago Press, Phoenix Books, 1967.

Fehrenbach, T. R. *Lone Star: A History of Texas and the Texans.* New York: Macmillan, 1968.

Ferber, Edna. *Giant.* New York: Doubleday, 1952; Cardinal ed., Pocket Books, 1954.

Finty, Tom, Jr. *Anti-Trust Legislation in Texas.* Dallas: A. H. Belo Co., 1916.

Flynn, John T. *God's Gold: The Story of Rockefeller and His Time.* New York: Harcourt, Brace, 1932.

Forbes, Gerald. *Flush Production: The Epic of Oil in the Gulf-Southwest.* Norman: University of Oklahoma Press, 1942.

Frantz, Joe. B. *Texas: A Bicentennical History.* New York and Nashville: W. W. Norton and Co. and American Association for State and Local History, 1976.

Fuermann, George. *Houston: Land of the Big Rich.* Garden City, N.Y.: Doubleday, 1951.

———. *Reluctant Empire.* Garden City, N.Y.: Doubleday, 1957.

Glasscock, Lucille. *A Texas Wildcatter: A Fascinating Saga of Oil.* San Antonio: Naylor Co., 1952.

Gould, Charles N. *Covered Wagon Geologist.* Norman: University of Oklahoma Press, 1959.

Grant, W. Vance, and C. George Lind. *Digest of Education Statistics, 1975 Edition.* Washington, D.C.: U.S. Government Printing Office, 1976.

Haley, J. Evetts. *Story of the Shamrock.* Amarillo: Shamrock Co., 1954.

Hamill, Curtis G. *We Drilled Spindletop!* Houston: priv. pub., 1957.

Harter, Harry. *East Texas Oil Parade.* San Antonio: Naylor Co., 1934.

He Admits, or the Confessions of Joseph Weldon Bailey. Houston: Harris County Democratic Club, 1908.

Heilbroner, Robert L. *The Quest for Wealth: A Study of Acquisitive Man.* New York: Simon & Schuster, 1956.

Henriques, Robert. *Bearsted: A Biography of Marcus Samuel, First Viscount Bearsted and Founder of "Shell" Transport and Trading Company.* New York: Viking Press, 1960.

Hewins, Ralph. *Mr. Five Per Cent: The Story of Calouste Gulbenkian.* New York: Rinehart & Co., 1958.

Hidy, Ralph W., and Muriel E. Hidy. *Pioneering in Big Business, 1882–1911. History of Standard Oil Company (New Jersey).* New York: Harper & Brothers, 1955.

History of Petroleum Engineering. New York and Dallas: American Petroleum Institute, 1961.

Horlacher, James Levi. *A Year in the Oil Fields.* Lexington, Ky.: The Kentucky Kernel, 1929.

House, Boyce. *Oil Boom: The Story of Spindletop, Burkburnett, Mexia, Smackover, Desdemona, and Ranger.* Caldwell, Idaho: Caxton Printers, 1941.

———. *Oil Field Fury.* San Antonio: Naylor Co., 1954.

———. *Roaring Ranger: The World's Biggest Boom.* San Antonio: Naylor Co., 1951.

———. *Were You in Ranger?* Dallas: Tardy Publishing Co., 1935.

Hunt, H. L. *Alpaca Revisited.* Dallas: H. L. H. Products, 1967.

———. *H. L. Hunt Early Days.* Dallas: Parade Press, 1973.

———. *Hunt Heritage: The Republic and Our Families.* Dallas: Parade Press, 1973.

Ickes, Harold L. *The Secret Diary of Harold L. Ickes: The First Thousand Days, 1933–1936.* New York: Simon & Schuster, 1953.

Ironside, Roberta Louise. *An Adventure Called Skelly: A History of Skelly Oil Company Through Fifty Years, 1919–1969.* New York: Appleton-Century-Crofts, 1970.

Irving, Clifford. *Fake: The Story of Elmyr de Hory, the Greatest Art Forger of Our Time.* New York: McGraw-Hill Book Co., 1969.

Jackson, John A. *Wise County: 25 Years of Progress.* Dallas: priv. publ., 1972.

James, Marquis. *The Texaco Story: The First Fifty Years, 1902–1952.* N.p.: The Texas Company, 1953.

Johnson, M. L. *The Bailey Investigation, Disgrace to Democracy: How Governor Campbell & J. L. Peeler Cut Bait While Oily Joe Fished Up the Suckers.* Austin: priv. publ., 1907.

Johnson, Thelma, et al. *The Spindle Top Oil Field: A History of Its Discovery and Development.* Beaumont: George Norvell, 1927.

Jones, John P. *Borger: The Little Oklahoma.* N.p.: The Author, 1927.

————. *Ten Years in the Oil Fields.* El Dorado, Ark.: n. pub 1926.

Jones, Peter d'A. *The Robber Barons Revisited.* Lexington, Mass.: D. C. Heath & Co., 1968.

Kielman, Chester V., compiler and ed. *The University of Texas Archives: A Guide to the Historical Manuscripts Collection in the University of Texas Library.* Austin: University of Texas Press, 1967.

Kilman, Ed, and Theon Wright. *Hugh Roy Cullen: A Story of American Opportunity.* New York: Prentice-Hall, 1954.

King, Carl B., and Howard W. Risher, Jr. *The Negro in the Petroleum Industry.* The Racial Policies of American Industry, Report No. 5. Philadelphia: University of Pennsylvania Press, 1969.

King, John O. *The Early History of the Houston Oil Company of Texas, 1901–1908.* Houston: Texas Gulf Coast Historical Association, 1959.

————. *Joseph Stephen Cullinan: A Study of Leadership in the Texas Petroleum Industry, 1897–1937.* Nashville: Vanderbilt University Press & Texas Gulf Coast Historical Association, 1970.

Kirstein, George G. *The Rich: Are They Different?* Boston: Houghton Mifflin Co., 1968.

Knight, James A. *For the Love of Money: Human Behavior and Money.* Philadelphia: J. B. Lippincott Co., 1968.

Knowles, Ruth Sheldon. *The Greatest Gamblers: The Epic of American Oil Exploration.* New York: McGraw-Hill Book Co., 1959.

La Cossitt, Henry. *Twenty Who Did: Successful Business Patterns of Twenty Young American Companies and Their Leaders.* New York: Hawthorn Books, 1958.

Larson, Henrietta M., and Kenneth Wiggins Porter. *History of Humble Oil & Refining Company: A Study in Industrial Growth.* New York: Harper & Brothers, 1959.

Lea, Tom. *The King Ranch.* Boston: Little, Brown, 1957. 2 vols.

Leven, David D. *Done in Oil: The Cavalcade of the Petroleum Industry from a Practical, Economic and Financial Standpoint.* New York: Ranger Press, 1941.

Lundberg, Ferdinand. *The Rich and the Super-Rich: A Study in the Power of Money Today.* New York: Lyle Stuart, Inc., 1968; Bantam Books, 1969.

Marcus, Stanley. *Minding the Store: A Memoir.* Boston: Little, Brown, 1974.

Martin, Robert L. *The City Moves West: Economic and Industrial Growth in Central West Texas.* Austin: University of Texas Press, 1969.

McBeth, Reid Sayers. *Pioneering the Gulf Coast: A Story of the Life and Accomplishments of Capt. Anthony F. Lucas.* New York: n.pub., 1918.

McDaniel, Ruel. *Some Ran Hot.* Dallas: Regional Press, 1939.

Medders, Margaret. *The Medders Story.* Memphis: Marest Publishing Co., 1973.

Miller, Ann, with Norma Lee Browning. *Miller's High Life.* Garden City, N.Y.: Doubleday, 1972.

Miller Max. *Speak to the Earth.* New York: Appleton-Century-Crofts, 1955.

Miller, Thomas Lloyd. *The Public Lands of Texas, 1519–1970.* Norman: University of Oklahoma Press, 1971.

Moore, Richard R. *West Texas After the Discovery of Oil: A Modern Frontier.* Austin: Jenkins Publishing Co./The Pemberton Press, 1971.

Morris, Willie. *North Toward Home.* Boston: Houghton Mifflin Co., 1967.

Mott, Frank Luther. *American Journalism: A History, 1690–1960,* 3rd ed. New York: Macmillan Co., 1962.

Myres, Samuel D. *The Permian Basin, Petroleum Empire of the Southwest: Era of Discovery, from the Beginning to the Depression.* El Paso: Permian Press, 1973.

Nevin, David. *The Texans: What They Are—And Why.* New York: William Morrow & Co., 1968.

Nevins, Allan. *John D. Rockefeller.*One-volume abridgment of Nevins' *Study in Power,* as presented by William Greenleaf. New York: Charles Scribner's Sons, 1959.

Notice of Sale and Prospectus for Board of Regents of The University of Texas System and Board of Directors of the Texas A&M University System Permanent University Fund Bonds. New

Series, 1975. N.p.: University of Texas System, 1975.

Oates, Stephen B. *Visions of Glory: Texans on the Southwestern Frontier.* Norman: University of Oklahoma Press, 1970.

O'Bryan, Patrick. *The Great Conroe Oil Field.* [Houston]: n.pub., n.d.

O'Connor, Richard. *The Oil Barons: Men of Greed and Grandeur.* Boston: Little, Brown & Co., 1971.

Owen, Edgar Wesley. *Trek of the Oil Finders: A History of Exploration for Petroleum.* Tulsa: American Association of Petroleum Geologists, 1975.

Owens, William A. *Fever in the Earth.* New York: G. P. Putnam's Sons, 1958.

Parker, George [George Stoker]. *Oil Field Medico.* Dallas: Banks-Upshaw & Co., 1948.

Parten, J. R. *The Texas Oil Case.* Austin: Independent Petroleum Association of Texas, 1933.

Perry, George Sessions. *Texas, A World in Itself.* New York: Whittlesey House, 1942.

Perryman, W. L., Jr. *Address Before the New York Society of Security Analysts, February 8, 1960.* [Dallas]: General American Oil Company of Texas, 1960.

Pettengill, Samuel B. *Hot Oil: The Problem of Petroleum.* New York: Economic Forum Co., Inc., 1936.

Pope, Clarence C. *An Oil Scout in the Permian Basin, 1924–1960.* El Paso: Permian Press, 1972.

Pratt, Wallace E. *Oil in the Earth.* Lawrence: University of Kansas Press, 1943.

Rees Goronwy. *The Multimillionaires: Six Studies in Wealth.* New York: Macmillan Co., 1961.

Richardson, Rupert Norval. *Texas, The Lone Star State.* Englewood Cliffs, N.J.: Prentice-Hall, Inc., 1943. Rev, 3rd ed. 1970.

Rister, Carl Coke. *Oil! Titan of the Southwest.* Norman: University of Oklahoma Press, 1949.

Rogers, John William. *About Oil in Spain: The Story of Valdebro, a Happy Venture in Spanish-American Co-operation.* Madrid: [Valdebro], 1958.

———. *The Lusty Texans of Dallas.* New York: E. P. Dutton & Co., 1960.

————. *The Story of General American Oil Company of Texas.* [Dallas: General American Oil Company of Texas, 1955.]

Rundell, Walter, Jr. *Early Texas Oil: A Photographic History, 1866–1936.* College Station, Texas: Texas A&M University Press, 1977.

Russell, Francis. *The Shadow of Blooming Grove: Warren G. Harding in His Times.* New York; McGraw-Hill Book Company, 1968.

Sampson, Anthony. *The Seven Sisters: The Great Oil Companies and the World They Made.* New York: Viking Press, 1975.

Schwettmann, Martin W. *Santa Rita: Oil from Santa Rita No. 1.* Austin: n. pub., n.d.

————. *Santa Rita: The University of Texas Oil Discovery.* Austin: Texas State Historical Association, 1943.

Senter, E. G. *The Bailey Case Boiled Down.* Dallas: Flag Publishing Co., 1908.

Sewell, Gerald, and Mary Beth Rogers. *The Story of Texas Public Lands: A Unique Heritage.* [Austin]: Texas General Land Office & J. M. West Texas Corp., [1973].

Solberg, Carl. *Oil Power.* New York: Mason/Charter, 1976.

Spence, Hartzell. *Portrait in Oil: How the Ohio Oil Company Grew to Become Marathon.* New York: McGraw-Hill Book Company, 1962.

Spindletop: Symbol of Free Enterprise. Preprint of a Series of Speeches Commemorating the 50th Anniversary of the Discovery of the Spindletop Oil Field, Beaumont, Texas. Beaumont: Spindletop 50th Anniversary Committee, 1951.

Spindletop, Where Oil Became an Industry. Official Proceedings of 50th Anniversary Program of Discovery of Beaumont Oil Field, 1901. Beaumont: Spindletop 50th Anniversary Commission, 1951.

Spratt, John S. *The Road to Spindeltop: Economic Change in Texas, 1875–1901.* Dallas: Southern Methodist University Press, 1955.

Starbuck, Edwin Diller, ed., et al. *Lives That Guide.* New York: World Book Co., 1939.

Steward, Maxwell S. *The Big Foundations.* Public Affairs Pamphlet No. 500. New York: Public Affairs Pamphlets, 1975.

Swanson, E. B., compiler. *A Century of Oil and Gas in Books: A Descriptive Bibliography.* New York: Appleton-Century-Crofts, Inc., 1960.

Tait, Samuel W., Jr. *The Wildcatters: An Informal History of Oil-Hunting in America.* Princeton: Princeton University Press, 1946.

Texas Almanac, 1972-1973. Dallas: A. H. Belo Corp., 1973.

Texas Legislature, House. *Proceedings and Reports of Bailey Investigation Committee.* Austin: Von Boeckmann-Jones Co., 1907.

Thompson, Craig. *Since Spindletop: A Human Story of Gulf's First Half-Century.* [Pittsburgh: Gulf Oil Company, 1951.]

Thompson, Ernest O. *How the Railroad Commission of Texas Operates.* Testimony, House, Committee on Interstate and Foreign Commerce. Washington: n.pub., 1957.

Tinkle, Lon. *Mr. De: A Biography of Everette Lee DeGolyer.* Boston: Little, Brown & Co., 1970.

Tolbert, Frank X. *The Story of Lyne Taliaferro (Tol) Barret, Who Drilled Texas' First Oil Well.* [Dallas]: Texas Mid-Continent Oil & Gas Association, 1966.

Tompkins, Walker A. *Little Giant of Signal Hill: An Adventure in American Enterprise.* Englewood Cliffs, N.J.: Prentice-Hall, Inc., 1964.

Tugendhat, Christopher. *Oil, The Biggest Business.* New York: G. P. Putnam's Sons, 1968.

U.S. Congress. House. 73rd Congress (Recess). *Hearings Before A Subcommittee of the Committee on Interstate and Foreign Commerce. Sept. 17-22, 1934.* Washington: U.S. Government Printing Office, 1934. 4 parts.

———. Senate. *Hearings Before a Special Committee Investigating Petroleum Resources—The Independent Petroleum Company, 79th Congress, 2nd Session, March 19, 20, 21, 22, 27, and 28, 1946.* Washington: U.S. Government Printing Office, 1946.

Vagtborg, Harold. *The Story of Southwest Research Center: A Private, Nonprofit, Scientific Research Adventure.* San Antonio: Southwest Research Institute, 1973.

Vernon's Annotated Revised Civil Statutes of the State of Texas. St. Paul: West Publishing Co., 1969.

Warner, C. A. *Texas Oil and Gas since 1543.* Houston: Gulf Publishing Co., 1939.

Webb, Walter Prescott. *The Great Frontier.* Boston: Houghton Mifflin Co., 1952.

———, and H. Bailey Carroll, eds. *The Handbook of Texas.* Austin: Texas State Historical Association, 1952. 2 vols.

Wendt, Lloyd, and Herman Kogan. *Bet A Million! The Story of John W. Gates.* Indianapolis: Bobbs-Merrill Co., 1948.

White, Owen P. *The Autobiography of a Durable Sinner.* New York: G. P. Putnam's Sons, 1942.

Who's Who in America, 38th ed. 1974–1975. Chicago: Marquis Who's Who, 1974. 2 vols.

THESES AND DISSERTATIONS

Crouch, Thomas W. "Texas Crude Oil Pipelines to 1955." M.A. Thesis, University of Texas at Austin, 1959.

Dolman, Wilson E. "Public Lands of West Texas, 1870–1900." Ph.D. Thesis, University of Texas at Austin, 1974.

Eakens, Robert Henry Seale. "The Development of Proration in the East Texas Oil Field." M.A. Thesis, The University of Texas, 1937.

Herring, Dal Martin. "Oil Patch Tales." M.A. Thesis, Sul Ross State College, 1965.

Martin, Elizabeth Kathryn. "Lexicon of the Texas Oil Fields." Ph.D. Thesis, East Texas State University, 1969. 2 vols.

Parker, Edith Helene. "History of Land Grants for Education in Texas." Ph.D. Thesis, University of Texas at Austin, 1952.

Smith, Jesse Guy. "The Bailey Controversy in Texas Politics." M.A. Thesis, University of Chicago, 1924.

Wagner, Jimmie. "The Ranger Oil Boom." M.A. Thesis, Southern Methodist University, 1935.

Winfrey, Dorman A. "A History of Rusk County, Texas." M.A. Thesis, University of Texas at Austin, 1951.

ARTICLES

"A Deal Done In," *Time* (June 17, 1966), p. 62.

"A History of Texas Anti-Trust in Oil," *Texas Observer* (September 18, 1959), pp. 1–3.

Acheson, Alex. L. "Wildcatter Has 9 Lives," Dallas *Times Herald* (December 24, 1967), p. C-5.

Alexander, Louis. "Louis Alexander Calls on Bob Smith," *Oil*, Vol. xx, No. 4 (April, 1960), pp. 13–17.

Allen, Lew. "Oil Wildcatters," *New York Times* (July 30, 1922), Sect. 7, p. 3.

Alsop, Stewart. "America's New Big Rich," *Saturday Evening Post* (July 17, 1965), pp. 23–27, 36–46.

Amory, Cleveland. "The Oil Folks at Home," *Holiday* (February, 1957), pp. 52–57, 133, 134, 136, 139, 141–42.

Ashby, Lynn. "The Wildcatter's Wildcatter," *Texas Monthly* (November, 1974), pp. 67, 162.

"Back to Market," *Time* (June 9, 1967), p. 84.

Bagdikian, Ben H. "Houston's Shackled Press," *Atlantic* (August, 1966), pp. 87–93.

Bailey, Patrick. "56 Dry Holes Led to Success," Dallas *Times-Herald* (July 11, 1971), pp. 47A ff.

———. "Flashy Rudman Likes to Win Often," Dallas *Times- Herald* (June 27, 1971), p. D9.

"Benedum's Boom," *Business Week* (January 17, 1948), p. 23.

Bigbee, North. "D. Harold Byrd's Role as East Texas Field Pioneer Is Recalled," *Texas Oil Journal* (September, 1955), pp. 12–13.

" 'The Biggest Thing Yet'?" *Time* (December 5, 1949), pp. 91–92 ff.

"The Billionaire," *Newsweek* (July 15, 1957), pp. 169, 172.

Brown, Stanley H. "The Big Deal That Got Away," *Fortune* (October, 1966), pp. 164–66, 178, 180, 184, 188, 190, 192.

Broyles, William, and Alex Sheshunoff. "How First National Passed Republic and Other Stories of the Banking Game," *Texas Monthly* (May, 1974), pp. 44–48 ff.

Buckley, Tom. "Just Plain H. L. Hunt," *Esquire* (January, 1967), pp. 64–69 ff.

Buckley, William F., Jr., "Speaking Out: God Bless the Rich," *Saturday Evening Post* (December 30, 1967), pp. 4 ff.

———. "The Trials of the Very Rich," Shreveport *Times* (Dec. 8, 1974).

Burka, Paul. "So Close, So Far," *Texas Monthly* (April, 1976), pp. 26–28 ff.

Busch, Noel F. "Dizzying, Dazzling Houston," *Reader's Digest* (April, 1975), pp. 114–18.

Castro, Tony. "Mr. Brown of Brown & Root: Power and Money in Houston," *Texas Observer* (July 25, 1975), pp. 15–16.

———. "Power and Money in Houston," *Texas Observer* (July 4, 1975), pp. 3–5.

" 'Chief Roughneck 1972' Is W. A. 'Monty' Moncrief," *Lone Star Steel Company Starlight* (October, 1972), p. 1.

Conaway, James. "Oil: The Source," *Atlantic* (March, 1975), pp. 60–70.

Davidson, Chandler. " 'The Texans' and Other Myths," *Texas Observer* (June 18, 1976), pp. 3–5.

"Death and a Changing Industry Thin Oil's Multi-millionaires," *Business Week* (October 10, 1959), pp. 30–32.

DeGolyer, E. "Anthony F. Lucas and Spindletop," *Southwest Review*, vol. XXXI (Fall, 1945), pp. 83–87.

Deterling, Del. "Hay System for Fewer Backaches and Headaches," *Progressive Farmer* (June, 1975), pp. 16–17.

Dugger, Ronnie. "John Connally: Nixon's New Quarterback," *Atlantic* (July, 1971), pp. 82–86, 88–90.

———. "Oil and Politics," *Atlantic* (September, 1969), pp. 66–78, 82–88, 90.

Dupuy, William Atherton. "Once More 'Hot Oil' Gushes Ruinously," *New York Times Magazine* (January 27, 1935), pp. 2, 15.

"East Texas Drowns Itself in Oil," *Review of Reviews* (August, 1931), pp. 78–79.

"East Texas, Oil Terror," *Business Week* (January 19, 1935), pp. 20–21.

Eckert, Fred J. "America's Richest Man—And How He Got That Way," *Family Weekly* (July 12, 1964), p. 6.

[Eckhardt, Bob]. "Oil Prices and Inflation," *Texas Observer* (May 24, 1974), pp. 16–18.

Elliott, Keith. "Gas Fever on the Border," *Texas Parade* (June, 1975), pp. 12–20.

"Exploiting Texas: An Editorial," *Texas Observer* (April 18, 1959), pp. 1, 5.

"Five Noted Thinkers Explore the Future," *National Geographic*, Vol. 150, no. 1 (July, 1976), pp. 68–74.

Frantz, Joe B. "Southwestern Collection," *Southwestern Historical Quarterly*, Vol. LXXVII, no. 3 (January, 1974), pp. 399–414.

Gaines, James R., et al. "A Scandal for the Hunt Clan," *Newsweek* (March 24, 1975), pp. 26–27.

Gambrell, Herbert. "James Stephen Hogg: Statesman or Demagogue?," *Southwest Review*, Vol. XIII, No. 3 (April, 1928), pp. 338–66.

Gard, Wayne. "Hot Oil," *New Republic* (January 30, 1935), pp. 326–27.

Garnett, Edward B. "Oil Is King in the Texas Panhandle," *World's Work*, Vol. LV (December, 1927), pp. 168–74.

"Gassing Game," *Texas Monthly* (April, 1976), pp. 54, 56.

"Geological Firm Works Night and Day to Locate Promising Oil Land; Here's Interesting Story of Outstanding Etex Firm," (Quitman, Texas) *Wood County Democrat* (July 27, 1950), pp. 6, 8.

"George Strake Featured Speaker at Houston's Executive Night Program," *The Landman* (February, 1965), pp. 16–25, 66–77.

Goddard, Ruth. "The Wildcatter of Running Duke," *Texas Star* (January 16, 1972), pp. 10–11.

Gould, Charles N. "The Beginning of the Panhandle Oil and Gas Field," *Panhandle-Plains Historical Review*, Vol. VIII (1935), pp. 21–36.

Gray, George W. "The Roaring Tides of the Oil Fields," *New York Times Magazine* (September 20, 1931), pp. 4–5.

Grover, John. Four-part series on "Texas Jillionaires," Los Angeles *Mirror* (August 30–September 2, 1954).

Hager, Dorsey, " 'Lady Luck' or 'Law of Probabilities' Played Lead Part in Discovery of Many Oil Fields," *Oil and Gas Journal* (January 3, 1935), pp. 50–51.

"Halbouty, 'Born Across Two Railroad Tracks,' Ranks Today as Outspoken Industry Champion," *Business & Energy International* (June 1, 1976; 2nd quarter), p. 26.

Herndon, Booton. "Thomas Walker Murray: Crap-Shooting Wildcatter," *True* (May, 1959), pp. 18–20, 22, 24, 26, 28, 100–1.

"He's Half Wildcatter, Half Big Businessman," *Business Week* (November 14, 1964), pp. 103–4 ff.

"Hot Oil Cooler," *Business Week* (December 22, 1934), p. 11.

House, Boyce. "The Colonel Left Tracks," *Saturday Evening Post* (June 5, 1937), pp. 18–19 ff.

———. "It Was Fun While It Lasted," *Saturday Evening Post* (October 16, 1937), pp. 14–15 ff.

"Hunt Strikes Ink," *Newsweek* (January 18, 1965), p. 49.

Hurt, Harry III. "The Most Powerful Texans," *Texas Monthly* (April, 1976), pp. 73–77, 107–23.

Isaac, Paul E. "Municipal Reform in Beaumont, Texas, 1902–1909," *Southwestern Historical Quarterly,* Vol. LXXVIII, No. 4 (April 1975), pp. 409–30.

Ivins, Molly. "The Texas Research League," *Texas Observer* (February 1, 1974), pp. 3–5

Johnson, Arthur M. "The Early Texas Oil Industry. Pipelines and the Birth of an Integrated Oil Industry 1901–1911," *Journal of Southern History* (November, 1966), Vol. 32, no. 4, pp. 516–28.

Johnson, Bobby H. "Oil in the Pea Patch: The East Texas Oil Boom," *East Texas Historical Journal,* Vol. XIII, No. 1 (Spring, 1975), pp. 34–42.

"Keeping a City in Good Shape," *Business Week* (June 6, 1964), pp. 10–14.

King, John O. "The Early Texas Oil Industry: Beginning at Corsicana, 1894–1901," *Journal of Southern History,* Vol. 32, no. 4 (November, 1966), pp. 505–515.

King, Larry L. "Who's Number One in the Permian Basin?" *Texas Monthly* (June, 1975), pp. 70–73, 84, 87.

"King of the Wildcatters," *Time* (February 13, 1950), pp. 18–21.

"King Ranch Riches Multiply," *Business Week* (December 7, 1946), pp. 22, 24, 26, 28.

"The Laborer and His Hire—Another Standard Oil Lesson," *Hearst's Magazine* (February, 1913), pp. 174–88.

Lewis, Alfred Henry. "The Hon (?) J.W. Bailey," *Cosmopolitan Magazine* (April, 1913), pp. 601–5.

Lincoln, Freeman. "John Mecom's Delightful Dilemma," *Fortune* (June, 1957), pp. 169–72 ff.

Louis, A. M. "America's Centimillionaires," *Fortune* (May, 1968), pp. 152–55 ff.

Lubar Robert. "Henry Holt and the Man from Koon Kreek," *Fortune* (December, 1959), pp. 104–9 ff.

Lynch, Dudley. "Excitement in Frustration," *Midwest: Magazine of the Chicago Sun-Times* (January 14, 1973), pp. 32, 34.

———. "The Frustration Fields Gang Rides Again," *Southwest Scene: The Dallas Morning News Sunday Magazine* (December 10, 1972), pp. 14–19.

"The Mail: Oil and Politics," *Atlantic* (December, 1969), pp. 42 ff.

Marcosson, Isaac F. "The Black Golconda," *Saturday Evening Post* (April 19, 1924), pp. 16–17 ff.

"Marrying for Money?" *Family Weekly* (October 20, 1974).

"Maxima," *Texas Observer* (February 1, 1974), pp. 6–7.

May, Francis B. "The Energy Economy: Drilling for Oil in Texas, 1866–1974," *Texas Business Review* (September, 1974), pp. 218–22.

Mayo, E.W. "The Oil Boom in Texas," *Harper's Weekly* (June 22, 1901), pp. 624–25.

McWhirter, William A. "How Art Swindlers Duped a Virtuous Millionaire," *Life* (July 7, 1967), pp. 52–61.

"Meadow's Luck," *Time* (May 19, 1967), pp. 94, 97.

"Men We Are Watching: The Lion in a Snare," *The Independent* (January 24, 1907), pp. 208–9.

"The Midas Touch of John Mecom," *Business Week* (October 10, 1964), pp. 90–92 ff.

Miller, Herman P. "Millionaires Are a Dime a Dozen," *New York Times Magazine* (November 28, 1965), pp. 50–51 ff.

Moncrief, W. A., and R. C. Cowan. "A Different Kind of Oil Pollution," *Atlantic* (May, 1975), pp. 49–50 ff.

"Moncrief Recalls Core Looking Like Oil-Dipped Brown Sugar," Longview *Daily News* (January 26, 1966), Sect. 2, p. 11.

"More Texas Oil," *Business Week* (March 27, 1948), p. 22.

" 'Most Valuable Senator,' " *New Republic* (April 8, 1957), p. 2.

Nevin, David. "A People Out for Stars, Not Peanuts," *Life* (July 1, 1966), pp. 50 ff.

Nordyke, Lewis. "Heap Big Uncle Frank," *Saturday Evening Post* (July 29, 1944), pp. 20–21 ff.

"New Kind of Oil Boom in Texas," *Business Week* (September 24, 1955) pp. 186–88 ff.

Northcott, Kaye. "Creeping Socialism off Texas Coast," *Texas Observer* (February 1, 1974), pp. 7 ff.

"Now, a Silver Rush," *Newsweek* (February 25, 1974), p. 83.

O'Bryan, Patrick. "Men of Houston: George W. Strake," *Houston Town* (October, 1958), pp. 42–44.

Olsen Jack. "The Big Itch They Call Little John," *Sports Illustrated* (January 11, 1965), pp. 50–54 ff.

Owen, Russell. "New Boom Town," *New York Times Magazine* (April 15, 1951), pp. 54–55.

Owens, William A. "Gusher at Spindletop," *American Heritage* (June, 1958), pp. 34–39 ff.

"Parten Proves Movie Industry Saying: The Bigger They Are, The Nicer They Are," *Business & Energy International* (June 1, 1976; 2nd Quarter), p. 25.

Pederson, Rena. "A Day in the Lives of the Hunts," *Dallas Morning News* (September 14, 1975), p. 30-A.

Phillips, David Graham. "The Treason of the Senate," *Cosmopolitan Magazine* (July, 1906), pp. 267–76.

"*Playboy* Interview: H. L. Hunt," *Playboy* (August, 1966), pp. 47–49 ff.

Porterfield, Bill. "H. L. Hunt's Long Goodbye," *Texas Monthly* (March, 1975), pp. 63–69 ff.

―――. "The Lonely Search for Oil," *Texas Monthly* (November, 1974), pp. 62–66 ff.

Reinert, Al. "Bob and George Go to Washington or the Post-Watergate Scramble," *Texas Monthly* (April, 1974), pp. 52–61.

"Richest of All," *Fortune* (May, 1968), p. 157.

Rundell, Walter, Jr. "Texas Petroleum History: A Selective Annotated Bibliography, *"Southwestern Historical Quarterly*, Vol. LXVII, no. 2 (October, 1963), pp. 267–78.

Sheehy, Sandy. "Problems in Paradise," *Houston City Magazine* (April, 1978), pp. 57–61.

Sherrill, Robert G. "H. L. Hunt: Portrait of a Super-Patriot," *The Nation* (February 24, 1964), pp. 182–95.

Sladek, Jean. "Our Saint Came Marching In," *Alcade: The University of Texas at Austin Alumni Magazine* (January, 1974), pp. 8–11.

"Sold Arabian," *Texas Monthly* (April, 1975), pp. 46–47.

"Standard, Humble Merger Revealed," *Texas Observer* (September 11, 1959), p. 5.

"Standard Not Barred," *Texas Observer* (September 18, 1959).

"Surprise Package," *Time* (December 17, 1965), p. 80.

Taylor, Lonn. "Miss Ima Hogg," *Texas Observer* (September 5, 1975), pp. 10–11.

Terry, Dickson. "A New Bunyanesque Type," *Texas Observer* (February 28, 1955), p. 6.

―――. "Clint Enjoys His Private Island," *Texas Observer* (March 28, 1955), p. 6.

―――. "Hugh Roy Says He's Selfish," *Texas Observer* (March 7, 1955), p. 6.

―――. "West Gets a Bang Playing Policeman," *Texas Observer* (March 14, 1955), p. 6.

"Texaco Goes East," *Business Week* (May 25, 1946), p. 56.

"Texanize It!," *Texas Observer* (July 26, 1974), p. 8.

"Texans on Wall Street," *Time* (June 16, 1961), pp. 80–84.

"The Texas Accent," *Nation* (June 25, 1973), p. 805.

Tolbert, Frank X. " 'Richest Man'—? Dallasite Doubts It," Dallas *Morning News,* April 4, 1948, Sect. 4, p. 1.

T. R. B. "Success Story," *New Republic* (May 27, 1967), p. 2.

"Vade Mecum," *Time* (July 24, 1964), p. 81.

Walker, Stanley "Where Are They Now? Mr. Davis and His Millions," *New Yorker* (November 26, 1949), pp. 35–49.

"Walter Bedford Sharp," *Fuel Oil Journal* (January, 1913), pp. 10–12.

Warner, C. A. "Texas and the Oil Industry," *Southwestern Historical Quarterly*, Vol. L. No. 1 (July, 1946), pp. 1–19.

West, Richard. "Texas Monthly Reporter: Succession at the King Ranch," *Texas Monthly* (December, 1974), pp. 10–11.

Whalen, Richard J. "Who Owns America?", *Saturday Evening Post* (December 30, 1967), pp. 17–21.

"Where Texas Falls Short," *Business Week* (July 29, 1967), p. 32.

White, Owen P. "Piping Hot," *Collier's* (January 12, 1935), pp. 10–11, 30–31.

White, Theodore H. "Texas: Land of Wealth and Fear. II. Texas Democracy—Domestic and Export Models," *The Reporter* (June 8, 1954), pp. 30–37.

Willey, Day Allen. "The Status of the Southwestern Oil Industry," *Review of Reviews* (January, 1904), pp. 56–63.

" 'You Have Made Yourself a Deal,' Said Monty Moncrief," *Petroleum Independent* (November–December, 1972), pp. 6–8, 11.

NEWSPAPERS

Austin *American.* November 23, 1928; April 19, 1929; April 25, 26, 29, May 2, 3, 1933.

Bridgeport *Index.* Oil & Gas Supplement, 1972.

Conroe *Daily Courier.* August 19, 1975.

Dallas *Morning News.* March 24, 1889; September 14, 1930; February 4, 1931: March 29–31, 1947; February 4, 1963; November 25, 1966; July 11, 1973; June 3, 1974; November–December, 1974; January, 1975–June, 1976.

Dallas *Times Herald.* December 24, 1967; June 27, 1971; February 4, 1974; March 8, 1975.

Electra *News.* Anniversary Edition, March 29, 1923.

Fort Worth *Star-Telegram.* July 29, 1971; November 17, 1974.

Galveston *Daily News.* September 16, October 27, 1906.

Gladewater *Gusher.* August 19, 1931.

Henderson *Times.* September 9, 16, 23, October 21, 1930.

Houston *Post.* March 27, 28, 1975.

Kilgore *News Herald.* August 24, 1941.

Los Angeles *Mirror.* August 30–September 2, 1954.

Memphis *Commercial Appeal.* June 7, 1970; September 7, 1973.

New York Times, May 7, 12, 1933; May 6, 30, June 15, 16, August 24, 27, 28, 1934.

San Angelo *Morning Times.* October 28, 1936. Anniversary Edition.

San Antonio *Express-News.* July 6, 1974.

San Antonio *Light.* March 16, 1969.

Shreveport *Times.* Dec. 8, 1974.

Texarkana *Gazette.* July 16, 1964; 1974–1976.

MISCELLANEOUS

"A Chronological History of Important Historical Events, Legislative Acts, Judicial Decisions, Orders, and Other Relevant Data Regarding The Railroad Commission of Texas," mimeo., Railroad Commission of Texas, n.d.

"Bibliography of Publications by Michel T. Halbouty," mimeo.

"Biographical Data and List of Club and Committee Memberships of R. E. Smith," mimeo., n.d.

"Biographical Sketch of W. A. Moncrief," mimeo, n.d.

"Brief Biography of Michel T. Halbouty," mimeo.

Clark, James A. "Outline of Personal History of Michel T. Halbouty," mimeo.

———. "Summary of Personal History of Michel T. Halbouty," mimeo.

"Carl Ernest Reistle, Jr.," mimeo, biographical sketch, n.d.

"History of the Texas Railroad Commission," mimeo.

"M. B. 'Bill' Rudman," mimeo, biographical sketch.

"Texas Mid-Continent Oil & Gas Association's Distinguished Service Award to W. A. (Monty) Moncrief by Herman P. Pressler at Its Annual Meeting in Houston, Texas, October 14, 1969."

"Texas Oil Scrapbook." Pioneers in Texas Oil Oral History Project, The University of Texas at Austin (PTO-UTA), Archives.

"This Week in D. C. with Henry B.," newsletter, U.S. Representative Henry B. Gonzalez, September 12, 1975.

"Wright Patman's 1924th, 1943rd, 1970th, 1975th Weekly Letters," November 21, 1974, April 3, October 16, November 20, 1975, newsletters of U.S Representative Wright Patman.

Index